BH
28%
SLC

W9-BTE-805

71041

LC
1034
.M56

Minimum competency
achievement testing

DATE DUE

Minimum competency achievement testing
LC1034.M56   29108

Jaeger, Richard M.
Wright Library

Minimum Competency Achievement Testing

Motives, Models, Measures, and Consequences

Edited by

Richard M. Jaeger
&
Carol Kehr Tittle

University of North Carolina at Greensboro

McCutchan Publishing Corporation
2526 Grove Street
Berkeley, California 94704

ISBN 0-8211-0909-X
Library of Congress Catalog Card Number 79-88823

© 1980 by American Educational Research Association; Chapter 1 © by David K. Cohen and Walter Haney.

Printed in the United States of America

Prologue

Goals, Hopes, and Intentions

The present literature on minimum competency testing is scattered, uneven in its quality, and imbalanced in its foci. This volume is an attempt to right those wrongs. Although it contains papers that address some of the thorniest technical problems that arise in competency testing, its offerings go well beyond mere technique. It is insufficient to consider only the "how" of competency testing. We must also ask why, when, for whom, to what ends, and with what eventualities. All of these questions, and more, are considered here.

If our best hopes are realized, this book will prove useful to a great many people who affect, and are affected by, minimum competency testing programs. Legislators bent on creating competency testing laws for their states, or on modifying existing laws, should benefit from a reflective review of papers that examine likely effects of competency testing on high school curricula, on the life-success chances of minority students, on teachers' roles and satisfaction, and on the organization of and power relationships in public shooling. In states that allow local school boards to determine competency requirements and assessment methods, school board members should find the same readings illuminating; they might, in addition, benefit from the case studies of competency testing in a number of states and local school systems. Measurement professionals responsible for designing competency testing programs will find suggestions on the solution of such technical problems as test design and standard setting. School administrators at all levels will find useful examinations of the ways competency testing programs are likely to affect their curricula, the psychological well-being of their students and teachers, and some of the most important policies that determine their authority in running the schools. Students of educational history and policy will find an analysis of the history of competency testing, its likely effects on the relationships between schools and other societal sectors, and the ways it is likely to alter schooling in the United States. Finally, although we have no delusions about the general public's interest in education policy or the pros and cons of testing, we hope that some parents and other concerned citizens—perhaps those who are most vociferous in their demands for school accountability—will find in these pages thought-provoking responses to questions on whether minimum competency testing is right or good for their children, their schools, or their communities.

The Structure of the Volume

The genesis of this book was a conference of the same title, held in Washington, D.C. on October 12-14, 1978, under the sponsorship of the American Educational Research Association. The conference was the second AERA Topical Conference devoted to a specific theme or area of study. The first, held in the fall of 1977, explored new developments in educational evaluation.

The Conference on Minimum Competency Achievement Testing included a number of invited papers, in addition to symposia developed from selected proposals submitted to the AERA in response to its call. Speakers discussed a wide array of topics related to minimum competency testing—from history and philosophy, to technical methods for setting competency standards, to procedures for management of a minimum competency testing program—and they represented an equally diverse array of institutional affiliations and backgrounds. State departments of education, local school systems, private research corporations, the federal government, and various universities were well represented.

Minimum competency testing involves more than a testing program with fixed standards of performance. Its motivations, operations, and consequences involve every facet of public and private elementary and secondary education, and it has profound implications for the whole of American society. The AERA conference and this book were designed to explore minimum competency testing in its broadest terms by considering issues previously left untouched, in addition to reanalyzing questions that have received a good bit of attention in earlier literature.

The pervasiveness of minimum competency testing is well documented by the authors of several papers presented here. It is everywhere, either in full-scale operation (in more than 12 states), under development, or under consideration (in all, involving 38 states). There are many more minimum competency testing programs in operation this year than last, and next year the number will increase again. A number of authors suggest that minimum competency testing is the stepchild of state legislatures and lay boards of education — either a reaction to what is perceived as a public cry for accountability, or an urge to legislate educational success without concern for methods or modes of achievement. For the most part, professional educators and measurement specialists have had little opportunity to affect competency testing policies. Their jobs have been to carry out the will of state boards of education or state legislatures, not to set the policies that define competency requirements and program operations.

The hurried development of minimum competency testing programs has necessitated educators' immediate attention to the pragmatic questions of competency definition, test development, standard setting, and program operations. Comparatively little attention has been directed to such larger issues as the need for minimum competency testing, the problems it seeks to solve, its likely effects on the structure and operation of the schools, and its consequences for those directly involved in elementary and secondary education, as well as for our larger society. The AERA conference and this book are attempts to fill that void.

Six parts compose this book. The first, entitled "Historical Bases and Policy Issues in Minimum Competency Testing," contains three major papers and two responses. In *Minimums, Competency Testing, and Social Policy*, David K. Cohen and Walter Haney describe the social and philosophical underpinnings of the minimum competency testing movement, and relate the movement to the philosophy of social welfare programs. Jenne K. Britell, in *Competency and Excellence: The Search for an Egalitarian Standard, the Demand for a Universal Guarantee*, contrasts minimum competency testing with other testing movements that have been prominent in the history of American education. In particular, she notes the novel features of minimum competency testing and describes their implications. The final major paper in this section is entitled *Policy Implications of Minimum Competency Testing*. It contains Joan C. Baratz's views on the ways minimum competency testing has affected and will affect control of public education, and her views on the value of elementary and secondary education for institutional access, further education, and life success. In addition, Dr. Baratz enumerates a plethora of policy issues that have not received the attention they warrant. Maxine Greene responds to Jenne Britell's paper by challenging some of her basic assumptions and definitions. She is far less sure that minimum competency testing will lead to any valued ends. Larry Cuban, in responding to Joan Baratz's paper, suggests that minimum competency testing may help schools to define more-defensible educational objectives and to discover more-effective strategies for the remediation of deficiencies. He admits that minimum competency testing may exact great social costs, largely at the expense of minority students currently in high school. The papers in Part I, then, seek to enhance our knowledge of the origins of minimum competency testing, both in terms of precedents in the testing movement and in terms of avowed societal goals and objectives, and to suggest the ways that minimum competency testing will alter relationships between schooling and other elements of American society.

In Part II, "Consequences of Minimum Competency Testing for the Schools, the Courts, and Society," three authors explore the potential impact of minimum competency testing on the elementary and secondary curricula, the likelihood of legal challenges to competency testing programs, and the relationships between basic skills achievement and students' latter opportunities for work and advanced education. Four respondents further illuminate these topics. The section begins with *Testing for Minimum Competency: A Legal Analysis*, by Paul L. Tractenberg. He reviews the legal bases for challenges to minimum competency testing programs, and then suggest program design features that would make such programs more or less vulnerable to legal action. In his paper on the *Impact of Minimum Competency Testing on Curriculum,* H. S. Broudy explores the possible consequences of such testing for the design of curricula, and projects competency testing developments in light of the public's perceptions of the purposes of schooling. Marianne Amarel, in her reaction to Broudy's paper, challenges his suggestion that some ultimate good may emerge from minimum competency testing. She sees the movement as a political attempt to wrest curricular control from teachers and place it at higher administrative levels. A second reaction to Broudy's paper is provided by W. James Popham. He agrees with Broudy's view that the public demand for competence may operate through minimum competency testing to the eventual benefit of curricula. In chapter six, Bruce K. Eckland examines the relationships between the types of basic skills currently measured by many minimum competency tests, and students' opportunities to enter the workforce or pursue additional education upon graduation from high school. His paper is entitled *Sociodemographic Implications of Minimum Competency Testing.* Robert W. Heath challenges Eckland's premises on the fundamental purposes of schooling, and suggests that only individual learners themselves can define skills that are truly functional. In another response, Ellis B. Page questions Eckland's conclusions on the relationships between reading and mathematical skills, and later opportunities for education and work. Page then suggests an alternative to current conceptions of minimum competency testing that would not require withholding high school diplomas, but would report each student's status on various testable skills. In sum, the papers in Part II suggest how minimum competency testing may alter elementary and secondary schooling, how those most adversely affected may use the courts to stop or modify the movement, and how such testing may influence students' opportunities to function in the larger society.

It is peculiar, but nonetheless true, that the prime actors in schooling have been virtually ignored in much of the literature on minimum competency testing. Part III is entitled "Implications of Minimum Competency Testing for Students and Teachers." This section contains some unique contributions on the ways minimum competency testing is likely to affect various groups: teachers, the broad group of students who participate in regular courses of instruction, and handicapped students (many of whom participate in regular programs within the limits of their abilities, under the mandates of Public Law 94-142). In *Minimum Competency Testing of Pupils: Psychological Implications for Teachers*, Jack I. Bardon and Clyde L. Robinette reveal that earlier literature has failed to consider the special needs of teachers, and that many minimum competency testing programs treat teachers as unthinking cogs in a factory model of education. They also elaborate on the likely negative consequences of continued inattention to teachers' needs. Theodore H. Blau reports on twenty-five years of clinical experience with children having difficulty in schools and on a recent survey of students' attitudes toward minimum competency testing in his paper, *Minimum Competency Testing: Psychological Implications for Students*. It is clear from his conclusions that this is a subject worthy of continued research and of specific attention during the planning and development of competency testing programs. Four papers that address the concerns of handicapped students complete this section. The first, by Kathleen S. Fenton, is entitled *Competency Testing and the Handicapped: Some Legal Concerns for School Administrators*. It contains a discussion of potential points of legal conflict between Public Law 94-142 and the requirements of minimum competency testing programs. *Test Scores and Individual Rights*, by Mary M. Kennedy, is the second paper on competency testing and handicapped students. Kennedy examines the philosophical bases of competency and the schools' obligation to handicapped students, within each of several assumptions and definitions. The third paper on competency testing and handicapped students is Louis C. Danielson's *Educational Goals and Competency*

Testing for the Handicapped. Danielson makes clear the need to define competencies that are functionally needed and realistic for various groups of handicapped students. Finally, Patricia A. Morrissey suggests specific ways that competency testing programs can be modified to accommodate the special needs of handicapped students in *Adaptive Testing: How and When Should Handicapped Students be Accommodated in Competency Testing Programs?*

Although minimum competency testing is in its infancy, it is already being used in a wide variety of contexts. Part IV, entitled "Case Studies of Minimum Competency Testing," contains three series of reports. The reports provide analyses of the development, implementation, and short-term results of minimum competency testing programs in a number of states, in a system of higher education, and in two local school systems. In addition, the role of the federal government in minimum competency testing is described.

The first series in Part IV describes competency testing in Florida, North Carolina, Oregon, and Virginia. These four states were selected for review because their competency testing programs differ in several important ways. Florida has been leading the accountability bandwagon for a number of years, and was the first state to institute demonstration of competence through testing as a high school graduation requirement. Florida's program is a model of tight, state-level control of competency requirements and performance specifications. North Carolina has come to minimum competency testing more recently, and operates under a legislative mandate that many would consider to be more enlightened than Florida's, but retains state-level control of all aspects of its competency testing program. Its program is unique in that the state legislature mandated some preliminary research prior to the use of competency tests for determining high school graduation. Oregon provides another example of an early move to competency testing, but its program differs markedly from those in Florida and North Carolina. A great deal of control is retained by local school systems. They specify competency requirements, standards, and methods of assessment within broad guidelines provided by the state. The fourth state considered, Virginia, has both a state-controlled and a locally controlled competency testing program. It is unique in this mixture, and its program is at an earlier stage of development than the other three state programs described in this section.

Although the federal government has thus far resisted congressional pressure to institute competency testing on a nationwide scale, the National Institute of Education has assumed an advisory, research, development, and dissemination role in minimum competency testing. The etiology of this action is described by Judith Sauls Shoemaker in a paper entitled

Minimum Competency Testing: The View from Capitol Hill. As is often true, the federal government provides a unique case that can neither be rationalized nor replicated. For the latter, we give thanks.

If competency testing is a good thing for elementary and secondary schools (as many legislators and state board of education members contend), why not apply it in state colleges and universities as well? Three papers in the second series of Part IV, by Haskin R. Pounds, Susan E. Ridenour, and R. Robert Rentz, describe just such an application in the Georgia state university system. They report on the purposes, political considerations, and design features of one of the largest and oldest competency testing programs in higher education. Their work may well serve as a model for other states, which are sure to turn to higher education as soon as their competency testing programs for grades K-12 are well under way.

Part IV concludes with two case studies of competency testing in two large cities: Los Angeles, California, and Portland, Oregon. Both districts have developed programs in response to relatively permissive state legislation, which demands little beyond setting some standards and determining ways of assessing individual students' abilities to meet those standards. These papers by Walter E. Hathaway and Robert Sallander suggest that competency testing at the local level is certainly feasible, and possibly useful.

The papers in Part IV are significant not only for the issues they address pragmatically, but also because of the issues they ignore. Many of the most weighty topics in the first three parts of this book are barely mentioned in the papers in Part IV: What is to be gained from minimum competency testing? How are the schools, the teachers, the students, and the community affected? What policies must be altered on the basis of test results?

The papers in Part V address some of the knottiest technical and procedural problems of competency testing: the definition of competency domains, the development and validation of instruments, and the setting of standards. Ronald K. Hambleton and Daniel R. Eignor present an extensive review of the literature on all three of these topics in their paper, *Competency Test Development, Validation, and Standard Setting.* They illustrate various procedures in great detail, and conclude with recommendations for best practice and with suggestions for further research. Fredrick L. Finch suggests a taxonomy for classifying competencies, and thus for defining the content of competency standards and measurement instruments, in a paper entitled *A Taxonomy for Competency Testing Programs.* The part concludes with a paper by Selina J. Ganopole, which presents a detailed procedure for setting competency standards.

Part VI is entitled "Alternatives to Present Conceptions of Minimum

Competency Testing." Its papers extend the typical approaches to competency testing along several dimensions. Robert A. Feldmesser suggests that all citizens be guaranteed the right to achieve minimum competence through an educating and certifying system that is separated from the high school and its diploma. Douglas E. Mitchell and William G. Spady contrast both competency-based and outcome-based education with the far narrower conception of minimum competency testing that is currently prevalent in our elementary and secondary schools. They call for more radical changes in curriculum definition, school organization, and certification of achievement. Finally, Thomas G. Sticht provides an illustration of competency definition through a detailed analysis of job demands in a military setting, and suggests that this example provides a model for competency definition in schools.

Acknowledgments

The organization of the AERA conference, and thus the structure and content of this book, were aided by the suggestions and counsel of many valued colleagues. At the risk of slighting many, we would like to mention a few whose suggestions were keenly appreciated, if not always accepted. Barbara Lasser of SWRL R and D, James Impara of the Virginia Polytechnic Institute and State University, Mary Hall of the Weyerhauser Foundation, Lorrie Shepard of the University of Colorado, and Leslie McLean of the Ontario Institute for Studies in Education provided detailed reactions to an early proposal for the design of the conference. W. James Popham, former President of AERA, suggested the theme of the conference during his term of office, and secured the approval of the AERA council. William Russell and the staff of the AERA central office provided invaluable assistance in organizing the conference, managing its logistics, and developing this book.

None of those acknowledged bear responsibility for any inaccuracies or shortcomings of this volume; the role of consultant is blessedly asymmetric in its shouldering of rewards and rebuffs. While we welcome the opportunity to acknowledge their contributions, we accept sole responsibility for the final presentation.

Contributors

Marianne Amarel is Senior Research Associate, Early Education Group, Educational Testing Service, Princeton, New Jersey.

Joan C. Baratz is Director, Education Policy Research Institute, Educational Testing Service, Washington, D.C.

Jack I. Bardon is Excellence Fund Professor of Education, University of North Carolina, Greensboro.

Theodore H. Blau is a clinical psychologist in private practice in Tampa, Florida; and former President of the American Psychological Association.

Jenne K. Britell is Executive Director for Program Planning, Educational Testing Service, Princeton, New Jersey.

H. S. Broudy is Professor Emeritus of Education, University of Illinois, Champaign-Urbana.

David K. Cohen is Professor, Graduate School of Education, Harvard University; and President, Huron Institute, Cambridge, Massachusetts.

Larry Cuban is Superintendent, Arlington County Public Schools, Arlington, Virginia.

Louis C. Danielson is Evaluation Specialist, Bureau of Education for the Handicapped, U.S. Office of Education, Washington, D.C.

Bruce K. Eckland is Professor of Sociology, University of North Carolina, Chapel Hill.

Daniel R. Eignor is Statistical Associate, Center for Occupational and Professional Assessment, Educational Testing Service, Princeton, New Jersey.

Robert A. Feldmesser is Senior Research Sociologist, Educational Testing Service, Princeton, New Jersey.

Kathleen S. Fenton is Education Program Specialist, Bureau of Education for the Handicapped, U.S. Office of Education, Washington, D.C.

Fredrick L. Finch is Senior Project Director, Test Development, CTB/McGraw-Hill, Del Monte Research Park, Monterey, California.

Thomas H. Fisher is Director, Assessment Section, Florida Department of Education, Tallahassee.

James J. Gallagher is Director, Frank Porter Graham Center, University of North Carolina, Chapel Hill.

Selina J. Ganopole is Assistant Professor, California State University, Northridge.

Maxine Greene is Professor, Division of Philosophy, the Social Sciences, and Education, Teachers College, Columbia University.

Ronald K. Hambleton is Professor of Education and Psychology, Laboratory of Psychometric and Evaluative Research, University of Massachusetts, Amherst.

Walter Haney is Staff Director, National Consortium on Testing, Huron Institute, Cambridge, Massachusetts.

Walter E. Hathaway is Evaluation Specialist, Portland Public Schools, Portland, Oregon.

Robert W. Heath is President, Nomos Institute, Berkeley, California, and Honolulu, Hawaii.

Marshall D. Herron is Director of Research and Assessment, Oregon Department of Education, Salem.

James C. Impara is Associate Professor of Educational Research, Virginia Polytechnic Institute and State University, Blacksburg.

Mary M. Kennedy is Acting Branch Chief, State Program Studies Branch, Bureau of Education for the Handicapped, U.S. Office of Education, Washington, D.C.

Douglas E. Mitchell is Associate Professor of Education, University of California, Riverside.

Patricia A. Morrissey is Educational Program Specialist, Bureau of Education for the Handicapped, U.S. Office of Education, Washington, D.C.

Ellis B. Page is Professor of Education, Duke University, Durham, North Carolina; and President-elect of the American Educational Research Association.

W. James Popham is Professor of Education, University of California, Los Angeles.

Haskin R. Pounds is Vice-Chancellor for Planning, Board of Regents of the University System of Georgia, Atlanta.

R. Robert Rentz is Associate Professor of Education, Georgia State University; and Director of the Regents' Testing Program in the State University System of Georgia, Atlanta.

Susan E. Ridenour is Assistant Director, Regents' Testing Program, Georgia State University, Atlanta.

Clyde L. Robinette is a graduate student, University of North Carolina, Greensboro.

Robert Sallander is Assistant Director, Research and Evaluation Branch, Los Angeles Unified School District, Los Angeles, California.

Judith Sauls Shoemaker is Senior Research Associate, National Institute of Education, Washington, D.C.

William G. Spady is Director, National Center for the Improvement of Learning, American Association of School Administrators, Arlington, Virginia.

Thomas G. Sticht is Senior Associate, National Institute of Education, Washington, D.C.

Paul L. Tractenberg is Professor of Law, Rutgers State University of New Jersey, Newark.

Contents

PART I
Historical Bases and Policy Issues in Minimum Competency Testing

The first paper in this part places the minimum competency testing movement within a broad social policy perspective; the second paper considers the movement as a part of the continuing search for standards and excellence in education. Taking these perspectives into account, the third paper examines the policy implications of minimum competency testing. These papers help us to understand the sources of ideas current in minimum competency testing, and to question the directions in which these ideas are leading us.

David K. Cohen and Walter Haney, in *Minimums, Competency Testing, and Social Policy*, provide us with several perspectives. First, the history of minimalism in social policy is examined from two viewpoints: equality and change. Then the idea of minimum standards is considered in relation to inputs (resources) and outputs (results). They note that testing for minimum competencies reflects an old tradition in this country—the persistent tendency in social policy to promote minimum levels of social welfare. They provide the particularly useful insight that, although social policy is minimalist in practice, it is typically conceived in egalitarian terms. This difference between terminology and practice often leads to disappointment with results.

Concern with results in education is exemplified by the evaluation studies which were prominent during the sixties and seventies. In these evaluations, the effectiveness of educational programs was measured in terms of outputs, not in terms of service delivery. The focus on students'

1

scores on standardized tests of achievement or ability has a long history. This history is examined by Jenne K. Britell in *Competence and Excellence: The Search for an Egalitarian Standard, The Demand for a Universal Guarantee*. Britell traces the "historic fascination" that Americans have had with education and with the measurement of its outcomes. She distinguishes between a standard of competence and a standard of excellence. Educational competence is defined as that level of performance that citizens require to function in their society. Educational excellence, on the other hand, is defined as the ideal standard, established apart from the criterion of function and attained by few. Specific standards of minimum competence are more difficult to define than general standards of either competence or excellence. Although definitions have not been plentiful, tests of minimum essentials have existed, according to Britell, for five decades.

Britell points out, as do Cohen and Haney, the difference between rhetoric and practice in American education. Although we have had a rhetorical commitment to a standard of excellence, the practical operation of the system has neither provided nor been expected to provide for universal attainment of excellence. Britell notes that the explicit commitment to standards of minimum competence represents a new stage in American education. She feels that minimum competency testing substitutes a more egalitarian standard for the older standard of excellence. She also recognizes that minimum competence may be a more realistic goal than attainment of excellence, given the variability among individuals and the limitations of current educational programs. More important, minimum competency testing provides a universal guarantee; it puts an unprecedented obligation on the schools to serve everyone.

In order to understand the present demands for minimum competency testing, Britell examines two themes in public education: the issue of educational control and responsibility, and the issue of choosing between the two priorities of competence or excellence. Britell traces the responses of American educators and psychologists to the challenge of educating generations of Americans through the development of new measures to assess mental ability. This movement was subverted by the view that mental abilities were innate and that schools had little responsibility for improving such abilities, as opposed to directing and selecting students within the educational system. While thus tracing the history of efforts to measure educational outcomes, Britell also notes that the current movement toward minimum competency testing is unprecedented in the extent to which testing programs are being implemented throughout the nation.

Britell also observes that the current movement shifts the burden of responsibility for the achievement of minimum competencies from schools to students. Cohen and Haney also note that the minimum competency testing movement establishes a social and educational policy that requires results, but shifts the responsibility for demonstrating results from institutions to individuals. Society is responsible for setting minimums, but individuals are primarily responsible for achieving them. As Cohen and Haney emphasize, there are two conflicting themes in minimum competency testing: the enhancement of educational equality, versus the stigmatization of the students who fail competency tests and the resulting development of a new means for status differentiation. Cohen and Haney are concerned with whether minimum competency testing can be successful, and they suggest that it represents old, unresolved technical problems in a new form. Their conclusion is echoed by Joan C. Baratz in *Policy Implications of Minimum Competency Testing.*

Baratz examines the current focus on test results, describes the diverse efforts by states to implement minimum competency testing programs, and discusses the policy implications deriving from these programs. The programs operate within a sociopolitical environment in which concern has moved from questions of equity based on inputs (What teachers? What dollars? What programs? What equipment?), to questions of quality based on outputs (What achievement levels? What minimum standards?). Given our history of efforts to reform the schools, and our general lack of success in these efforts, Baratz questions whether there is more to minimum competency testing programs than the rhetoric that has authorized them.

A review of the current programs leads to a number of policy questions, including such issues as the state's obligation to set and defend standards, the effect of such standards on equal educational opportunity, the adequacy of the standards, and the consequences of failing the test. The current furor in New York over plans to grant "certificates of achievement" instead of diplomas to all high school seniors who fail competency tests in reading and mathematics (*New York Times*, February 11, 1979, p. 36) indicates the conflict between the governing needs of boards of education and the educational needs of students. Although minimum competency testing programs have been legislated, these policy questions have not been thoroughly analyzed. Nor are there agreed-upon views to resolve the resulting conflicts, as illustrated by the differences in New York between the commissioner of education and the Board of Regents. The effect of minimum competency testing on equal educational opportunity, for example, is such that any program that places undue hardship on minority-group children will probably not be able to withstand the political and legal challenges it provokes.* Many of the issues which Baratz examines are elaborated in later papers, which focus upon legal, curricular, and social issues (Part II) and on the implications of competency testing for students, teachers, and special educational needs (Part III).

In response to Britell's paper, Maxine Greene reexamines Britell's definitions of competence and excellence. She also examines the theme of public demand for accountability, and emphasizes that only recently have we been able to distinguish between teaching and learning. We now know that the "notion of teaching, unlike learning, has, typically, intentional as well as success uses." She suggests that there may be less than perfect evidence for using public demand for minimum competency testing as a justification for an orientation to minimum competence. Greene also poses the broader question of the reason for the failures of schools. She would have us place less emphasis on the misapplication of tests and on the preoccupation with individuals of different ability, and she questions Britell's belief that there are guarantees for the kind of education that empowers individuals to teach themselves.

Similarly, Larry Cuban's response to Joan Baratz's paper questions some of her basic assumptions. Cuban, however, is more positive about the usefulness of state-mandated programs of minimum competency testing. Speaking from the viewpoint of a school superintendent, he poses several competing explanations for the origin of the minimum competency movement, but he supports Baratz's view of the superficiality of many minimum competency testing programs. Cuban also describes two particular consequences of these programs. The first is that schools obtain better definitions of specific objectives in basic skill areas; the second is that schools examine the availability of remedial services. He feels that little change will occur where schools do not have substantial financial support. Another important consequence Cuban notes is the social cost of excluding many students, most of whom are poor and members of minority groups, from receiving regular diplomas. Large numbers of minority students will have to pay directly the cost of ineffective schooling. On the positive side, however, Cuban anticipates that the younger brothers and sisters of currently failing students may benefit.

Perhaps Cohen and Haney are correct in asking their concluding question: "Can our institutions be trusted to do the work we believed they could?" The authors of the papers in Part I provide important perspectives within which to view the answer that minimum competency testing programs provide to this question.

---

*On July 13, 1979, a Federal district judge in Florida ordered a four-year delay in making the literacy test a requirement to receive a high school diploma. The delay was ordered to ensure that the "taint of segregation is removed from Florida's public schools" (*New York Times*, July 14, 1979, p. 5).

1 Minimums, Competency Testing, and Social Policy

David K. Cohen
Walter Haney

Administering tests to determine whether students have achieved "minimum competency" in particular subjects is a recent enthusiasm, but in certain respects it embodies an old tradition—to wit, the persistent tendency in U.S. social policy to promote minimum levels of social welfare. Social policy—by which we mean governmental assumption of responsibility for the common welfare—has generally taken shape in response to the sense that the welfare of some members of society has fallen below a minimal level of decency. It was such a belief that led Horace Mann and other reformers to campaign for the provision of public primary schooling. It was a similar belief about incomes that led later reformers to initiate welfare and social security payments. In fact, social programs as diverse as Medicare and public housing have been thought of as providing a decent minimum of services or facilities for those who could not do so for themselves. In most of these programs, the hope has been that a decent minimum would help people to a better start in the race of life. Social policy has grown enormously since its inception in the early nineteenth century, and a great deal of the continuing expansion is due to the setting of minimum standards in new domains or to an increase in minimums already provided.

Minimalism has not been without problems, and some of them are illuminating for students of minimum competency tests. One is a confusion about ends: social policy has been minimalist in practice, but it is typically conceived in egalitarian terms. This creates confusion concerning the character of policy, and often engenders disappointment

5

over the results. From their inception early in this century, for example, state aid programs for schools were organized to provide a minimum level of funding for all school districts within a state. Yet while the design was purely minimalist (appropriations were even called "foundation" grants), the programs were mostly understood and debated in egalitarian terms, as offering equality, rather than a decent minimum, of educational opportunity. As a result, when analysts and reformers weighed the programs' impact decades later, they judged them a failure, for of course fiscal inequality among districts within states persisted. Had the programs been evaluated in terms of their designed goal of providing a decent minimum, the judgment probably would have been very different.

Minimum protection is not, of course, inherently inconsistent with equality. In principle, raising floors in the provision of services would increase equality, as long as higher levels did not also rise. But in the United States, as minimums have been established and increased, the whole distribution has also shifted upwards. In education, for example, social policy began in the 1830s with efforts to provide free universal elementary schooling. Throughout the last half of the nineteenth century, the country gradually approached attainment of this goal. But as success grew nearer, eight years of elementary schooling increasingly came to seem inadequate. The reasons given for this included a decreasing demand for juvenile labor and a growing sense that economic progress required more years of formal training. At the same time, it became clear that if the minimum was left at eight years of elementary schooling, a rough educational equality soon would obtain among most Americans. For those who were at the bottom of the heap this would have been a great step forward, but for children in the growing lower-middle and middle classes, it would have meant the loss of any relative advantage that might accrue from minimum formal schooling.

The solution was more schooling for the children of families who desired it—preferably at public expense, but at their own expense if necessary. On the average, this preserved the relative advantage of middle-class families without sacrificing general attainment of the minimum. As elementary enrollment increased during the last half of the nineteenth century, more and more students attended high schools, and the number of these schools grew remarkably. At the beginning, most secondary students were from middle-class backgrounds, and their numbers grew as the elementary schools included more and more students from disadvantaged elements of U.S. society. There were some fierce debates over whether secondary schools should be supported by public funds, but the struggle was not a long one; in the latter half of the nineteenth century, secondary education was freely provided in more and more places. By the turn of the century, secondary school was rapidly becoming compulsory. And later in the twentieth century, as secondary schools began to include more than middle-class and academically inclined lower-class students, the same story was played out at a higher level: as the old ceiling (high school attendance) came closer to becoming a new floor, middle-class families began sending their children to college in record numbers.

Thus, one central problem of minimalist approaches in U.S. social policy has been the implication of publicly provided minimums in promoting social and economic competition. This implication is not surprising, for the indices on which social minimums are drawn are necessarily goods or services with wide social value; we do not extend services that no one much cares about. And in the U.S., competition for these goods and services is encouraged; personal success is judged in terms of the accumulation of such things as schooling, money, housing, and medical care. Assuring a minimum level in any sector has thus also entailed a rise in the acceptable levels of attainment for those above the minimum, who wish to preserve their real or imagined advantage.

We could, of course, imagine circumstances in which those above a new minimum would choose not to increase their advantage: the choice could be discouraged by criminal penalties or tax assessments, or long-term economic stagnation could make the costs prohibitive. But the fact is that no such circumstances prevailed in the century following the initiation of social policy in education. On the contrary, the ten decades between the 1830s and the 1930s saw remarkable economic growth and a flowering of the competitive ethic in American life. As a result, the provision of minimums in education and other social services seemed to operate as a signal that everyone's portion of such services must rise—or perhaps had already risen. Minimalism appears to have been a relatively conflict-free way of improving life for those at the bottom of the American heap, because economic growth allowed those above the bottom to improve as well.

The chief consequence of this competition has been to dampen the potential equalizing effects of minimalism, and to heighten the tension between egalitarian expectations and minimalist realities. For example, the state aid programs for schools steadily increased the minimum levels of provision, but only at the price of a similar escalation all along the distribution of schooling. Welfare payments have also increased over the years, but they have not kept pace with increases in real income. And although there has been a substantial increase in welfare programs since the 1930s, there is little evidence that this increase has reduced inequalities in the distribution of income. Minimalist policies are typically couched in egalitarian terms, but that is inappropriate. The policies were designed not to reduce inequality but to establish a minimum standard of social decency. Had they been intended to reduce inequality, some device to prevent inflation of the distribution of services would have been required. No such device was even contemplated.

One hope for minimum competency testing (MCT) programs—and part of the advertising in many places—has been that if minimum standards are established, academic achievement, especially of the disadvantaged, will improve. If MCT programs work, achievement would improve only insofar as the problems of these students are absolute, not relative—for example, illiteracy as opposed to slow reading. But to the extent that the problem of students at the lower end of test distribution is simply that they are lower in the distribution, some caution is warranted. For few cases in the history of U.S. social policy suggest that minimalism may reduce inequality.

Minimalism and Social Policy: Change

This analysis suggests other salient features of minimalism, such as its association with status inflation. As we noted above, many social policy minimums seem to mark a point that most members of society seek to exceed. At least in U.S. social policy, minimums appear to represent not a decent and broadly acceptable standard of provision, but rather a stigmatized standard acceptable only if applied to those inhabiting the lower reaches of society. As a result, particular minimums rapidly became obsolete. It was, for example, little more than a generation after elementary education became nearly universal that U.S. educators began striving to achieve universal secondary education. Time and time again, today's acceptable minimum became tomorrow's social disaster. In the 1930s, for example, $15 per week was considered to be an acceptable minimum family income. By the 1960s, even after accounting for the effects of inflation, this figure had more than doubled (Jencks et al., 1972, pp. 4-5). In the United States, economic growth and social competition have been so intense that social minimums became rapidly outdated.

But the rapid obsolescence of social policy minimums is not a given. A slowing of economic growth or a relaxation of social and economic competition could lead to much more stability—but might also make it much more difficult to obtain political consensus on decent minimums. For if our analysis is correct, one explanation for the relatively generous minimums in certain sectors of social policy may be the general recognition that many people can easily exceed the minimums. If that sense were to diminish sharply as a result of hard times or of the attainment of some "natural" ceiling, the story might change. Something of this sort could even now be occurring in education, where it seems that four years of college may remain as a rough ceiling for educational attainment, leaving little opportunity for continued status inflation into postgraduate school. Under these conditions, two developments occur. One is a gradual but steady decrease in gross inequality in educational attainment (measured by years of school completed). Another, contrary but related, development is internal differentiation of post-secondary schools, in which a variety of low-status options appear, such as junior and community colleges, proprietary vocational schools, and remedial schools. In an earlier time this differentiation occurred at the lower end of secondary education. The low-status options meet real demands from new students, but they also preserve status distinctions within a system that has seemingly reduced its inequality. It is a nice question whether inequality has been actually reduced or merely redefined. Indeed, in light of the greater equality in years of schooling, MCT might be viewed as a new means of status differentiation. From this perspective it is not surprising that MCT enthusiasts are eager to reestablish the social meaning of the high-school diploma.

Thus, minimalism is neither as simple nor as attractive an approach to social policy as it appears at first glance. Much of its appeal lies in the seeming self-evidence of a particular minimum at a particular time, yet this appeal is transitory. Social policy minimums are, in fact, remarkably relative, both because of unforeseeable historical changes and because of the more readily predictable obsolescence of policy minimums due to their implication in social and economic competition. In U.S. social policy, the minimalist approach owes its durability not only to the (flawed) belief that minimum protection will substantially reduce inequality, but also to the (illusory) belief that policy minimums are stable.

Minimums, "Inputs," and "Outputs"

Change has been a central feature of minimalism in social policy, but the change most important to our discussion is not a simple raising of floors nor a reaching of ceilings in the delivery of services. Rather, it is a shift in emphasis from delivering resources to securing results. For most of the history of U.S. social policy, efforts have focused on providing services: building better housing, reducing hazards to public health, improving schools' resources. It was, of course, assumed that providing these services would have results: better schools would produce better students; better sanitation would improve health and life; higher standards of housing would improve families' abilities to function socially and produce economically. But earlier in this century, these assumptions were rarely explicit. They were simply an essential part of a climate of opinion in which it seemed evident that by creating better institutions, men could make themselves healthier, wiser, and more humane. The aim of social policy seven or eight decades ago seemed so simple as to be beyond question: to provide decent services and better institutions in a society littered with evidence of need.

By the middle of the last decade, however, the link between providing resources and producing results had become less certain, and a good deal of skepticism marked public discourse. Health policy, for example, was no longer simply a matter of providing decent medical care and insuring against threats to public health. In the face of dramatically rising costs and often intractable problems, the issue came to be whether existing health care arrangements could efficiently produce the desired results. Productivity quickly became a central concern in social policy as attention shifted to the results of investment in the common welfare.

This shift of emphasis was nowhere as striking as in education. Extensive concern with results was first seen early in the 1960s in the efforts of civil rights activists to prove that disadvantaged children were treated poorly by schools. To show this, they demanded that test results be released school by school. The reformers assumed that the low performance resulted from schools' indifference or hostility, and hoped that making the results public would stimulate improvement. This concern with results carried over into the first wave of President Johnson's Great Society programs—notably Head Start and Title I of the 1965 Elementary and Secondary Education Act. These programs were also influenced by the Johnsonian enthusiasm for results-oriented "systems analysis" management techniques; and the upshot was an increasing emphasis, in the late 1960s, on outcome evaluation of social programs. Between 1966 and 1968, studies and evaluations multiplied at an astonishing rate: the Westinghouse-Ohio evaluation of Head Start, the G.E. Tempo Title I study, the Belmont system, the Follow Through evaluation, and the Head Start Planned Variation experiment are a few examples. Each weighed the impact of programs in terms of school output, not of service delivery. And all used one sort of output—students' scores on standardized tests of achievement or ability. By the end of the 1960s, test results were the focus of social policy in education.

But the new focus was not reassuring, for the new studies raised questions about the long-assumed connection between resources and results; they often reported that special programs seemed to have no special effects. This led to growing skepticism about schools' effectiveness, and about the wisdom of investment in education. These doubts were reinforced by a succession of large-scale studies examining the relationship between school resources and school outputs. The Coleman report and its academic progeny found little or no differential effectiveness among schools: differences in resources and facilities were unrelated to differences in student performances. In the popular (and mistaken) jargon, schools "didn't make a difference."

While that statement profoundly misconstrued the research, it nicely captured the sense of disillusion that had accumulated in the wake of all the attention to results. Writing in *Science*, Robert Nichols (1966) described the Coleman report as "literally of revolutionary significance . . . . These findings stand like a spear pointed at the heart of the cherished American belief that equality of educational opportunity will increase the equality of educational achievement." On the basis of the Coleman findings, an editorial in the same periodical charged that U.S. educators had no scientific basis for their activities (Morrisett, 1966). And the same period saw a similar phenomenon in other fields; research and analysis in health, manpower training, and drug-abuse programs revealed nonexistent or very modest connections between resources and results. The more closely this connection was examined, the more dubious it seemed. Many analysts began to think that traditional assumptions about the efficacy of resources had been groundless.

All this was a great shock, because it contradicted the old and honorable Enlightenment assumption that better institutions would produce better people. And in retrospect, the next step seems almost inevitable. If enhanced resources did not enhance results, then perhaps the way to get results was to insist on them somehow. While this approach did not violate inherited ideas about the relation between resources and results, it seemed to take into account the new evidence that the relation was not automatic.

The notion of insisting on results has been much discussed in various policy areas, but most of the action has been in education. Probably the first important step was performance contracting—that is, using money incentives to assure that teachers or students achieved specified levels of performance. Several experiments were set afoot, but the results were soon pronounced a failure (Gramlich and Koshel, 1975). Shortly thereafter, several lawsuits sought to establish that school districts have a constitutional obligation to bring students to some particular level of performance. The suits failed to persuade the courts. At roughly the same time, dozens of states implemented various "accountability" schemes, and several even tried to link state aid to local schools' achievement of some performance level. These schemes produced both paper and anxiety in the education establishment, but no other results were forthcoming.

The failure of these early efforts should not obscure the fact that they may signal a turning point in social policy—a shift away from aspirations to distribute resources more fairly, toward attempts to change the distribution of results. It is difficult to imagine a change of greater moment for social policy in education. One large element in the change is the potential for much greater state responsibility for the common welfare. The past has already seen considerable growth in state responsibility; providing a decent minimum of schooling, public health, welfare, and social security has vastly increased the services for which government is responsible, and as a result government has expanded. But trying to ensure that certain minimum social results are achieved—such as minimum competency in reading—would extend that responsibility far beyond its present bounds. Assuring results, after all, is much more difficult than delivering resources, and thus would carry government into realms of action hitherto unknown.

Were such a change in policy made, it might well alter the present balance between individual and social responsibility. So far, it has been the responsibility of the individual to produce outcomes in sectors like health and education; that of society was merely to provide sufficient resources—equal or compensatory—to ensure roughly equal opportunity. If, however, results are to be assured (that is, using whatever resources may be required to provide roughly equal outputs), much of the responsibility would have to pass to the state. That could be done directly, or through a social mechanism to motivate individual achievement, such as a system of reward or punishment for success or failure. Either alternative would be quite a change. Whether society assumes greater responsibility for producing outcomes, or for dispensing rewards and punishments, is of less consequence than the assumption of the responsibility itself.

To say that the change toward a results-oriented social policy would be momentous is not to say that it would work. The approach assumes, for example, that purposefully designed environments, or individual motivation, can be powerful enough to produce those better results we would like from schooling or health care. It also assumes that these more powerful environments or incentives could be managed by governments in ways consistent with liberty. And it may assume that we can learn enough about the social and individual processes by which results occur to engineer their production more successfully. Such assumptions are a major part of our intellectual inheritance, but they are not demonstrably true.

Minimum Competency Tests and a Policy of Results

So far, worries about such matters have not diminished enthusiasm for a results-oriented policy in education. On the contrary, the MCT movement suggests that enthusiasm is growing. Since the early 1970s, testing programs of this sort have become remarkably popular. As things now stand, a majority of states has taken some action in the direction of MCT, and many have operating programs. The programs differ in many respects—including the grade levels and subject involved, the role of the tests in decisions about graduation or promotion, and the presence or absence of remedial help. Nearly all of them seek at least two things: to define minimum learning outcomes for students in a variety of academic areas, and to insure that these standards are satisfied—but none make it clear how.

But while MCT derives from a results-oriented social policy, it also seems to be a move away from social responsibility for results. For while MCT leaves it to the state to set minimum standards, it shifts the burden of satisfying minimums from the state to the individual. Until now, U.S. social policy has been solidly founded on the notion that society is responsible for providing a minimum of goods or services to those in need. With MCT, however, society sets the standards while the individual (occasionally with some remedial help) is responsible for meeting them.

That is a point of great importance. Of course, some MCT programs do assume some responsibility for remedial work, and many educators now accept that environmental factors can impede children's ability to perform well on tests. But in the prevailing moral atmosphere, individual responsibility for intellectual work is still thought to be preeminent. At least for the time being, then, it is quite likely that those who fall below MCT minimums will be held primarily responsible for the failure. This marks a distinct change in ideas about the responsibility for achieving social policy minimums. MCT not only announces that the important success criterion is outcome; it also suggests that, while society is responsible for establishing minimum performance levels, individuals are responsible for attaining them.

Thus, while the new emphasis on results implies an expansion of social responsibility for welfare, the concept of individual responsibility for results embodied in MCT programs seems to promise a contraction of social responsibility. One wonders what to make of the seeming contradiction.

One possibility is that we are beginning a new, results-oriented epoch in social policy, in which confusion and contradiction are natural. In the second quarter of the nineteenth century, when the U.S. first moved toward public assumption of responsibility for primary schooling, there was a similar muddle. Some advocated the extension of state responsibility; others opposed it. Some early efforts to provide a minimum of public education produced governmentally operated schools; others relied on public subsidies to secular schools; still others, on public subsidies to religious schools. In at least one case, a private corporation ran the "public" schools. One could thus argue that, just as conceptions about the meaning of "public" and "responsibility" were quite unclear and sometimes contradictory at the outset of social policy in education, so now are ideas about the scope of responsibility for a social policy of results. Perhaps the confusions will clear up as experimentation settles into a pattern of expanding public responsibility for outcomes.

It is also possible that the seeming contradiction concerning responsibility for results reflects a deep ambivalence about the character of social policy. MCT may embody two contrary tendencies in U.S. social policy. One tendency is for society to assume responsibility for those who, for reasons unrelated to their own effort or ability, are unable to provide a minimal level of social decency for themselves; the other is to stigmatize the objects of social policy, and to use policy to that end. Certainly many social minimums in the United States have been thus stigmatized, as a result either of social and economic competition or of specific policy procedures. Earlier in this essay, for example, we explored how first elementary and later high school education came to seem inadequate, and thus in a sense to be stigmatized—to appear as under-education. This was the result not of policy as such, but of the interaction between intense competition over school attainment and a social policy of public provision of minimums (without valuing equality enough to restrict ceilings). In such cases, minimums acquire the status, in social and economic competition, of levels to be avoided by being exceeded.

There are, of course, also examples of policy taking a more direct role in creating a stigma. Public housing is stigmatized specifically because of the character of policy: what is provided is generally barren, ugly, and set apart from its surroundings. These qualities are habitually associated with stigmatized institutions: we say that a public housing project looks "like a prison" or "a state hospital." Public housing has the character of a last resort rather than that of adequacy. To take a more familiar case, policy has traditionally stigmatized recipients of welfare through: humiliating means-tests and application procedures; searches of recipients' homes without observation of constitutional guarantees; and programs of work-relief which make it plain that welfare recipients are being punished. In these different ways, policy sets its objects apart from society and marks them as inadequate and inferior.

It is not difficult to identify stigmatizing tendencies within MCT. The movement to extend social responsibility from resources to results may appear humane; but to set minimum standards without also assuming social responsibility for those who fall below them recalls the old tendency to stigmatize the objects of social policy. The new test minimums may resemble an educational means-test, which sets the debris of U.S. education apart from everyone else. There is, after all, a history of just such endeavors in education during the last seven or eight decades. Some of the most telling examples are the use of "general" curriculum tracks in secondary schools as a dumping ground; the use of special schools for the same purposes (New York City's "600" schools, for example); the role of special education classes in many school systems, at least until recently; and, of course, the use of ability grouping in elementary schools. In each case, policy created special categories intended to offer carefully designed treatment, support, or encouragement for those in need. Sometimes that happened. But often it did not, for reasons—whether fiscal, social or psychological—associated with the stigma attached to the "special" educational categories.

Minimum competency testing may thus reinforce the tendency in U.S. education to confuse special needs with what Erving Goffman termed "spoiled identity." States and districts may use the special categories not as a device for improving the condition of those in need and repairing their connections to everyone else, but as a means of separating and stigmatizing them.

Origins of Minimum Competency Testing

Is MCT, then, a progressive shift of attention in social policy toward providing outcomes, as a means of enhancing educational equality; or will it act as another means of status differentiation? Prediction would be foolish. Not only is the future resistant to our forecasts, but the two tendencies are not mutually exclusive. MCT embodies both now, and is likely to do so in the future. The question is, what balance may we expect between these durable tendencies in U.S. social policy? We may learn something on this point from a review of the circumstances in which the MCT movement arose. Is it due primarily to generous or to punitive impulses?

In some cases, the answer is neither. The spread of input-output conceptions of social organization is an example. The idea that schools, hospitals, and government agencies could be viewed as factories—as processing human raw material and creating human outputs, and therefore as being more or less efficient—owes a great deal to the influence of economic ideas, both scientific and popular, on the social sciences and social thought generally. Whether or not this way of thinking about social life is appropriate, it has contributed greatly to the intellectual and political climate in which MCT seems sensible. Similarly, it might be argued that education

is particularly vulnerable to results-oriented policy and evaluation, because, unlike other policy sectors, it is susceptible to measurement of
outputs as well as inputs. Students, after all, do take tests, and the results
are chiefly quantitative; whereas patients leaving a hospital are not scored
on an inventory of health, nor do social security recipients fill out an
annual twenty-item scale on the economic and social impact of the payments. More simply, no one can tell us how much health or, much less,
how much security he or she experiences. But anyone can tell us how much
education he or she has. Schooling is considered in discrete quantitative
entities—years, semesters, test scores—and in this respect is unlike most
other social services. This common quantitative language for discussing
achievement makes education particularly susceptible to input-output
analysis.

These factors help to explain why a results-oriented policy has taken
hold so quickly in education; but one must look elsewhere for evidence
on the possible political tendencies of MCT. One critical point is the extent
to which MCT takes responsibility for dealing with those whose competency is less than minimal. Florida's MCT scheme, for example, gave little,
if any, attention to the issue of remediation before the startling finding in fall
1977 that 40 to 50 percent of the students failed portions of the state test
(Fisher, 1978). Even in Massachusetts, which has one of the most liberal
approaches to MCT in the form of a program of "basic skills improvement," the signs are not auspicious. The aim of the program is to "improve
the attainment of basic skills competency by students . . . not to establish
a new condition for promotion or graduation" (Massachusetts State Board
of Education, August 1978). Yet the Massachusetts policy explicitly does
not establish a separate instructional program beyond the services normally provided in public schools. Indeed, it was predicated on the assumption that the basic skills improvement program would cost nothing extra.

Unhappily, there is evidence of either parsimonious or punishing
inclinations nearly everywhere. MCT has gained momentum in a climate
of scarce resources and scarcer patience with professionals and their
clients. Questions about the efficacy of social policy have taken on a
particularly pessimistic and even punishing aspect. California voters were
urged to vote for Proposition 13, for example, not just to react against
taxation, but also to defeat busing for school integration and to oppose
welfare payments. The pinched condition of most budgets in social
agencies is understood not only as a consequence of hard times, but also
as a reaction to liberal reform that "does not work." In the present climate,
the general worry about getting one's money's worth is not simply a comment on corruption or economic constraints, but part of a broad opposition to increased spending on social welfare programs of doubtful efficacy.

In such a climate the characteristic reflex is to blame both providers and recipients of social services for program failure. It would not be surprising if MCT provided more ammunition for this reflex.

The Viability of Minimum Competency Testing

One reason why MCT seems likely to encourage a punitive reaction is the scant evidence that minimum competency testing can be successful. It is, of course, impossible to be certain on this point. In 1860 public support for high schools seemed unwise to many Americans, and in 1954 the desegregation of southern schools struck most as entirely unworkable. The wisdom or workability of social innovations is rarely clear in advance. But although there can be no sure-fire forecast, one can identify some of the elements probably required for MCT to work. One element would be a face-valid conception of the minimum. In the 1930s a modest subsistence seemed a face-valid retirement income; this helped social security legislation to pass. In the 1840s, when most schools were primary schools, providing primary school for all had broad social face-validity. One might argue that if the minimum is seriously disputed and there is no generally accepted way to settle the dispute, minimalism will not work even if there is agreement on other points. President Nixon's abortive Family Assistance Plan may be an example of a minimum so lacking in broad social face-validity that it could not be made policy.

Does a minimum with broad social face-validity exist among educational outcomes? The answer is unclear, for while there is general uncertainty about what the right outcomes are, it is widely agreed that such skills as reading and mathematics are essential "competencies." There is no agreement, however, about what else is essential. Some state programs include little else, while others include social, personal, and attitudinal "competencies." These differences are unlikely to be resolved by argument or evidence. After all, education has many possible aims, and the past century has seen persistent disagreement about which of these deserved inclusion in the public agenda.

It does seem possible, though, that consensus could crystallize around a minimum core of skills, such as reading and mathematics. There are, of course, fundamental problems. Specialists disagree about how to define competency in reading: Is it decoding or comprehension? In math, there is disagreement about the virtues of what is termed problem-solving ability as opposed to computational skills. Nevertheless, the wide acceptance of the National Assessment of Educational Progress (NAEP) tests is encouraging evidence that a consensus is possible. These tests were the subject of bitter dispute, but after being adopted they gained widespread legitimacy. Thus, despite the disagreements, it is possible that a particular MCT battery will be widely adopted, seem workable, and *become* a socially valid minimum.

But to be workable, MCT probably would also have to have a simple and plausible way of determining whether the minimum has been achieved. In the case of input-oriented minimums this is fairly easy. One can know how many dollars the government pays a retired person, or whether primary schools are being provided, or how many children attend them. One can even know what proportion of all children in an age group attend, and how far they go. Each measure involves simple counting on indices widely known and believed to be definitive—dollars, or years of school, or numbers of people. The counting may be difficult, because it is on a large scale and even simple data may be hard to find; but at least it is not made more difficult by doubts about the conceptual character or validity of the measures. By contrast, decent housing is a minimum that is difficult to achieve because of conceptual problems. Ideas about what decent housing is seem to vary greatly, despite the long history of census work on the matter. Officials and commentators cannot agree on what the government ought to provide, or on the quality of what it did provide, in public housing.

Some minimums in education do satisfy this criterion, such as years of school completed. High school graduation, for example, was for a long time a face-valid measure of a social policy minimum. But most school outcome measures are not like this. The obvious case in education is tests. Despite general agreement among parents and professionals that what tests measure is very important, few agree on the right tests to use— for example, the Scholastic Aptitude Test or the New York Regents exams—or on what test level is the necessary minimum. While testing is seen as a legitimate activity, only rarely has a given test achieved pre-eminence in its own realm. For teachers, parents, students, and test experts can read different tests on the same subject and notice differences, but find no intuitively appealing or broadly accepted way of deciding which test is best. Of course, states with operating MCT programs use some sort of test, and other states are developing tests. But the tests are all different, in subject-matter focus, in difficulty, and in other respects as well. It is true, though, that MCT programs may simply preempt the field (as the New York Regents did) on a state-by-state basis. Thus, while confusion may be expected to continue with minimum competency testing, other considerations suggest that some tests may gain exclusive or near-exclusive dominance in their states.

Finally, and perhaps most problematic, a successful minimalist social program must have a relatively simple way of satisfying the minimum standard. The government, for example, has so far produced social security payments with remarkable accuracy and regularity. The same can be said of the provision of welfare payments, school resources, and health care. This does not mean that everything about the delivery of the goods and services in question is manageable, or even understandable. Not all influences on the size of social security payments are controllable by government. Nor can government control such variations in the character of the teaching force as generational changes in its values, or changes in the patterns of recruitment to the profession. But in all these areas, government has so far been able to understand enough and control enough to deliver the prescribed minimum input of money, or teachers, or housing, or medical care.

As everyone knows by now, the production of social policy outcomes is less reliable. If we understand influences on the provision of resources only imperfectly, we understand the creation of outcomes still less well. There is, of course, no question that schools are effective in teaching skills; algebra, French, and geography, like large areas of reading, do not spring spontaneously to mind; schools teach them. But there is a very weak understanding of why some students, teachers, classrooms, or schools are more productive than others in the same subjects. Thus far, all the evidence suggests that there are important differences in effectiveness, but that they have no uniform causes. They seem to be the result of complex interactions among individuals, social settings, times, and places. Thus, we know that establishing schools where there are none will create competencies where they were weak or nonexistent. And we know that a major increase in the amount of schooling (in a given subject) will increase average competencies across the board (or in that subject). But we know little about creating differential competencies within the same broad levels of provision.

What is more, if our understanding is weak, our ability to control the relevant factors is even more precarious. As the previous discussion suggests, we do not know what to control. Furthermore, controlling some of the things that might turn out to be relevant could violate laws and customs. Reformers have long argued, for example, that intense environments may be the only way to remedy environmentally induced inadequacies in academic skills; social theorists as diverse as Robert Owen and James Coleman have urged the creation of boarding schools for the poor. But such a policy would violate custom, and might lead to all the abuses we associate with other institutions designed for, or primarily populated by, the poor. In addition, many of the things that might have to be controlled in order to affect outcomes significantly may be uncontrollable within the present social order—such as early child-rearing practices, teachers' attitudes, verbal ability, and students' motivation.

VRJC LIBRARY

Taken together, these caveats suggest caution in thinking about the capacity of schools to satisfy MCT standards. There is, in addition, much discouraging evidence on this score from the last twenty years' experience with remedial and compensatory education: it seems quite likely that MCT programs, even if established in a spirit of generosity and social concern, may be unable to help many of those who fail. Without a reliable means of "remediation," one wonders what constructive purpose could be served by large-scale public announcements of failure. MCT may thus be caught between two problematic alternatives: reducing minimums to levels that would fail only a few in order to avoid stigma and the consequent reaction; or setting minimums higher, with the likely result that both the schools and the students are blamed for the ensuing failures.

Conclusion

In a certain sense, then, MCT simply presents old unsolved problems in new form. Standardized tests have never resolved disagreements about the nature of subject matter, because subject-matter specialists cannot resolve them. And standardized tests cannot decide what competency is; they can define competency only relatively by referencing all scores to an average or criterion score. Competent students are those who do better than other students or than required by the criterion. One might reasonably argue, in fact, that MCT took these old problems, removed them from the obscurity to which they were carefully consigned, and enshrined them as the centerpiece of the new policy. It seems a curious approach.

Yet while the technical viability of MCT is no small concern, this has not been our sole or even chief focus. Instead we have tried to locate MCT within the broader context of U.S. social policy. We have argued that the new testing movement represents a curious blend of old and new. It embodies old themes—the emphasis on minimalism, the ambivalence between stigmatizing and helping tendencies in social policy—but gives them a paradoxical new twist. MCT seems progressive because it promises to extend public responsibility from providing resources to providing results. Yet it seems conservative because it promises to contract public responsibility by shifting the burden of achieving competency from society to the individual. MCT programs will stigmatize the students who fail to learn, and by implication at least, the schools that fail to teach, even though experience and research strongly suggest that the test instruments are of doubtful quality, and that we are far from being able to remedy the failures thus revealed. If the matter were not so serious it would be laughable:

the only reliable way we have of reducing failure in MCT programs is to reduce the cutoff points on the tests.

The problems discussed in this essay seem unlikely to recede. The last two decades have seen a remarkable increase in concern about results in social policy; but as time has passed hopes have dwindled. No idea has been more central to U.S. social policy than the inherited notion that many social defects can be remedied by improving the environment, and nothing has been more unsettling than the evidence that creating new institutions, or providing more resources, does not always or even usually improve results. As evidence on this point has accumulated, questions about inherited liberal doctrine have mounted. Some commentators have portrayed the evidence as a sign of crisis in liberal social policy—even, perhaps, of its impending collapse. While that strikes us as a little premature, it is difficult to overstate the concern and pessimism consequent on the shift of attention to policy outcomes.

The outlook for MCT programs is thus not a happy one. Because of their inability thus far to do a convincing job in remedial education, schools will probably be unable to remedy the failures that MCT programs will define. And that will probably simply worsen the situation MCT programs were intended to correct. The failure of programs aimed at improving results may discredit the test instruments that reported the failure; it may further undermine confidence in the schools that were to produce the results or remedy the failure; or it may encourage onlookers to blame the students. None seems particularly appealing.

In some respects, then, the most hopeful sign would be that the reports of MCT programs were simply ignored. Certainly much worthy information meets this fate, and one should not underestimate the public's ability to yawn at a critical juncture. But if the current enthusiasm for school outcomes continues, we cannot expect understanding to keep pace. There is now great uncertainty about long-standing assumptions in social policy—especially about the extent to which social service institutions can produce the results they have advertised. This has led to confusion, both about the possible scope of social policy and about the potential effectiveness of social services. The confusion is of course not yet untangled, nor should we expect it to be in the near future. Basic questions have been raised, and it will take a long time for new experience and new investigations to put these questions in better focus. In the meantime it makes sense to realize that MCT, like many other current policy initiatives, may be more a symptom of the disruption of our ideas about social policy than a solution to this disorder. MCT is part of a large but somewhat incoherent effort to come to terms with unsettled ideas about the effectiveness of social services, and with greater dissatisfaction than we have previously known.

Every new effort to produce results appears as a declaration, but in a sense the declaration is a question, perhaps even a worry: Can our institutions be trusted to do what we believed they could?

References

Fisher, T. H. Florida's approach to competency testing. *Phi Delta Kappan* 59 (1978): 599-602.

Gramlich, E. M. & Koshel, P. P. *Educational performance contracting*. Washington, D.C.: Brookings, 1975.

Jencks, C., Smith, M., Acland, H., Bane, M., Cohen, D., Gintis, H., Heyns, B., & Michelson, S. *Inequality: A reassessment of the effect of family and schooling in America*. New York: Basic Books, 1972.

Massachusetts State Board of Education. *Policy on basic skills improvement*. Boston: Massachusetts Department of Education, August 29, 1978.

Morrisett, L. W. Preschool education. *Science* 153 (September 9, 1966): 3741.

Nichols, R. C. Schools and the disadvantaged. *Science* 154 (December 9, 1966): 3754.

2 Competence and Excellence: The Search for an Egalitarian Standard, the Demand for a Universal Guarantee

Jenne K. Britell

Introduction

In the papers that follow, others will analyze the various issues evoked by the current use of a standard of minimum competence: the lack of consensus on its substance; the rational or irrational basis for the chosen levels; the demand for and resistance to such a standard; the success or failure of efforts to quantify competence; and the struggle for political control of the requirements. These issues have also marked earlier efforts to evaluate the achievements of public elementary and secondary schools.

Americans have a historic fascination with educational yield and its measurement. Neither educators nor the critical public, however, has ever defined the *nature* of the educational standards that American schooling should achieve. This failure to specify has marred discussions of the

In the preparation of the address, the author was fortunate to have the assistance of the following: William H. Angoff, Henry S. Dyer, John J. Fremer, Jr., Jules M. Goodison, Albert P. Maslow, Elizabeth I. Mayer, Genevieve C. Montagna, William W. Turnbull, Lee S. Waks, Cheryl J. Weiner, and E. Belvin Williams. Through Maxine Green's criticism, I have become aware of the possible misinterpretation of my term, "the training of the mind." By "training," I intend *discipline*, a skill learned both from others and from one's own experience. This quality is critical to the achievement of educational competence and the consequent ability to function—that is, "to apply skills learned to other situations that require communication, examination of alternatives, and decision." I believe discipline of the mind is consistent with Greene's concept of the abilities necessary to communicate, examine alternatives, and to make decisions; it is also consistent with Dewey's and Ryle's views, which she cites.

standard of competence and the standard of excellence. The two are not intrinsically in conflict, although some contemporary discussants pose them as alternatives. Competence differs from excellence in *character* as well as in *level*. Competence is the state of adequate performance of a task. It usually is not comparative. One is competent or incompetent in relation to the required performance, not in relation to others' achievements. Excellence is both an absolute state of achievement and the highest level of performance attained by a few (relative to the many).

In my discussion of the history of a standard of minimum competence and its assessment in public elementary and secondary education, I define educational competence as that level of performance that citizens require in order to function in the society in which they live. The competence required in one kind of society, therefore, will differ from that required in another. In the United States, the society is technologically advanced and remains committed to democratic government. To "function" here is to apply the skills learned to other situations that require communication, examination of alternatives, and decision. This competence differs from the objective of the earlier life adjustment movement, which also stressed "usefulness in life." Educational competence is rooted in educational achievement. It requires the training of the mind; it is not anti-intellectual. I define educational excellence as the ideal standard, established apart from the criterion of function and at a level currently attained by the few: in essence, the Platonic Pure Form.

The specific standard of *minimum* competence may be more difficult to delineate than the general standards of either competence or excellence, for two reasons. First, it requires unprecedented attention to definition, if we intend more than only basic skills in academic subjects; and many of the new statutes do not limit the schools' obligations to basic skills. Second, it requires precision and consensus on the choice of levels. Past commentators have recognized the difficulty of specifying the minimum level; the difficulty existed whether one sought to assess achievement or aptitude. In 1936, E. F. Lindquist noted: "There are few if any high school or college courses for which the minimum essentials have been authoritatively described in a form sufficiently specific to make possible the construction of such tests."[1] In 1949, Dewey Stuit counseled guidance personnel in their use of aptitude test scores to advise prospective graduate school applicants: "Unfortunately there is no simple answer to the question of what constitutes a minimum level of aptitude for success in a professional school. If all professional schools followed exactly the same curriculum, observed the same standards, and could enroll student populations of the same qualifications, it would be possible to set minimum specifications for admissions to these training programs."[2] Yet despite the difficulties, minimum competence has been assessed in elementary and secondary education for some time, although the term "minimum competence" has appeared frequently in the literature only within the past five years.[3]

Let me illustrate. First, tests of minimum essentials of academic subjects have existed for five decades. The initial rationale for such measures was similar to that put forth by contemporary advocates of basic skills assessment. Many testing experts have opposed these tests; they have argued that the tests fail to recognize differences in individual learning growth and also lack comparability. (One developer's "minimum" is not another's.[4])

Second, tests of minimum competence in which the pass-fail system operates have been and still are important. In this category are some credit-by-examination programs, such as the Tests of General Educational Development (GED) and the College Level Examination Program (CLEP).

Third, tests traditionally used for selection have at times certified a minimum level of competence. The New York State Regents Examinations initially had this function when they were established for elementary schools (1865) and high schools (1878). In the latter instance, the Regents Examinations were analogous to the high school examinations now required in some states. In 1901, the College Board established the passing score of 60 (on a scale of 100) for its achievement tests for college admissions; it thus certified the minimum acceptable level of knowledge of a subject.

Fourth, the use of cutting scores in admissions and placement processes represents a present standard of minimum competence.

Fifth, the concept of minimum mental competence (as opposed to minimum achieved competence) has been used to identify that level below which the individual is assumed unable to perform certain tasks. Tests such as the Stanford-Binet have this functional use. This is relevant because of the schools' historic use of individual and group intelligence tests. In contrast to the present, such tests stressed mental capability rather than educational achievement.

Sixth, there is the similarity noted by Gray between Piagetian theory and criterion-referenced measurement; criterion-referenced measures are the most frequently used instruments in the present assessments of minimum competence.[5]

In addition, an implicit minimum level has been used in operations in which the explicit emphasis has been on achievement relative to the highest level. Examples include age-grade equivalents, promotion standards, and ability grouping and grading, as practiced by school systems or within individual classrooms.

Thus the assessment of minimum competence is not new. Some of the present furor may therefore stem from the newly explicit respectability of the goal of *minimum* competence and the attempt to mandate its achievement. This recent emphasis contrasts with the earlier stress on the "highest standards" (never clearly defined). In American education, however, rhetoric often has differed from practice. There has long been a rhetorical commitment to the standard of excellence, but in practice, the operation of an educational system that neither provided nor expected to provide for the universal attainment of excellence. Such attainment has been impossible with the finite resources, finite time, and educational structure that exist. These realities have not allowed the educational system to deal with the range of individual differences of styles and rates of learning in a manner and to the extent required to achieve universal excellence.

The explicit imposition of the standard of minimum competence represents a new stage in American education.

First, it substitutes a more egalitarian standard for the standard of excellence. It is an effort to reconcile proved individual differences with the political demands for equality of achievement in a society that espouses equality of opportunity.

Second, it recognizes that minimum competence may be the most realistic educational goal, given the variability among individuals and the limitations of our current educational programs.

Third, it provides a universal guarantee. It places an unprecedented obligation on the schools to serve everyone. In this sense, the imposition of a standard of minimum competence reflects the political demands of the 1960s that the public educational system serve its entire constituency. I distinguish here between the significance of the standard and some of the abuses of practice, chiefly the use of the test when there is no opportunity for remedy. Such abuse shifts the obligation to achieve the minimum standard from the school to the student.

In the next section of this paper, I shall trace the evolution of the present demand for minimum competence through two interrelated historical themes in American public elementary and secondary education.

First, there is the issue of *educational control and responsibility*. Though educators have accepted ultimate public control, they have continually struggled with the public for the power to establish specific requirements. The Boston School Committee encountered resistance to its written examinations in 1845. The New York State Regents were opposed in their efforts. At various times in the twentieth century, college admission requirements and the College Board's examinations have been considered inappropriate determinants of high school curricula.

The controlling public also has increased its demands that educators and schools assume a greater responsibility for results. Educational practitioners have been criticized more for their failure to meet public expectations than for their failure to manage public funds. Horace Mann spoke of "the perilous coast where the hopes of so many parents and so many children have been wrecked."[6] In a 1936 study, I. L. Kandel compared American and European attitudes toward education. Americans believed "schools must meet the actual and immediate needs and abilities of children." Americans were also "accustomed to more direct participation in educational affairs and less influenced by respect for educational and social traditions."[7]

Administrators and teachers rarely have challenged these demands until they have failed to meet them. In the twentieth century, the public has demanded precise evidence of educators' success and precise explanations of their failure. Educators have responded with quantitative discussions of educational quality. The measures have permitted differentiation among levels of ability and among levels of academic performance; they have not provided for the concomitant differentiation of competence. The public has accepted such measurement and now suspects any evidence or argument that is not quantitative. Preoccupation with the gauge has distracted further from efforts to define educational standards.

Second, there is the issue of *choice between the two educational priorities of competence and excellence.* While absolute choice is not necessary, society must still establish a priority—with regard to the concentration of energy, value, and resources. The three are not the same. For example, even when we have concentrated resources on the average student, we have *prized* the most able. The choice has become more difficult as a result of the greater knowledge of individual differences and of the demands of a technologically dependent nation that competes with other countries. Ultimately, the choice has always required interpretation of two American fundamental values: equality of opportunity and equality of individuals. Whatever our practices, we have not relinquished the rhetorical commitment to these principles; thus they must be considered in any discussion of choice.

In 1907, the National Education Association (NEA) established the Committee on the Provision for Exceptional Children in the Public Schools. Benjamin Ide Wheeler, president of the University of California, stated a position that continually has been debated in the twentieth century: "Our democracy involves no proposition of equality of achievement but straightforwardly and supremely equality of opportunity. . . . It established no standard size of foot or brain. . . . It proposed to give every man a real chance to make the most possible out of his single life."[8]

In 1936, Kandel argued that equality of opportunity did not mean identity of opportunity.[9] In 1961, John W. Gardner asked "Can we be equal and excellent too?"[10] We have never successfully defined equality of opportunity in a manner that satisfies everyone.

The Schools' Obligation: Competence or Excellence?

A competent electorate was the earliest justification for a publicly-supported school system. Because the polity was primarily white and male, these groups received the attention and controlled the definition and assessment of competence. The terms "proficiency," "sufficiency," and "competence" were used to describe the objective of public education. Where "excellence" appeared in the general discussion of public education, it was not separate from competence.

From the beginning, the controlling public sought evidence of money well spent. In 1709, Boston established a committee of "gentlemen of liberal education" to inspect the schools and to "inform themselves of the methods used in the teaching of the scholars and to inquire of their *proficiency*."[11] In 1789, the Massachusetts General Court required that selectmen and others "shall inquire into the proficiency of scholars"[12] in the schools. These examinations were oral; pupils were chosen by the masters; and of significance for the future, the level of proficiency was neither specified nor debated.

In 1845, the Boston School Committee developed and administered written examinations in history, astronomy, arithmetic, and geography to some members of the first class, selected by the masters. For the first time, the masters and teachers did not have prior access to the examinations. Horace Mann, secretary of the Massachusetts Board of Education, described the Boston School Committee's objective: "The method of examination tests in a most admirable manner the *competency* or *sufficiency* of the teaching which the pupils have received; for as a workman is not taught any art or handicraft until he can execute it, so a child is not taught any principle until he can explain it or apply it" (italics added).[13] Mann reported the committee's disappointing conclusion: "The Grammar Schools of Boston have not the excellence and usefulness that they should possess." Only 45 percent met the desired level in history; 39 percent in astronomy; 35 percent in arithmetic; and 34 percent in geography.[14] (Actual conditions were even worse, since only the best scholars, determined by the master, had been examined.) Mann's final comment fits our contemporary litany: "In other towns, where teachers were receiving far inferior compensation and where an improved system of schools had but recently been organized, the pupils would be found to be far superior to the pupils in the Boston schools."[15]

The Boston School Committee consequently recommended changes in the method of instruction, more stringent requirements for teachers, greater accountability from the masters, and examination of a larger sample of pupils.

The public demand for evidence of educational competence continued. Written examinations at both the elementary and secondary levels proliferated in the second half of the nineteenth century. Chicago introduced an examination for high school admissions in 1856 and later utilized it in promotion. The aforementioned Regents Examinations appeared. After 1875, high schools moved from a pass-fail system to a five (A-B-C-D-F) or three-point (E-P-F) scale. After 1900, most elementary schools reorganized their grading practices to fit similar patterns.[16]

But the precision was far less than it appeared. There were few efforts to examine the content of the public expectation, to achieve consistency across evaluations, or to consider the comparative or absolute nature of the standard of competence. From contemporary reports, one can conclude that the standard represented both a comparative assessment (based on others' performance) and the judge's ideal of performance. Grades also reflected the teachers' opinion of an individual's appearance, behavior, and family background.

The years from 1890 to 1917 were years of change in the methods and criteria by which quality was judged in American life. The principle of quality control was developed; uniformity was introduced; better records were kept; structure and consistency were increasingly valued. Education was expected to conform to the new ways. In retrospect, Max McConn, dean of Lehigh and a leading educational reformer during the twenties and thirties, described the period from 1890 to 1915 as the "Age of the Standard" in education: "To set standards and to enforce standards and to raise them even more was nearly the whole duty of teachers and principals and presidents."[17]

The social context within which educators operated had changed, and the school systems also were changing. Educational administrators faced problems that would recur throughout the twentieth century: there were not enough teachers or classrooms; there were varying practices; teaching was inconsistent and often poor; and there was a growing, increasingly heterogeneous student population. A pattern of educational behavior developed that also would recur throughout the twentieth century. First, educational leaders recognized the need for reform; second, they moved slowly to institute reforms; third, the public learned of the debacle; and fourth, educators were on the barricades, and they sacrificed deliberate action for immediate defense.

In 1897, in the first of the new educational exposés, Joseph Mayer Rice reported that children were not competent in spelling. Later, he reported that neither were they competent in arithmetic. Rice based his conclusions on the results of tests that he had devised and administered. In these tests, Rice stressed application of the skill learned in the classroom.

Rice was only the first. As a result of public demand for concrete evidence of educational quality, the U.S. commissioner of education, Elmer Ellsworth Brown, enlisted experts to explain the Office of Education's annual statistical report. E. L. Thorndike wrote the introduction to the 1907 analysis; George M. Strayer, the introduction to the 1908 edition. Thorndike set forth very clearly the audience of the *Report* and of American education: "I shall try to show in some measure what these statistics reveal that is of interest and significance; first, to all intelligent citizens; second, to the half-million men and women who are engaged in the work of teaching; and third, to those teachers, clergymen, editors, statesmen, and other students of education who lead public opinion and should possess expert knowledge."[18]

The public, particularly school boards and educational critics, read the tables. Leonard Ayres, director of the Russell Sage Investigation of Backward Children, expressed concern because "students and critics of our public schools are paying more and more attention to the record of the figures printed in the annual reports of superintendents and school boards."[19] The "record," especially of the high retardation* and elimination, testified more to the schools' failure than to their success. Simon Patten noted in 1911: "It is not the schools vs. graft but the schools vs. street cleaning, pure water, tenement house inspection, the prevention of disease or the reduction of infant mortality. The advocate of pure water or clean streets shows how much the death rate will be altered by each proposed addition to his share of the budget. Only the teacher is without such figures."[20]

To remedy this circumstance, in 1912 the National Education Association (NEA) established the Committee on Tests and Standards of Efficiency. George M. Strayer, the chairman, explained its goal: "From such measurements, it will be possible to describe accurately the accomplishments of children and to devise a series of standards which will be applicable to varying groups of children and to different social demands."[21]

Educational achievement tests of various school subjects were developed. With these, administrators and teachers assessed the degree of attainment of the standard. The measure provided evidence; it therefore took precedence over the definition of the standard. Despite warnings on the lack of standardization and on the uncontrolled sample populations,

---

*Defined as grade level of two or three years below age.

the tests proliferated.[22] Many communities instituted school surveys in which these tests were used. By 1918, there were 84 tests for elementary school and 25 for secondary school. Annual sales of tests became significant. Monroe reported sales of 900,000 copies of one test and sales of 200,000 of at least two others.[23] Fourteen cities established bureaus of educational research in part to analyze test data.

With tests of educational achievement, educators could not solve the problem of how to classify children by *ability*. The problem was not limited to the United States. In the 1903 *Report of the U.S. Commissioner of Education*, a writer estimated that "probably one percent [of pupils in each country] are so dull and defective that they cannot be taught in the ordinary school classes."[24] Although Boston, Philadelphia, Springfield, and Chicago had special classes before 1900, school administrators needed better methods of sorting their students.

The early work of American psychologists on the measurement of mental ability was not responsive to the educators' problem. Led by James McKeen Cattell of Columbia, American psychologists initially sought to assess intelligence with the use of psychomotor tests.[25] In contrast, Alfred Binet began with the problem that also faced American administrators—the separation of normal from dull students. After fifteen years of experimentation, Binet developed a scale of various tasks of mental performance for use in the Paris schools. American psychologists knew of Binet's work from its inception, because Binet was the editor of *L'Année Psychologique* (which was referenced in the *Psychological Index*). Moreover, American psychologists (including Edmund Huey of The Johns Hopkins University) studied with Binet; and Edward Hamilton Buchner reported on Binet's work annually after 1905 in the *Psychological Bulletin*.

Psychology was a growing profession; the number of Ph.D.'s was increasing, and psychologists welcomed every opportunity to illustrate the value of their work. In pupil classification, psychologists found an area in which they could be relevant, and educators welcomed their assistance. Lightner Witmer, often considered the founder of American clinical psychology, felt that the psychological expert's participation in investigations of retardation would "furnish standards of reference to judge the extent we fail to educate the rising generation of this country."[26]

In the years from 1908 to 1917, American psychologists expanded on Binet's research; they revised the scale and developed new measures. In the Stanford revision, Lewis Terman took the mental quotient—the ratio of mental age to chronological age (developed in 1912 by William Stern, a German psychologist)—and multiplied it by 100 to produce the IQ. By 1917, individual intelligence tests, such as the Binet, were used in schools, clinics, hospitals, immigration centers, and the New York City Police Department. In the last instance, the *New York Times* described the City's effort. "If the policeman is uncertain, he may march his suspect up an alley and apply a Binet test. . . . A mental standard of recognition will be inculcated, so that officers on duty may be immediately aware of a mental or moral defective when confronted with one."[27]

The concept of the competence produced by education now was redefined in terms of the amount of mental ability an individual possessed. More ability was better, and little consideration was given to whether there was a corresponding increase in competence.

By 1918, there was a shift in the focus of the accountability of educators. The goals of educational effectiveness and competence to function were replaced by the goals of educational efficiency and the identification of differentiated levels of mental ability and educational achievement. Educators and commentators debated about the appropriate education for individuals of different ability rather than the requisite education for all. Some educational leaders objected to the position of the "statistical-standard-scale-test advocates."[28] Others advised colleagues, "The passion for testing efficiency will not slack until every element and factor of the teaching process has been submitted to rigorous quantitative measurements."[29]

The apparent success of the military classification program during World War I provided additional support for these new goals. At the war's conclusion, many of the psychologists who had worked on the group intelligence tests returned to education. Group tests of intelligence, modeled on the army Alpha and Beta, soon appeared in the schools. Educators also adopted two of the assumptions that had guided the military use of intelligence tests: the equating of levels of mental ability with levels of competence, and the immutability of intelligence. Mental ability and competence became synonymous—"A" men were more competent than "C" men, and "A" students with IQs of 150 were more competent than "C" students with IQs of 100. Few pointed out that the war had ended before "A" men had demonstrated their superior competence. If ability were innate, schools had a different obligation. V.A.C. Henmon explained: "Before long we will consciously recognize that the school can be more effective if it gives up the attempt to accomplish impossibilities by training and allows the function of directing, guiding, and selecting to assume larger proportions."[30] This was an insidious argument that for a time subverted the responsibility of the educational system to provide for all children.

Unquestionably, educational administrators and teachers had a dilemma. They wanted to provide a better education; like the public, educators had been shocked by the 25 percent illiteracy rate revealed by the Alpha testing. They had too many students in their schools. They wanted to break the "lockstep" that forced all children through a single program, regardless of ability or rate of learning. They had to explain their failures. Finally they had to be good managers.

Interestingly, educators did not duplicate, to any extent, the World War I testing effort in the actual measurement of competence. The Committee on the Classification of Personnel in the Army, chaired by W. V. Bingham, had developed a series of proficiency tests to assess the required level of competence in various trades: auto mechanic, electrician, sheet metal worker, structural steel worker, and electrical lineman. In the preparation of the test, the committee had sought assistance from skilled mechanics, labor union officials, plant managers, the U.S. Civil Service, the U.S. Labor Department, and army officers. The selected items were administered to individuals of different levels of competence (experts, journeymen, apprentices, and novices) prior to the establishment of the range of performance. Approximately 130,000 recruits were examined with one or more of the 83 oral, 40 graphic, or 30 performance tests. Only in the testing of clerical skills, however, did this proficiency approach appear in education.[31]

During the 1920s, the results of intelligence tests became an easy explanation to fulfill the educational responsibility that the public demanded. Because of the correlation between intelligence and achievement test performance, some now claimed that schools with large numbers of pupils with low intelligence test scores could not be compared on achievement test performance with schools with pupils with higher IQs.

Education which only nurtured existing qualities, however, posed a philosophical challenge to the democratic belief in the power of education. While few denied that individuals differed, many did not accept the conclusion that the schools of a democracy should train some to lead and some to follow. Some took issue with the theory of immutability. They soon were able to support their philosophical arguments with new research, which demonstrated the impact of social, economic, and cultural factors on test performance.[32]

By the end of the twenties, American education was uncertain of its purpose. Schools had diverse programs for the achievement of standards, but the standards had not been examined as often as their attainment had been measured. Some programs grouped students according to ability; others provided individualized programs of instruction. Educators continued to use intelligence tests, but testing experts and educational researchers began to emphasize that the tests did not reflect innate, immutable ability. Some former advocates of the racist interpretation of intelligence, like Carl Campbell Brigham, now reversed their position. Finally, many began to question the accepted purposes of testing; some argued that examinations should serve primarily a guidance rather than a certification purpose.[33]

The thirties provided an opportunity for change. Despite the economic problems, the decade was a period of unparalled examination, attention to educational problems, and reform. The new concept of evaluating education was substituted for the earlier one of testing students. Its advocates now sought to tie the assessment of a student's progress to underlying educational objectives. Many new activities created a milieu in which the values could be explored and defined. Educational and psychological measurement experts had a better understanding of the limits of tests, and they reexamined earlier conclusions on group and individual performance. The American Psychological Association, the Progressive Education Association, the National Society for the Study of Education, and the NEA considered the issues of professional responsibility and future purpose. At meetings of the Educational Records Bureau and at the annual invitational conference of the American Council on Education, speakers discussed the new research.

The issue of the assessment of competence was raised directly and indirectly in various research and testing efforts. These included the *Study of Schools and Colleges in Pennsylvania* and the *Study of Examinations and Their Substitutes*, sponsored by the Carnegie Foundation, and the *Study of the Relation of Schools and Colleges* (the Eight Year Study), conducted by the Progressive Education Association. There were new tests, such as the Cooperative Tests of the American Council on Education, the measures developed by Ralph Tyler and others to evaluate the Eight Year Study, and the Iowa Every-Pupil Tests of Basic Skills and Iowa Tests of Educational Development, developed primarily by E. F. Lindquist.

Finally, educators seemed ready again to assume responsibility for the education of *all* their pupils and to consider the ultimate objective of the educational process. Would the public to whom they were accountable permit them to do so?

World War II ended these deliberations. The military, however, continued the effort to define educational competence. The U.S. Armed Forces Institute (USAFI) developed the Tests of General Educational Development for both high school and college course equivalence. The military also used a standard of competence to classify military tasks.

After World War II, educators had to serve a larger population as a result of a new national commitment to expanded opportunity. Educational leaders readily accepted the new responsibility. They failed again, however, to clarify the public expectations or to consider the limitations of their system.

Soon there was more evidence of education's failure than its success. Educators seemed to provide neither competence for everyone nor excellence for a few. The critics, like the public, differed over which goals should be preeminent. Arthur Bestor reported that the "discontent with training" noted by university faculties was "equally widespread among doctors, engineers, clergymen, lawyers, and other professional men. Businessmen are dismayed at the deficiencies in reading, writing, arithmetic and general knowledge displayed by the high school graduates they employed. Parents are alarmed at the educational handicaps under which their children are obliged to labor as they enter upon the serious business of life."[34]

Because of the threat of Soviet supremacy, the public demanded, however, that educators concentrate on those who excelled. Admiral Rickover exemplified this position: "In the final analysis, our cherished American standard of living depends on the work of a relatively small group of skilled professionals."[35]

For philosophical and practical reasons, however, the articulation of such a philosophy and the operational practices that followed have never gained acceptance. The problem with this position has increased as we have become aware of the vast differences in basic opportunity. In the 1960s, national policy turned to the issue of remedy, in response to the growing political power of racial and ethnic minorities and a new national social conscience. Courts and civil rights groups questioned the use of certain selection devices; in essence, they asked whether the chosen measure and level were evidence of competence. Again, the failure of definition plagued both educators and the public. Some debated the need for standards; others debated the impact of the sixties on the standards; still others debated the appropriate level; few examined their nature. Despite the pressure for eliminating, and the actual elimination of some grading practices, and despite the institution of open admissions, public accountability still demanded evidence of educational achievement. The proposal for the National Assessment of Educational Progress (1964) and the evaluation requirements of the Elementary and Secondary Education Act (1965) testified to the continued interest.

In the 1971 report, *Statewide Assessment Programs*, Henry Dyer and Elsa Rosenthal reported that assessment efforts were in a "highly fluid state."[36] One began to hear demands for specific accountability, for the delineation of the schools' responsibility for results. In the seven years since the report on state assessment programs, the demands for accountability have increased. In the lack of specificity, the current movement for minimum competence and its assessment is only a replay. In the universality of the requirement, however, the current movement is unprecedented.

Conclusion

There is disagreement on the underlying motive for the development of American public education: some view it as a fundamental principle in the successful operation of a democracy; others, as the way in which the Corporate State ensures a well-disciplined, unquestioning work force suitable to the technological system. Yet we have not chosen an Orwellian solution; we continue to accept the Jeffersonian view that ignorance and freedom are incompatible. We still believe "schooling makes a difference," as Irving Lorge concluded.[37] Unquestionably, schooling is only one aspect of the process and the opportunities that constitute education. Nonetheless, it has been the area in which we have chosen to concentrate most of our resources and virtually all of our expectations.

Earlier, I stated that the standard of minimum competence is a more egalitarian and realistic standard than we have had in the past. The standard also places a far greater responsibility on the schools than we have ever imposed. It is greater because it is explicit and because it includes every pupil. The new demand also changes the historic relationship in American education between the standards of competence and excellence. The two are not so nearly synonymous as they once were; neither are they different levels of a single dimension as they more recently have been; competence and excellence are now separate and equally important. We are unlikely to achieve minimum competence for everyone without an educational system that is excellent. Furthermore, once we have achieved this goal, we will require far greater, more diverse opportunities for individuals to achieve excellence.

Notes

1. Herbert F. Hawkes, E. F. Lindquist, and C. R. Mann, *The Construction and Use of Achievement Tests* (Washington, D.C.: American Council on Education, 1936), p. 36.

2. Dewey B. Stuit, Gwendolyn S. Dickson, Thomas F. Jordan, and Lester Schloerb, *Predicting Success in Professional Schools* (Washington, D.C.: American Council on Education, 1949), p. 14.

3. Prior to the discussions of the past few years, little had been written about the educational use of a standard of minimum competency. A search of the *Psychological Abstracts* computer index revealed very few articles written before 1970. A survey of previous *Psychological Abstracts* indices revealed no use of the term. Oscar Buros never discussed "minimum competency tests" in any of the *Mental Measurements Yearbooks*. A search of card catalogues at teacher-training institutions revealed a dearth of early literature (although the issue of teacher competency has received a great deal of attention). The 1974 publication of the

Education Writers Association, *Tests and Testing*, did not contain the term "minimum competency testing" in its glossary. Until recently, the *Annual Report of the U.S. Commissioner of Education* did not contain any discussion of minimum competency testing.

4. E. E. Cureton, "Minimum Requirements in Establishing and Reporting Norms on Educational Tests," *Harvard Educational Review* 11 (May 1941): pp. 287-289.

5. William M. Gray, *Review of Educational Research* 48 (Spring 1978), pp. 223-249. Gray concludes: "Despite differences Piagetian theory and CRM share a general purpose—that of diagnosing behavior. CRM holds promise of alleviating some of the undesirable practices of present-day testing; Piagetian theory delineates an approach to assessing and theorizing about mental processes that offers a viable alternative to the behavioristic approach currently in vogue . . . Piaget's developmental levels provide a very effective means of determining just how a child conceptualizes and interacts with his world, and would appear to provide a psychological basis for CRM that is consistent with the precepts of that system" (p. 249).

6. Horace Mann, quoted in Otis W. Caldwell and Stuart A. Courtis, *Then and Now in Education*, 1845:1923 (New York: World Book Company, 1924), p. 271.

7. I. L. Kandel, *Examinations and Their Substitutes in the United States* (New York: The Carnegie Foundation for the Advancement of Teaching, 1936), p. 9.

8. Benjamin Ide Wheeler, "Call Nothing Common," *NEA Addresses and Proceedings* (Winona, Minn.: NEA, 1907), p. 136.

9. Charles W. Eliot had earlier expressed a similar view: "The vague desire for equality in a democracy has worked great mischief in democratic schools. There is no such thing as equality of gifts or powers, or faculties, among either children or adults." (Kandel, *Examinations and Their Substitutes*, p. 32).

10. John W. Gardner, *Excellence: Can We be Equal and Excellent Too?* (New York: Harper & Row, 1961).

11. Kandel, *Examinations and Their Substitutes*, p. 22.

12. Ibid., p. 23.

13. Horace Mann, quoted in Caldwell and Courtis, *Then and Now*, p. 242.

14. Ibid., pp. 49-50.

15. Ibid., p. 247.

16. Most discussions of grading do not specify the date when American schools first began to use a differentiated scale. In general the Rev. George Fisher, an Englishman, is credited with the first use of a scale (of 1-5, with one the best and five the poorest) in 1864. Fisher analyzed samples of various subjects including writing, spelling, mathematics, grammar, and composition. The work of individual students was then graded according to its similarity to the quality of the samples.

17. Max McConn, "The Uses and Abuses of Examinations," in Hawkes, Lindquist, and Mann, *Construction and Use of Achievement Tests*, p. 447.

18. E. L. Thorndike, in the *Report of the U.S. Commissioner of Education*, 1907, Vol. 2, p. 523.

19. Leonard P. Ayres, "Measuring Educational Progress through Educational Results," *School Review* 20 (May 1912): p. 301.

20. Simon N. Patten is quoted in Joseph S. Taylor, "Measurement of School Efficiency," *Educational Review* 44 (November 1912): p. 349.

21. George M. Strayer, "By What Standards or Tests Shall the Efficiency of a School or School System Be Measured?" *NEA Addresses and Proceedings*, (Winona, Minn.: NEA, 1912), p. 560.

22. Walter S. Monroe, "Existing Tests and Standards," in National Society for the Study of Education, *Seventeenth Yearbook*, Part I (Bloomington: Public School Publishing Company, 1918), p. 72. Monroe cautioned that the term "standardized" should be examined carefully. "In all cases, it should be remembered that any standard, which is simply a statement of the consensus of present practice, is open to the criticism that we must not assume that what is, is what should be."

23. Ibid., p. 71.

24. David I. Lincoln, "The Education of the Feebleminded in the U.S.," in *Report of the Commissioner of Education*, 1902, Chap. 47, p. 2191.

25. In 1895, the American Psychological Association had established the Committee on Physical and Mental Tests, chaired by Cattell.

26. Lightner Witmer, "The Study and Treatment of Retardation: a Field of Applied Psychology," *Psychological Bulletin* 6 (April 1909): p. 121.

27. "Psychology Squad Announced for Police Department," *New York Times*, October 30, 1915. In a November 1 editorial, the *Times* took some credit for the innovation, citing its earlier remarks "on the superiority of the 'new psychology' to the 'third degree' as a means of getting the truth out of people suspected of crime." ("Policemen to Learn Psychology," *New York Times*, November 1, 1915.)

28. William H. Maxwell, "Efficiency of Schools and School Systems," NEA *Addresses and Proceedings* (Ann Arbor, Mich.: NEA, 1915), p. 398.

29. Fred Newton Scott, "Efficiency for Efficiency's Sake," *School Review* 23 (January 1916): p. 36.

30. V. A. C. Henmon, "The Measurement of Intelligence," *School and Society* 13 (February 5, 1921): p. 157.

31. Philip H. DuBois, *A History of Psychological Testing* (Boston: Allyn and Bacon, 1970), p. 86.

32. Many took issue with this theory of immutability. William Bagley, John Dewey, and Walter Lippmann are perhaps the best known challengers. In 1922-1923, Bagley, Dewey, and Lippmann wrote a series of articles including: William Bagley, "Educational Determinism or Democracy and the I.Q.," *School and Society* 15 (1922): pp. 373-384; John Dewey, "Mediocrity and Individuality," *New Republic* 33 (1922): p. 35; idem, "Individuality, Equality, and Superiority," *New Republic* 33 (1922): p. 61; Walter Lippmann, "The Mental Age of Americans," *New Republic* 32 (1922): pp. 213-215; idem, "The Mystery of the 'A' Men," *New Republic* 32 (1922): pp. 246-248; idem, "The Reliability of Intelligence Tests," *New Republic* 32 (1922): pp. 275-277; idem, "The Abuse of Tests," *New Republic* 32 (1922): pp. 297-298; idem, "Tests of Hereditary Intelligence," *New Republic* 32 (1922): pp. 328-330; idem, "A Future for Tests," *New Republic* 33 (1922): pp. 9-11. Charles Judd, dean of the School of Education, the University of Chicago, and Thomas Finegan, Pennsylvania superintendent of schools, attacked the theory at the 1923

meeting of the NEA. Judd warned: "There is an intoxication of enthusiasm which is sometimes as inconvenient for the public as other forms of unbalanced irrationality. That tests have been advertised for purposes to which they were and are inadequate is certainly true." Charles Judd, "Educational Research and the American School Program," *NEA Addresses and Proceedings* [Washington, D.C.: NEA, 1923], p. 173. Finegan lauded Bagley's "scholarly and masterly treatment of the subject." He called the criticism "opportune and courageous" and felt Bagley had raised "several timely and pertinent issues in regard to the proper function and limitations of educational tests and measurements." (Thomas E. Finegan, "Educational Progress in 1922," *NEA Addresses and Proceedings* [Washington, D.C.: NEA, 1923], p. 520.) Frank Freeman attacked the theory in several articles throughout the decade. Herbert Alexander, a graduate student at Stanford, reanalyzed the Alpha data, and found a high correlation between schooling and test scores. (Herbert Alexander, "A Comparison of American States in Army Alpha and Socioeconomic Status," *School and Society* 16 [1922]: pp. 388-392.) Lippmann cited Alexander's work in "A Defense of Education," *The Century Magazine* (November 1923): pp. 99-101.

By the end of the decade, several others had challenged the misinterpretation of the Alpha data. Yoder noted, "Within the past two years [there have been] a half-dozen books and no less than half a hundred articles portraying the results of twenty or thirty investigations." There were three distinct views: (1) those in support of racial superiority and inferiority "usually adducing additional evidence to support the thesis," (2) those considering "race inferiority possible but not adequately demonstrated and balance arguments for and against," (3) those "highly critical of the means used to demonstrate race inferiority and of the results so obtained and generally insisting upon racial equality." Yoder then observed: "As a whole, the attitudes of the various writers presenting these three viewpoints of the problem are quite changed from those which the exponents of the same contentions showed ten or even five years ago. *The race superiority enthusiasts appear to be on the defensive, speaking generally.*" (italics added). Yoder commented on "their striving furiously to amass more of the usual evidence . . . ignoring the fact that it is the quality rather than the quantity of evidence which is under fire." The second group, Yoder noted, "show the reserve and objectivity of a group that feels it has the majority of scientific opinion. . . " The third group "has the fire of enthusiastic discovery about it combined with an idealistic zeal aiming at what it considers scientific inaccuracy and fallacy." (Dale Yoder, "The Present Status of the Question of Racial Differences," *Journal of Educational Psychology* [1930]: p. 463).

33. Kandel, *Examinations and Their Substitutes*, p. 66.

34. Arthur E. Bestor, *Educational Wastelands* (Urbana, Ill.: University of Illinois Press, 1953), p. 4.

35. H. G. Rickover, *Education and Freedom* (New York: E. P. Dutton & Company, 1959), p. 121.

36. Henry S. Dyer and Elsa Rosenthal "An Overview of the Survey Findings," in Educational Testing Service in Collaboration with Education Commission of the

States and Education Resources Center, *State Educational Assessment Programs* (Princeton, N.J.: Educational Testing Service, 1971), p. ix.

37. Irving Lorge, "Schooling Makes a Difference" *Teaches College Record*, 46 (May 1945): p. 483.

Response to
"Competence and Excellence:
The Search for an Egalitarian Standard,
the Demand for a Universal Guarantee,"
by Jenne K. Britell

Maxine Greene

Definitions of Competence and Excellence

As Jenne Britell sees it, the development of a standard of minimum competence is fundamentally egalitarian in meaning and intent. Once such a standard is precisely defined, she believes, all our children will be guaranteed equality of educational achievement (if, that is, the schools live up to their obligations). Compared with earlier emphases on aptitude testing and on the equating of competence with mental abilities, the concern for minimum competence represents a break with traditional commitments to a "standard of excellence." The preoccupation with "achievement relative to the highest level" led, according to Britell, to inequities, inefficiencies, and widespread failures on the part of public schools. Oriented to a "universal attainment of excellence," which was—from any realistic point of view—impossible, the schools were never able to deal effectively with individual differences nor with the meaning of equal opportunity. They never, Britell suggests, took the responsibility for all their pupils; and it followed that thousands upon thousands fell below an acceptable level of achievement.

I understand the uses of stipulative definitions; but one of my difficulties with Britell's argument is that I do not find her definitions to be (to use Israel Scheffler's words) "formally coherent and pragmatically well-chosen,"[1] at least not in every case. My difficulties cluster around her definition of educational competence "as that level of performance that citizens require to function in the society in which they live," and her definition of excellence as "an absolute state of achievement" or a "Platonic Pure Form." Where the understanding of competence is concerned, I share with Chris Pipho the belief that "school skills" are not necessarily identical with "life skills," and that transfer from school to "life" or to "job" is not necessarily automatic.[2] But, when Britell talks about "level of performance," she does not mean anything so specific as performance on the job. "To 'function'," she writes, "is to apply the skills learned to other situations that require communication, examination of alternatives, and decision."

I agree with her that this goes beyond what was meant by "life adjustment." I agree with her, too, that to function in this way involves using the mind. However, she says it "requires the training of the mind"; and her use of the term "training" may explain as well as complicate her stipulated definition of "competence." Like Gilbert Ryle, I distinguish training rather sharply from teaching.[3] Training involves drilling, "putting," as Ryle puts it, "the pupil through stereotyped exercises which he masters by sheer repetition." Or it involves plain habituation, getting people to do "low-level things" more or less automatically. All this may constitute a foundation for or a first step toward teaching; but teaching is a matter of equipping persons with the knacks and procedures they need to make "independent moves" of their own.[4] Now I realize full well that Jenne Britell does not have mere drill or habituation in mind when she speaks of "training the mind." Nor is she confining herself to the rudiments or the basic skills when she uses the term "competence." But if, like John Dewey, she were to consider mind as a "Verb,"[5] or if, like Ryle, she were to conceive competences as capacities that develop variously when people begin teaching themselves, she might treat differently the presumed transfer from school achievement to what she describes as "situations that require communication, examination of alternatives, and decision." To communicate effectively demands the ability to understand other points of view, to consider diverse interests and attitudes, and to articulate ideas and beliefs in ways appropriate to various listeners. To examine alternatives and make decisions requires the ability to assess situations as situations holding alternative possibilities for action, to anticipate consequences, and to evaluate predicted ends in the light of principles. It is difficult for me to translate such abilities into minimum competences; but I am suggesting that the insertion of the term "training" into this context may obscure and oversimplify what is actually involved. The notion of training carries with it a conception of discrete skills and habits; it *reduces* communication and decision making to more or less stereotyped behaviors, presumably trainable behaviors. This may, a reader is bound to think, be the only way complex activities (in usually unpredictable situations) can be translated into competences.

I have similar trouble with the term "excellence" which, along with "competence," structures the argument in Britell's paper. For one thing, if excellence is viewed from a Platonic vantage point, it means something other than "absolute standard." Admittedly, Plato's conception of education did depend on the existence of absolute models; and he did delineate (through the idea of the "divided line") the levels of knowledge and perfection that have haunted philosophers ever since. But, at least in *The Republic*, all individuals had the potential for conversion. When Plato talked about the art of effecting conversion, the effort "not to put the power of sight into the soul's eye, which already has it, but to ensure that, instead of looking in the wrong direction, it is turned in the way it ought to be,"[6] he had all human types in mind. Granting the existence of a standard, I would still insist that in classical thinkers there was a conception of multiple excellences. I recognize the inequities associated with what Britell sees as a preoccupation with "levels of ability and performance"; but I think it makes a difference to presume (as John Gardner did, for instance)[7] that there is a range of human excellences. There have always been perceived levels in American education; there have been conceptions of hierarchy which ranked persons in terms of merit as well as achievement; but I doubt that there has been even a "rhetorical commitment" to a single standard of human excellence of consequence for the schools.

The Theme of Public Demand for Accountability

Obviously, much depends on historical context; and the historical background is, after all, Jenne Britell's major concern. The main themes she develops seem to me to have to do, first, with the recurrent demands of American publics for some sort of accountability, some way of verifying what the schools were doing where the achievements of children were concerned. They have to do, second, with the important fact that, at least since the First World War, educational leaders have tended to be more interested in "the appropriate education for individuals of different ability rather than the requisite education for all." It seems clear enough that, ever since the eighteenth century, examinations and tests were devised in response to public demand. I am struck by the fact that (to use Horace Mann's language) the "competency or sufficiency of the teaching" was the focus of attention. It was taken for granted that effective teaching guaranteed learning and the application of what was learned. Actually, we have learned relatively recently to distinguish between teaching and learning. We know now that the "notion of 'teaching,' unlike 'learning,' has, typically *intentional* as well as *success* uses."[8] That means that teaching must be understood as a purposeful activity, involving an element of trying to reach a goal that may or may not be attained. The general assumption, in Horace Mann's day, was that teachers who knew their subjects had the "aptness to teach." They understood how to manage their classrooms, and could not but equip the young with the skills and behaviors they required. "Lessons, as far as it is possible," wrote Horace Mann, "should be so adjusted to the capacity of the scholar, that there should be no failure in a recitation, not occasioned by culpable neglect."[9] With so much confidence in the teacher, neither he nor the public troubled themselves about irremediable differences among children, the crippling effects of poverty, or the lack of stimulation at home. Parents demanded training in good habits, in the rudiments of literacy, and in the skills presumably needed for the pursuit of success: thus, given a proper organization of the schools, adequately prepared teachers, and a decent "mix" of students, they were assured that their children would succeed (except in cases of total obduracy).

As Britell suggests, the demands put upon the schools by a "controlling public" changed during 1890-1917. Industrialization, urbanization, and alienation of various kinds estranged people from their schools until the years after the First World War; yet what Britell calls "the content of the public expectation" was seldom assessed. The social changes that took place early in the present century (new waves of immigration, mass production, increasing mechanization, and the rest) undoubtedly turned educators' attention to the need to assess achievement and, later on, to predict it (and thereby to classify and sort children, as Jenne Britell points out). Although I am not sure what segment of the public was represented by the NEA's Committee on Economy of Time in Education, the committee's report, in 1911, stressed the need to acquire "those habits, skills, knowledges, ideals, and prejudices which must be made the common property of all. . . . "[10] Nor am I sure to which public the so-called "cult of efficiency"[11] responded; nor Franklin Bobbitt's 1924 effort to build a curriculum that would, on the basis of a scientific classification of all human activities, prepare all children for effective adulthood in the existing social world.[12] Britell places considerable emphasis on "public demand for concrete educational evidence" and indicates that the present interest in minimum competency assessment is a response to what is viewed as a "mandate" from a public which now insists that schools meet their obligations and thus expands those obligations as never before. She also says that, in these days, the public is suspicious of nonquantitative evidence and wants the type of measurement procedures that assess competence rather than levels of ability. This may be; but I would hesitate to accept it as a given, just as I would hesitate to accept the claim that the "scientific management" movement of the 1920s was an expression of public sentiment. I do not question the unease among the public regarding test scores and some apparent declines in literacy; and I am fully aware of the ways in which a technological *ethos* shapes both language and expectation. Nevertheless, I remain skeptical about the notion of "explicit demand" as a justification for an orientation to minimum competence. To assert that, and to assert, at the same time, that minimum competence "may be the most realistic universal educational goal" and that it provides a "universal guarantee" is to set aside the nagging questions respecting gauge and standard. It is, as well, to ignore arguments like those eloquently presented by Gene Glass and others—charges having to do with the arbitrariness of trying to derive criterion scores, the authoritarian character of "absolute evaluation in education," and the superiority of what Glass calls "comparative evidence."[13] Such arguments can be answered, of course; indeed, some have tried to answer them. I would suggest to Jenne Britell, however, that too many questions remain open for such sweeping claims to be made.

The Theme of Educating Individuals of Different Ability

With regard to the second theme (the predominant interest in "appropriate education for individuals of different ability"), I would also want to qualify some generalizations. In the first place, I am not convinced that differentiated education for "excellence" is necessarily the opposite of "requisite education for all." Britell believes this to be the case, I think, because of her view of equality—or, perhaps, her view that a commitment to "equality of opportunity and equality of individuals" is fundamental to the American value system. It seems evident to me also that traditional notions of equal opportunity were exposed as insufficient during the 1960s. If we learned anything in education, we learned that it is simply not equitable to take people who are unequal (in economic or social status, or in physical endowment, for example) and expect them to succeed in a course of schooling under the same conditions as their more advantaged brothers and sisters. Certainly, many people are still objecting to selective admissions, affirmative action, and the like; and many others are proclaiming the futility of remedial programs. Nonetheless, there is some acknowledgment that equality does not mean sameness or identity. If there is to be fairness, distinctions have to be made. When discussing fairness (or justice), R. S. Peters has written that the basic notion "is that distinctions should be made if there are relevant differences and that they should not be made if there are no relevant differences or on the basis of irrelevant differences."[14] Using a criterion much like this, people argue for integration, since differences in color are irrelevant when it comes to providing a decent education. Or they argue for equal rights for women, on the grounds that difference in sex is an irrelevant ground for discriminating in employment or on the job. However, where Head Start and other compensatory programs were concerned, deficits due to environmental attrition, lack of stimulation, and the like were considered as causes of relevant differences in the capacity to learn. Since the making of distinctions of that sort involves the making of categories, those persons singled out as being entitled to compensation or remediation were categorized in terms of "levels of ability." It seems to me that, were it not for such deliberate equalizing of opportunity, there would be no hope of eventually equalizing achievement; and I hope that is what Britell has in mind when she talks about the "opportunity for remedy." But there remains the matter of standards. When ought compensatory or remedial action stop?

The Goals of Education and the Failures of Schools

The last critical point I want to make takes me back into the past. Is it indeed the case that, as Britell suggests, there has been a continuing stress on "the highest standards," and that competence has been equated with excellence? Is it indeed the case that a "requisite" education for all has been subordinated to consideration of "achievement relative to the highest level"? And is disinterest in (or perplexity about) a minimum to be treated as a *reason* for the failures of our schools?

Some light may be thrown by a comparison of Thomas Jefferson's conception of public education with Horace Mann's. It is well known that Jefferson's Bill for the General Diffusion of Knowledge was developed in the belief that the best protection against tyranny would be "to illuminate, as far as practicable, the minds of the people at large. . . . " It is also well known that he differentiated between the kind of education necessary for the "laboring" and for the "learned" and placed particular emphasis on the education of "those persons, whom nature hath endowed with genius and virtue," who would be "rendered by liberal education worthy to receive, and able to guard the sacred deposit of the rights and liberties of their fellow citizens. . . . "[15] Clearly, his was a proposal for selective education, with considerable stress on what Britell calls a "standard of excellence." Nevertheless, he wrote that "Nobody can doubt my zeal for the general instruction of the people. I never have proposed a sacrifice of the primary to the ultimate grade of instruction. Let us keep our eye steadily on the whole system."[16] It seems evident that what was "requisite" for Jefferson was the protection of individuals in the free exercise of their natural rights, and the breaking through of class barriers and prejudices to facilitate the discovery of those "endowed with genius and virtue," no matter what their birth or wealth "or other accidental condition or circumstance. . . . " As for minimum competences, he proposed that, in the schools of Virginia, all children should be taught reading, writing, and arithmetic; "and the books which shall be used therein for instructing the children shall be such as will at the same time make them acquainted with Graecian, Roman, English, and American history."[17] The difficulty, of course, was that minimum meant, for most children, all that there would be. Jefferson, explaining the selection that followed three years of public schooling, said that "twenty of the best geniuses will be raked from the rubbish annually . . ."; and, having used such a metaphor, left us a rather chilling image of what minimal education might turn out to be.

By the time Horace Mann became secretary of the Massachusetts State Board of Education, the Jacksonian revolution had taken place, the factory system had spread, and the dream of a freeholder or agrarian society had ebbed away. His religious and philanthropic motives accounted for Mann's interest in educating all the children in a common school, in developing "the faculties of perception, comparison, calculation, and causality" in every one, as well as in overcoming degeneracy. Education, because it could counter the "tendency to the domination of capital and the servility of labor" by equipping all the young to *create* wealth, would become "the great equalizer of the conditions of men."[18] The universal, egalitarian values which Jenne Britell associates with the pursuit of minimum competences were foremost in Mann's beliefs. He did not concern himself with "levels" or the "highest standards." Every child was to be given a moral education and taught independence and self-control. Every child was to be taught the useful arts and the habits of good health. Obviously, his expressed hopes were inordinate. When he spoke of the school, he said that "if administered in the spirit of justice and conciliation, all the rising generation may be brought within the circle of its reformatory and elevating influences," that the "pliant and ductile" materials on which it worked could be shaped into an endless variety of forms.[19] Yet, as Britell indicates, the achievement levels (when tested) were often not acceptable. Class divisions did not disappear, as Mann thought they would; the gulf between "poverty and profusion" remained as wide as it had ever been.

Was this because the level of required competence was set too high? Was it because there was insufficient differentiation? Was it because of inadequate support, poorly trained teachers, or too much stress on "control"? Was it because standards were never clearly defined, or because the schools did not take enough responsibility? The same questions can be asked with respect to achievement at the turn of the century and during the ensuing years. I am not convinced that the preoccupation with "individuals of different ability" or the misapplication of IQ tests affected the attainment of minimum competence; nor am I convinced that these emphases indicated a lack of universality, a neglect of "all the children."

I do not question Jenne Britell's conclusion that the widespread demand for accountability makes acceptance of quantitative assessments more likely. I do question her belief that there are guarantees. Public education that is oriented to achievement rather than to what Lawrence Kohlberg calls "development"[20] and to what Dewey called "growth and more growth"[21] is not likely to become the kind of education that promotes cognitive maturity or an ongoing quest for meanings; nor is it likely to be the kind of education that empowers individuals to teach themselves. I shall leave to others the task of proposing alternatives to minimum competence assessment. But I want an excellent voice to sound before I conclude. It is the voice of Immanuel Kant, who said something I believe to be relevant today: "Parents," he said, "usually educate their children in such a manner that, however bad the world may be, they may adapt themselves to its present conditions. But they ought to give them an education so much better than this, that a better condition of things may thereby be brought about in the future."[22] I can only hope. I insist that there are no guarantees.

Notes

1. Israel Scheffler, *The Language of Education* (Springfield, Ill.: Charles C. Thomas, 1960), p. 15.
2. Chris Pipho, "Minimum Competency Testing in 1978: A Look at State Standards," *Phi Delta Kappan*, May 1978, p. 586.
3. Gilbert Ryle, "Teaching and Training," in *The Concept of Education*, ed. R. S. Peters (New York: The Humanities Press, 1967), pp. 105-119.
4. Ibid., p. 114.
5. John Dewey, *Art as Experience* (New York: Minton, Balch & Co., 1934), p. 263.
6. Plato *Republic* 7. 518 (ed. F. M. Cornford [New York: Oxford University Press, 1945], p. 263.)
7. John Gardner, *Excellence: Can We Be Equal and Excellent Too?* (New York: Harper & Row, 1961), pp. 131-157.
8. Israel Scheffler, "Conditions of Knowledge," reprint in *Modern Philosophies of Education*, ed. John Paul Strain (New York: Random House, 1971), p. 298.
9. Horace Mann, "The Education of Free Men," in *The Republic and the School*, ed. Lawrence A. Cremin (New York: Teachers College Press, 1957), pp. 46-48.

10. Lawrence A. Cremin, *The Transformation of the School* (New York: Alfred A. Knopf, 1961), p. 193.

11. Cf. Raymond E. Callahan, *Education and the Cult of Efficiency* (Chicago: University of Chicago Press, 1962).

12. Cremin, *Transformation of the School*, pp. 199-200.

13. Gene V. Glass, "Minimum Competence and Incompetence in Florida," *Phi Delta Kappan*, pp. 602-603.

14. R. S. Peters, *Ethics and Education* (Chicago: Scott, Foresman and Co., 1967), p. 61.

15. Thomas Jefferson, "The General Diffusion of Knowledge," in *Crusade Against Ignorance: Thomas Jefferson on Education*, ed. Gordon C. Lee (New York: Teachers College Press, 1972), p. 83; ibid., p. 84.

16. Ibid., p. 81, editor's note.

17. Ibid., p. 95.

18. Horace Mann, "Report for 1848", in *Two Hundred Years of Educational Thought*, ed. Henry J. Perkinson (New York: David McKay Co., 1976), p. 86.

19. Horace Mann, "The Education of Free Men," *The Republic and the School*, p. 80.

20. Lawrence Kohlberg and E. Turiel, "Moral Development and Moral Education," in *Psychology and Educational Practice*, ed. G. Lesser (Glencoe, Ill.: Scott, Foresman & Co., 1971).

21. John Dewey, *Democracy and Education* (New York: The Macmillan Company, 1916), pp. 49-62.

22. Immanuel Kant, *Education* (Ann Arbor: University of Michigan Press, 1960), p. 14.

3　Policy Implications of Minimum Competency Testing

Joan C. Baratz

Introduction

There is a curious but persistent American cultural belief that, for want of a more precise definition, I have identified as the "information will make you free" thesis. The basis of this tradition is the notion of American "know-how"—that optimistic and, at times, naive view that all that stands between a problem and its solution is the proper information (some would say the appropriate technology). While this cheerful belief in the problem-solving potency of good will and technology pervades all aspects of American life, nowhere is it more dramatically and persistently visible than in education. The present craze for setting minimum standards is a case in point which deserves attention.[1]

The first two papers of this volume addressed from an historical perspective the question of setting minimum standards and made some effort to determine the social and political implications of the "minimum competency movement." Two distinct views were presented. David Cohen perceived minimum competency as one more example of the shabby treatment the less fortunate and less powerful receive from their government, while Jenne Britell was optimistic, viewing minimum competency as a bright promise for the disadvantaged.

I approach the topic from a third, perhaps more cautious (some might say cynical) position. To me the question is not so much whether the minimum competency movement is good or bad, but whether it has any substance beyond its rhetoric and political posturing. The education landscape is littered with reforms and innovations that attracted a great deal of interest in the media and at professional meetings only to be discarded when a new fad came along. Although many see the active role of state legislatures in proposing bills and passing laws about standard setting as a sign that minimum competency is an educational reform more permanent than previous efforts, one need only examine the history of other statewide accountability laws to understand that enactment of broad-based legislation is hardly synonymous with educational reform.

In this presentation, therefore, I will examine the minimum competency testing phenomenon by posing three questions: (1) Why focus on testing as the source of reforming education? (2) How diverse, and "underdeveloped," are statewide minimum competency programs? (3) What policy implications flow from the present testing environment?

Before proceeding, however, it is necessary to forewarn you of my biases about minimum competency testing:

(1) The tests do not provide new information. There is no likelihood that the tests will reveal difficulties not already apparent in American public education. In fact, our perceived difficulties are what caused these tests to be mandated in the first place, and the political realities (that is, developing a test which produces an "acceptable" failure rate) will assure that implementing the tests creates no serious shock waves.[2]

(2) Minimum competency testing is not a major educational reform. In the past, tests, in themselves, have not succeeded in producing greater accountability or change in educational procedures. As Chall has aptly observed:

The strong faith in state competency testing . . . should give us pause. Is it possible that these new competency tests can accomplish what the years of standardized achievement testing have not? Is it possible that these new tests can alert the schools to pupil failure while the standardized achievement tests given regularly in almost every school in the nation could not? Was John Doe a functional illiterate after 12 years of schooling because the achievement tests he took in school failed to reveal his reading problem? Or did his problem stem from failures in implementing the test results? If so, might not the same occur with the best of tests regularly administered and interpreted? (Chall, 1978, p. 10)

The present minimum competence movement is somewhat anomalous in that the ends and the means are one and the same. The test which sets the explicit standard is seen as the process for reforming the system at the same time that proof of the reform is performance on the test.

(3) There is more sound than substance to many minimum competency programs. In his presentation, David Cohen outlined three criteria that were critical to developing a feasible minimum competency standard. These included: a shared definition of the standard to be set; a technology capable of measuring the standard; and an educational system capable of imparting the knowledge required to pass the standard.

As this paper will attempt to demonstrate, these criteria are not met in current efforts to create minimum competency testing programs. A close examination of the programs, following former Attorney General Mitchell's advice, "watch what I do, not what I say," leaves one with the distinct impression that these programs are the product of the fabled emperor's tailors.

(4) Minimum competency testing is not a right-wing, reactionary coup. A glance at the history of education reveals that diverse political ideologies have always been present and active within it. While there has been a generally conservative trend in education in the late 1970s, plainly shown by the back-to-basics movement, current broad-based support for minimum competency testing should not be interpreted as an abandonment of all that is near and dear to liberals. Quality education, after all, is not anathema to citizens who care about opportunity and equity.

(5) Minimum competency testing will not last as a distinct phenomenon any more than performance contracting or "new math" have persisted as central foci of educational change. New fads (or at least new terms to describe allegedly basic changes in practice or procedure) tend to fly through the educational profession, but they tend also to be short-lived. In 1973, statewide system accountability, along with management by objectives, was the watchword and the promise for change.

(6) Standardized testing programs will remain a part of American education. Aside from the current interest in minimum competency testing, achievement testing of school children is a multimillion dollar industry that is rather like General Motors and "the military-industrial complex" — not likely to fade away despite continued attacks.[3]

(7) The clamor for accountability will continue. There is a taxpayer revolt and a consumer impetus behind much current criticism of the educational system.[4] Earlier efforts to make teachers accountable through test data were unsuccessful; present efforts to change the system through student accountability are likely to face similar difficulties.[5]

This shift between extremes resembles an oscillating pendulum: we attribute educational problems to *either* teachers *or* students. The subtler, mingled causes of educational problems have, so far, eluded attempts to isolate and address them before political reaction grasps a simple explanation, applies a simplified solution, and reactivates the cycle of faddish remedies. Nonetheless, as long as the notion persists that schools are no good, new demands for accountability and reform are likely to occur.[6]

Why the Interest in Minimum Competency Testing?

It is impossible to understand the persistent faith in testing as both diagnostic and palliative without touching on the sociopolitical context of the contemporary educational system.

Historians and philosophers of education have discussed in considerable detail society's need to fit a corporate, capitalist culture to an educational system that supports such a society and socializes its future adult citizens and workers.[7] To that end, we have seen education policy preoccupied with "the cult of efficiency" (Callahan, 1962), with the link between school and work, and with sorting students to assure a qualified work force to sustain the system.

As Cohen and Lazerson indicate:

[The development of education in the United States in the twentieth century] has to be understood in the framework of the schools' adaptation to large-scale corporate capitalism and the conflicts this engendered. Infusing the schools with corporate values and reorganizing them in ways seen as consistent with this new economic order has been the dominant motif. . . . The schools' role has been to socialize economically desirable values and behavior, teach vocational skills, and provide education consistent with students' expected occupational attainment. . . . Schooling came to be seen as work or the preparation for work; schools were pictured as factories, educators as industrial managers, and students as the raw materials to be inducted into the production process. . . . The corporate society required an academic meritocracy that selected students on the basis of ability and educated them accordingly. The great inequities in this selection system were a function of the students' presumed occupational destination and could not be squared with prevailing ideas of equality. (Cohen and Lazerson, 1972, p. 47)

This incompatibility within testing—a "people sorter" that sustains the corporate system, but creates an elite that contradicts our ideal of equality—is fundamental to its continuously controversial and conflict-ridden history.

While the "factory-sorting" model dominates educational policymaking, it has been challenged by (among others) those educators and policymakers who believe that such a system undermines the American democratic ideal. Social scientists espousing an egalitarian position questioned the tests' validity and suggested that poor performance was produced not by a student's flawed or limited ability but rather, by the cultural biases inherent in the test (that is, the test was technically inadequate). The egalitarian notion of education assumed several things: children come to school with equal potential to learn; differential test scores represent the limited and/or different early experiences of the test takers;[8] and education must focus on how to teach children with these different sets of experiences.

While the credibility of test scores and their utility for sorting students regarding access to educational opportunities was challenged, no one questioned the standard for excellence implicitly set by the tests. Nobody asked whether students selected for a particular program should learn what the program claimed to teach; the egalitarians were complaining that tests unfairly excluded certain students from the program. It is important to understand that the challenge to the meritocratic principles (which were embedded in the corporate capitalist educational model) was primarily a criticism of *access*, not of program quality or the appropriateness of subject matter. The egalitarians assumed that new ways would be found to teach the necessary information. They focused on how to teach culturally diverse children, not on what to teach them.

During the late 1960s and early seventies, educational testing was conceived as a social indicator to be used in judging the system, rather than as a measure of the child. Statewide assessment programs were developed in order to inform the policy process and alert educational decision-makers to actual and potential problems.[9]

These assessment programs, along with other indicators such as the steady national decline of SAT scores, began to raise questions about the credibility of the educational system. Businessmen were complaining that they saw few employable public school graduates. Newspapers carried accounts of high school students who were barely literate, and courts were presented with education "malpractice" suits by plaintiffs who claimed not to have received an education despite 12 years in the public schools.[10]

While some scholars have challenged the notion that children are learning less today than in the "good old days," the prevailing public opinion is that students are not learning. This deep skepticism has pushed us toward certifying students by means of standardized tests.

Concentration on a minimum standard for certification neutralizes the egalitarian criticism of tests as promoting both elitism and limited access, while assuring a "quality" product of potential workers. It is difficult to argue against quality (of course, those who urged greater access to educational opportunity never intended that access lead to the sham of interpreting attendance as a measure of learning).

Since quality education has become our goal, minimum competency testing has gained nationwide acceptance as the vehicle for achieving that end. Concern has moved from questions of equity based on access (to teachers, dollars, programs, equipment), to issues of quality based on outputs (what achievement level, what minimum standard). The central issue has therefore shifted from whom schools teach to what schools test. Education, standard setting, and testing have become synonymous.

How Diverse Are Statewide Minimum Competency Testing (MCT) Programs?

Over thirty states have enacted or considered legislation or school board rulings regarding minimum competency testing. There is great diversity among these programs regarding: (1) scope of the MCT program (extent and source of state authorization); (2) definition of competencies (Who decides what is assessed at what level?); (3) program administration (who is tested, by what methods, how many times; and how target student groups are treated); (4) consequences of MCT programs ("early exit," promotion, graduation and certification, and remedial assistance); and (5) dissemination of testing results. Each of these features, which illustrate the degree of variation among states, is briefly discussed below.

Scope of MCT Programs

States differ in their articulation of competency requirements. Some are defined in detailed mandates, authorized legislatively, and affect all aspects of competency-based education: assessment of basic skills, grade promotion, and high school graduation. Most MCT mandates, however, are either broad policy rulings of the state school board or brief statutes that leave details to local districts, with or without state guidelines.

Florida, Colorado, and Utah exemplify the range of differences in this regard. Florida legislation imposes uniform statewide standards and testing of basic skills and functional literacy in a competency certification program encompassing assessment, grade promotion, and graduation. Colorado legislation makes the local district requirement of competency tests contingent upon certain provisions of benefit to the student. A state board ruling in Utah establishes a competency-based graduation requirement; localities formulate standards, measurements, and grades.

Generally, state programs in competency-based graduation can be divided into three categories: (1) statewide requirement with uniform state standards and measurement; (2) statewide requirement with local standards and measurement; and (3) statewide requirement with state standards and measurement, but with local option to participate (See table 1).

Table 1. Authorization for Setting Standards

	Statewide Requirements		Local Options		Other*
	State Tests	Local Tests	State Tests	Local Tests	
Alabama	—	—	—	—	X
Alaska	—	—	—	X	—
Arizona	—	X	—	—	—
California	—	X	—	—	—
Colorado	—	—	—	X	—
Connecticut	X	—	—	—	—
Delaware	X	X	—	—	—
Florida	X	X	—	—	—
Georgia	X	X	—	—	—
Idaho	—	—	X	—	—
Indiana	—	X	—	—	—
Kansas	X	—	—	—	X
Kentucky	X	—	—	—	—
Louisiana	—	—	—	—	X
Maine	X	—	—	—	—
Maryland	—	—	—	—	X
Missouri**	X	—	—	—	—
Nebraska	—	—	X	X	—
Nevada	X	—	—	—	—
New Jersey	X	—	—	—	—
New Mexico	X	—	—	—	—
New York	X	—	—	—	—
North Carolina	X	—	—	—	—
Oregon	—	X	—	—	—
Rhode Island**	X	—	—	—	—
Tennessee	X	—	—	—	—
Texas	—	—	—	X	—
Utah	—	X	—	—	—
Vermont	—	X	—	—	—
Virginia	X	X	—	—	—
Washington**	X	X	—	—	—
Wyoming	—	X	—	—	—

*Programs under study or development with test details to be defined.
**Information as of December 1977.

Definition of Competencies

States vary in terms of who sets standards, what is assessed, and how much one must know. With respect to defining competencies and setting standards, most states have recognized the need for political acceptability, and have authorized mechanisms for building a consensus involving various political and social interest groups. These mechanisms include task forces, advisory committees, hearings, surveys, and citizen review panels, all of which help determine the type and level of knowledge and proficiencies considered necessary for promotion or graduation.[11]

Different states assess different things. Basic skills, functional literacy, and survival or life skills are terms for a variety of accomplishments commonly measured under minimum competency programs (See table 2). Some state programs also judge academic skills or subject-area proficiencies.

Basic skills and functional literacy refer to reading, writing, math, and their application to routine tasks of the adult world. Survival or life skills may be confined to the routine application of basic skills, or they may be broadened to include a number of objectives. Among them are citizenship, leisure skills, lifelong learning, and attitudes toward school. In Montana, the public identified the appreciation of "beauty" and "cooperation" as skills to be assessed.

Mastery, satisfactory performance, and grade equivalency—all of which specify how much must one know—are among the various levels of minimum competency required. States vary in these cutoff levels. In Florida, getting 70 percent of the tested items correct constitutes mastery; in Arizona, achieving the equivalent of 9th-grade reading ability is the minimum performance necessary for high school graduation; and in Denver, getting approximately 60 percent correct on test items is considered the minimum necessary for graduation.

Levels of competency or cutoff scores are established by professionals in some states, and are subject to review by lay panels. In some programs, minimum standards are set uniformly at the state level; in others, deference is given to local autonomy. Districts either have sole discretion to determine the minimum standards, or exercise various options the state provides. Setting no standard may be one of these options.

The rigorousness of the standards is subject to a number of considerations. The professional judgment of educators is often tempered by their practical calculations of such questions as whether the cost of remedial programs for the large number of students who might fail a rigorous test would be prohibitive. Reflecting a similar sensitivity, a National Academy of Education (1978) report opposed statewide test requirements because a "respectable" test would result in such a high

Table 2. Areas Tested in State MCTP

	Basic Skills	Functional Literacy	Other*
Alabama	X	X	—
Alaska	—	—	a
Arizona	X	—	X
California	X	—	—
Colorado	X	—	—
Connecticut	X	—	—
Delaware	X	X	X
Florida	X	X	X
Georgia	X	X	—
Idaho	X	—	—
Indiana	—	—	a
Kansas	X	—	—
Kentucky	X	—	—
Louisiana	X	—	—
Maine	X	—	b
Maryland	X	X	—
Missouri	X	—	c
Nebraska	X	—	—
Nevada	X	—	—
New Jersey	X	—	—
New Mexico	X	—	X
New York	X	—	—
North Carolina	X	X	—
Oklahoma	X	—	—
Oregon	X	X	X
Rhode Island	X	—	—
Tennessee	X	—	—
Texas	—	—	a
Utah	X	X	—
Vermont	X	—	X
Virginia	X	X	—
Washington	X	—	—
Wyoming	—	—	a

*Other refers to (a) local option on skills to be tested (Alaska, Indiana); (b) state programs currently under development, pending local or state definition of skill areas (Maine); or to (c) states with competency tested beyond basic skills and functional literacy (Missouri).

failure rate that the requirements would be "politically impossible" to maintain.

Program Administration

State testing programs also differ in various administrative aspects such as phase-in periods, grades tested, types of tests, and special provisions for bilingual and handicapped students.

Phase-in Periods

The period between the date of enactment and the year in which the first graduating class is affected varies among state programs. The majority provide a phase-in period of 3-5 years (See table 3).

Apart from the notice to students provided by an adequate phase-in period, this developmental stage allows opportunities for preparing

Table 3. Phase-in Periods for Competency-Based Graduation Requirements

State	Year Enacted	Year Effective	Phase-in Period
Alaska	1977	—	—
Arizona	1973	1976	3 years
California	1977	1981	4 years
Colorado	1975*	—	—
Delaware	1976	1981	5 years
Florida	1976	1979	3 years
Georgia	1977	1982	5 years
Idaho	1977	1982	5 years
Maryland	1977	1982	5 years
Nevada	1977	1982	5 years
New Mexico	1977	1981	4 years
New York	1976	1979	3 years
North Carolina	1977	1979	2 years
Oregon	1972	1978	6 years
Utah	1977	1980	3 years
Vermont	1976	1981	5 years
Virginia	1978	1981	3 years
Wyoming	1977	1980	3 years

*Colorado's legislation enables minimum competency testing for graduation which is contingent upon a number of provisions concerning remedial assistance and opportunities for retakes. It does not mention a period after which the competency requirements become effective.

students to meet the new demands. For example, Georgia provides state funds during the five-year developmental phase so that districts can undertake special instruction in how to teach life-role competencies necessary for graduation. Pilot districts are given $25,000 per year to develop programs teaching life-role skills.

Grades Tested

Programs vary as to the grade at which testing begins, and the number of opportunities for retakes. As indicated by table 4, all existing programs provide multiple opportunities for testing; the majority administer tests between grades 9 and 12. It should be noted that almost all state MCT programs have a prior and separate assessment program which provides an early identification of competency needs (Campbell, 1973).

Special Provisions for Bilingual and Handicapped Students

Most programs are still resolving details regarding special exemptions and requirements for targeted student populations such as handicapped and bilingual students. Much of the concern expressed in this regard has focused on the handicapped.

In a survey of states with minimum competency testing for graduation—including nine states with large bilingual populations—Baratz (1978) found that: (1) none of the state requirements categorically excludes

Table 4. Grades Tested in State MCT Programs

State	Grade	State	Grade
Alaska	local option	Nebraska	5-12
Arizona	8, 12	Nevada	3, 6, 9, 12
California	10, 11	New Jersey	3, 6, 9, 11
Colorado	9-12	New Mexico	10-12
Connecticut	9	New York	9-12
Delaware	11	North Carolina	11, 12
Florida	3, 5, 8, 11, 12	Oklahoma	3, 6, 9, 12
Georgia	9-12	Oregon	local option
Idaho	9-12	Rhode Island	9-12
Indiana	3, 6, 8, 10	Tennessee	11, 12
Kansas	2, 4, 6, 8, 11	Utah	local option
Kentucky	3, 5, 7, 10	Vermont	K-12
Louisiana	8	Virginia	9-12
Maine	local option	Washington	K 8
Maryland	9-12	Wyoming	local option
Missouri	8-12		

bilingual students; (2) few states are currently addressing or have addressed the competency needs of bilingual students; (3) where categorical exemptions or waivers are granted, they are usually granted to special students and to the severely handicapped; (4) except in Denver, no special assistance is provided to bilingual students under current MCT provisions; and (5) where local standards and measurements are allowed, state policy sometimes recognizes that differential standards may be set and differential diplomas awarded.

Types of Tests

The means of determining graduation competencies vary from paper-and-pencil testing, to certification by a panel, to demonstration of competence in the context of actual social situations. State programs in California, Oregon, Utah, Virginia, and Arizona merely require the "demonstration" of competencies, leaving local districts the option of arriving at specific standards and methods of assessment. Under some programs, districts may either (1) develop local methods of evaluating competencies within state-defined objectives or competency areas, as in Oregon, or (2) administer local tests subject to quality control through a statewide uniform test, as in Delaware.

Consequences of MCT Programs

The consequences of minimum competency testing also differ among states. Possible outcomes of minimum competency testing include early exit from high school, graduation and certification, promotion, or remediation.

Early Exit for Graduation

Early exit, conceived as an option for bright or bored students who are on the verge of leaving the school, is a variation of a minimum standards program for high school graduation. The popularity of the early exit concept appears slight, primarily because of its effect in lowering the age of compulsory school attendance and its potential effect on average daily attendance (ADA). Early exit programs exist in Florida and California. Their feasibility has been under consideration in Arizona, Arkansas, and Kansas.

Graduation and Certification

Currently, 22 states are in various stages of implementing competency-based high school graduation programs, and 21 more are actively considering such state requirements.[12] However, except for Arizona, Colorado, Florida, New York, and Oregon, most state programs will not be effective until the 1980s. Depending on the particular state, different types of certificates may be used to distinguish those who meet the minimums from those who do not (such as a regular high school diploma; a differentiated high school diploma; a certificate of competency; or a certificate of attendance).

Promotion

An interest in high school graduation standards has been coupled with a growing concern for setting minimum proficiency requirements for grade promotion. While some states are contemplating standards for elementary grade promotions, others have set requirements for promotion into high school.

Although competencies are assessed for grade promotion, none of the current programs mandate retention on the basis of competency failures. Remediation is the usual outcome. Where retention is a possibility, as in Maryland and Nevada, it is at the local district's option. States with grade promotional competency requirements include Arizona, Delaware, Florida, Michigan, Nevada, Virginia, and Tennessee. States contemplating such requirements include Arkansas, Michigan, and Ohio.

Remedial Assistance

Programs differ as to whether students who do not pass the minimum standards requirement receive remedial help; who is responsible for providing the help; who pays for it; and what is included in the remedial program. Wyoming and Utah, for example, do not mandate remedial help. In states where remediation is required, it is almost always the financial responsibility of the local district. In Florida, however, $10 million has been appropriated by the state legislature for remedial programs.

Remedial assistance may be provided in several forms: as part of regular classroom instruction (Maryland); as special instruction (New Jersey); as a special summer session (Denver); as pupil-parent-teacher conferences with individualized instruction (California); or as special preparatory classes in the competencies to be measured (Denver).

Dissemination of Testing Results

Although test data from MCT programs are student-oriented, the information released to the public and policymakers will nevertheless be taken as a report card for each school or school system. The controversy over the release of the numbers of graduates (or the numbers passing or failing competency requirements) may be more intense than the controversy provoked by the reporting of any other assessment data. The experience in Florida indicates the scope of media attention that competency test results may provoke when the state reports the numbers and racial composition of students passing or failing the statewide functional literacy exams.[13]

Few state programs currently have explicit guidelines concerning the collection and reporting of test data. The lack of clear requirements for reporting minimum competency data is partially due to the developmental stage of most state programs. Thus far, only four states specify reports of minimum competency data: Arizona,[14] Florida, New York, and Maryland.

A review of the status of MCT programs indicates: (1) the public wants some indication from schools that students can read, write, and figure; (2) the policymakers have addressed this demand with broad legislation but with little money; (3) the student bears the burden of the consequences of testing; (4) the statewide programs are all in their developmental stages—there is a good deal of rhetoric about promotion and graduation, but little evidence of withheld diplomas or massive retentions; and (5) the public demand for standards is being countered by the reluctance of teachers and other educational interest-groups to embrace tests as a way of improving education.

What Are the Policy Issues Related to Minimum Standards?

The questions inherent in the existing standards involve broad legal issues—such as discriminatory labeling and equal educational opportunity—as well as policy issues to be considered below, such as consistency in educational standards, the validity of the skills tested and the performance standards imposed, and the extent of a state's legal obligation to its students.

What Is a State's Responsibility?

What is the obligation of a state toward students who reach graduation age and cannot pass the tests? Is it fair to withhold a diploma in one district for failure to display 9th grade competency, when in another jurisdiction within a state, 8th grade competency is sufficient for a diploma? Where standards, measurement, and remedial aid are not uniformly prescribed throughout a state because of deference to local control, will the differential effect on diverse student groups raise issues about equal educational opportunity?

The question of a state's responsibility is crucial. While the obli-obligation to educate has historically been relegated to the states, what constitutes an education has not, heretofore, been made explicit by any state. Educational obligations, as defined by the states, have been articulated in terms of input: pupil/teacher ratios, curriculum offerings, building requirements, and teacher certification. Output obligations are vaguely expressed in terms such as "high quality" and "thorough and efficient." In the past, courts have been reluctant to address equal educational opportunity issues from an output perspective (Tractenberg, 1974; Tractenberg, n.d.). Nonetheless, the imposition of minimum standards set by states might well provide criteria for holding accountable not only the student, but the system as well.

In setting standards, the system not only states what children must know, but what it presumes it can teach. Responsibility for teaching thus rests with the school system; learning rests with the child. Yet if it is reasonable to assume that in setting educational standards the system operates from the belief that its students can be taught the standards, then standard setting can be seen as a contract between the system and the students.

Any failure rate above 5 percent might be seen as an indictment of present school practices and an indication that the system needs to provide something else to children. When upwards of 40 percent of the children fail a minimum standards test, it clearly indicates the system's failure to teach, rather than the children's inability to learn.[15]

A system that sets standards must ultimately be able to demonstrate that every reasonable effort has been made to give children the opportunity to learn. Therefore, setting standards for children means setting standards for the educational system. The system must be able to demonstrate that it is responsive to and acting upon the information it gathers regarding a student's educational progress. Without some formalized system for responding to the failure of children, MCT programs will be vulnerable to legal attack.[16]

What Is the Effect of MCT Programs on Equal Educational Opportunities?

What is the relationship between MCTs and equal educational opportunity, particularly if tests are shown to affect adversely a disproportionate number of minority-group students? Is there a correlation between competency certification and the socioeconomic or racial grouping of students who achieve mastery?

On its surface, the shift of focus—from questions of equity based on inputs of the system to questions based on outputs of the student—appears to be a major change of policy and an attempt to undermine the sixties' definition of equity and access. Nevertheless, the concern that MCT programs might destroy previous gains and do grave damage, especially to minority children, seems unwarranted. Several considerations support this assertion: (1) unfortunately, there are no major gains in the education of minority-group children that are jeopardized by an MCT program; (2) many of the "input" factors from the sixties and early seventies are well-embedded in law (if not always in administration) and cannot be ignored merely because another issue, minimum competency testing, has captivated public discussion and debate; and therefore (3) any MCT program that places undue hardship on minority-group children will probably not be able to withstand the political and legal challenges it provokes.

A look at the present "status" of minimum standards setting, however, leads to the conclusion that present discussions of testing are alarming not so much because they threaten the system (that is, cause great new harm to students and/or destroy local control), but because they indicate the "poverty" of educational establishment efforts to suggest credible alternatives for educating poor, minority-group children. There is no cause to believe that the minimum standard craze hurts children any more than what we have been doing in the past; just as it is politically necessary to pass legislation setting standards, so it is politically infeasible to have a majority of students fail them.

What Constitutes a Standard?

What constitutes "mastery" or "satisfactory" performance in "survival skills"? Even if we assume that educators can discern how much mastery is needed to be successful—survive—in life, what type of test questions attest to that mastery? Will the system teach the test? Will minimum standards thus turn into maximums?

Setting the standard requires attention to legal, technical, and political issues. Gaffney and Schember (1977) have identified legal responsibilities (regarding obligations not to discriminate and to assure due process) which will require that test development minimally meet "best practice" standards and that care be taken that test results do not, on their face, disproportionately affect minority-group children. In addition the test, to comply with due process requirements, must also assess what the school has taught. From a practical political perspective, those who develop and implement the program must seek broad-based, representative support for the test. Therefore, the "standard" is ultimately likely to be a value judgment buttressed by political realities and refined by statistical technology.

Who Will Pay for the Consequences of Poor Performance?

Is the desire for quality education which is inherent in standard setting accompanied by adequate compensatory programs for the special needs of minorities and other subgroups? Who will bear the burden of remedial education for students who fail these tests? Will the costs of remedial education be disequalizing to efforts at equalization of state aid? What happens to students who do not succeed in passing the tests? What is to be done with below-"average" students—for example, fifteen-year-olds still unable to pass elementary proficiency exams? Will school employees be held accountable? Will competency standards combine with the trend for accountability, and thus bring public pressure for educational malpractice legislation? (In Florida, a legislative proposal is pending to dismiss instructional personnel who fail to raise student achievement to the minimum standards.)

As our review of MCT programs indicated, many of the programs do not require remedial assistance for students who fail the tests, nor is there widespread policy to provide additional funds for students who fail.[17] If MCT programs are to have any hope of improving education (to say nothing of withstanding judicial review), it seems imperative that policymakers develop an educational system that is accountable not merely because it administers periodic tests, but because it uses the information from tests to provide additional and different resources to children who are not achieving the specified goals. The MCT program must, at a minimum, assure that the educational progress of children is monitored so that if procedure A is not effective, procedure B is provided, and so on, until the goals are achieved.

Will a Focus on Testing Corrupt the Utility of the Test?

As test scores begin to be used for other than diagnostic purposes, they become vulnerable to misuse and cheating. Stories abound about teachers "teaching the test," principals allowing extra time for completion of the test, and certain pupils being excused from taking the test in an effort to assure more positive test results for schools.[18]

This is the problem Donald Campbell identified as "use-related distortion." He found that "the more any quantitative social indicator is used for social decisionmaking, the more subject it will be to corruption pressures and the more apt it will be to distort and corrupt the social processes it is intended to monitor." (D. Campbell, 1975, p. 35) As Campbell illustrated, a vivid example is yielded by comparing our regard for voting statistics and for census data. Elaborate precautions surround elections to ensure their honesty; surrounding census taking there are comparatively few evaluative safeguards, and these are easily evaded. Yet we tend to suspect voting statistics, but to trust the census. Why? Because votes are continually *used* to make important social decisions—they have the ultimate consequence of distributing resources and power, while only of late has the census begun to be used for similar purposes. Minimum competency testing has a similar volatility. As test results come to be used for distributing real resources, they will inevitably be subject to the type of corruption identified by Campbell.

Conclusion

In writing this paper I was sorely tempted to take the initial section presenting my biases and move it here, enabling me piously to state my biases as conclusions. Nonetheless, the prejudices I mentioned earlier are not the product of "whole cloth"; they do emerge from careful examination of previous educational reforms and of accountability through testing. The question presently before policymakers and educators is whether, in responding to the policy issues identified here, we can benefit from past experience and surmount the political, administrative, legal, and technical obstacles that have frustrated previous reforms. I am hopeful, but, given past experiences, I am not optimistic.

Notes

1. In the past three years, over 30 states have enacted legislation or passed school board resolutions regarding the setting of standards. Demands for these laws have generally come from the public and the business community, while opposition to them has been voiced primarily by education interest groups. See Pipho, 1978.

2. Test development and field testing can assist in determining the "difficulty level" of items and adjustments made. For political issues, see discussion in the National Academy of Education, 1978.

3. The attacks on testing are usually generated by test use; however, the resolution of controversies is usually technical (to make the test better) rather than stopping the testing. See Baratz, J., 1978.

4. For further discussion see Ravitch, 1978.

5. The use of test scores as a punishment or incentive for performance is not a new concept. In the early 1970s an attempt was made to use statewide assessment data to hold teachers accountable for their performance. This effort ran into much opposition from teacher organizations and was soon abandoned. See Skerry, 1976.

6. One recourse is to change the public's perception of reality, which the NEA is presently attempting in a Maryland school district through a carefully orchestrated public relations campaign (complete with singing commercials) designed to inform citizens "What's Right with Our Schools?" (*Washington Post*, October 1, 1978).

7. See the writings of education historians such as Colin Greer, Michael Katz, Joel Spring, Marvin Lazerson, and Clarence Karier.

8. There has been a continuing debate as to the viability and functionality of many of the behaviors identified as characteristic of poor, minority-group children. Their behaviors have been labeled "pathological" and "limited" by some social scientists, but "culturally different" by others. See Baratz, S. and Baratz, J. 1970.

9. Campbell, 1973. The actual policy uses of such data were not as widespread as originally anticipated. See Thant and Baratz, 1978.

10. *Peter W.* v. *San Francisco Unified School District*, 1976; and *Donahue* v. *Copaigue*, 1977.

11. The importance of citizen review is illustrated in Florida. An administrative ruling in a grievance procedure brought by a parent found the Florida Functional Literacy Exam null and void because the cutoff scores had not been reviewed by a citizen panel.

12. The number of states with MCT programs varies according to how and when the data are collected, and by whom. For example, Pipho (1978) includes Maine as a state with minimum competency requirements although the state requirement is for one-time testing of 11th graders, with the results to be studied for policy determination regarding high school graduation requirements. (The study group recently decided against such a requirement.) Others include states with purely local programs locally initiated, developed, and administered in the absence of a statewide policy or mandate (for example, Gary, Indiana). Numbers used here are based on programs initiated or required by the state, either as a statewide mandate or as legislation and policy.

13. Over two-thirds of the black students in the state failed the math test. The NAACP went to court to stop implementation of the program, and a subsequent ruling based on administrative procedures voided the test results.

14. Arizona's minimum competency program, which has been in effect since 1976, requires all results to be reported to the legislature with an analysis and a recommendation on improving the quality of reading achievement. However, until 1978, Arizona did not aggregate state-level data.

15. The Florida experience is a case in point. Problems with metric measurement was one explanation for the difficulty with the test.

16. Tractenberg (n.d.) discusses the vulnerability of school districts that impose standards but do not provide services for students who do not meet the standard.

17. For problems of using test scores for distributing funds, see Feldmesser, 1975.

18. Problems with cheating in test procedures and score reporting were chronicled in the *Washington Post*, "Improprieties Found in School Testing," September 29, 1978.

References

Baratz, J. 1978. Cultural bias and the use of tests: a double-edged sword. In *Speaking out: the use of tests in the policy arena*. Princeton: Educational Testing Service, pp. 9-20.

Baratz, J. July 1978. In setting minimal standards have we abandoned concerns for equity and access? Paper presented at the Wingspread Conference, Racine, Wis. Excerpts in *Principal* 58, no. 2 (1979): 11-41.

Baratz, S. and Baratz, J. 1970. Early childhood intervention: the social science base of institutional racism. *Harvard Educational Review* 40, no. 1: 29-50.

Callahan, R. 1962. *Education and the cult of efficiency*. Chicago: University of Chicago Press.

Campbell, D. 1975. Assessing the impact of planned social change. In Gene Lyons (ed.), *Social research and public policies*. Hanover, N. H.: University Press of New England.

Campbell, P. 1973. *Statewide assessment programs.* Princeton: Educational Testing Service.

Chall, J. 1978. Minimum competency testing. *Harvard Graduate School of Education Association Bulletin* 22, no. 3: 9-12.

Cohen, D. and Lazerson, M. 1972. Education and the corporate order. *Socialist Revolution* 2, no. 2: 47-72.

Donahue v. *Copaigue Union School Free School District*, 407 N.Y.S. 2d 874 (Supreme Court, App. Div., Sec. Dept. 1978) Affirming, Index 77-1128, Opinion 8/31/78.

Feldmesser, R. 1975. *Use of test scores as a basis for fund allocation*, Final Report. Washington, D.C.: National Institute of Education.

Gaffney, M. and Schember, D. 1977. Promotion and graduation testing requirements and the legal obligations of the education system. In Baratz, J., and Gaffney, M. "Legal and education issues of competency testing for promotion and graduation: Can a policy capable of withstanding judicial scrutiny be devised?" Proposal to the National Institute of Education.

Improprieties found in school testing. September 29, 1978. *Washington Post.*

National Academy of Education, Committee on Testing and Basic Skills. 1978. *Improving educational achievement.* Washington, D.C.: National Academy of Education.

Peter W. v. *San Francisco Unified School District.* 1976. 60 Cal. App. 3d 814, 131 Cal. Rptr. 854 (Ct. App. 1976).

Pipho, C. 1978. *Minimum competency update.* Denver: Education Commission of the States.

Ravitch, D. March 1978. The new testing movement: what it means. Paper presented at the National Conference on Achievement Testing and Basic Skills, U.S. Department of Health, Education and Welfare, Washington, D.C.

Skerry, P. 1976. *Statewide assessment and the policy process: the New Jersey experience.* Washington, D.C.: Education Policy Research Institute of Educational Testing Service.

Thant, T. and Baratz, J. 1978. Test data and politics: a survey of state testing programs and policy uses. Mimeographed. Washington, D.C.: Education Policy Research Institute of Educational Testing Service.

Tractenberg, P. n.d. The legal implications of statewide pupil performance standards. Mimeographed.

Tractenberg, P. 1974. Reforming school finance through state constitutions: *Robinson* v. *Cahill* points the way. *Rutgers Law Review*, special issue no. 3: 365-463.

What's right with our schools? October 1, 1978. *Washington Post.*

Response to Dr. Baratz:
"Policy Implications of
Minimum Competency Testing"

Larry Cuban

Dr. Baratz states her biases before moving into the body of her paper. I, for one, find it useful to know where the writer stands. With that in mind, let me share some of my biases about minimum competency testing. (1) After assessing the weaknesses and strengths of state-mandated programs, such as in Virginia, I find such tests a useful tool for a school board to improve a school system's performance with marginal and low-achieving students. (2) The accountability impulse that brought us minimum competency testing, its most recent manifestation, is longstanding (almost a decade and a half old); this impulse will continue to generate other political mandates imposed upon school boards and superintendents. (3) Minimum competency testing will have substantial consequences, both positive and negative, for instruction, curriculum, school organization, and teacher performance. Inevitably, my reactions to Dr. Baratz's paper will be colored by these biases.

Dr. Baratz, like most of us, searches for the origins of the minimum competency movement. She locates it in the ideological conflict between egalitarians, who challenged the meritocracy embedded in the "corporate capitalist model," and supporters of the model. The vocabulary of "corporate capitalist model" comes directly from the revisionist view of the educational past and is currently popular. But there are competing explanations for the movement surfacing now. Dr. Baratz does not suggest these other possible explanations, such as the cyclical fascination of educators and social engineers with accountability, or political pressure that is episodic, erratic, and external to schools.

Since Dr. Baratz is seeking the origins of this testing passion, she is basically asking a set of historical questions. Her answers should, at the least, meet the following tests: (1) Does the explanation account for why minimum competency testing erupted on the educational landscape as suddenly as it did? (2) Does the explanation answer why there was a rapid diffusion of minimum competency testing to almost two-thirds of the states in less than three years? (3) Does the explanation link minimum competency testing to similar phenomena and thereby become plausible for an institution like education, which is notoriously afflicted with cyclical patterns? I don't think her theory of conflict between egalitarian advocates and supporters of meritocracy passes these test questions.

Her few paragraphs, however, on what happened in the 1960s and 1970s is a fair but superficial description that explains the minimum competency movement, especially when she points out that educational testing became a social indicator to be used in judging the performance of school systems. The elusive why of all this, unfortunately, was unexplored.

When Dr. Baratz moved into describing state efforts to legislate minimum competency programs, she provided a most useful, spare summary of the movement. The movement's unevenness, the underdeveloped quality of many states' efforts, the shocking superficiality of some programs, and the rapidity of its spread—all of these are clearly and compactly stated.

Drawn from this summary, her conclusions seem both plausible and sensible. I differ, however, with her last conclusion concerning the resistance of teachers and other educational interest groups. While that resistance may be a fact, she presents no evidence to make that point. Since the NEA and the American Federation of Teachers have staked out opposing positions on standardized tests and minimum competency testing, I would like to have more substantial evidence of overt opposition by teachers before this conclusion is reached.

In the final section of her paper, Dr. Baratz moves from her excellent summary of state programs to the policy implications of the movement. Rather than speak of policy implications, I prefer to deal with the consequences—both actual and anticipated—of minimum competency testing, as seen from the vantage point of one school district in the second year of such testing.

Dr. Baratz sees the imposition of minimum standards by the state as establishing criteria holding both the student and the system accountable. The standards clarify, she suggests, who does what and who is responsible for what. I think she is right. The process of the state coercively clarifying for each school district their primary mission in specific terms—defining what schools are to teach students—has already begun to produce specific objectives in basic skills areas in systems where such targets were lacking. It has forced school systems to assess the remedial services that were available in the high school, to identify earlier checkpoints in diagnosing low-achieving students in their school career, and to discover where gaps existed in order to establish a coherent process of identifying and serving low-achieving students.

I see these consequences occurring in districts that have some extra resources to devote to this process; but they will not materialize necessarily, I fear, in school districts already hard-pressed to provide minimum school services to meet the everpresent, conflicting demands of their communities. Without substantial state support of compensatory services to financially strapped districts, little behavioral change will occur in school districts doing minimum competency testing. (Of course, I refer only to the experience of one district in a state where no funds have yet been provided to local districts, neither for remedial services nor for back-up programs to help low-achieving students leap the hurdle of a graduation test.)

When Dr. Baratz turns to the policy implications for minority students, I feel she passes over the issue too quickly. She understands clearly that the cutoff point on state-mandated tests can be set at any level to produce a politically safe failure rate. But whatever that rate is (and while it will not be a majority, even a 20-25 percent failure rate is shocking), over the next five years large numbers of low-income black, Hispanic, and white students will fail. These students would have ordinarily received a regular diploma upon completion of the course of study; now they will not receive a diploma. They will be tagged as failures. Or, if they do receive a diploma, it will be devalued and resemble an attendance certificate. The social costs of excluding many students, most of whom are poor and members of minority groups, from receiving regular diplomas cannot be calculated yet.

In other words, in the next few years there will be large numbers of minority students who will have to pay directly the cost of ineffective schooling. This is an inevitable consequence of any minimum competency test mandate that is projected for a graduating class two to three years away.

How does one calculate the costs of putting on the streets more students, who will now have the school-stamped stigma of failure, to join the already large pool of unemployed youth? I am not as confident as Dr. Baratz that court cases or class action suits will save these young men and women.

Ironically, I anticipate that the younger brothers and sisters of those students who fail the test, and thus receive either a devalued diploma or none at all, may benefit. Dr. Baratz suggests this when she points out that the educational progress of children should be closely monitored. I anticipate that improved early identification procedures, monitoring of individual students' progress, and repeated skill testing will mushroom rapidly in many school systems. And if they do, the only reason for the spread will be the whip of minimum competency testing and the public prodding that will stem from test results on annual display for the community.

The technology of skill-deficit identification, teaching, testing, and reteaching is both familiar and well-enough embedded among school staffs to be implemented in most school systems. In our district, for example, it took about a year to conceptualize, organize, and begin implementing an identification and monitoring program once the state mandated the graduation requirements. Of course, a number of these pieces were already in practice; but minimum competency testing prodded us into pulling together a coherent, sequential system. Again, this is one system's experience; the redirection of available resources will dictate how much can be done in other places.

The policy implications that Dr. Baratz outlines in her paper are important ones. Obviously, she cannot cover all the consequences that might flow from a state-mandated program. Nor can I. However, I would like to suggest a few other policy consequences that I anticipate or already see emerging.

The advocates of minimum competency testing felt that a political decision (that is, state legislation of graduation tests of competency) would affect the entire process of education. Based upon my limited experience, I think the advocates will be more right than wrong in their hunch. There is a long, rich history of tests shaping what is taught.

I anticipate that there will be both a narrowing of content and a crisper uniformity in curriculum, especially for marginal and low-achieving students; there will be even more emphasis on cognitive skills and less on nonacademic areas; grade-by-grade objectives keyed to test items will be developed in school systems in order to demonstrate that there is a rational basis to pass students on to another grade or to retain them; and grade-by-grade objectives will establish tighter linkages between state and local tests and what is actually taught. There will be a slow but steady drift back toward ability grouping, especially at the secondary level, and a slow but cautious embrace of academic tracking. Pressures for these changes have already occurred. Whether any of these anticipated policy consequences will benefit children more than the existing system benefits them is another question—one to which I do not know the answer.

Historically, there have been few times when externally imposed political mandates have jolted schools like the accountability impulses of the last decade and a half. The last comparable one was the turn-of-the-century centralization of school board authority and the rise of the superintendent as educational expert, all as an answer to poor student performance. This movement resulted in new state laws and city charters reforming the governance of public schools. We are still studying the policy implications of that political solution (that is: change the governance of schooling and educational performance will improve).

My guess is that the policy effects of state-mandated minimum competency testing will continue to permeate schooling and change its

VRJC LIBRARY

character as did the political reforms at the turn of the century. We are at the beginning, rather than the end, of the policy effects of minimum competency testing.

PART II

Consequences of Minimum Competency Testing for the Schools, the Courts, and Society

In this section, authors of three major papers and four respondents explore the ways minimum competency testing is likely to affect what is taught in our schools, the bases for legal challenges to competency testing, and the relationships between students' competency test performance and their later opportunities for education and work.

In *Testing for Minimum Competency: A Legal Analysis*, Paul Tractenberg begins by identifying six legal bases for challenging various aspects of a minimum competency testing program. Both the federal and state constitutions contain due process clauses that protect citizens in two ways. Guarantees of substantive due process require the state to act in a reasonable manner, and solely in areas that are demonstrably related to legitimate state interests. Charges might be brought, on the basis of denial of substantive due process, that competency test content does not represent what has been taught in the schools. Guarantees of procedural due process require the state to act fairly when it deprives citizens of liberty or property. Procedural due process challenges might form the basis of claims that the test scoring rules are unfair. The second legal basis for actions against competency tests lies in the equal protection clauses of the federal and state constitutions. Such clauses protect groups from unfair treatment, whereas due process clauses guarantee the rights of individuals. Evidence of unjustified differential classification of groups on the basis of competency test results might be used in legal actions founded in equal protection clauses. Most state constitutions contain clauses that guarantee students access to public education. Thus education becomes a "right" for students and a legally mandated obligation of the state. If such clauses can be used to define education as a "fundamental right," challenges to competency testing based on denial of equal protection would be materially strengthened. The fourth element of the legal armamentarium is the set of education statutes that exist outside state constitutions. These laws often amplify constitutional education clauses and proscribe the actions of state education authorities. In a number of states, such statutes describe the required design and operation of minimum competency testing programs. Opportunities for legal action on the basis of noncompliance are obvious. A fifth basis for legal challenge is the set of state education regulations typically issued by state educational authorities. Such regulations do not constitute law, but often have the force of law. Their potency for supporting legal challenge may be almost as great as that of state education statutes. The final basis for action is the vast history of court decisions that defines our common law. Past actions of the courts in other test-related cases establish precedent for all manner of legal challenge to competency testing programs.

Having identified the legal foundations for court action on competency testing, Tractenberg considers the testing program design options discussed in Henry M. Brickell's paper, "Seven Key Notes on Minimum Competency Testing," which appeared in the proceedings of four regional conferences on competency testing sponsored by the National Institute of Education, and which was reprinted in the May 1978 issue of *Phi Delta Kappan*. For each design issue raised by Brickell, Tractenberg identifies the option that is least vulnerable to legal challenge. Considering the types of competencies to be required, for example—a choice among school skills, life skills, basic skills applied to life-role situations, and so on— Tractenberg suggests that "basic skills" competencies would be least subject to challenge on the basis of due process or equal protection clauses of federal or state constitutions. Basic skills are taught in most (if not all) elementary schools; they typically form the substance of the curriculum in the early years of school, so that students receive adequate notice of the expectation that they acquire basic skills; and the case for inherent bias in basic skills is considerably weaker than the case that could be developed against, say, competencies defined in terms of life-role experiences.

Tractenberg's model of the least vulnerable minimum competency testing program is consistent with the programs presently operating in many of the states—he would have us test basic skills knowledge; use pencil-and-paper tests for measurement; test periodically, beginning in the early grades; use consistent statewide competency standards, but perhaps allow local educational agencies to adopt supplementary standards; set unitary standards by subject area, rather than many standards for different groups of students; set standards that are educationally defensible, rather than set standards using political or fiscal bases exclusively; set standards that apply to each student, not standards that apply to schools (as might be done in a statewide assessment program); and provide opportunities for remediation of students' deficiencies, but fail those who don't ultimately meet minimum standards. As we shall see in the remaining papers in this section, however, a minimum competency testing program that maximizes legal invincibility may not be most desirable from educational and sociological perspectives.

In his 1963 paper, "A Model for School Learning," John B. Carroll identified time devoted to instruction as an important determiner of student achievement. Among others, Wiley and Harnishfeger (1974) confirm Carroll's supposition that the greater the time devoted to instruction in a subject, the greater will be the students' achievement in that subject. These findings are relevant to the impact of minimum competency testing on the high school curriculum, because total instructional time is limited. In an age of increasing teacher militancy, and regulation of the length of the school day and school year through tightly negotiated contracts, additions to the high school curriculum without compensatory reductions are unlikely. If minimum competency criteria are defined solely in basic skills terms, and high schools attempt to remediate students' deficiencies during the regular school day, some time presently devoted to other subjects must be lost. And we can expect some consequential effects on student achievement in these subjects.

Harry Broudy's paper, *The Impact of Minimum Competency Testing on Curriculum*, begins by questioning both the meaning and the utility of minimum competency testing. Broudy suggests that the term carries a multiplicity of meanings, that such testing will only be useful for measurement of rote recall and other didactics, and that the only predictable outcome of minimum competency testing is that testing companies will gain income. He sees minimum competency testing as a political activity, and suggests that the political consequences of such testing, including the ultimate viability of public education, may be far more important than its curricular consequences.

Broudy next explores the implications of the schools' adopting a kind of "functional literacy curriculum," consistent with the narrow, basic-skills definition of competencies adopted by many states and school districts. He finds such a curriculum severely deficient in elements needed to equip students to be truly functional in life—elements to provide personal adequacy, occupational adequacy, and civic adequacy—which he claims most parents and taxpayers really demand when they argue for functional literacy. Adults who can adequately cope with life require education, not training, he insists—education based on the broad and rich five-strand curriculum detailed in Broudy, Smith, and Burnett (1964).

After suggesting that a public and professional commitment to education that goes beyond the "three R's" has typified American public education, Broudy states that minimum competency testing may indicate a withdrawal from this commitment. At worst, he suggests, minimum competency testing may lead us to a two-tiered system of schooling: a kindergarten through sixth-grade curriculum for the children of the masses, and a kindergarten through twelfth-grade curriculum (perhaps in nonpublic schools) for the children of the monied classes who can afford such special instruction. Thus his most chilling scenario includes the demise of universal, egalitarian public education through grade twelve as a hope, if not a reality, in the United States. Although Broudy does not suggest it, the synergism of minimum competency testing, of busing schoolchildren on a metropolitan areawide basis for purposes of racial desegregation, and of the rise of voucher plans to compensate parents for enrollment of their children in nonpublic schools (A referendum is expected to appear on the statewide ballot in California in 1980.) may well cause the demise of our current public educational system.

Broudy concludes with a more positive scenario than the one described above. He predicts that educators and the public will quickly realize that strict attention to basic skills achievement, or a narrow conception of functional literacy, is inadequate. They will recognize that students must participate in the full richness of the five-strand curriculum if they are to become adequately functioning adults. This will bring about a far broader definition of minimum competency, and a renewed interest in education and schooling, to the ultimate benefit of both.

In her reaction of Broudy's paper, Marianne Amarel is far less sanguine on the prospects for some ultimate good arising from minimum competency testing. Acknowledging that minimum competency testing need not inevitably lead to a basic skills curriculum, she points to the abundant evidence of such movement in school systems and states that have embraced minimum competency testing thus far.

Amarel views minimum competency testing as a move to wrest control of education from individual teachers and to place it at superordinate administrative levels such as central offices of school systems or state departments of education. She is convinced that such a movement will have profoundly negative educational consequences, since it restricts teachers' options in determining achievement criteria, setting standards for achievement, choosing the content to be assessed, and selecting techniques for assessment. Citing evidence that control of assessment means control of curriculum, Amarel notes that centrally controlled assessment programs often lead to prescriptive instructional programs. Thus school systems and states restrict teachers' abilities to control instruction, yet at the same time they hold teachers accountable for student performance.

Amarel agrees with Broudy on the need for a broad curriculum that fosters far more than rote, didactic learning, but she claims that such a curriculum is impossible in the absence of teacher control. Only when teachers have the option of responding to the unique needs, interests, questions, and abilities of individual learners, is it possible to go beyond rote learning, according to Amarel.

Instruction that emphasizes component skills alone (the primary content assessed in many basic skills competency tests) fails to capitalize on the existing knowledge of students. Amarel suggests that such instruction is most damaging to students who may not have a rich storehouse of experience to begin with—typically students of lower socioeconomic levels—so that minimum competency testing may ultimately exacerbate the problems of socioeconomic discrimination in our schools.

Amarel concludes that minimum competency testing has the potential of affecting in a negative way not only the content of our curriculum, but the process of instruction as well. She foresees the possibility that, as curricular content is highly restricted, teachers will be made ineffective automatons. As does Broudy, she suggests that such limited schooling is most likely to be visited upon children from lower socioeconomic classes.

W. James Popham's reaction to Broudy's paper is one of cautious optimism. He agrees that the day-to-day curriculum of the schools will be shaped to match the content of minimum competency tests whenever test content is sufficiently clear to allow curriculum definition. If a minimalist interpretation of functional literacy persists, Popham further agrees that a two-caste system of public education may ultimately result.

Although he acknowledges that current interpretations of the meaning of basic skills and functional literacy are decidedly narrow in most school systems and states, Popham suggests that continued public demand for higher-order learning in the schools will lead to reform of competency standards. The public's demand for truly functional graduates who can become successful and independent citizens and workers will force the development of assessment devices for measurement of a broader array of criteria, and these, Popham hopes, will force the enrichment of the curriculum in the directions Broudy demands.

In these first papers, then, we see the seeds of tension between those responsible for the schools' curriculum and administrators intent on

avoiding lawsuits over competency testing programs. A narrow definition of competency, which safeguards a competency testing program from
legal challenge, is likely to restrict the curriculum in ways that undermine
the schools' educational goals, to further widen the present achievement
disparity between the children from higher and lower socioeconomic
classes, and, at worst, to cause the demise of K-12 public education.

Other important questions relate to the effects of denying a high school
diploma to students who do not meet minimum competency standards.
Test validity and interpretive validity loom large among these questions.
These and other issues are considered in the remaining papers of this
section.

Bruce Eckland examines the relationships of scores on basic skills
tests in reading and mathematics (The tests used in his study are similar
to the minimum competency tests used in several states.) to later employment, income, and college-going rates of high school graduates. In his
paper entitled *Sociodemographic Implications of Minimum Competency
Testing*, Eckland suggests that preparation for work and preparation for
further schooling are the "primary functions" of secondary education.
He asks whether use of minimum competency tests in determining which
high school students will be awarded a diploma will have any effect on
students' prospects on these two key educational outcomes.

Eckland's primary data source is the National Longitudinal Study of
the High School Class of 1972, completed under the sponsorship of the
National Center for Education Statistics. Using these data, he found that
scores on reading and math tests had no relationship to the employment
rates of white students within four months of high school graduation.
However, both reading and math test scores were related, in the expected
direction, to the employment rates of black high school graduates.

Searching further, Eckland found that levels of part-time employment
were not related to basic skills test performance in high school for either
black or white graduates, and that test performance was also unrelated
to weekly income for graduates of either race. Citing work by Peng and
Jaffe (based on a four-years-post-graduation follow-up of students originally tested as part of the National Longitudinal Study), Eckland reports
virtually no relationship between scoring in the lower vs. the upper quarter
of the distribution on either of the NLS basic skills tests on the one hand,
and unemployment rates, mean hours worked, or weekly income ($175
for those in the upper quarter, vs. $173 for those in the lower quarter)
on the other hand, *four years after* high school graduation. These data
apply only to high school graduates who did not enter college.

As might be expected, NLS test scores were highly related to college-
going rates for both blacks and whites. However, denying high school

diplomas to those who score poorly on the tests would have far greater effects on the college-going rates of blacks than on those of whites. For example, Eckland shows that refusal to grant high school diplomas to those in the lowest 10 percent of the NLS score distribution (thereby precluding their entering college) would reduce the white college-going rate from 54 percent to 53 percent, but the corresponding rate for blacks would drop from 48 percent to 38 percent. Eliminating the lowest 20 percent of the distribution would have a negligible effect on the college-going rate of whites (54 percent to 52 percent), but would reduce the rate for blacks from 48 percent to 31 percent. Thus the present 6 percent difference in the college-going rates of blacks and whites would be increased to 21 percent.

Based on these data and others, Eckland concludes that high school graduation serves an important credentialing function in U.S. society, but that acquiring the kinds of basic skills measured by the NLS tests (and by implication, a large number of the presently-adopted minimum competency tests) has little relationship to either employment or income for those who do not go to college. That such skills are important for those who attend college may be as much an artifact of our admissions procedures as an indication of their fundamental necessity.

In his reaction to Eckland's paper, Robert W. Heath rejects Eckland's premises that the primary functions of secondary schooling are to prepare students for work and for more schooling, and that reading and computation are essential for functioning in adult life. In Heath's view, preparation for work and additional schooling is "an inadequate conception of the social functioning of schooling." Heath cites Eckland's data as prima facie evidence of the unessential nature of reading and math skills for adult functioning. It is interesting to note that both Heath and Eckland ignore the restriction of the cited NLS data to those who do not enter college.

Heath states that academic competencies are, for the most part, merely ritualistic criteria for most adults; that is, they do not meet a utilitarian need, as defined by those adults. In Heath's view, functional competencies can only be defined by individuals for themselves, in the context of their immediate needs, and in particular circumstances. They are both subjective and objective. So the very idea of the state defining minimum competencies that apply to all high school students at all times is ritualistic and disfunctional for many students.

Heath recommends that the states assess the performance levels of individuals on a large sample of competencies that are deemed functional by a large number of people in society. This assessment could be used to define performance norms, so that adults and students could be informed of their own performance deficits, compared with large numbers of persons in the general population. Individuals would thus have data that would be useful to them in defining their own needs. The process of need definition would take place through a series of dialogues with educators, as suggested in the works of Paolo Friere. In such dialogues, individuals would retain the power to make their own decisions on functional competencies and performance deficits, but educators would have the power of data on societal performance, educational treatments, remediation costs, and so on.

This approach to competency-based education would, in Heath's view, provide liberation for individuals, and break down the oppression, cultural stereotyping, and cultural imperialism that accompanies our present systems of competency testing.

Thus, for reasons other than those identified by Eckland, Heath agrees that minimum competency testing as presently defined in most states and school systems may cause more harm than good. His proposed alternatives, although philosophically appealing, raise a number of practical problems. For example, students may not be able to identify the competency needs that they will have as adults; the relationships between school-generated skills for children and adult competencies are tenuous at best (of course, this same problem exists in conventional competency-based education programs as well); even if students can define their own needs, the schools may find it impossible to respond to them on an individual basis.

In a second review of Eckland's paper, Ellis B. Page holds to a meritocratic view of the value of a high school education, and attempts to refute Eckland's findings on statistical grounds. He begins by claiming that the NLS data cited by Eckland apply only to a special, nonrepresentative group of individuals. Because the data apply only to non-college-going youth, Page suggests that the lack of relationship between test scores and later employment and income data results from a statistical artifact.

Page suggests that the regression of "true ability" on test score is flatter for the non-college-going group than would be the case in the entire population of high school seniors. He then argues that high scorers among the non-college-going group result largely from measurement error, and that these students do not possess a high level of true ability. If this is the case, Page concludes that society is reacting appropriately by not rewarding the high scorers with higher incomes and higher employment rates.

Page's argument assumes that society can detect and will reward true ability, not a measured estimate of it. The balance of his statistical argument rests on his assumption of a model in which those who are in the highest half of a true ability distribution go to college, and those who are in the lowest half do not. To the degree that this assumption is violated—as it undoubtedly would be in practice, since colleges do not have true ability measures to use in selection—Page's conclusions are greatly weakened.

Page further assumes that the National Longitudinal Study test data are so unreliable that, for any comparisons of blacks and whites, they fail to account for true racial differences; he points out that each group will regress toward its own true-score mean.

Finally, Page suggests that the eventual earnings of high school graduates are not accurately reflected by their earnings only four years beyond graduation—the data reported by Eckland. He cites data reported by Olneck (1977) in support of this contention, and states that Olneck found positive correlations between test performance, income, and later education, in contrast to Eckland's results.

Page agrees that using minimum competency tests in determining which students will receive the high school diploma will likely reduce the college-going rates of black students, assuming uniform cutoff scores are adopted. He suggests that use of different cutoff scores would likely result in reverse-discrimination suits filed by groups held to a higher standard. As a solution to this problem, Page suggests the use of "scaled certification," a plan in which minimum competency test performance would not be required for high school graduation, but competency test scores would be printed on the face of each student's high school diploma.

Page has presented his counterarguments in a persuasive manner, but he ignores the fundamental discrepancies and lack of predictability that have always been evident in educational and psychological measurement. Even in the best studies of prediction of college performance, test scores predict about 33 percent of the variance in any practical criterion (for example, first-year college grade point averages). Tests of cognitive skills measure only a fraction of the abilities that are evidently required for success in college or in any occupation. Similarly, problems of cultural bias remain as intractable today as they have been throughout the history of measuring differences among individuals in this and other cultures. It is a disservice to those who want to use tests for improving, rather than constraining, education to treat tests as more powerful and infallible than is truly the case.

References

Broudy, H. S., Smith, B. O., and Burnett, J. R. *Democracy and excellence in American secondary education.* Chicago: Rand McNally, 1964.

Carroll, J. B. A model for school learning. *Teachers College Record, 64,* 1963, 723-33.

Wiley, D. E., and Harnishfeger, A. Explosion of a myth: quantity of schooling and exposure to instruction, major educational vehicles. Report No. 8, *Studies of Educative Processes.* Chicago: CEMREL, Inc., 1974.

4 Testing for Minimum Competency: A Legal Analysis

Paul L. Tractenberg

The burgeoning minimum competency testing movement has generated a growing body of literature. Most of it has described developments in the states,[1] or discussed educational, political, psychometric, or fiscal problems.[2] Many articles and papers have mentioned, almost casually, the possibility that the establishment of minimum competency testing programs might have legal implications. These have usually been conceived of in connection with educational malpractice litigation.[3] The theory is that if a state or local school district establishes minimum competency standards, it thereby obligates itself to ensure that at least all "educable" students perform at or above those levels. Students who fail to achieve such levels may have legally enforceable rights against the educational system and its officials.

Only a few recent articles and papers have sought to deal in some detail with legal issues related to competency testing or the establishment of minimum pupil performance standards.[4] In the main, these writings have dealt with the general concept of competency testing rather than with the details of actual or potential programs.

This paper will update and expand upon those earlier efforts. It consists of three sections: the first provides an overview of relevant legal provisions and theories; the second applies those provisions and theories to the various elements of state minimum competency testing programs; and the final section offers some projections about legal developments and about the minimum competency testing movement generally.

I. Relevant Legal Provisions and Theories

There are six categories of legal provisions which may prove relevant to minimum competency assessment programs. Three are constitutional in origin: federal and state due process clauses; federal and state equal protection clauses; and state education clauses. The fourth is statutory—those provisions of the state's education laws which directly or indirectly bear upon the establishment and operation of a minimum competency testing program. The fifth is regulatory—relevant policies, rules and regulations of the state education authorities. The sixth is the "common law"—legal principles that have evolved through litigation. Each of those sources of law will be considered briefly.

i. Federal and State Due Process Clauses

The Fourteenth Amendment to the U.S. Constitution, and most state constitutions, contain a due process clause. The federal clause provides that no state[5] shall "deprive any person of life, liberty, or property, without due process of law." The judiciary has construed due process to have substantive and procedural aspects.

Substantive due process, still in existence (although significantly diminished in legal importance),[6] requires that the action of the state be rational and reasonably related to a legitimate state objective. If, for example, it could be proven that a state's minimum competency testing program was testing students on material never taught in the schools, students who failed on that test to demonstrate their competency might credibly assert a violation of their right to substantive due process.[7]

Procedural due process requires that the state act in a fair manner when it deprives a citizen of liberty or property. In connection with a minimum competency testing program, procedural due process might require, for example, a procedure under which students with "failing" scores be permitted to challenge the scoring of the test or the validity of the test itself.

Both substantive and procedural due process require a showing that a person has been deprived of liberty or property by action of the state. Students could assert that denial of a "regular" diploma, or of promotion or graduation under a minimum competency testing program, constitutes a deprivation of "property." Courts have found that students have a property interest in their education, such that physical exclusion from school, even for a short time, requires due process procedures.[8] Whether retention in grade or failure to graduate would be a deprivation of a property interest is less clear.[9]

Students might also argue, although with far more difficulty, that the operation of a minimum competency testing program deprives them of a liberty interest. They would base this argument upon the stigmatization allegedly occurring as a consequence of their classification as below minimum competency or as ineligible for promotion, graduation, or a regular diploma.[10]

It should be remembered, though, that proof of deprivation of a liberty or property interest, of itself, does not condemn the state's action; it obligates the state to act fairly and rationally. Indeed, during the past several years the trend in the federal courts has been to expand governmental prerogatives and discretion, and to afford correspondingly reduced judicial protection to aggrieved citizens.[11] Yet some state courts have resisted this trend in interpreting their state constitutional due process clauses.[12]

ii. Federal and State Equal Protection Clauses

Equal protection is a constitutional principle related to due process. Both require governmental rationality and fairness in treatment of citizens. The federal equal protection clause also derives from the Fourteenth Amendment. It prohibits any state from denying "to any person within its jurisdiction the equal protection of the laws."

The focus of the equal protection clause is on irrationality toward groups rather than toward individuals, however. A challenger of state action must show that it classifies persons and provides differential treatment to them without adequate justification. In the federal courts, as well as in some state courts, the burden of justification required of the state for differential treatment increases with the importance of the interest that is subjected to such treatment. The courts declare that "fundamental" interests impose upon the state the burden of showing a compelling reason for, and no available alternative to, the differential treatment. This "strict scrutiny" approach is also invoked by "suspect" classifications, such as those based upon race. Interests of lesser importance, or classifications not based on a suspect characteristic, result in a lesser burden on the state—perhaps only the need to prove that the classification is rational, even if not the best means to achieve the state's objective.

An equal protection challenge to a minimum competency testing program would likely proceed along one or both of the following lines: (1) that, to the extent black or Hispanic students were disproportionately represented among those falling below the minimum competency level, the program classified students racially or ethnically—a suspect classification—and should be subjected to strict scrutiny; or (2) that the program lacked even a rational basis because, for example, the test was technically invalid[13] or it covered material not taught in the schools.[14] The argument that strict scrutiny should be applied because of the fundamental nature of education is unlikely to succeed in the federal courts. The United States Supreme Court ruled to the contrary in 1973.[15] Several state courts have reached a different conclusion, however, under state equal protection clauses.[16]

Recent United States Supreme Court decisions also have created problems for an equal protection challenge based upon racial or ethnic discrimination. The Court has ruled that a statistically disproportionate effect, while relevant, is insufficient to demonstrate a racial or ethnic classification. Challengers of state action must prove, by direct or circumstantial evidence, that there was an intention to create such a classification.[17] That may be a formidable task in the context of a minimum competency testing program.

iii. State Education Clauses

Most state constitutions contain clauses which make education an obligation of the state. Frequently these clauses define, at least in a broad manner, the quality or extent of the required education.[18] Some state courts have ruled that these clauses give students a legally enforceable right to that quality or extent of education.[19]

State education clauses may be relevant in two ways. First, they may establish that education is a fundamental interest under the state constitution's equal protection clause.[20] Second, the education clauses may be directly relevant to a challenge relating to minimum competency testing. Depending upon the constitution, statutes and regulations, and judicial interpretations of a particular state, it may be possible to argue that achievement of minimum competency is part of a student's constitutional right to education (perhaps as elaborated by statutes or administrative regulations). In such a state, the *absence* of a minimum competency assessment program could be challenged in the courts.[21] Additionally, a program which imposed sanctions on students for failure to achieve minimum competency levels, without providing adequate remedial help and opportunities for retesting, could be attacked under the state education clause.[22]

iv. State Education Statutes

Among the voluminous education statutes of most states, there are likely to be a number of provisions relevant to minimum competency efforts. Of course, in an increasing number of states there are provisions which establish minimum competency testing programs.[23] A possible line of legal argument is that a program, as implemented, does not comport with statutory requirements. Alleged noncompliance may take many forms, ranging from blatant failure to meet specific requirements (such as failing to institute testing by a date specified in the statute) to more complex issues of qualitative inadequacies (for example, a failure to provide educationally sufficient remedial programs for students who fall below the minimum competency standards).

The vehicle by which legal challenges of this type could be brought is the mandamus action, a request that the court order public officials to carry out their legal responsibilities. In some states there may be technical problems with using this vehicle for some challenges; mandamus is available only to require public officials to perform ministerial, as opposed to discretionary, functions. That is to say, in those states mandamus actions may be more readily available to deal with total defaults, as in the failure to implement any minimum competency testing program, than with qualitative shortcomings in programs undertaken.

Other, more general provisions of state education laws will be relevant too. For example, states commonly have statutory provisions which carry forward and amplify their constitutions' education clauses. In New Jersey, which has a constitutional guarantee of a "thorough and efficient system of free public schools,"[24] the statutes implement that guarantee in a variety of ways. The commissioner of education is charged with responsibility "to inquire into and ascertain the thoroughness and efficiency of operation of any of the schools of the public school system of the state and of any grades therein by such means, tests and examinations as to him seem proper."[25] More pointedly, a recent statute defines the "goal of a thorough and efficient system of free public schools" to be "to provide to all children in New Jersey, regardless of socioeconomic status or geographic location, the educational opportunity which will prepare them to function politically, economically and socially in a democratic society."[26] Finally, the New Jersey Legislature has provided that:

A thorough and efficient system of free public schools shall include the following major elements, which shall serve as guidelines for the achievement of the legislative goal . . . : . . . c. Instruction intended to produce the attainment of reasonable levels of proficiency in the basic communications and computational skills; . . . e. Programs and supportive services for all pupils especially those who are educationally disadvantaged or who have special educational needs; . . . j. Evaluation and monitoring programs at both the state and local levels.[27]

Such provisions, stopping short of explicit establishment of a minimum competency testing program,[28] provide a basis for asserting that only by incorporating an effective minimum competency testing program into its evaluative and instructional efforts can a state meet its statutory obligations.

v. State Regulations

In some states, education regulations formally promulgated by state education authorities have the force of law. They can form a basis for legal challenges relating to minimum competency testing programs in much the same way as statutes. Indeed, because regulations tend to deal with educational programs in greater detail than do statutes, they may provide a stronger basis for legal action. The more specific and detailed the prescription by a legislature or state education body, the more limited and mechanical the judicial intervention can be. If, for example, state regulations provide in detail for a minimum competency testing program pursuant to the authority of a more general statute, failure of the state or local school districts to implement that program fully can be challenged. The education authorities may defend by asserting that despite the specificity of the regulations, they should be permitted some flexibility; or they may seek to modify the regulations; or they may argue that the challengers have to exhaust available administrative remedies.[29] All of these, however, are matters well within the traditional competence of courts to resolve.

In states where administrative regulations are not given the force of law, or in cases of administrative actions (such as guidelines or policy statements) not having the status of formal regulations, the substance of the administrative judgment should still have weight in a legal proceeding. The administrative position represents the expert view of the state's educational authorities. As such, a court would likely find it highly relevant to an interpretation of broad constitutional or statutory provisions.

vi. The "Common Law"

The final source of law which may be influential in judicial consideration of a minimum competency testing program is the "common law." Under the Anglo-American legal system, this is judge-made law. Courts will tend to follow prior judicial decisions in similar cases under the doctrine of *stare decisis*. In confronting a new case, therefore, a court will consider—along with relevant constitutional, statutory, and regulatory provisions—the judicial precedent, especially cases decided in the same jurisdiction.

Many bodies of precedent are relevant to minimum competency testing programs. For example, as indicated previously, federal and state courts have dealt extensively with, and given content to, constitutional concepts such as due process rights of students, equal protection aspects of pupil classification by testing, educational segregation, and equality of educational opportunity. In many states, related education statutes and regulations have been judicially construed.

II. Applying the Legal Theories to
Minimum Competency Testing Programs

Existing and potential minimum competency testing programs reflect a variety of perspectives and approaches.[30] In this section, I will consider the legal implications of some of the main variations on the central theme. As a point of departure, I will use the "seven key notes"—elements of a minimum competency testing policy—identified by Henry M. Brickell in a paper prepared for the Education Commission of the States, and the National Institute of Education.[31] Brickell's "key notes" are: (1) the competencies to be required; (2) the means of measuring them; (3) the point(s) at which they will be measured; (4) the number of minimums which will be set; (5) the levels at which minimums will be set; (6) whether the standards will be for schools or for students; and (7) the consequences of failing to meet the minimums.

i. The Competencies to Be Required

Brickell suggests that there are five broad categories of competencies from which a choice might be made. These are: (1) basic skills; (2) school subjects; (3) life areas; (4) basic skills applied in each school subject; and (5) basic skills applied in each life area. The policy choice is even more complex, however. Defining the categories of "basic skills" and "life areas" involves still further policy judgments.[32]

Consideration of the legal implications of the various alternatives may influence the policy decision. In general, the substantive due process concept of rationality, the equal protection concept of nondiscrimination, and the state constitutional, statutory, and regulatory requirement of a certain quality or quantum of education are the relevant legal theories.

On one level, focusing on competency in school subjects may comport most easily with the due process and equal protection concepts so long as: (1) the competency testing relates to subjects which the students actually have had a reasonable opportunity to master; and (2) the selection of subjects taught generally, or chosen for competency testing, is non-discriminatory (in the sense that it is not skewed in favor of particular socioeconomic, racial, or ethnic groups.)[33]

However, the choice of school subjects as the basis for a minimum competency testing program might pose greater legal difficulties under certain state educational quality requirements. Those requirements may dictate that minimum competency be defined in terms of life, as opposed to school, skills. In New Jersey, the state's education clause has been interpreted to require "that educational opportunity which is needed in the contemporary setting to equip a child for his role as a citizen and as a competitor in the labor market."[34] To the extent that a minimum competency testing program is geared to comport with such a constitutional requirement, it is questionable whether testing competence in traditional school subjects is sufficient.[35]

Testing competence in "life areas" rather than in school subjects may seem to be more responsive to a mandate such as New Jersey's. However, such a choice might raise serious substantive due process and equal protection questions. If life skills, as such, are not taught in the schools, students may be able to challenge the competency testing program on the ground of arbitrariness. How can they be refused promotion or graduation, be required to receive remedial assistance, or be stigmatized as "incompetent" based upon a test which covers material they were not directly taught? Moreover, a substantial potential for discrimination exists in the selection of "life areas." Certain life areas or skills may be relevant to, and derived from, the life experience of certain groups of students but not others.[36] To construct a competency test for all students based upon such life areas would be discriminatory.

Choosing basic skills as the focus of a minimum competency testing program would resolve many of these legal difficulties. Skills are denominated as "basic" because they are used in school and in life. Especially in the lower grades, the basic skills are themselves school subjects. Thereafter they are instrumental for more advanced subjects. Although reading, mathematics, and written and oral communication arguably may not be well taught in some schools, it is inconceivable that anyone could argue that they are not taught at all. Thus, the prospects of a substantive due process challenge would be minimized. A discrimination argument based on equal protection also has little chance of success. Among the whole range of school subjects, those dealing with the basic skills are most likely to be perceived as neutral toward various racial or ethnic groups.[37] More substantial questions may be raised about whether a basic skills focus meets the educational quality standards of state constitutions, statutes, and regulations. To the extent that the basic skills selected are demonstrably relevant to effective citizenship and to competition in the labor market, a minimum competency testing program based upon those skills should survive a challenge.

Brickell suggests that competency also could be tested in the basic skills as applied either to school subjects or to life areas. Although applying the basic skills to life areas may strengthen the argument that the minimum competency testing program meets state requirements of preparing students for "life," such an approach may reintroduce equal protection-based discrimination issues discussed previously.

On balance, therefore, it appears that a minimum competency testing program which emphasizes the basic skills, without applying them to school subjects or to life areas, is most likely to withstand legal challenge.[38] This assumes, of course, that there have been reasonably effective educational opportunities equally available to all students, and that the testing instruments and procedures used are fair and valid.

ii. The Means of Measuring the Competencies

Brickell suggests four broad choices for measurement of the competencies: (1) actual performance in later school or job situations; (2) simulated performance in situations resembling those to be encountered later in school or on the job; (3) school performance by the student at the time competency is to be measured; and (4) paper-and-pencil tests.

The legal touchstone for evaluating these alternatives is the concept of validity.[39] Under both due process and equal protection doctrine, tests, of whatever type,[40] must satisfy standards of objectivity, reliability, and validity.[41] Due process is implicated if the use to be made of the test threatens to deprive students of their rights to liberty or property. Evidence that the use of the test stigmatizes students who fail, or requires their attendance at remedial programs, will be germane to an alleged deprivation of their liberty interest.[42] A denial of promotion or graduation which is based on the test results is the clearest support for deprivation of a property interest.[43] Yet even if a court could be persuaded that some students had been deprived of their liberty or property rights, the students still would have to prove that the test or related procedures was not procedurally or substantively fair.

An equal protection challenge would proceed most forcefully if a suspect classification were evident. Preliminary results of some minimum competency testing programs suggest that they have a racially disproportionate effect—a far higher percentage of black than white students fall below the competency levels. Under the federal Constitution's equal protection clause, such a statistical showing was previously sufficient to establish a *prima facie* case of racial discrimination, and, thus sufficient to shift a heavy burden of justification onto the educational authorities. Recently, however, the United States Supreme Court determined that an intent to discriminate, rather than merely a discriminatory effect, had to be proven in order to establish a racial classification.[44] An intent to discriminate can be proven by circumstantial evidence, including statistical data, as well as by direct evidence.[45] It is not clear, however, how heavy a burden that ruling will place upon challengers of a minimum competency testing program.

If no suspect classification can be established, and if the federal courts adhere to the view that education is not a fundamental interest, then the classification of students into those who have achieved competence and those who have not can be justified by showing that it has a "rational basis." The validity of the testing instrument will still be part of the showing of rationality, but the overall burden on the school authorities will be substantially lighter than under a strict scrutiny approach. That is especially likely given the recent tendency of the federal courts to defer to public officials' judgments.[46]

Applying these legal principles to the broad choices outlined by Brickell suggests that standardized paper-and-pencil tests may have certain legal advantages over the other alternatives. This is especially true if the minimum competency testing program focuses on basic skills as opposed to life skills. In terms of objectivity, a paper-and-pencil test oriented to basic skills is likely to be preferable to performance or school-product measures which, in most instances, would be evaluated by school staff. In terms of technical validity, standardized paper-and-pencil tests likely will have the advantage of broader-based and better organized validity studies. Indeed, in the basic skills there already exist a variety of tests with reasonably good track records which can be used or adapted to minimum competency testing programs. Despite these advantages, the predictive validity of paper-and-pencil tests is not beyond challenge. The argument would be that success or failure on a paper-and-pencil test of achievement in the basic skills does not correlate highly with attainment of the state's educational goals—successful performance as a citizen and as a competitor in the job market. However, that argument may fail—either because a sufficiently high correlation can be shown, or because a court may rule that another type of validity (such as face, content, or construct) provides adequate support for the use of the test.

On balance, then, the potential legal problems of the performance or product-related measures are greater than those of the paper-and-pencil test, and their educational or public policy advantages are uncertain.

iii. The Point(s) at Which Competencies Will Be Measured

Brickell suggests that competencies could be measured during school or at the end of schooling. The point at which measurement occurs may depend upon the purpose and format of the particular minimum competency testing program. For example, a minimum competency testing program geared to promotion from grade to grade obviously would be administered toward the end of the particular school year. A high school graduation competency requirement, on the other hand, might result in testing at the end of the student's public school career.

Choosing the time(s) for measurement of competencies raises several important legal issues—primarily the notice aspect of procedural due

process and the outcome aspects of the states' educational quality requirements. Assuming that denial of graduation or of a regular diploma is a
deprivation of a property right, the education authorities must act in conformity with procedural due process, one element of which is adequate
notice. Notice of the denial hardly would seem adequate if it were to take
the form of a test administered, and results announced, at the end of a
student's last year in high school. The student would be unable to avoid
the deprivation without suffering substantial injury.[47] From an educational
point of view, too, such an approach has little to commend it. A sound
program would involve periodic testing of competencies beginning early
in a student's educational career. As will be discussed subsequently,
students identified as having deficiencies should be given special assistance suited to their needs. Additionally, if deficiences are widespread, an
evaluation of the school system's curriculum and instructional effectiveness should be mounted.

Even if a minimum competency testing program were found not to
deprive students of a property interest,[48] state educational quality requirements might still impose an early testing obligation. If the public schools
are required to gear their instruction toward producing effective citizens
and competitors in the labor market, one logical way to judge them is
pragmatically. Are their graduates competent actually to function as
citizens and as competitors in the labor market? Waiting until the end of
the last year in school to assess those competencies, without allowing a
meaningful opportunity for improvement, would seem an ineffective and
perhaps irrational means of carrying out the state mandate. As such,
the competency testing could be challenged as a denial of the state's educational quality guarantee.

iv. The Number of Minimums Which Will Be Set

The possibilities regarding the number of minimums range from a single
minimum competency level for all students at a particular grade level
throughout the state, to a separate standard for each student, based upon
that student's perceived abilities and background. Between those poles
are other possibilities: multiple statewide standards for groups of students
categorized by one or more criteria (such as demonstrated or projected
intelligence, facility with English,[49] existence of a handicap,[50] socioeconomic background,[51] nature of the school district and the community
in which it is located,[52] and the district's educational expenditure level);[53]
either single or multiple standards established by each school district;[54]
one or more statewide standards augmented by additional, and perhaps
higher, competency standards established by local districts.

As Brickell points out, there are educational problems generated either by a single standard applied to all students or by differential standards for each student. A single standard may be both too difficult and too easy, given wide variations in student ability and performance. Differential standards require that each student's performance capacity be estimated, with the dual problems of the so-called self-fulfilling prophecy phenomenon, and the possible inaccuracy of ability tests as predictors of achievement. Moreover, if high school graduation or the granting of a "regular" diploma is conditioned upon demonstration of adequate competence, graduation or the diploma would have little, if any, uniform meaning, even at the lower end of the scale.

These sorts of educational and public policy concerns have legal analogs. A single statewide competency standard, applicable to all students of a particular grade level throughout the state, may raise several legal issues. First, if the standard were established on the basis of "average" past performance of students within the state, and if the consequence of failing to achieve the standard were sanctions against the student (such as nonpromotion, nongraduation, or withholding of a regular diploma), then, almost by definition, approximately half the students in the state would be consigned to failure and, perhaps ultimately, to sanctions. Those students might well question the fairness and rationality of that system on due process grounds. On the other hand, if, as is more likely, the statewide standard were established at a substantially lower level so that a high percentage of students could achieve it, then questions would be raised about the standard's conformity with the state's educational quality responsibilities. In New Jersey, for example, as previously discussed, the state is charged with constitutional and statutory responsibility for ensuring that all students have an educational opportunity reasonably designed to permit them to function as effective citizens and competitors in the labor market. Instruction geared to the students' attainment of reasonable proficiency in the basic skills is an essential element of the state's responsibility. "Reasonable proficiency" should be defined in terms of the demands of citizenship and of the job market. A statewide minimum competency standard designed to measure actual proficiency in the basic skills would have to conform to such "reasonable proficiency" levels. If not, the minimum competency testing program would fail to adequately implement the constitutional and statutory educational quality requirements.

Another source of legal challenge might be the racially or ethnically differential impacts of a statewide standard. The details of such a challenge have been discussed already. It is sufficient to add here that the differential impact will likely be most pronounced if there is a single statewide standard.

Resorting to multiple standards will not necessarily eliminate this or other legal questions, however. If, for example, performance expectations for minority students were consistently and automatically reduced because of their racial, ethnic, or socioeconomic status, legal challenges might be forthcoming. Even broader challenges to individualized standards are likely, though. These could be based upon either due process notions of arbitrariness or irrationality in the establishment of the standards, or upon state educational quality requirements. In the former case, the focus would be on the mechanisms by which the standards were established. The strength of the challenge would depend upon the care exercised by the state or local district education authorities in establishing the minimum competency levels. If, for example, the standards for each pupil were determined by an individual teacher acting impressionistically, rather than on the basis of carefully articulated criteria, the system would be extremely vulnerable.

Differential standards in the basic skills might also be vulnerable under some state education clauses. In some states, those clauses have been construed to require provision of both equality of educational opportunity, and a certain minimum quality and extent of education. Proficiency in the basic skills is increasingly being perceived as a cornerstone of the state's educational obligation to students. A minimum competency testing program should be an integral part of the state's discharge of that obligation; it should help to shape the entire instructional effort. To the extent that the program is based upon differential competency standards for individual pupils, obvious issues are raised about the equality of educational opportunity being afforded. The student considered to have low capacity may meet his or her competency standards with a relatively low level of performance. Yet the educational system may interpret that to mean that it has met its instructional responsibilities to that student. A student perceived to have higher capacity and correspondingly higher competency standards probably will be entitled to greater instructional effort, at least if he or she fails initially to meet the standards.

The quality requirements of state education clauses may be implicated, too, if the performance standards for some students are set below proficiency levels reasonably necessary for effective functioning as a citizen or in the job market. Differential standards may be questioned especially in regard to their relevance to the job market. The proficiency demands of the job market are neither static nor determined in a vacuum. To a significant extent they are based upon the levels of skills generally available in the pool of applicants. Thus, formally establishing higher performance standards for some students (and gearing the instructional program accordingly) will tend to elevate the expectations of the job market, and further disadvantage those students whose performance falls below those thresholds.

On balance, considering educational, public policy, and legal issues, the soundest minimum competency testing program would be one which provided common statewide proficiency standards in the basic skills for all students (except perhaps for those who were determined, because of mental retardation, serious English language limitations, and so forth, to be unable to meet such standards) and which required or permitted local districts to establish additional standards. The "additional" standards could be higher standards than the state's in the basic skills or, perhaps, standards in other subject-matter areas. This conclusion presupposes that the statewide standards establish a performance floor reasonably related to post-secondary school requirements. It also presupposes that local districts develop their own standards in full conformity with the legal, educational, and public policy considerations discussed in this paper.

v. The Levels at Which the Minimums Will Be Set

There are many ways in which a state or local school district can approach the task of establishing minimum competency levels. Some of the problems have been hinted at already.

Level setting can be approached politically or fiscally. The education authorities can decide that no more than a certain percentage of students can fall below the minimum competency levels because a higher percentage of failure would be embarrassing and erosive of public support. That might lead to the policy conclusion that no more than 5, 10, or 20 percent of the students should perform below standards. The standards and measurement instruments would be developed to meet that objective.

Alternatively, the education authorities or fund appropriators might decide that, if all failing students are to receive remedial instruction, there are funds available to provide adequate remediation to only a certain percentage of the students.[55] Again, the standards and measurement instruments would be geared to achieve that result.

Although these approaches may be rational from political and fiscal perspectives, they are subject to serious legal challenge from the perspective of students' educational rights. At least in those states where students have a clear constitutional or statutory right to a certain quantum of education, these approaches lack a rational connection to fulfillment of the state's obligation.

In those states as a matter of law, and perhaps elsewhere as a matter of educational policy, a different approach to establishing minimum performance levels would be indicated. Instead of beginning with political or fiscal judgments of what is a desirable result of applying minimum competency standards (and working backward to determine the standards), the policymakers would decide upon the desired and necessary educational outcomes—that is, what minimum performance levels are appropriate to graduates of their schools, or are necessary to permit them to function effectively in the post-secondary school world. This decision could be based, as Brickell recognizes, on a definition of "successful" or "minimally competent" adults and the skills they possess. Once this definition has been developed, education authorities could work backward in successive stages to establish minimum competency standards for high school graduation and for earlier junctures of students' educational careers.

Although legal and public policy questions surely could be raised about the way in which education authorities carried out this approach,[56] the approach itself is much more compatible with the states' educational obligations.

vi. Whether the Standards Will Be for Schools or for Students

Thus far this paper has proceeded on the assumption that minimum competency standards will be established for students rather than for schools. That orientation is not inevitable. A minimum competency testing program might be established to determine how well schools and school districts are performing on the whole.

The practical differences between these two approaches are substantial. As Brickell points out, the choice between them will determine:

. . . whether you will write test items all students can pass or only most students can pass; whether you will test everybody or only a sample; whether you will report results to each individual parent or only to the general public; whether you will settle for a school program that reaches 70% of the students even if that 70% misses, for example, every single "disadvantaged" child; and whether you will modify every unsatisfactory program or fail and recycle every unsatisfactory graduate.[57]

A focus on schools and school districts would reduce some legal difficulties but might increase others. To the extent that such a focus would reduce or eliminate sanctions against individual students or groups of students (by not denying them promotion, or graduation, or regular diplomas, or by not publicly identifying them as below competency levels), due process and equal protection concerns would be lessened. Arguments based on deprivation of a liberty or property interest, or on invidious discrimination would be far less credible. The thrust of the minimum competency testing program would be on school or school district accountability, and the response to inadequate performance presumably would be a programmatic or personnel-oriented response.

That may be a rational and appropriate approach unless the state's constitution, statutes, or regulations impose a clear educational quality requirement directed to the rights of each student. In that event, as previously discussed, a minimum competency testing program which was not designed to ensure that each student had an opportunity to achieve reasonable proficiency in the basic skills would be suspect. Failure of the program to lead to special educational assistance for individual students who fell below the specified standards would be the clearest indication of its invalidity.

vii. The Consequences of Failing to Meet the Minimums

This final key note follows directly from the prior discussion. Brickell suggests six possible consequences for students who fall below minimum competency standards, and six parallel consequences for schools whose students fail to perform adequately. They are as follows: (1) verify the findings independently; (2) provide several more chances; (3) lower the standard to meet their performance; (4) remediate so that they can pass (or redesign school programs to match successful programs); (5) refuse to promote or graduate them (or refuse to let schools operate until they can meet the standard); and (6) promote or graduate them with a restricted diploma or a certificate of attendance (or let schools operate but refuse to accredit them).[58]

The prior discussion made clear that the preferable, and in some states the required, response to particular students who have failed to meet minimum competency levels is to direct appropriate educational assistance to them. This may take the form of remediation for the individual students; it may also involve school or districtwide programmatic or personnel responses. Surely if a substantial percentage of a school's or district's students is failing to meet statewide or local standards, the overall educational program, including the quality of the instructional staff, should be evaluated and perhaps upgraded.

Lowering the minimum competency standards because "too many" students have failed to meet them[59] is an unacceptable response, for both public policy and legal reasons.

If students who fail to meet the competency standards are provided with appropriate remedial assistance, and if the program is otherwise fair and rational,[60] then ultimately they could be refused promotion or graduation, or be promoted or graduated with a restricted diploma or a certificate of attendance. From a due process perspective, these students may have been deprived of a liberty or property interest by that action, but the state is permitted to do so if it acts fairly and rationally. From an educational quality perspective, the state cannot be required to *guarantee* educational results for all students. The state can be held, however, to provision of an appropriate educational opportunity for all students. Educational results, as measured by an effective minimum competency testing program, are relevant to a determination of whether the educational opportunity is appropriate. In legal terms, evidence of inadequate pupil performance should shift to the education authorities the burden of demonstrating that, nonetheless, they have been providing all students with appropriate educational opportunities. The result is consistent with sound public policy and with the discharge by educators of their professional responsibility.

III. The Future of the Minimum Competency Testing Movement

According to some commentators, the minimum competency testing movement may already have peaked.[61] Others believe that it will continue to expand and to develop.[62] In either event, its effects will be felt by public school systems and by students for years. Whether the movement will improve education and educational outcomes by promoting more responsible and effective teaching, administering, and studying, or whether it will merely victimize those who are held accountable by it, cannot yet be determined.[63] The answer to that crucial question will turn upon the quality of policy making which shapes the minimum competency testing movement. It will also depend upon the care and skill exercised in implementing the policy thrusts. Legal principles, and the threat or actuality of litigation, may come to play an important role in the evolution of minimum competency testing programs. Hopefully, by requiring rationality, fairness, and objectivity, but not making impossible demands, this role will be a positive one.

As this paper has described, the failure of states to adopt minimum competency testing programs could lead to challenges under state constitutional and statutory education provisions. More likely, legal challenges will focus on inadequacies of programs adopted by the states, either in their basic concept or their implementation. Although school authorities may be haunted by the spectre of malpractice suits brought by students who are performing below minimum competency standards, suits directed at improving educational programs are more likely to succeed. Meanwhile, educators and researchers should undertake some preventive maintenance—they should try to head off legal challenges by fashioning minimum competency testing programs, and by carrying out related research, in the most careful manner possible. If they do so, the law will have been an important, if relatively silent, partner in educational reform.

Notes

1. See, for example, C. Pipho, "Minimum Competency Testing in 1978: A Look at State Standards," 59 *Phi Delta Kappan* (May 1978): 585-588.

2. See, for example, A. Wise, "Minimum Educational Adequacy: Beyond School Finance Reform," 1 *J. of Education Finance* (Spring 1976): 468; J. Baratz, "In Setting Minimal Standards Have We Abandoned Concerns for Equity and Access," (an unpublished paper presented at Wingspread Conference - Educational Policy Research Institute, Washington, D.C., July 1978); E. Kelley, "The Politics of Proficiency," (an unpublished paper prepared for the National Institute of Education, 1977); B. Anderson, "The Costs of Legislated Minimal Competency Requirements," (an unpublished paper prepared for the National Institute of Education, September 1977). Also see the May 1978 (Vol. 59-No. 9) issue of *Phi Delta Kappan* which contains a series of articles on minimum competency testing.

3. "Educational malpractice" refers to claims that a school district and its professional staff have failed to fulfill their duties to a student or class of students as measured by pupil performance levels. The leading example of such a case is *Peter W.* v. *San Francisco Unified School Dist.*, 60 Cal. App. 3d 814, 131 Cal. Rptr. 854 (1976). In *Peter W.*, the plaintiff, an 18 year old high school graduate, argued that the school district was negligent because of its failure to teach him to read and write adequately. However, the trial court and the intermediate appeals court rejected the plaintiff's claim. Moreover, despite the fact that in California, at the time the *Peter W.* case was filed, there was a statutory requirement that students read at the 8th grade level in order to qualify for high school graduation, the California Supreme Court refused to consider the case.

4. M. McClung, "Competency Testing: Potential for Discrimination," 11 *Clearinghouse Review* (1977): 439; P. Tractenberg, "The Legal Implications of Statewide Pupil Performance Standards," (an unpublished paper prepared for the National Institute of Education and the Education Commission of the States, September 1977). See also S. Sugarman, "Accountability through the Courts," 82 *School Review* (1974): 233; Note, "Educational Malpractice," 124 *U. Pa. L. Rev.* (1976): 755.

5. The term "state" includes not only state governments but also other state and local government bodies, including school districts.

6. The U.S. Supreme Court, until 1937, struck down numerous state laws as not having a "real and substantial relationship" to permissible state purposes and therefore as violating "substantive due process." The most notorious example of such activity was *Lochner* v. *New York*, 198 U.S. 45 (1905), where the Court struck down New York's maximum hour legislation for bakery employees. The breakthrough case where the Court applied the now common and more relaxed "rational basis" test was *West Coast Hotel Co.* v. *Parrish*, 300 U.S. 379 (1937). Since that time, other than in cases dealing with civil rights and civil liberties, virtually no state law has been invalidated by the Supreme Court as violating "substantive due process."

7. See McClung "Competency Testing" [*supra* n. 4].

8. For example, *Goss* v. *Lopez*, 419 U.S. 565 (1975).

9. The right to be promoted or graduated can be distinguished from the right to attend school in at least two respects. First, the right to attend school is explicitly provided by the laws of most states; the right to be promoted or graduated is usually implicit. Second, the right to attend school is less obviously conditioned upon conformity with school rules than is the right to be promoted or graduated premised upon adequate academic performance. Despite these distinctions, however, courts still might rule that the right of students to be promoted or graduated is a property interest under the due process clause. The consequence of this ruling would not be to give students an absolute right to be promoted or graduated; rather, retention in grade or failure to graduate a student would have to be carried out in conformity with the due process clause.

10. Stigmatization, as infringing on a protected liberty interest, was recognized in *Wisconsin* v. *Constantineau*, 400 U.S. 433 (1971). See also *Board of Regents* v. *Roth*, 408 U.S. 564 (1972); P. Tractenberg, "Selecting 'Educationally Deprived' Students for Title I: a Review of the Legal Issues," (an unpublished paper prepared for the National Institute of Education, 1977) pp. 59-62. However, the U.S. Supreme Court narrowed the definition of stigmatization to require the "alteration of legal status which, combined with the injury from defamation, justified the invocation of procedural safeguards." (*Paul* v. *Davis*, 424 U.S. 693, 708-9 [1976]).

11. See, for example, *Rizzo* v. *Goode*, 423 U.S. 362 (1976); Brennan, "Address to the New Jersey Bar" (May 22, 1976) [reprinted in 33 *Guild Practitioner* (1976): 152].

12. See, for example, *People* v. *Brisendine*, 13 Cal. 3d 528, 531 P. 2d 1099, 119 Cal. Rptr. 315 (1975).

13. For a competency test to meet technical requirements, it must be shown that it is both *valid* and *reliable*. *Validity* refers to whether the test actually measures the characteristic that it claims to measure. *Reliability* refers to whether the test measures that characteristic consistently. In the case of competency testing, an *invalid* reading test might actually be measuring writing skills. An *unreliable* reading test might give a student who took the test twice, using two different forms of it, a high score when he or she used form "A" and a low score when he or she used form "B". See American Psychological Association, *Standards for Educational and Psychological Tests and Manuals* (1966) [revised and renamed in 1971], pp. 25 *et seq.*

14. This also could be the basis for a due process challenge—namely, that the state was acting irrationally. See discussion of due process above.

15. *San Antonio Independent School Dist.* v. *Rodriguez*, 411 U.S. 1 (1973).

16. See, for example, *Serrano* v. *Priest*, 18 Cal. 3d 728, 557 P. 2d 929, 135 Cal. Rptr. 345 (1977); *Horton* v. *Meskill*, 172 Conn. 615, 376 A. 2d 359 (1977).

17. In *Washington* v. *Davis*, 426 U.S. 229 (1976), the Court held that disproportionate racial impact of a test is insufficient to establish an unconstitutional racial classification; a discriminatory purpose must be shown. Several subsequent Supreme Court decisions shed light on how that purpose may be shown. See, for example, *Village of Arlington Heights* v. *Metropolitan Housing Development Corp.*, 429 U.S. 252, (1977). In light of this narrowing construction of the equal protection clause, challenges based upon Title VI of the Civil Rights Act of 1964

and its implementing regulations may be preferable. The U.S. Supreme Court indicated in *Washington* v. *Davis* that disproportionate racial impact of a test might be sufficient to constitute violation of Title VI. See McClung, "Competency Testing" [*supra* n. 4], p. 442, n. 42.

18. State constitutions' education clauses include: 1) "thorough and efficient"— N. J. *Const.* art. VIII, §4, ¶1; Ohio *Const.* art. VI, §2; Pa. *Const.* art. III, §14; W. Va. *Const.* art XII, §1; 2) "high quality"—Ill. *Const.* art X, §1; Mont. *Const.* art. X, §1 (3); Va. *Const.* art. VIII, §1; and 3) "uniform"—Cal. *Const.* art. IX, §5; Idaho *Const.* art. IX, §1; Wyo. *Const.* art. VII, §1.

19. See for example, *Robinson* v. *Cahill*, 62 N.J. 473, 509, 303 A.2d 273, 292 (1973); *Horton* v. *Meskill*, 172 Conn. 615, 649, 376 A.2d 359, 374-75 (1977); *Seattle School District No. 1* v. *Washington*, Civ. No. 53950 (Thurston County Super. Ct., Wash., Jan. 14, 1977).

20. *San Antonio Independent School District* v. *Rodriguez*, 411 U.S. 1, 33 (1973).

21. Tractenberg, "The Legal Implications of Statewide Pupil Performance Standards," [*supra* n. 4], pp. 32 *et seq.*

22. Ibid.

23. As of March 15, 1978, 33 states had taken some type of formal action to establish minimum competency standards and in the remaining 17 states, legislation or administrative action was being considered. See Pipho, "Minimum Competency Testing" [*supra* n. 1], p. 585.

24. N.J. *Const.* art. VIII, §4, ¶1.

25. N.J. *Stat. Ann.* §18A:4-24.

26. N.J. *Stat. Ann.* §18A:7A-4.

27. N.J. *Stat. Ann.* §18A:7A-5.

28. New Jersey also has statutory provisions mandating establishment of statewide pupil proficiency standards in the basic skills. N.J. *Stat. Ann.* 18A:7A-6 *et seq.*

29. In New Jersey, for example, the commissioner of education has jurisdiction to "hear and determine, without cost to the parties, all controversies and disputes arising under the school laws. . . or under the rules of the state board or of the Commissioner." N.J. *Stat. Ann.* 18A:6-9. Under the doctrine of "exhaustion of administrative remedies," quite strictly applied in New Jersey, generally anyone who wishes to challenge an education-related matter must bring the issue before the commissioner. Only after rulings by the commissioner and the State Board of Education could an appeal to the courts be taken.

30. See, for example, C. Pipho, "Minimum Competency Testing" [*supra*, n. 1]. See also R. Noonan & L. Rubin, "Statewide Minimum Pupil Proficiency Standards: a Survey of the States" (an unpublished study done under NIE Grant C-76-10105, July 1977).

31. H. Brickell, "Seven Key Notes on Minimum Competency Testing," 59 *Phi Delta Kappan* (1978): 589.

32. Brickell refers, in passing, to "basic skills" as including reading, writing, and arithmetic and to "life areas" as including citizenship, work, and family. Ibid., p. 589.

33. For example, testing students who had just entered a bilingual educational

program in subjects that required substantial English knowledge would be discriminatory. Similarly, a social studies testing program which dealt exclusively with the political affairs of Puerto Rico would be questionable.

34. *Robinson* v. *Cahill,* 62 N.J. 473, 515, 303 A.2d 273, 295 (1973).

35. This would, of course, not be the case if the traditional curriculum was modified to include "life skill" subjects.

36. For example, reading and understanding a subway map might favor urban students, whereas reading and understanding a road map might favor suburban students.

37. Controversy has, however, been generated about the legitimacy of testing the competency of black students in "white" English. The claim is made that "black" English has its own methods of expression and rules of construction, and that is what should be evaluated.

38. This does not mean that other choices are legally barred, but only that they may lead to more troublesome legal issues.

39. Validity has both a generalized meaning of suitability and appropriateness and a technical psychometric meaning. As to the latter, see n. 13 *supra.*

40. Although paper-and-pencil tests may be most commonly used, a whole range of measurement devices are considered to be tests and are, therefore, subject to validity requirements.

41. See n. 13 *supra.*

42. See n. 10 *supra.*

43. See n. 9 *supra.* As indicated, retention in grade or refusal to graduate a student, although the strongest argument for deprivation of a property interest, is not without some question.

44. *Washington* v. *Davis,* 426 U.S. 229 (1976). See n. 17 *supra.*

45. In *Village of Arlington Heights* v. *Metropolitan Housing Development Corp.,* 429 U.S. 252, (1977), the Court listed a number of factors that may be considered in establishing discriminatory intent. These included: (1) historical background; (2) the specific sequence of events leading up to the challenged decision; (3) departures from normal procedural sequences or typical substantive results; and (4) the legislative or administrative history. Idem, pp. 267-8.

46. *Ingraham* v. *Wright,* 430 U.S. 651, (1977); *Rizzo* v. *Goode,* 426 U.S. 362 (1976). See also Tractenberg, "Selecting Students for Title I," [*supra* n. 10], pp. 13 *et seq.*

47. Even if remedial help were provided and retesting were available, the student would be injured by a delay in graduation or in receipt of his or her diploma. Moreover, remedial assistance may be more effective at an earlier age when the educational deficit is less pronounced.

48. That might occur either because a court ruled that denial of graduation or of a regular diploma was not a deprivation of property, or because a particular minimum competency testing program was structured for purely diagnostic purposes, with no direct sanctions attached.

49. Students with limited English-speaking ability are totally exempt from minimum competency testing programs in many states. For a detailed treatment of the matter and recommendations as to establishment of basic skills standards

for such students, see Bilingual Minimum Standards Committee, *Research Report and Policy Recommendations* (Trenton: State of New Jersey, June 1978).

50. In some states, including New Jersey, all students who have been classified as handicapped are excluded from the minimum competency testing program.

51. Many studies have dealt with the correlation between socioeconomic status and educational achievement. See, for example, U.S. Office of Education, U.S. Dept. of Health, Education and Welfare, *Equality of Educational Opportunity* (OE-3800) (1966) [the "Coleman Report"]; C. Jencks, *Inequality: A Reassessment of the Effect of Family and Schooling in America* (New York: Basic Books, 1972). J. McDermott & S. Klein, "The Cost-Quality Debate in School Finance Litigation: Do Dollars Make a Difference?" 38 *Law & Contemp. Prob.* (1974): 415.

52. For example, the New Jersey Department of Education divides the state's school districts into the following nine "district factor groups": urban, suburban, and rural; and whether each of the preceding are of high, moderate, or low socioeconomic status. In addition, a tenth category of "seashore" is included because of the large seasonal fluctuations in the populations of seashore resort communities.

53. For a recent discussion of the results of school district expenditure disparities, see B. Levin, "Current Trends in School Finance Reform Litigation: A Commentary," *Duke L. J.* (1977) 1099, 1114-26.

54. In addition to multiple standards based on categorization of students as indicated above, school districts might establish a different standard for each school.

55. Under this approach, legislators or educational authorities would determine how much money was available for all remedial efforts and how much would be required for each student. By simple division of the latter amount into the former, a number of students would be derived which would be used in determining the competency level desired.

56. Questions could be raised about: (1) the adequacy and appropriateness of the educational authorities' determination of adult minimum competencies; (2) their translation into school-related proficiencies; and (3) the testing instruments used to measure them.

57. H. Brickell, "Seven Key Notes" [*supra* n. 31], p. 592.

58. Ibid.

59. Measurement instruments, and perhaps the minimum competency standards themselves, can be modified if, based on field testing or otherwise, valid educational or psychometric judgments indicate that modification is required to implement the state's goals. Safeguards should be erected, however, to prevent this from being an open door to dilution of standards. If standards were lowered so that they no longer were reasonably related to the demands of citizenship and the job market, they could be challenged on legal theories discussed previously.

60. Some of the primary elements of a fair and rational system are: (1) carefully developed, nondiscriminatory standards; (2) valid measurement instruments and procedures; (3) an opportunity for verification of the initial evaluation results; and (4) evaluation early enough to permit remedial assistance (or program redesign) and reevaluation. Some commentators have also suggested that minimum

competency testing programs should be phased in, so that students substantially through the educational process do not have new and onerous standards imposed upon them. See M. McClung, "Competency Testing," [*supra* n. 4].

61. New Jersey Department of Education, *Report of the New Jersey State Committee on High School Graduation Requirements* (Trenton: N.J. Dept. of Ed., December 1977), p. 32.

62. For example, a bill before the New Jersey legislature would require high school students to pass minimum competency examinations prior to graduation. (S.B. 1154, N.J. Sen. [1978]).

63. In general, the state minimum competency testing programs which have been put into effect conform relatively well to the legal strictures outlined in this paper. They tend: (1) to focus on basic skills at least initially; (2) to use standardized paper-and-pencil tests for measurement purposes; (3) to provide periodic measurement of competencies throughout the students' educational careers; (4) to establish statewide group minimums, often with local supplementation; (5) to set minimums for students and perhaps for schools; and (6) to provide remedial assistance to students who fail to achieve the minimums. Many problems have begun to emerge, however. Among them are minimums set at levels which seem to be based more on political or fiscal judgments than on educational judgments, and remedial programs which are under-funded and inadequately or inappropriately conceived. See R. Noonan & L. Rubin, "Statewide Proficiency Standards," [*supra* n. 30].

5 Impact of Minimum Competency Testing on Curriculum

H. S. Broudy

Because of the great variety of views about the meanings, validity, relevance, and consequences of minimum competency testing, and because of the plethora of schemes and mandates for implementing it, the safest prediction about its effects is that it will produce the babel of discussion and the chaos of practice that are characteristic of innovations in the American public school.[1]

I shall have virtually nothing to say about standardized achievement testing as such. I am inclined to favor objective tests for end-of-lesson, end-of-course, and end-of-school outcomes insofar as they are the outcomes of didactics. It seems to me that when content is clearly and explicitly taught for recall or recognition, that recall or recognition can be adequately sampled and measured. How much more than this can be inferred from such test results is another matter. Robert Stake (1976) and Gene Glass (1978) are probably right in arguing that test results do not warrant inferences to criteria of scholastic achievement, its causes, or its remedies.[2] These logical niceties, however, will do little to dampen the political enthusiasm for this kind of testing and inference. The commodity-production schematism and the mentality corresponding to it are virtually impossible to keep out of education.

The impact of the minimum competency testing movement on curriculum is no more predictable than on other phases of schooling—financial, demographic, and political—except that one commentator is quite confident that it will cost money, perhaps lots of it (Anderson, 1978, p. 41), and another writer predicts that test developers, researchers, and educational administrators will be given "new business, financed with public money," which will "justify and serve their positions and prerogatives" (Kelley, 1978, p. 40).

Two sorts of questions anent the effect of minimum competency testing on curriculum arise: one is the extent to which the issues are curricular; the extent to which the issues are political is the second. If the answer to the latter query is 100 percent, then we had better let the political currents flow from day to day, vote to vote, and keep afloat as best we can. If it is less than 100 percent, then there may be a small area that is not dominated by political pressures. It might, for example, leave room for tradition. The subject-matter curriculum enjoys a long and somewhat stormy history; the problem-solving curriculum history is shorter but no less stormy. The return to basics recurs at fairly regular intervals. There may even be room for some logical and epistemological considerations. For example, the criteria for "good" physics are not decided by a vote of the general public; they are determined by a consensus of the learned, albeit no votes are taken. The authority for deciding what is good in physics resides with qualified physicists. A community has the right to ask: "What is physics (even good physics) good for?" Or as the vulgar would have it, "Who needs it?" If there is disagreement among the taxpayers, then the majority rule would apply. But does the public have the right to decide what is good physics? Does it have the right to decide the shape and content of the curriculum? Is the public's right restricted to whether a subject is taught, or does it extend to what in that subject shall be taught? Is there a body of knowledge or principles in the custody of some learned guild which removes some curricular decisions from the political process, *de jure* if not *de facto*?

How many of the current controversies on minimum competency testing are about curriculum? For example, consider the following questions: (1) To what extent will the minimum competency testing movement decrease the time and attention given to the other strands of the curriculum (a) for all pupils; (b) for some pupils; and (c) which strands are most likely to suffer? (2) Will the tests serve as screening devices to determine the opportunities and requirements in other areas of schooling? (3) If the tests are used to identify a school population that cannot increase its proficiency beyond a given minimum, should opportunities for further schooling be denied them: (a) in public school systems; (b) in special streams of public school systems; (c) in institutions other than public school systems? (4) If the minimum competency testing program is used to identify a noneducable youth population, will this have an effect on the compulsory school attendance laws now on the books? (5) Could or will the minimum competency testing programs be used to effect a clearer division between instructional activities and those psychological and social activities considered necessary to get children "ready" for instruction? Could such a division affect the allocation of resources and the mission of the schools? (6) To what extent will the movement be used, wittingly or not, to undermine "public" education?

Of all these questions, only the first is directly concerned with the content of the curriculum, but in the light of what has been said about the numerous variables involved, one hesitates to make predictions. The remaining questions are chiefly in the ideological-political realm; that is, Which social groups will benefit or suffer if the testing movement is used in certain ways? Again there is no way of knowing that they will be used in these ways or that the consequences will be the same in different localities. We shall have to wait and see.

One way to get at the curriculum issue is to suppose (not predict) that the testing movement will tend to force the public school curriculum more into activities directed toward functional literacy. One can then explore the meanings of functional literacy, the kinds of schooling required by the several meanings, and see how it compares with other concepts of the curriculum. Or, one might speculate on the compatibility of the functional literacy curriculum with the values that are assumed to constitute the rationale of the American public school system. On an even more general level of discussion, the functional literacy curriculum may be measured against a conception of human nature: the good life of the individual in the good society. This would amount to a philosophy of the curriculum, or at least a theory of the curriculum. There are many such theories, and since there is no acknowledged learned guild to adjudicate their respective claims, one can only present a theory and hope it will be noticed.

A general education curriculum would include the following strands: (1) symbolics of information—skills of reading, writing, computation, and interpreting aesthetic clues; (2) basic sciences—mathematics, physics, biology, chemistry; (3) developmental studies (a) of the cosmos—earth science, astronomy, meteorology; (b) of the social institutions—family, government, schools; (c) of culture—arts, technologies; (4) problem solving—individual and collective; and (5) exemplars of knowledge and value as contained in the humanistic classics of the culture. The rationale for these strands has been set forth in some detail elsewhere (Broudy, Smith, and Burnett, 1964).

The several strands together are designed to furnish the individual with the skills of using linguistic, quantitative, and imagic symbols to build a conceptual system and an imagic store that will supply "educated" contexts for problem solving, feeling, judging, and communicating.

This curriculum leaves out a great many subjects frequently offered in many secondary schools and contains items not taught in many elementary or secondary schools. It is general, in that it is generalizable for further schooling and for out-of-school life. It is a curriculum for educating man as man (*pace feminists*), but the details need not detain us.

A Brief Catechism

Do all children "need" this kind of curriculum? No, only children who are to become "educated" adults do.

Does every child have a "right" to become educated? Only if a society commits itself to granting this right to every child.

Has our society made this commitment? Many educators have thought so, and have construed the mission of the public schools as implementing that right.

This does not mean that they have all translated that right into the particular strands of the curriculum mentioned above. Nevertheless, there has been a general agreement in rhetoric and sentiment that the public schools, envisioning universal attendance from grades K-12, would prepare us all for occupational, civic, and personal adequacy—that is, for being good citizens in a democratic, humane, high-achievement society. This agreement clearly committed the public schools to a curriculum that went well beyond the three R's for *all* children, especially when compulsory attendance was extended into early adolescence.

The notion that the children of all citizens should not only be encouraged but even forced to acquire an education was a radical sentiment. It meant abandoning a tradition of early British and American schooling that prescribed an intellectual-literary curriculum for the children of the classes and a vocational one, laced with piety and social docility, for the children of the masses—if and when the masses could be persuaded or forced to send their children to school. The extent to which the children of the masses were allowed to undertake the curriculum of their social "betters" largely determined their upward social mobility. It also gave this country a citizenry that could tune its consciousness to the demands of large-scale machine industry, mass production, and high technology.

Is our society now withdrawing from this broad commitment to universal, free, and, up to a point, compulsory schooling? I can find no univocal answer to this question in the general or professional press. Some of the advocates of minimum competency testing say that functional literacy is the least the schools ought to guarantee to, and demand from, everyone; but some seem further to think that until universal literacy is successful, no other program should be provided at public expense. Many voters seem ready to accept the latter interpretation, perhaps because they believe that the schools, willy-nilly, have identified a school population which cannot be taught or will not learn anything beyond minimal functional literacy, and partly because they believe that the school has neglected teaching functional literacy while doing something else.

One may be pardoned, therefore, for venturing the conjecture that by a diversity of routes—minimum competency testing, tuition credits for private elementary and secondary schools, voucher systems, legislation and funding for a host of special programs—we may be returning to a two-tiered system of schooling: a six-grade common school with minimal functional literacy as its goal, what might be called an Underclass *Volkschule*, and a grade 7-12 college or preprofessional preparatory school for those who have the scholastic aptitude to continue beyond the *Volkschule*. Or we might develop a K-6 *Volkschule* terminal curriculum stressing functional literacy for the children of the Underclasses and a K-12 curriculum for the children of the Overclasses. Of course, private versions of all sorts of schools and vouchers would be available, presumably to give parents choice and to encourage greater responsibility for their children's schooling. The latter argument, so attractive to the fashionable neo-laissez-faire ideologists, simply forgets that compulsory schooling at public expense was adopted largely because so many parents did not send their children to school.

This is only one aspect or manifestation of the ebbing public confidence in its social institutions and in the redemptive power of social legislation. The promises of the civil rights legislation and the Great Society programs of the 60s have not been fulfilled. As columnist John Roche remarked recently, "It seems as if every American Crusade ends up as a racket." The disillusion with the power of the schools to cure the effects of centuries of racial discrimination, with the military's ability to win wars at will, not to mention the general belief that we are all involved in a great battle royal in which everyone is ripping off everyone else, are variations on the same theme. A more charitable, yet even more melancholy, interpretation of the current anomie is the intimation that no social organization can function efficiently if the numbers involved increase beyond a critical figure. The costs of administration, and of anticipating, monitoring, and correcting subversion, once the number of units goes above the critical point, seem to be embarrassingly close to exceeding the benefits generated.

Functional Literacy as a Curriculum

In the light of this informal catechetical exercise, what is there to say about the effect of minimum competency testing on the curriculum?

If it should come to pass that functional literacy is regarded as a necessary and sufficient curriculum for a considerable portion of the school population, it will be appropriate to ask the following questions: Is functional literacy (defined as the ability to read utility bills and classified ads, to write a letter of application, do simple sums) adequate to the demands made on the individual by a modern technological society? Can such a society survive on this level of proficiency? Will practice and drill in the mechanics of the three R's in fact produce functional literacy, even at this modest level?

Literacy means using the symbolic skills to send or receive messages—information. How does this occur? A symbol stands for something and recalls it to consciousness. Consider the assertion: "The cat is in the tree." Which cat is *the* cat? And in which tree? Is it a real or imaginary cat? Translating the words into their respective lexical equivalents does not answer these questions. The subject has to supply contexts and particular data to fix the meaning of the sentence. If it is the neighbor's gray cat, then the chances are quite good that it is in the apple tree in the neighbor's yard—that being the only tree in the immediate vicinity. But why make the report at all? So what if the cat is in the tree? What context makes the assertion significant?

Mechanical identification of printed words with their phonetic equivalents and their standard referents is not what is ordinarily meant by reading comprehension, let alone *functional* literacy. Whoever doubts this conclusion need only hand a non-English-speaking reader a dictionary and ask him to be functionally literate about the locution: "They worked around the clock."

The point is that *other strands of the curriculum* are needed to provide context-building resources that make literacy possible, in any save the barest mechanical sense. If acquisition of these resources is restricted, even intensive instruction in the mechanics will not produce literacy. There is reason to believe that failure in reading may owe as much to the poverty of images and other associative resources as to inadequate mechanics.

But, it will be objected, if pupils cannot master the mechanics of reading, how can they penetrate and learn the other strands of the curriculum? Well, how do nonliterate people acquire their store of images and concepts? They do so by using spoken language, their senses, and their imagination. Does one need reading for radio, television, movies and illustrated magazines? Reading can enlarge and refine the image and concept store if it is used to study the disciplines—the sciences and the humanities. It is in the five strands of the general curriculum of the school that one learns this use. Reading is a necessary condition for education only if it is a key to these disciplines, which encase the culture and which contain the resources for cultivating the mind. And mastery of the three R's is certainly not a sufficient condition for their being used in this way. For although "key-door," "foundation-edifice" are correlative pairs, in life, keys are not always used to open doors, and foundations on which nothing further is built do in fact exist. If the minimum competency mandates encourage or force the schools to make the mechanics of reading dominate the rest of the curriculum, or tie minimum competence to tests that measure only the mechanics of reading and computation, it will prove to be a hollow victory for everyone concerned.[3]

What meaning shall be attached to functional literacy? For it does have a wide range of meaning indeed. For one thing, it depends on the sphere in which one wishes to be literate. If one defines functional literacy to mean only reading utility bills, filling out applications, reading the classified ads, checking the supermarket checker, and reading interest charges on mortgages, then it seems incredible that we should need anything like a K-12 school system to provide it. Surely with appropriate behavior modification techniques, this could be "taught" to all but the severely brain-damaged child and adult in a few years. Surely with advanced technology and Madison Avenue know-how, this problem can be managed. As an extreme but not entirely fanciful suggestion, one might enact and enforce a law that prevented anyone from operating a motor vehicle until he or she could pass a proficiency test at this level of functional literacy.

But how far will this minimal requirement take the individual into occupational, civic, or personal adequacy in a culture such as ours? Even the well-intentioned college graduate finds it difficult to understand what is going on in his own state, let alone the nation and the world. It is what one reads *with* that makes sense out of what is read in the press, books, or seen on the television screen. I doubt very much that the strange behavior of the public at the polls, or in the marketplace, or in the home will be corrected by "functional literacy," or that it can be explained by ineptness in the three R's. Far from being able to dispense with all but minimal functional literacy in our prescription for high school graduates, we should be frightened to despair at how much one needs to learn, to know, in order to understand our world and to make some pretence of coping rationally with its predicaments.

Functional literacy, however, can be defined in much broader terms than reading utility bills or filling out tax forms. It can mean being able to use language in all its forms to enlarge knowledge, clarify thought, enrich the imagination, and guide judgment. So defined or characterized, functional literacy is the equivalent of a general education, which, on my view, cannot do with fewer than the five strands listed above.

This suggests not the kind of minimum competency testing that is being mandated, but rather a professional responsibility to identify after-the-fact acts of competence and of incompetence for each individual—as good teachers do. It also suggests devising tests of the ability of the high school graduate to use knowledge acquired in school as educated adults are expected to use it, namely, for the interpretation of situations and events of all kinds, some of which come to them in the form of print.

I have no illusions about the objectivity or validity of tests. As indicated earlier, I do think they are useful for assessing end-of-school or end-of-course outcomes of didactics, but their usefulness for assessing the ability of a person to use his schooling is very limited.[4] This is so because the interpretive, associative, and applicative uses of schooling are rarely exact reinstatements of the content as learned. I have explored Michael Polanyi's notion of tacit knowing to help explicate the sense of "knowing with" as differentiated from "knowing how" and "knowing that" (Polanyi, 1967).

Here it may be sufficient to point out that when we are asked to read a paragraph about the exploration of space, research on DNA, medical discoveries, a review of a new play, an art exhibition, a concert, the cause of inflation and the decline of the value of the dollar in Japan, we respond "with" contexts and associations acquired from many sources. By having adults respond to carefully selected materials from actual publications (major newspapers and nontechnical magazines), we might be able to identify the "knowing with" components that are crucial to understanding, which is interpretation. It might also be possible to relate the responses to materials known to have been studied in school.

Each of the five strands of the curriculum is responsible for producing contexts or stencils that will make materials on the salient issues of the day intelligible, albeit not necessarily make the issues solvable by the reader or the society itself. We should concentrate our efforts on devising tests that would enable us to judge whether these responsibilities have been discharged, and schools that take seriously their curriculum in general education should welcome them.

Tests of end-of-course and end-of-school outcomes taught by rote for exact recall will not do this adequately; neither will artificial tests of reasoning, inference, and analysis. Not the former because, for the associative and interpretive uses of schooling, precise recall of materials studied may not be necessary and perhaps not even helpful. The latter are inadequate because the interpretive tasks of life are rarely reducible to simple logical exercises. School integration, busing, equal opportunity, taxation policy, and virtually all national and international social issues are reported in language that carries a high but tacit cognitive, imagic, emotive load. How well one senses which modes of knowledge, which criteria, which instances are "relevant" to an issue, let alone decisive, is a response that one would like to judge directly, rather than through highly schematized questions. The issue we are discussing today is about as good an example as any of how much more is involved in its comprehension than simple linguistic and logical skills.

In other words, it may not be necessary to give up the ideal of universal education or to make a travesty of our commitment to it in order to satisfy the public's desire for accountability. Indeed, the minimum competency testing movement might just prod our educational leadership to become interested in education.

Summary

This paper has devoted more space than was perhaps desirable to isolating the curriculum issue within the complex of questions raised by the minimum competency testing movement. Most of these questions call for predictions as to what would happen to the existing curricula if the movement succeeded. The bewildering diversity of definitions, circumstances, and approaches to the problem make it unlikely that such predictions will amount to anything more than guesses.

Commonsense interpretations of the public mood and the ways of government justify a general expectation that the movement will lead to constriction of school offerings in favor of instruction in the three R's, and the exclusion of those who have difficulties with the three R's from any other R's. Conceivably, we might regress (in the name of innovation to be sure) to a two-tiered system of public schools with minimal functional literacy for the masses—a sort of Underclass *Volkschule*—and a more standard curriculum for the children of the classes.

For the moment, the important task is to assess the functional literacy curriculum against a curriculum designed to provide general education in a modern democratic society. I have tried to show that literacy itself presupposes more than mechanical mastery of the three R's and that for the current "proficiency" criteria of functional literacy, a K-12 school system is superfluous.

To be genuinely functional, literacy requires all strands of the curriculum; it was suggested that "tests" of adult uses of schooling might give us an entry into the accountability of schools for general education.

Notes

1. For documentation on the kinds and extent of the diversity, one should consult Miller (Note 1), which is a report of four conferences on minimum competency testing; one should also consult a special issue of *Phi Delta Kappan* 59 (May 1978), based upon it. The conferences were sponsored by the Education Commission of the States and the National Institute of Education. They were replete with assorted experts and representatives of numerous constituencies.

2. Glass says, "no one knows how well a person must read to succeed in life or what percentage of the graduating class ought to be able to evaluate compound interest payments" (1978, p. 602).

3. "Reason and evidence provide little, if any, justification for the belief that minimum competency testing will help poor students learn or poor teachers to teach" (Wise, 1978, p. 598).

4. I agree with Stake that "evaluation should be relevant to education, not rote performance, but we don't have a technology of measurement oriented toward education" (1976, p. 347, note 4); but I believe it is time to develop one.

References

Anderson, B. D. Costs of legislated minimal competency requirements. In B. S. Miller (ed.). January 1978. *Minimum competency testing: a report of four regional conferences.* St. Louis: CEMREL, Inc.

Broudy, H. S., Smith, B. O., & Burnett, J. R. 1964. *Democracy and excellence in american secondary education.* Chicago: Rand McNally.

Glass, G. V. Minimum competence and incompetence in Florida. 1978. *Phi Delta Kappan* 59: 602-605.

Kelley, E. W. January 1978. The politics of proficiency. In B. S. Miller (ed.), *Minimum competency testing: a report of four regional conferences.* St. Louis: CEMREL, Inc.

Miller, B. S. (ed.). January 1978. *Minimum competency testing: a report of four regional conferences.* St. Louis: CEMREL, Inc.

Polanyi, M. 1967. *The tacit dimension.* New York: Doubleday.

Stake, R. E. May 1975. Statement prepared for a panel on testing in the Royal Oak (Mich.) District.

Stake, R. E. 1976. Making school evaluations relevant. *North Central Association Quarterly* 50: 347-352.

Wise, E. E. 1978. Minimum competency testing: Another case of hyper-rationalization. *Phi Delta Kappan* 59: 596-598.

Comments on H. Broudy's
"Impact of Minimum Competency
Testing on Curriculum"

Marianne Amarel

Harry Broudy will venture no specific predictions about the effects of minimum competency testing on the public school curriculum. He is content to raise a fistful of questions that have hardly been considered, let alone resolved—questions that remind us that the institutionalized testing of minimum competencies has the potential to influence decisions about who will be educated, for how long, and to what ends.

Lacking Professor Broudy's restraint, I will risk a bit of soothsaying. I predict that we shall see few, if any, thoughtfully and judiciously implemented minimum competency testing programs in the near future. As auguries go, this is not a very bold one. A little random reading in the ballooning literature on the topic, and of Broudy's surely partial list of unresolved social policy issues, forces the realization that the understandings and conditions necessary for sound implementation of minimum competency testing are not immediately at hand.

So much for consulting the tea leaves. To move on to firmer ground, I join Broudy in the view that omens point to the constriction of school curriculum, arising in part from a widespread preoccupation with basic skill training aimed at the attainment of functional literacy. With no grounds for dissent, I will simply add a thought or two to Broudy's analysis, mentioning in particular some ways that minimum competency testing may influence and perhaps alter the role of the teacher.

Let me begin by absolving minimum competency testing from either full blame or full credit for the increased concern with basic skills. This trend cannot be solely attributed to competency testing, nor should it be seen as its inevitable consequence, there being no conceptual imperative for the emphasis on basic skills in the notion of competency-based education. For example, a variety of *social* goals, concerned with the way students function as members of groups, or *personal* goals, related to the quality of the students' own development, might equally well be selected as the competencies that schooling seeks to promote, and as the achievements it ultimately wishes to assess. These options, however, have not been exercised by the bulk of the school systems that have instituted minimum competency bases for promotion or graduation.

I see the impetus for minimum competency testing as stemming, in good part, from a desire to regulate teacher and student performance more closely. While the intent to exercise control is relatively clear, the reasons for pulling on the reins are less so. The chorus urging competency testing on the schools does *not* chant with one voice, as Broudy has already observed. Some view such control as a strategy that ensures the schools' keeping faith with the commitment to a universal education of acceptable quality. Others, however, would use it as a way to legitimize the withholding of educational opportunity from a portion of the student population. However intended, I believe that choosing minimum competency testing as the mechanism for getting a firmer grip on school functions will have some inexorable consequences. It is a strategy that shifts the evaluation of instruction from teachers and schools to points more distant from the student—often several administrative layers away from the classroom—to district and state administration. It removes from the teachers' domain the major components of evaluation: standard setting and criteria setting, the choice of specific content to be assessed, as well as the technique and manner of assessment. Even the determination of how evaluation results are to be used is taken away from the school and teacher.

On the face of it, minimum competency testing is an indirect mechanism for regulating teacher and student performance, in that it neither prescribes nor offers pedagogical alternatives for shaping student learning. It is interesting to note, then, that the spread of minimum competency testing is being paralleled by an increase in highly prescriptive instructional programs. These programs are most visible at the early grades, and are often specifically aimed at children with low academic achievement scores. Variously called diagnostic/prescriptive, individualized, or "direct instruction" programs, they have several features in common. Frequently, the prescription extends to the knowledge or skill domain to be taught (primarily basic skills), to the instructional sequence to be followed (usually linear), to the units of instruction (usually small and discrete), to the instructional process to be used (largely drill and practice), and to the specification of the diagnostic or evaluative tools to be used (frequently paper-and-pencil tests). The professional autonomy of the teacher in a fully implemented program of this kind is diminished, since the teacher's role here calls for little active judgment or decision making. It is a paradox of the press for accountability that, just when teachers are being held increasingly responsible for the achievement scores of their students, their authority over their own practice is being undermined, since both instructional means and ends are more closely prescribed.

Although turning the teacher into a mere educational functionary may be ideologically distasteful to some, a case might be made for the transformation if it proved effective in promoting the kind of literacy Broudy has written and spoken about. But there is, as yet, no convincing empirical evidence that it does, nor much theoretical support that it can. The weight of what we know about human learning and cognition is not on the side of constricting the teacher's work. In recent years, rather substantial support has been accumulated for viewing the learner as an active, purposeful agent, who constructs, orders, and stores experiences so as to make sense of the world and gain competence in dealing with it. Knowledge is not ingested and retained the way it is encountered; rather, it is formed into personally meaningful representations by the learner. Learning thus may be seen essentially as a voluntary process, which may be guided, supported, and facilitated, but not mandated. This suggests that prespecifying the means, routes, and, to a degree, even the content of learning for diverse groups of students is inadvisable.

Traditionally, it has been the role of the teacher to negotiate the terrain between the abilities and qualities of the student and the demands of the learning task. Instructional programs that do not incorporate the teacher's knowledge of the students must, of necessity, set limited aims. Such programs tend to focus on curricular goals that do not depend on a high degree of pedagogical skill, but on instruction through rote, repetition, or other didactic routines. The effectiveness and scope of didactic instruction is, of course, a major combat zone of education today. My bias matches Broudy's in doubting that rote instruction in the mechanics of the basics skills can lead to even limited literacy. Reading, that most basic of basic skills, makes this point best. There are, no doubt, components of the skill of reading that are amenable to training, and most children can eventually be taught to transform written words into sounded words. But this skill alone is a long way from reading, if we define reading as the recovery and reconstruction of meaning that is embedded in text. Seen this way, reading is, of necessity, dependent on the availability to the reader of an existing context of knowledge and understanding. Most children come to learning how to read with a sufficiency of such knowledge—they have a grasp of the spoken language and a good deal of world-knowledge that they derived from experiences with the material and social realities of their world. The continued enrichment and extension of this context of meanings is the prime function of education, and reading can become one of the means for its ongoing development.

But when reading is taught in such a way that access to the child's available meaning structures is blocked—as when the instructional emphasis is on fragmented component skills, with little or no use of meaningful reading material—the purpose of reading may become obscured.

The commonly found drop in reading scores at the upper grades, when tests shift from assessing component skills to assessing comprehension, reflects the problem. This is particularly true for children whose environments provide relatively few opportunities for building the broad contexts needed for academic reading. Ironically, these are the children who stand a greater chance of receiving an education that is narrow in scope and restrictive in method.

It should be evident that I understand the notion of curriculum to include the practice as well as the content of instruction. In the education of young children, the means and the substance are often difficult to separate, and may be equally consequential. Minimum competency testing has the potential of affecting all aspects of the curricular process. Broudy's formulations on the nature of literacy, with their implications for the teaching role, point up an area of vulnerability at the intersection of the curriculum and of competency testing. Narrowly conceived testing programs may desiccate the curriculum for some children, and bring about a further segregation of schooling along social-class lines. Such programs can deflect us from what is still an avowed public commitment: the adequate preparation of children to become contributing members of any sector of society, not merely the one preordained by their social origins.

Curriculum and Minimum Competency: A Reaction to the Remarks of H. S. Broudy

W. James Popham

It is always a pleasure to encounter an educational essay in which one sees the results of a fine mind at work. Such pleasure is heightened all the more when that mind has been steeped in decades of astutely observing America's educational system in operation. We are the beneficiaries of this delightful mix as a consequence of Professor Broudy's applying his experience to analyze minimum competency testing's probable impact on the schools' curriculum.

Philosophers, of course, are supposed to be cerebral folk. And Broudy's work has, through the years, represented first-rate philosophy. It is interesting, therefore, to see where his cerebration takes him when he is directed to worry about how curriculum might be affected by the minimum competency testing movement.

Fears, Tears, and Tiers

Although Broudy's essay is peppered with thought-provoking insights, I found myself most intrigued by his concerns about whether advocates of minimum competency testing were unwittingly nurturing the return to a two-caste system of education—one for the classes and one for the masses. Although I have encountered no architect of minimum competency testing programs who intends the creation of such a dual system of education as a hidden mission, parents are often unable to discern where their progeny are headed.

Yet, as Broudy contends with characteristic sagacity, we might well end up with two educational emphases, only one of which spells education with an upper-case E. Much of this depends, as he points out, on "what meaning shall be attached to functional literacy." Shall we conceive of a functionally literate young adult as one who can merely monitor the supermarket checker or, instead, as one who can "use language in all its forms to enlarge knowledge, clarify thought, enrich the imagination, and guide judgment?" The more we move toward a notion of functional literacy reflecting the latter conception, the less we must concern ourselves about the societal perils of a two-class educational system, since functional literacy in its broadest meaning can be equated with Broudy's five-stranded notion of general education.

But few of the people I have encountered in the minimal competency testing marketplace are arguing for such a broad conception of minimum competency. It is only natural that, since educators will be held accountable via their students' successes or failures, those educators will tend to set out instructional challenges that they have a chance of meeting.

Broudy opines that, if we take the minimal meaning of functional literacy, such literacy could be taught to all but the severely brain-damaged in a few years. Well, this is precisely the level of functioning the public currently doubts is being taught to high school graduates after a *dozen* years of schooling. The public is screaming for minimum warranties, not an enlightened conception of functional literacy. We do, indeed, need to worry about the prospect of a split-level educational edifice.

Curriculum Relevance

Broudy gives only passing attention to a curricular issue that may, albeit circuitously, impinge on his concerns about a reductional curriculum. That issue revolves around the impact that the tests employed in minimum competency testing programs will have on the day-to-day curriculum of the schools. In my judgment, the prospects are certain that in states or districts where the certification tests are described with sufficient clarity to permit targeted instructional design, the curriculum will become more and more test-valid.

This is a fairly safe prediction, since there will be positive consequences for those curriculum designers who match their curricula to the certification tests' emphases, and negative consequences for those who don't. Only in settings where certification tests are so amorphous that no curriculum implications are present will we fail to see the curriculum molded to match the tests. Such situations will be encountered chiefly when the tests selected for certification of high school graduates are run-of-the-mill, nationally standardized, norm-referenced achievement tests. But in any minimum competency testing setting where the sought-for competencies have been fairly well stated, we can expect that at least part of the curriculum will become coterminous with the test's emphases.

Now if Broudy's yearning for a more enlightened notion of functional literacy is not realized, as I suspect will be the case, what will be the effects of the curriculum's gravitation toward the tests? At worst it will confirm the critics' dire predictions that minima will become maxima; that is, less profound aspirations will crowd out more profound ones. At best, however, it may force educators to realize that they must provide more than rhetoric to support loftier curricular aims.

It runs counter to human frailties to establish tests (with significant human consequences) to support minima but to provide only talk to support maxima, and then expect people to get truly excited about the promotion of higher-order aims.

I am suggesting that the curricular impact of minimum competency testing programs may illuminate the necessity to create tests which measure higher-order skills and understandings, and then to establish at least some sorts of sanctions associated with students' performance on those measures.

Clearly described tests, matched with meaningful consequences, will influence curriculum. They ought to. The opportunity before us is whether we can marshal the intellectual and financial resources necessary to cause this sort of assessment-curriculum reformation.

Pessimism Repudiated

Professor Broudy concluded his analysis on a note of optimism. I have concluded my analysis of his analysis on a note of optimism. That a person of Broudy's insights and experience can remain optimistic makes me optimistic that our pooled optimism may not be misplaced.

6 Sociodemographic Implications of Minimum Competency Testing

Bruce K. Eckland

When asked to review the sociodemographic consequences of minimum competency testing, the first question that came to my mind was: Consequences for *what* and for *whom*? The schools, the teachers, the students, or society at large? The growing literature on outcome-based education, although providing some clues, largely ignores what the social consequences actually are, or might be, for any of these groups. What one finds are fleeting statements about youngsters not being able to perform at a level that is "functional in society"; about competency tests discriminating against blacks and other minorities; about large numbers of students who will be so discouraged by failing the tests that they will drop out of high school; about remedial programs that will lead to resegregation within the school or to other forms of tracking; and about all those above-average students who will be lulled into complacency by low minimum standards. None of these statements has much factual basis, yet all certainly deserve our attention. In my review, I have not even found any evidence or thoughtful discussion on the central question of whether or not minimum competency testing would have any impact on what many writers have long thought to be the two primary, although obviously not the only, social functions of secondary education. These are preparation for work and college.

As described by Martin Trow, a major transformation of American secondary education occurred during the 1950s and 60s, bringing into sharp focus the dual functions of the comprehensive high school (1961).

These were, on the one hand, to prepare youth for useful tasks and *terminal* diplomas, and, on the other, to prepare a growing proportion of students for *college*. Trow argued that the rise of mass higher education led directly to an increased emphasis on college preparatory programs in most secondary schools, while retaining the general and vocational tracks for the less academically motivated, terminal students.

In light of these two broad functions of schooling, what I consider in this paper is the correlation between success on minimum competency tests, like reading and math, and success in life, as measured by access to jobs and access to college. The connections between this performance and the primary functions of secondary education have not been closely examined, and they need to be.

Can we just assume, for instance, that the main reason so many young people, especially blacks, cannot find decent jobs is because they graduate from high school without being able to read or to compute? Or take another example. Can we assume that sending the bottom 10 or 20 percent of all 12th-graders on these tests into the world without a diploma would have no effect on college enrollments or on the life-success chances of these students? Questions of this kind, I believe, are important to have answered and, as I will show, the answers are not self-evident.

The public's expectations of education are largely pragmatic. Above all, parents want schools to prepare their children to become responsible and productive adults, a role which is still largely defined in terms of *work* and not necessarily good citizenship, not promoting personal development, and certainly not athletics, even though the latter continues to dominate the world of adolescents. I am not saying that citizenship, personal development, and athletics are not valued by adults. Rather, I am saying that the main measure of success in life for most people is pecuniary, that a technologically oriented society places a heavy premium on the possession of certain kinds of intellectual competence, and that at least some of the relevant skills presumably are learned in school. The competency-based education movement is partly the response of a public who believe that their children are being short-changed in such traditional subjects as reading, writing, and math, and that these skills are strongly related to success in the world of work.

If these basic skills are the most important outcomes of elementary and secondary education, as many would claim, then what is the actual connection between achieving them and getting a well-paying job or going to college? If a student completed twelve years of schooling with a certificate of attendance instead of a diploma, would it really matter? Are the basic skills that many minimum competency tests measure all that important today, or is it the diploma itself that counts?

The Data

The data for this report come from the National Longitudinal Study (NLS) of the high school class of 1972. The NLS is the first in a program of longitudinal studies sponsored by the National Center for Education Statistics (NCES). The first baseyear survey was conducted by Educational Testing Service (ETS) in spring of 1972, with over 1,000 participating schools and data collected on about 18,000 graduating seniors. Followup surveys of these students were conducted by the Research Triangle Institute (RTI) in fall 1973, 1974, and 1976, with response rates averaging well over 90 percent.

The sample is representative of all public and private high schools in the nation, but is accompanied by an oversampling of schools composed of low socioeconomic and minority students. Thus, the 1972 NLS is the first large-scale data from which national estimates can be derived for trends among different racial groups in their transition from school to work or to college.

Before turning to the results, I will describe the NLS test battery. Of the six subtests that were administered in the baseyear survey, I believe three measure the same kinds of basic skills that generally are included in most minimum competency tests—that is, mathematics, reading comprehension, and vocabulary.

The 25-item math test was judged not to be speeded; it was of "middle difficulty" according to the ETS staff that constructed the tests, and it had an estimated reliability of .87. Most of the items involved computations, but did not tap algebraic, geometric, or other higher-level skills. Of equal relevance here is that some of the items in the math test dealt with applied skills, such as the use of monetary figures, temperature reading, and measuring in feet and inches. In other words, while not designed for the purpose, the math test no doubt included items that would likely be found in many minimum competency tests at grade 12.

The NLS reading and vocabulary tests were somewhat less reliable (estimated reliabilities of .80 and .78, respectively). Partly for this reason, and the fact that they measure similar abilities, I have combined their standard scores in computing the deciles to be reported here. The 15-minute reading test consisted of 5 short passages and a total of 15 items. It too was judged by ETS not to be speeded and was of "middle difficulty" for 12th-graders. The 5-minute vocabulary test also contained 15 items and was judged not to be speeded, but was "somewhat difficult" for the group even though ETS claims that the items in this test were purposely selected to avoid academic or collegiate bias.

In table 1, decile distributions on the math and combined verbal tests are

Table 1. Racial Distribution of NLS Test Scores

Deciles**	Math Test		Reading Tests*	
	Whites (N=12301)	Blacks (N=1952)	Whites (N=12301)	Blacks (N=1952)
1	5.8%	28.9%	5.4%	29.3%
2	7.5	20.9	7.4	21.6
3	8.7	14.9	8.8	14.6
4	9.7	11.1	9.8	10.7
5	10.3	9.0	10.4	7.6
6	11.0	5.3	11.0	6.6
7	11.4	4.6	11.4	4.4
8	11.6	2.6	11.9	2.3
9	11.8	1.7	12.0	1.6
10	12.1	1.0	12.0	1.3
Totals	100.1%	99.8%	100.0%	100.0%

*Combined scores on reading comprehension and word analogy tests.
**Deciles are computed from the total NLS baseyear sample, which includes other racial-ethnic minorities not listed here.

presented separately for blacks and whites. Consistent with past studies, as well as with earlier reports from Florida and other states that have begun using minimum competency tests, most blacks fall into the lower three deciles on both exams. It therefore is easy to understand why the issue of competency testing has become so highly politicized along racial lines in some states, and why it is important to examine just what kind of impact, if any, these programs could have for different racial groups.

The Results

The first group I wish to consider is those who do not go to college immediately after high school. Can we find any evidence to support the common assumption that the reason some high school graduates cannot find a job that pays a decent wage is because our schools have failed to provide them with such essential skills for adult life as being able to read and to compute? To examine this question, we look first at unemployment rates for the NLS sample several months after graduation (in October 1972), then at hours worked per week by those who found jobs, and finally at what those who were working full-time were earning. Students who were enrolled in college in October 1972 have been deleted from this part of the analysis in order to make the results more interpretable.

The overall unemployment rate, as shown in table 2, was over three

Table 2. Unemployment Rates by Decile on the NLS Math
and Verbal Tests

	Percent Unemployed*			
	Math Test		Reading Tests	
Deciles	Whites	Blacks	Whites	Blacks
1	11% (440) **	36% (309)	13% (437)	34% (351)
2	10% (612)	27% (226)	9% (575)	28% (212)
3	10% (648)	30% (135)	10% (649)	23% (127)
4	10% (708)	27% (103)	8% (674)	33% (80)
5	8% (662)	21% (68)	10% (665)	25% (52)
6 to 10***	9% (2269)	16% (69)	9% (2339)	22% (88)
Totals	9% (5339)	29% (910)	9% (5339)	29% (910)

*All respondents who were "looking for work" as of the first week of October 1972, expressed as a proportion of those who were determined to be in the labor force and not enrolled in college.

**Figures in parentheses are the numbers of persons in each decile upon which the percentages are based.

***Because of the small size of the sample for blacks, the upper five deciles have been combined here and also in the next two tables.

times higher for blacks than for whites, 29 versus 9 percent, a finding that is generally consistent with recent Department of Labor reports on youth unemployment. Is the high unemployment rate among blacks related to the fact that these young people, even though they have completed 12 years of schooling, do so poorly on basic skills competency tests? Only partly. As shown in the table, a large gap between blacks and whites exists at all levels of competency, although it diminishes somewhat at the upper levels. For example, among blacks and whites who scored in the lowest decile in math, the ratio is about 3 to 1, whereas it drops to about 2 to 1 in the higher deciles.

More important, the relationships between employment and math and reading ability are negligible for whites but are moderately positive for blacks. There was only a 2 percentage point difference in unemployment for whites who fell in the lowest decile on math and those who scored in the upper half of the distribution. However, for blacks, the difference was much more marked, with 36 percent of those in the lowest decile unemployed compared with 16 percent unemployment for those in the upper half of the distribution on the math test. It appears, then, for some unknown reason, that the basic skills being measured here are important for black high school graduates but not for whites when it comes to finding a job. While these racial differences are interesting, do not overlook the more surprising finding that for the majority of the population, if you are a high school graduate and white, your tested reading and computation competency has almost no effect on your employability.

The critics among you, of course, will rightly want to know more about these respondents. Since most young people who do not go to college or get married actually do find work after high school, you may feel that making a good living is more important than being employed within a few months of high school graduation. Before examining wages, though, let us look at hours worked. As it turns out, one out of four seniors who found jobs and were not going to college were employed only part-time (defined as working less than 35 hours per week). Given this rather high rate of part-time employment among the NLS respondents, the amount of time worked could be as important an economic indication as any other, in the first year after high school. Is it related to basic skills competency? Table 3 shows no consistent pattern between test scores and part-time employment. As a whole, students in the lower deciles were no more likely than those in the upper deciles on the math and reading tests to be working part-time.

Table 4 is based on average weekly wages for persons employed full-time. Again the results show that ability to read or to compute, as measured on the NLS tests, makes no difference at all. About one-half

Table 3. Part-Time Employment by Decile on the NLS Math and Verbal Tests

| | Percent Working under 35 Hours per Week* | | | |
| | Math Test | | Reading Tests | |
Deciles	Whites	Blacks	Whites	Blacks
1	27% (319) **	29% (166)	22% (294)	22% (203)
2	22% (453)	26% (141)	26% (423)	29% (122)
3	23% (487)	25% (87)	20% (483)	28% (95)
4	24% (519)	27% (64)	26% (520)	30% (46)
5	25% (529)	18% (45)	23% (518)	23% (31)
6 to 10	30% (1781)	34% (56)	29% (1850)	35% (62)
Totals	26% (4088)	27% (559)	26% (4088)	27% (559)

*All respondents working under 35 hours per week as of October 1972, expressed as a proportion of those who held jobs (excluding students enrolled in college).
**Figures in parentheses represent the numbers of persons in each decile upon which the percentages are based.

Table 4. Wage Rates by Decile on the NLS Math and Verbal Tests

| | Percent Earning 100 Dollars or Less per Week* | | | |
| | Math Test | | Reading Tests | |
Deciles	Whites	Blacks	Whites	Blacks
1	49% (181) **	52% (87)	46% (188)	49% (123)
2	49% (272)	51% (81)	47% (243)	50% (68)
3	48% (306)	37% (46)	45% (316)	44% (41)
4	47% (309)	55% (38)	50% (309)	43% (23)
5	46% (327)	56% (25)	46% (311)	59% (17)
6 to 10	47% (1001)	32% (25)	48% (1029)	47% (30)
Totals	47% (2396)	48% (302)	47% (2396)	48% (302)

*Wages as of October 1972 for all persons working 35 hours or more per week and not enrolled in college.

**Figures in parentheses represent the numbers of persons in each decile upon which the percentages are based.

of both whites and blacks who held full-time jobs were earning $100 or less per week. Moreover, those in the lower deciles on math and reading were no worse off than those in the upper deciles. The results are essentially the same for blacks and whites.

In summary, if a student does not go to college, what he or she scores on a basic skills competency test in math or reading simply does not appear to matter economically. At least one student in ten can figure on being unemployed for some period after high school, with the chances of unemployment being much greater for blacks. If the graduate finds work, he or she has a one-in-four chance of working only part-time, and if working full-time a one-in-two chance of earning $100 or less per week. Being able to read or to compute well will help you find a job, but only if you are black, and it will not help you to earn more money, whether you are white or black.

These were the conditions for new high school graduates in 1972 and they did not change much in the next four years. Using data from the third NLS followup survey, Peng and Jaffe recently compared the progress of all students who never went to college and who were in the upper and lower ability quartiles, based on essentially the same standardized test scores used here (1978). As of October 1976, 4.5 percent of those in the upper quartile and 6.8 percent of those in the lower quartile were unemployed and looking for work. In terms of number of hours worked, the average was 41.5 hours per week in October 1976 for persons in the highest test score quartile and 41.6 per week for those in the lowest quartile. Finally, persons in the highest test score quartile earned $175 on the average per week, while those in the lowest quartile earned $173 per week. The relationship between test scores and economic success or failure (or, more precisely, the almost total lack of such a relationship) has remained unchanged for the class of 1972 with the passage of four years.

If such basic skills as math and reading do not count for much in the world of work for recent high school graduates, perhaps they do in another way, through higher education. After all, the best jobs, and ultimately the highest wages, are associated with having a college degree. Certainly who goes to college is related to some minimum competency in the basic skills. Assuming this to be true, what then would be the impact on current rates of college attendance if a substantial number of students failed to pass the tests and, as a result, did not receive a high school diploma? And, would the effects be the same for whites and minorities? The answers depend on several things. In particular, they depend on the relationship between college attendance and the kinds of skills being measured by such tests, and on the distribution of test scores according to race. For example, if high school students who would be predicted to fail a minimum competency test in reading or math were not planning to go, or were not being admitted to college anyway, there would be little need for concern. Let us see if this is the case.

Table 5 shows the rates of college attendance for the NLS sample separately for blacks and whites who fall into each decile on the math and verbal tests. College attendance, incidentally, is defined here in terms of all persons who enrolled in an academic program in college at any time within 4½ years after high school. First, it is obvious by looking down the columns of the table that there is a very strong and almost perfect monotonic relationship between test scores and who goes to college. This is not surprising. In other analyses of the NLS data, it also has been discovered that the scores are more predictive of who goes to college than were any other background or school-related variable we have examined, with the exception of a student's stated plans as a senior (Thomas, Alexander, and Eckland, 1979). Particularly interesting is the fact that a composite measure of the NLS test scores correlates more highly with college attendance (.45) than does rank in class (.37). Since colleges uniformly give far more attention to high school grades than to standardized tests in their admissions processes it is not clear why the tests take on such importance. One possible explanation is that, due to grade inflation and social promotion, students rely more heavily on their own (or the tests') assessment of their ability to do college work than on their school

Table 5. Rates of College Attendance by Decile on the NLS
Math and Verbal Tests

| | Percent Who Went to College* | | | |
| | Math Test | | Reading Tests | |
Deciles	Whites	Blacks	Whites	Blacks
1	14% (551)**	32% (459)	15% (512)	27% (455)
2	22% (755)	35% (316)	23% (739)	40% (331)
3	29% (889)	49% (236)	30% (900)	49% (225)
4	35% (1018)	48% (174)	36% (1022)	57% (174)
5	42% (1071)	63% (134)	45% (1108)	60% (117)
6	51% (1170)	72% (82)	54% (1185)	75% (104)
7	62% (1234)	88% (80)	60% (1208)	79% (76)
8 to 10***	79% (3957)	90% (89)	77% (3971)	85% (88)
Totals	54% (10645)	48% (1570)	54% 10645)	48% (1570)

*Defined as any enrollment at any time within 4½ years (by October 1976) after high school.
**Figures in parentheses are the number of students upon which the percentages are based. The numbers are restricted to students who participated in the 1972 baseyear survey and responded to the first three followups.
***Because of the small size of the sample for blacks, the 8th, 9th, and 10th deciles have been combined.

grades when deciding whether or not to continue their education after high school. Another possibility is that we are dealing with a form of pluralistic ignorance. That is, students may *believe* that colleges give substantially more weight than they actually do to standardized tests, and then *act* accordingly. In any case, the acquisition of basic skills in math and reading, as measured by the NLS tests, is an exceedingly important determinant of who goes to college, as demonstrated in table 5. This is true for both blacks and whites.

In the case of whites, the college-going rates for those in the bottom deciles are so low that removing them from the pool of students normally eligible for college would have little effect on total enrollments. For example, if the standards used for failing persons on a minimum competency test in math were set at a level whereby 10 percent of all students failed, the percentage of whites attending college would remain virtually unchanged. (The drop would be less than 1 percent from the current rate of 54 percent.) Even raising the standard another full decile would not have much impact. It would effectively lower the overall rate of college attendance for whites from 54 to 52 percent, as shown in table 6.

The consequences for blacks, however, would be markedly different,

Table 6. Current and Projected Rates of College Attendance, by Race

	Percent Who Go to College		
	Whites	Blacks	Difference between Groups
Current Rate	54%	48%	6%
If no students in the lowest decile in *math* went to college	54%	38%	16%
If no students in the lowest decile in *reading* skills went to college	54%	40%	14%
If no students in the lowest *two* deciles in *math* went to college	52%	31%	21%
If no students in the lowest *two* deciles in *reading* went to college	52%	31%	21%

both because about half of all blacks in the 12th-grade score in the lowest two deciles on these tests, and because the rates of college attendance for blacks at this level are much higher than they are for whites. Consider the bottom decile on the math test. Three out of ten blacks score at this level, yet 32 percent of these students go to college. In contrast, only 14 percent of the whites who score in the bottom decile go to college and proportionately few whites fall into this decile. Thus, if the bottom line on minimum competency tests were set at a level whereby only 10 percent of all students failed, the results could still be disastrous for blacks. The predicted drop in the college attendance rate, based on the findings for the math test alone, would be 10 percentage points (from the current 48 percent rate to 38 percent). Looking at the results in another way, a 10 percent failure rate in math would increase the black-white differential in college attendance from the present 6 percentage points to 16 percentage points.

Discussion

In conclusion, then, although minimum competency tests of basic skills in math and reading apparently have little effect on the employment or wages of students entering the labor force after high school, they do have a strong bearing on who goes to college and, thus, on the long-run socioeconomic attainment process. Such ominous results as the possibility of lowering the college attendance of blacks by 10 to 15 percentage points would occur only if the cutoff points on the tests were uniformly applied (no double standards), the tests actually were used as a basis for awarding a high school diploma (as many are proposing), and eligibility for college actually required obtaining a diploma. Any one of these conditions, of course, could be circumvented. For instance, colleges could alter their admissions requirements in the name of affirmative action, and some doubtlessly would.

More than likely, however, most states probably will find mechanisms by which to pass all but a very small minority of their students, perhaps all but 2, 3, or 4 percent. As some districts are finding, one way to do this is to remove from the pool of students who are required to take the examinations those who are certified as "mentally handicapped." Depending on how liberally this is defined, this exemption could resolve part of the problem for certain groups. Another solution is to maintain "reasonable" standards of competency and invest a good deal of effort in seeing that students meet them. This, of course, is the central objective of competency-based education, but it remains to be achieved.

What I find difficult to comprehend, particularly in light of our ignorance about the relationship between academic skills and adult life (and thus the validity of the tests), is the political process by which standards of minimum competency are to be traded off against whatever is a politically tolerable number of failing students, if standards are set much above the 8th-grade level. Almost everyone seems to admit that the passing scores on criterion-referenced tests in high school are currently being set quite arbitrarily. This means that each state or school district, whichever is setting the standards, is at liberty to control the consequences by ultimately turning to some norm-referenced standard. If the standard is set such that 5 percent of whites and 30 percent of blacks fail, which is what could easily happen, there will be real trouble holding the minimum line. In all probability, the standards will be lowered or by-passed, even if they already are considered by the test experts to be at a "minimum competency" level. What school administrators may find particularly troublesome is following the political need to set standards for high school graduation at the elementary school level, in order to avoid failing too many students, and then being criticized for imposing such low educational standards for a diploma.

One last point. The sociodemographic stakes ultimately will depend on how faithfully diplomas are denied to persons who fail the tests. As the results from the NLS show, the consequences could be especially severe for minority students, since failing the test could mean not going to college for many of them. On the other hand, for whites who did not go to college, we found no relationship between test performance and either unemployment or wage rates. Does this mean that being denied a diploma has no effect on employment? Not necessarily. One of Bachman's central findings after following a national sample of high school students through adolescence and into adulthood a few years ago (1978) was that, although *wages* did not show a clear association with having received a high school diploma, the school *dropouts* had much higher rates of unemployment. It appears that the high school diploma mainly serves a credentialing function in American society, a certificate to hold a job or to go to college. It hurts not to have one.

If an individual also obtains the basic skills and competencies that the diploma was thought to verify, so much the better, but only if he or she is college bound. Otherwise it appears to matter very little just how one obtains a diploma, including obtaining one by social promotion. The only important thing is to get it, or most employers will not hire you.

Will minimum competency testing give more meaning to the high school diploma in the future? Perhaps. In one sense, the diploma already has too much meaning, in that employers use it indiscriminately as a screening device. They erroneously assume that it is telling them something important about the competence of its holder, when it probably is not. It is unfortunate that the results do not come out on the side of human capital theory of economics, in support of structural-functionalism in sociology, and on the side of those of us who still believe in the meritocracy. However, they do not, and I find this more disturbing than any of the present battles over minimum competency testing. The tests will come because we do not know how else to defend what we are doing in education, and perhaps they are a good thing.

References

Bachman, J. G. *Adolescence to Adulthood.* Ann Arbor, Mich.: Institute for Social Research, 1978.

Peng, S. and Jaffe, J. "A Study of Highly Able Students Who Did Not Go to College." Technical Report. Research Triangle Institute, September 1978.

Thomas, G. E., Alexander, K. L., and Eckland, B. K. "Access to Higher Education: The Importance of Race, Sex, Social Class, and Academic Credentials." *School Review* 87 (February 1979), pp. 133-56.

Trow, M. "The Second Transformation of American Secondary Education." *International Journal of Comparative Sociology* 2 (1961), pp. 144-66.

Reactions to Bruce Eckland's Paper: "Sociodemographic Implications of Minimum Competency Testing"

Robert W. Heath

Reactions to papers on controversial issues are inevitably shaped by one's frame of reference and context. With the hope that it will aid in understanding my reactions to Professor Eckland's paper, I will preface these comments with an indication of the perspectives that influence my response.

For nearly a year now, I have been directing a needs-assessment study of adult education in the state of California. This study is very much a part of the competency-testing movement analyzed in this volume. Because this study addresses *adult* competency, however, it imposes some unique considerations. First, competency must be viewed in more than academic terms; being a competent adult involves considerably more than the exercise of reading and mathematical skills. Once attention is directed to the concept of adult functional competency, implications for the school-age population become apparent. If competencies essential to functioning in society can be identified, should these competencies not be addressed by the schools?

Another consideration imposed when studying the educational needs of adults is that of the *autonomy* of the learner. Unlike children, adults cannot be compelled to attend school nor to study subject matter not of their own choosing. To attract adult students, the school (or other agency) must offer an educational opportunity that meets a need that is recognized and acknowledged by the potential student. Once attention is directed to the concept of the educational *needs* of adults, the implications for elementary and secondary education follow. Could it be that many of our educational failures (particularly with children of low-income and ethnic minority families) can be traced to a mismatch between curriculum and students' needs? I believe the data presented by Professor Eckland demonstrate just that.

A second frame of reference for my reactions has been formed by working on a series of curriculum evaluation projects in the state of Hawaii during the past three years. These projects, dealing with multicultural, bilingual, English, and consumer education curricula, have demanded a cross-cultural approach. In a state with no ethnic majority and an extremely large population of recent immigrants from Polynesia, Micronesia, and Asia, cultural differences simply cannot be ignored. Though the children of Hawaii are being educated for participation in American society, the educational system cannot assume that the school-age population has a predominately white, middle-class, Western background.

As various cultural groups encounter this public education system, it becomes dramatically evident that these cultural differences result in very different educational needs. The elementary-grade bilingual education program in Hawaii seems to be a success with Korean children and, simultaneously, a failure with Samoan children. Though different ethnic or socioeconomic groups may demonstrate the same level of performance (especially on achievement tests) on a particular competency, it does *not* follow that they have the same educational needs.

My reactions to Professor Eckland's paper are influenced then by these two perspectives: the concept of *functional* competency in contrast with academic *minimum* competency, and the cultural and subcultural determinations of educational needs.

These reactions will focus first on two premises of the study, and then on three major findings. In his opening paragraph, Eckland identifies a generally accepted premise that schools have two primary social functions, "preparation for work and college." A case is made for this premise largely on the basis of "the public's expectations." A second premise, in the discussion of results, is that the "essential skills for adult life" are "being able to read and to compute." I will argue that "preparation for work and college" is an inadequate conception of the social function of schooling and that reading and computation are not the essential skills of adult life.

The findings that seem most important to me are:

(1) As shown in table 2, roughly the same employment gap between blacks and whites exists at all levels of competency. The percent unemployed is about three times as large for blacks as for whites at all deciles of the NLS test scores.

(2) "If you are a high school graduate and white, your tested reading and computation competency has almost no effect on your employability." The data in table 2 show *no* relationship between test scores and unemployment rates.

(3) "Being able to read or to compute well . . . will not help you to earn more money, whether you are white or black." The data in table 4 show *no* relationship between test scores and "Percent Earning 100 Dollars or Less per Week."

These results seem to me to controvert the two premises specified and to have profound implications for minimum competency testing. Reading and math, as tested, cannot be the "essential skills for adult life" if attainment of these skills is unrelated to employment, earnings, and reduction of the disadvantage of minority status. To set minimum competency standards in terms of such achievement measures is to perpetuate and probably magnify the problems resulting from this fallacy.

It may be useful to distinguish between academic *minimum* competencies and *functional* competencies. Academic minimum competencies are those required by an educational institution for the award of a diploma, a degree, or promotion in grade level. The particular skills and the performance levels required are determined largely by tradition, convention, or "norms." Academic minimum competencies are required by educational institutions with little evidence that these competencies have utility outside those institutions. That is, these competencies are largely *ritualistic*. To identify them as such does not imply that such ritualistic competencies are unimportant. Our culture, like all others, must have its social rituals to insure social cohesion and cultural continuity.

A competency, at a particular level of performance, is *functional* when it meets a need of a person with particular characteristics (gender, age, ethnic group) in a particular set of circumstances. The competencies needed to function as an adult (or a child) in any society may be assigned to two categories: *utilitarian* and *ritualistic*. Utilitarian competencies include, for example, those needed to obtain goods and services, to use the communication and transportation systems, to maintain health and safety, to function interpersonally, and to participate in the legal and political processes. Ritualistic competencies include, for example, those needed to obtain diplomas and degrees, to participate in the common ceremonies and holidays, to demonstrate socially tolerable morality and "good taste," and to recognize the common standards of beauty and excellence that contribute to social cohesion. The data presented by Eckland may suggest that the existing curricula and corresponding measures of achievement are out of balance for most of the population, with too much emphasis on ritualistic learning and too little on utilitarian competencies.

A *competency* is an attribute (for example, a skill, information, or attitude) of an individual that *may* serve to meet one or more needs of that person. Thus a person may have competencies that are not exercised (and thus are not *functional*) because they do not meet an existing need. While a single competency may meet more than one need, several competencies may be required to meet another need. Moreover, a single competency may be manifested by a number of corresponding performance indicators.

A competency may be exercised at various *performance levels*. Depending on the need to be served, different performance levels of a given competency may be functional for different people, and even for the same person under different circumstances. For example, an Olympic swimming competitor and a recreational swimmer exercise different performance levels of the same competency.

As defined, a competency is *functional* only when it meets a *need* of an individual. *Need* is the most critical concept, and the most difficult to define, in this context.

The "discrepancy model" is the one most frequently encountered in the contemporary educational literature on needs assessment. Scriven and Roth (1978) have discussed this model.

In reviewing the literature of needs assessment, it became obvious that the term 'need' was usually being defined (implicitly if not explicitly) as the discrepancy between a target state and an actual or present state regardless of whether the topic under discussion was an entity, institution, or other system. . . .

More generally, this definition has commonly been taken to justify the identification of wants assessments with needs assessments. But children who need dental care rarely want it, patients who want laetrile rarely need it. Needs assessments are not at all the same as market surveys; both determine objective conditions, but wanting is a condition that people are by definition aware of, while in the case of needing, they may not. Thus a definition which refers to goals etc. is too bound to what people are conscious of to be satisfactory. Humans needed vitamin C long before they knew it.

As Scriven and Roth (1978) point out, the discrepancy model of needs assessment is laden with conceptual and practical weaknesses. Clearly one can recognize the need for food, safety, or education without an explicit statement of an ideal state. Yet, to determine the difference between *what is* and *what should be* requires knowledge of a target, goal, or ideal state.

In the context of identifying functional competencies "needed" by adults, this "discrepancy" formulation seems unsatisfactory. Some questions left unanswered are: (1) How is it to be determined when a person needs a particular competency, and who is to make this determination? (2) If a "want" is of sufficient intensity, does it become a "need"? (3) Can one "need" a competency without knowing it? (4) Since many "treatments" may be available to meet a particular need, how is the "best" treatment to be selected? (5) Is it not possible that needs (especially for competencies) can be met without any contrived treatment, for example, by maturation?

It seems evident that it is both possible and useful to assess the performance level of individuals on criteria that may be presumed to correspond to competencies that are *functional* to large numbers of people.

That is, it is possible to assess, with considerable rigor, *performance deficits* on a broad range of competencies on representative samples of specified populations. In fact, considerable research effort in the past few years and our own current project involve just such endeavors.

The work of Paulo Freire (1970) and of his critics (Stanley, 1972) and followers has done much to broaden our understanding of educational needs. This literature suggests that the identification and the understanding of a *need* for a competency are accomplished with greatest validity through a *dialogue*.

Dialogue is not the prescription of "higher-order" (that is, institutional or societal) needs to the individual. Yet much curriculum is obviously designed to meet the needs, not of the individual being educated, but of the society and the institutions surrounding the individual.

In authentic dialogue, a power relationship is inherent. That is, the individual has the power: (1) to disbelieve, ignore, or reject the educator's statement of a need or performance deficit; (2) to reject the educator's identification of educational "treatments"; and (3) to reject the educator's estimate of the client's context, values, and status. The educator has power associated with the possession of information on: (1) the status of performance deficits; (2) the educational treatments possible; and (3) the possible costs, side effects, availability, and immediacy of treatments.

It is possible to assess, for an individual or a group, the level of performance on one or more indicators representative of a particular competency. Determination of a *performance deficit* does not, however, establish the existence of an educational need, nor does it automatically suggest a particular educational treatment.

Assuming that a performance deficit has been determined, and that authentic dialogue has been initiated, the educator and the client (student) enter into an exchange of information. To identify a need for some educational treatment, the client must be aware of a deficit, must come to perceive the deficit as undesirable, and must think it possible to reduce the deficit. No one, however well-intentioned, can determine for individuals their educational self-interest. The educator can, however, provide the client with information regarding the available treatments corresponding to various performance deficits. The educator may also provide information about the costs, side effects, immediacy of effect, and convenience of available educational treatments. These considerations lead to a decision *by the client*: (1) to raise the performance level to one of competency, and (2) to accomplish this through the use of a particular treatment.

Only when the client has made this decision can it be said that a *need* for a particular educational treatment exists. Under these conditions, a need may be said to be both objective and subjective. That is, the assessment of performance deficits is objective, and the belief of relevance to the individual's self-interest is subjective.

Functional competency involves more than the mechanistic application of isolated skills to meet biologic needs. Functional competency implies a perception of "reality." This act of perception involves both objective (reading, computing) and subjective (belief, attitude) behavior. Individuals who are functionally competent in a particular respect do not perceive themselves to be powerless or helpless in that respect. Rather, they have the power (competency) to transform their own reality in that respect. They know themselves to be *inherently* capable of changing themselves and of contributing to changes in their own social, economic, environment, especially as they acquire specific competencies that meet authentic needs.

Functional competency makes the individual resistant to "cultural imperialism,"—that is, to the internalization of stereotypes of oneself that are "oppressive" (limiting or constraining). Such stereotypes include an "old" person, a woman, a redneck, a Chicano, an educator, a black, and a poor or lower-class person. Those who increase their functional competencies become correspondingly less "oppressed" and less "oppressive." Rather, they become more "conscious" or "literate."

This conception of functional competency does not imply a static or utopian social order. Instead, it views competency-based education as individual liberation that is irrelevant to theories of political or economic organization. Because of the uniqueness and variety of every individual, no person will ever perfectly "fit" society. The diversity of individuals and the continuously changing self and changing society preclude any final state of functional competency. Therefore, there can be no universal or final operational definition of functional competency. However, the process of striving for functional competency can be made increasingly nonoppressive and humane.

References

Freire, P. *Pedagogy of the oppressed.* New York: Seabury Press, 1970.

Scriven, M., & Roth, J. *Needs assessment.* Unpublished manuscript (available from the Evaluation Institute, University of San Francisco), February 1978.

Stanley, M. Literacy: The crisis of a conventional wisdom. In S. M. Grabowski (ed.) *Paulo Freire: a revolutionary dilemma for the adult educator.* Syracuse: Syracuse University Publications in Continuing Education, 1972, pp. 36-55.

Minimum Competency, No Competency,
or Scaled Certification?

Ellis B. Page

One can see very strong arguments on both sides of the debate about minimum competency testings (MCT). On the one hand, there is a growing despair about the granting of diplomas to students who, often enough, do not possess skills even appropriate to high school, let alone suitable for the twelfth grade. On the other hand, there is a mounting concern about the strange line which will be used for any cut-score: a line essentially arbitrary and virtually impossible to defend. I will argue that there is a third way, termed "scaled certification," which permits us to escape both of these disturbing and dangerous horns of our dilemma. But first let us examine some of the interesting and provocative data which Eckland (1978) provides elsewhere in this volume. Seldom has there been a time in education when we were more in need of good data to guide our footsteps! And we shall see just how Eckland's data, and his interpretation of them, fit into the current debate about MCT, or into any advocacy for a third alternative, such as scaled certification.

Let us extract certain summary statements made about these data. For convenience we shall number these: (1) ". . . if you are a high school graduate and white, your tested reading and computation competency has almost no effect on your employability." (2) "Table 3 shows no consistent pattern between test scores and part-time employment." (3) ". . . if a student does not go to college, what he or she scores on a basic skills competency test . . . simply does not appear to matter economically." (4) " . . . a composite measure of the NLS test scores correlates more highly with college attendance (.45) than does rank in class (.37)." (5) "It appears that the high school diploma mainly serves a credentialing function in American society, a certificate to hold a job or to go to college." (6) "It is unfortunate that the results do not come out . . . on the side of those of us who still believe in the meritocracy."

Nevertheless, I find that I am one of those who, despite Eckland's valuable data, do "still believe in the meritocracy," and also in these competency tests as showing something about important social abilities. Is there any evidence on our side?

First, consider a 1947 set of data on the men who took the Army General Classification Test, with occupations ordered by median scores on IQ tests. These are seen in figure 1, which is a classic graph (Stewart, 1947; adapted in Stanley & Hopkins, 1972, p. 351). If these occupations

IQ SCORE

CIVILIAN OCCUPATION	N	68 76 84 92 100 108 116 124 132
Accountant	216	
Teacher	360	
Lawyer	164	
Stenographer	206	
Bookkeeper	302	
Pharmacist	78	
Draftsman	139	
Clerk, general	2,063	
Radio repairman	198	
Cashier	168	
Salesman	859	
Store manager	385	
Telephone repairman	62	
File clerk	119	
Airplane mechanic	115	
Artist	82	
Photographer	70	
Musician, instrumental	161	
Toolmaker	147	
Shipping clerk	408	
Printer	192	
Stock clerk	791	
Machinist	617	
Policeman	172	
Sales clerk	2,362	
Electrician	435	
Meat cutter	691	
Sheet metal worker	462	
Welder	236	
Plumber	222	
Auto mechanic	1,693	
Bricklayer	213	
Carpenter, general	1,004	
Baker	334	
Painter, general	680	
Truck driver, heavy	3,473	
Tailor	74	
Cook	653	
Laborer	7,805	
Barber	166	
Miner	502	
Teamster	284	
Farm worker	7,475	
Lumberjack	236	
Men in general		

10th percentile   Median   90th percentile

25th percentile   75th percentile

Figure 1. Scores on the Army General Classification Test for Occupational Groups Converted to Deviation IQ Equivalents (Data from Stewart, 1947; adapted in Stanley & Hopkins, 1972)

are stripped of their scores and ranked for "status" or "prestige," we know that they will fall in a very similar order (Herrnstein, 1973). And study of the occupations suggests something more: the correlation of these test scores with *status* will be higher than with *income*. (That is, plumbers will often earn as much as teachers, but will have lower scores, and lower prestige.) Indeed, in a study by Olneck (1977), the correlation of "Test Score" with "Initial Occupation" (classified by social status) was .445, whereas it was only .359 with "Earnings." Nonetheless, Olneck's data yielded a residual correlation of test scores with earnings, after partialing out the effects of education, of .185. In at least one large study, then, it is *not* evident that scores (via education) served only a "credentialing function." Olneck's findings are more concordant with our traditional views that intelligence is valuable in the world of work, and that there will be at least *some* remuneration for that extra value.

How may we explain the apparent discordance of the NLS results reported by Eckland and the results cited above? There are a number of artifacts in the particular data set he selected, which should probably be acknowledged. In the first place, these test scores themselves were not known to anyone, and therefore could not be used in college selection. Thus, NLS scores served no "credentialing function." The math test, for example, would serve only as an indicator of some *background* ability (in math or in general aptitude and achievement); selection to college would be more related to such background ability than would employability or income. Let us greatly simplify the selection, and suppose that, in some group of high-schoolers, just the *top half* of the students (classified by true ability) went to college, and that the others looked for work. Now let us imagine the effects of this selection on the measured math score, with its inevitable errors. Such a situation is pictured in figure 2.

In figure 2, we graphically observe some phenomena which are often neglected. In the noncollege group, the strong, steep slant of the bivariate distribution of "true overall ability" and NLS math test score, expected for the total high school group, will no longer be so apparent. To the contrary, the slope of the regression line will be much smaller than that of the total group's line. Now, if we think of the economic advantage being accorded to *true* ability (and it will surely not be influenced by the secret NLS score), then we would not expect the *apparently* high-ability students in the noncollege group to do unusually well. This should not wipe out their advantage altogether, but it should lessen it to a considerable extent. In short, the high-decile noncollege test scores simply do not reflect the same true ability as in the general population, but indicate instead, something considerably lower. The net effect of this recognition is to weaken Eckland's conclusions that your competency to read or to compute

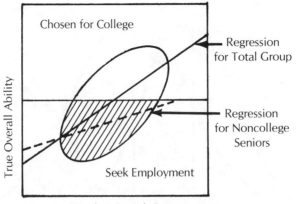

Figure 2. Why Math Scores Are Farther from True Ability among the Noncollege Sample
Here we make the simplifying assumption that the top one-half of the seniors (in true ability) are selected for college, and the others seek employment. Then we see, among the lower group, a lower regression, and a greater deviation (especially at high measured levels) from the true ability levels of the larger population.

has almost no effect on your employability and that competency simply does not particularly matter economically. It is not, after all, the true "competency" we are seeing in this group, but an artificially *elevated* estimate of it.

Similar artifacts exist for the data reported by race. The data from Eckland's table 1 show slightly more than one standard deviation difference on math and on verbal tests between the blacks and whites sampled. If we take "total overall scholastic ability" to be some composite of measures correlated with these test scores, then the comparisons of his tables 2, 3, and 4 are seen to be curiously biased. A suggestion of this bias is shown here in figure 3.

The conclusion from figure 3 is this: When Eckland "controls" for measured math decile or verbal decile in racial comparisons, he is not, in fact, adequately controlling for overall school ability (as might be measured in SATs and various achievement tests). To the extent that performance on the job would reflect overall ability, one would expect continued racial differences. (This would be easily demonstrated by

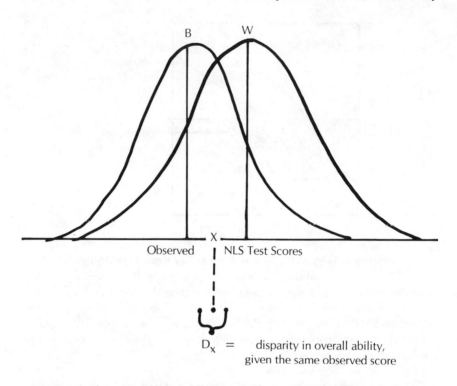

D$_x$ =   disparity in overall ability,
            given the same observed score

Figure 3. Differential Bias of Observed Test Scores
Each population regresses toward its own overall school ability. Therefore, given an observed test score X̂ on one of the NLS measures, we may predict a disparity D$_x$ on the overall ability, for any observed score X. This disparity will be greater at the extremes of the distribution than at the place shown.

looking at the regressions of verbal on math tests for the two groups, or the regressions of math on verbal tests.) The bias would be still more apparent after removing from these two groups the college-bound half of the students.

There are still other problems with the NLS data Eckland analyzes, which would make his conclusions of uncertain comparability with the findings of others. One may question whether, even five years out of high school, we have a suitable estimate of eventual earnings. Olneck's timing may be sounder, since his criterion is a year of earnings during the subjects' *maturity*, after long-range career patterns were better established. Furthermore there is more to occupational status than simply the wage earned.

And the data do not allow for certain expectable confoundings of sex. I would like to believe, then, that the NLS data do not adequately disprove a theory of at least partial meritocracy, with test score related to ultimate job status and social influence, even for those who do not continue to college. No doubt many researchers will be eager to study forthcoming data from these same NLS subjects, on their longer-range occupational accomplishments. It will be most interesting to see whether, as these become more and more notable in variation, the results, apart from schooling, will be more in line with those of Olneck and others, and more concordant with the rough occupational hierarchy shown here in figure 1.

But let us speculate with Eckland about the effects of minimum competency testing. On this point, too, his data are worth our serious consideration. From his table 1, it is obvious that any "respectable" cutoff score will result in a denial of diplomas to many more blacks than whites. It is further obvious that, if MCT scores are to have continued validity, we had better take them as they are, and not build in racial adjustments (such as Jane Mercer has frequently advocated). But when we use such cutoff scores, their net effect will be to produce an untenable political situation in which, as Eckland predicts, huge numbers of black college students like those presently enrolled would not be eligible for admission; they would never have "graduated" from high school. I don't foresee a happy future for those school districts or those states that are using MCT cutoffs, without some racial adjustments for the awarding of high school diplomas.

But consider such adjustments. If blacks are awarded high school diplomas with a lower cutoff score than that used for whites, successful legal actions by white students and their parents would surely result, under the charge of reverse discrimination. The ultimate result, in such case, would again be a short and unhappy life for the MCT program.

Or consider another plan, such as that being worked out in Connecticut, where students may be "identified" some years before their 12th grade as being below acceptable standards, and where there will be programs aimed at their remediation. For reasons apparent in our figure 3, such programs will *appear* to have greater success with whites (as measured on post-tests) than with blacks. This will lead many to believe that the programs themselves have racial bias, though much of such apparent bias will be purely a statistical artifact caused by the regression from the qualifying tests to different racial means. For such programs, too, one may predict a short and unhappy life, especially if the schools follow through with the threatened cutoff scores by refusing to award diplomas. And if they do not, then the system will continue to award "meaningless" diplomas, assuring no one of any competence, minimum or otherwise.

Scaled Certification

As argued elsewhere (Page, 1978), I believe that by far the preferred solution to the problem of MCT will come from "scaled certification." Under such a plan, conventional awarding of diplomas (certificates of attendance and program completion) to all departing seniors would be continued. On such diplomas, there would appear a profile of scores from a short test battery, together with a total score. These would be expressed in T-scores, with an interpretation in percentiles on established state or national norms. Such tests would be repeatable for students dissatisfied with their scores, in much the same way that students today repeat the SAT or ACT tests for college admission, or repeat the GRE tests for admission to graduate school. And the test scores could be summarized over time.

As a program for discussion, I would propose tests much like the current ACT, with four scores: English, math, social studies, and natural sciences. A total score might be based on a weighting according to judgment (see the work on the *bentee* in Page, 1972, 1974; and Page & Breen, 1974a, 1974b). In designing the instruments, in norming them, in controlling for security, reliability, and validity, and in retesting, I would recommend following fairly closely the very successful practices of the ACT and the College Entrance Examination Board.

If such a program were instituted, it might have some interesting bearing on the NLS data shown by Eckland. For one thing, if such a profile of scores were available to employers, there might be a much more discriminating selection of teenagers for work, and a better fit of worker to the work. Particularly, abler black graduates might be hired more often than at present, exactly because the potential employer would have increased confidence that such applicants were *not* in the bottom deciles of national ability. The point is this: The racial data from tables 2 and 3 do not reflect any employer knowledge of the test scores shown. Therefore, they probably had little basis for choosing the abler graduates, except for surface impressions, in which social class and race might play an unfairly heavy role. Good test scores might provide, in other words, some degree of "emancipation" for applicants otherwise unfairly stigmatized by race. This is a speculation which, at the least, deserves some further study.

Proper use of scaled certification, then, might help in the maintenance or reestablishment of that meritocracy which most of us, including Eckland and myself, would like to foster.

References

Herrnstein, R. J. *IQ in the meritocracy.* Boston: Little, Brown, 1973.

Olneck, M. R. On the use of sibling data to estimate the effects of family background, cognitive skills, and schooling: Results from the Kalamazoo Brothers Study. In Taubman, P. (ed.), *Kinometrics: Determinants of socioeconomic success within and between families.* Amsterdam: North-Holland, 1977, pp. 125-159.

Page, E. B. Seeking a measure of general educational advancement: The bentee. *Journal of Educational Measurement,* 1972, *9*(1), 33-43.

Page, E. B. 'Top-down' trees of educational values. *Educational and Psychological Measurement,* 1974, *34*(3), 573-584.

Page, E. B. Escaping the minimum competency dilemma: Scaled certification. *CAPT Newsletter,* May 1978, *3*(5), 6-12.

Page, E. B., & Breen, T. F. III. Educational values for measurement technology: Some theory and data. In Coffman, W. E. (ed.), *Frontiers in educational measurement and information processing.* Boston: Houghton Mifflin, 1974a, pp. 13-30.

Page, E. B., & Breen, T. F. III. Factor analysis of educational values across two methods of judgment. *Proceedings* of the XV Congreso Interamericano de Psicología, 1974b, pp. 106-107.

Stanley, J. C., & Hopkins, K. D. *Educational and psychological measurement and evaluation.* Englewood Cliffs, N.J.: Prentice-Hall, 1972.

Stewart, N. AGCT scores of Army personnel grouped by occupation. *Occupations,* 1947, *26*, 5-41.

PART III
Implications of Minimum Competency Testing for Students and Teachers

As a number of writers have commented, the current minimum competency testing movement tends to shift the responsibility for attaining competence from society at large to the individual student. A number of papers in this section examine the implications of that shift for the psychological well-being, educational development, and survival of students. But prior to that examination, classroom teachers, another group central to the process of competency testing, is the focus of a paper by Jack Bardon and Clyde Robinette entitled *Minimum Competency Testing of Pupils: Psychological Implications for Teachers*. It is ironic that earlier discussions of minimum competency testing have frequently ignored both students and teachers, despite their clear position at the "center of the action."

Bardon and Robinette state that to understand the consequences of testing pupils we need to examine what has been said about teachers, why there has been a lack of attention paid to teachers, and the mechanistic model of education underlying the reasons for this lack of attention to teachers and teaching. They point out that taking the teacher for granted, as though instruction and curriculum exist apart from their implementation through teaching, is a bit like assuming an automobile can drive without a driver. Legislation on minimum competency testing seemingly views the teacher as a means to an end, ignoring the reality of schooling and how the process of teaching and learning takes place.

On the benefit side, Bardon and Robinette suggest that teachers may experience some positive results from competency testing. The testing may enhance student motivation and direct attention to remedial efforts. Counterbalancing (or perhaps, overbalancing) these possible positive aspects, are the negative ones. These include teachers' loss of curricular freedom, economic penalties due to increased emphasis on remediation and the expense of testing itself, and decreased attention to students who are above minimum competency levels. These authors also examine unresolved issues, such as the specter of creating another category of special education. Although they conclude that minimum competency testing is here to stay, "at least for a while," they make a number of recommendations on ways its adverse effects can be minimized. They emphasize that the needs of teachers and their morale cannot be ignored as if they do not exist.

Including a major emphasis on teacher needs and morale is consonant with the emphasis in the second paper, *Minimum Competency Testing: Psychological Implications for Students*, by Theodore H. Blau. Blau found, in a review of available literature, that there is almost no reference to the student and the student's needs. In his analysis, minimum competency testing is a classic case of "blaming the victim." Under the guise of "helping" the victim, it is necessary to examine the victim carefully, scientifically, and so on, and to find a solution to the dilemma within the victim. This concentration ignores and avoids the basic social causes of the problems being addressed. Blau has examined over 2,000 school children in the past twenty-five years, many of whom were not "doing well" in school. Recently he has asked students about Florida's minimum competency testing program in one of the few studies which has examined student perceptions of minimum competency testing. Blau states that the greatest problem in working with students was to convince them that the tests could be used for them rather than against them in some way. He has much to say to those who will be working with minimum competency testing programs, and he concludes with a series of recommendations to improve current student evaluation schemes. He bases these recommendations upon a view of the student as protagonist.

The needs of a special group of students, those who are handicapped and are subject to Public Law 94-142, the Education of All Handicapped Children Act, are examined in the remaining four papers in this section. Kathleen S. Fenton, in her paper, *Competency Testing and the Handicapped: Some Legal Concerns for School Administrators*, draws attention to the individualized education program (IEP) which is required for each handicapped child under Public Law 94-142. Administrators will have to be concerned with the extent to which IEP goals reflect the regular education program, and with the relationship between the IEP and the child's eligibility or preparation for any minimum competency testing program. Due process, under Public Law 94-142, requires notice of pending action, informed consent, opportunity for resolution of conflicts through informal means, and the right to formal appeal in an impartial hearing. When test results are used to certify individuals for graduation, administrators and legislators need to be aware of these legal requirements for the education of handicapped children.

Similar issues are explored in more depth in the paper by Mary M. Kennedy, *Test Scores and Individual Rights.* Kennedy examines three issues: the first is whether education is a right of the individual, to be exercised at her or his discretion, or whether society is responsible for assuring individual accomplishments; if society is responsible, the second issue is what competencies could be universally required; and the third, the issue of the extent to which society can reasonably assume responsibility for assuring that all individuals acquire these competencies. The special case of the handicapped student brings forcefully into view the problem of defining minimum competencies and the different contexts within which individuals function after schooling.

Louis C. Danielson, in his paper, *Educational Goals and Competency Testing for the Handicapped,* explores the diversity of environments in which minimum competencies may be required. A retarded adult's survival in a halfway house may be an appropriate level of functional competence for that person. Competency testers need to demonstrate a relationship between test performance and post-school functioning. The needs of handicapped children and adults have been largely ignored to date in the definition of minimum competency testing programs. Patricia A. Morrissey, in her paper, *Adaptive Testing: How and When Should Handicapped Students be Accommodated in Competency Testing Programs?* does begin a discussion of possible areas of accommodation and suggests tentative guidelines for accommodation. Her paper will be valuable to those who are concerned with developing and administering minimum competency testing programs, especially where there is an attempt to work with the handicapped.

In Part IV, a number of case studies of minimum competency testing programs are presented. Although the writers in Part III have tried to draw our attention and concern to the major participants in minimum competency testing programs, it is of interest to note that the case descriptions in Part IV by and large are not concerned with teachers and students, and they particularly ignore special groups of students.

7 Minimum Competency Testing of Pupils: Psychological Implications for Teachers

Jack I. Bardon
Clyde L. Robinette

Introduction

The available literature on minimum competency testing of pupils is notable for what it does not say about teachers. Teachers appear to be shadow figures in all the hoopla, diatribe, genuine concern, and enthusiasm generated by this new national educational pastime. We could identify no single source in the literature on minimum competency testing that centers its attention on teachers or teaching. To understand the psychological consequences on teachers of testing pupils, we need to examine what little has been said about teachers, why there has been a lack of attention paid to teachers, and the mechanistic model of education underlying the reasons.

When reference has been made to teachers or to teaching, it has tended most often to be negative. Minimum competency testing of pupils has been cited, for example, as a means to persuade those teachers to do better who fail to teach basic skills or who are unproductive in other ways (Reilly, 1978; Wise, 1978). The problems lower-grade teachers create for teachers in the higher grades when they fail to teach basic skills have been mentioned (National Academy of Education, 1978). Some believe that teachers and other educators, left to their own devices, will simply try to protect themselves and will do little about improving pupil competency (Hentoff, 1978). And, it has been said that teachers resent the minimum competency testing movement because they want people to believe that students cannot learn, as justification for their poor teaching (Clark, 1978).

In all fairness, some comments were found that could be construed to be mildly positive toward teachers, indicating awareness that teachers are not entirely to blame for pupil failure to learn. When new demands are made on teachers, it has been said that more training and professional development should be provided (National Academy of Education, 1978). Time to prepare has been pointed out as desirable, so that teachers can learn to teach somewhat differently to reflect new course objectives (McClung, 1978). The importance of adding instructional resources to get the job done has been duly noted (Chall, 1978).

How does it happen that such a curious lack of attention to teachers should occur? Taking the teacher for granted, as though instruction and curriculum exist apart from their implementation through teaching, is like assuming an automobile can drive without a driver. Furthermore, believing that training or professional development per se will make the teacher teach better is also naive, as inservice education is also teaching, and the nature of its activities and how it is provided are critical to the success of its offerings and intentions (Hauserman, 1978).

Much of the rhetoric associated with minimum competency testing appears to be punitive toward teachers who have not taught well and toward pupils who have not learned. We believe that teachers have been both implicated and ignored partly because those outside the public schools who have promoted minimum competency testing do not trust teachers or their judgment (National Academy of Education, 1978) and see the movement as a way of forcing teachers to do what they will not do on their own. Teachers are to be made to teach. It is assumed that they can if only they will try. The reform movement was not created by educators, but rather was an attempt on a broad front to force teachers to be better teachers—to change by mandate what did not occur in the ordinary course of events (Chall, 1978; Pipho, 1978).

Pupils who have not learned include at least two varieties: those who will not learn and those who have not been taught properly. Teachers, while not often mentioned directly, are by implication treated as one of the central causes and contributors to both these pupil conditions.

For many persons the minimum competency testing movement is an emotional one, based on deep convictions about the nature of teaching, or based on frustration with the educational system for not guarding against incompetency in its graduates. For the lay public, the institution of education tends, often, to be made more personal by interpreting "education" as "teacher." In other words, the teachers' culpability and responsibility to do better are so deeply ingrained in the logic and "psychologic" of the reform movement, that those who write or speak about reform feel no necessity to point out the obvious.

For those educators, other professionals, and technical specialists with special concerns in carrying out the legislative mandates on competency testing, the teacher is not often central. Some are deeply involved in the many problems of measurement. Others are analyzing the broad and far-reaching implications of the movement for social and educational policy.

In so far as we have been able to identify a model in the existing literature, the model for minimum competency testing is primarily a mechanistic one; a form of input-output production. Tests are devised. They are administered. Those who fail are forewarned. Better teaching and remediation may be demanded. Retesting is done. Ultimately, the pupil passes or fails. The burden of failure is on the student in some instances, or on the teacher in others, or maybe both. When it is on the pupil, it is a form of "blaming the victim" (American Friends Service Committee, 1978). When it is on the teacher, it is a form of blaming the machinery. The model seemingly views the teacher as a manipulable mechanical device that can be repaired if need be, as a means to an end. But it ignores the reality of schooling and minimizes how, in fact, teaching and learning take place (Good, Biddle & Brophy, 1975; Good & Brophy, 1973; Jackson, 1968). We need next to inquire about the responses of teachers to the minimum competency movement to date.

Teacher Reactions

States vary so greatly in their approaches to minimum competency testing that generalities about teacher reactions and the effects of programs on teachers are difficult to make (Pipho, 1978). Competency standards offer potential benefits to teachers, and they present problems. The extent to which teachers will be glad the movement has happened or sorry they ever heard of it will depend on a number of factors. These include: the particular approach taken in their respective states; pupil results and public reaction to these results, especially after the programs have been in effect for a reasonable period of time; and the extent to which legislation and the public offer support to the schools for programs, with support translated to mean some form of material assistance as well as other indications that teachers' morale, esteem, and psychological well-being are receiving consideration.

Surprisingly little reaction from teachers to the competency testing movement has been forthcoming, at least formally, through writing and public pronouncement. It is suspected that teachers have not engaged the issue because: (1) competency testing has happened already in their states, and they have survived (Educational Testing Service, 1978); (2) it has not yet happened in their states, and they are unsure of specifics and of how competency testing will impinge on their teaching; (3) they do not see themselves as the bad teachers who will be implicated; (4) in their collective wisdom, they assume that what Seymour Sarason has reminded us—that the more things seem to change the more they really stay the same—holds for minimum competency testing also (Sarason, 1971); that is, if nothing is done, nothing much will happen; (5) they are still caught up in the implementation of P.L. 94-142, The Education of the Handicapped Act (Public Law 94-142, 1977), and are too busy figuring out what that law means for them to worry too much about the next educational reform.

What little could be located in the literature about teacher reaction suggests that competency testing is threatening to some because it adds to their already poor image (Utz et al., 1974). Some others are concerned because it may create additional work without relief from assignments already undertaken (Thompson, 1974; Wood, 1978). High school teachers are concerned that they were not trained to teach basic subjects (Huff, 1977). Some teachers view competency testing as a back door to a state or nationally imposed curriculum or as a step toward evaluation of teachers (National Education Association, 1978).

So far, we have tried to make the case that the teacher is important to the success of minimum competency testing programs, but that the teacher has been viewed as an intervening variable in an "input-through-put-output" mechanical model. Any serious attempt to ensure levels of minimum competency that are acceptable to the public as worthy of a high school diploma requires attention to teacher attitudes, behaviors, rewards, and expectations. If minimum competency comes to mean minimal—so much so that the public regards it as inadequate—the teacher will not matter, nor will the movement. All will recognize that nothing has changed in public education. But if standards are set high enough so that many pupils must strive to reach the minimum level, and if the competencies involved are both basic and intricate, clearly requiring exposure to instruction and instructional support, teachers will matter—matter more in fact, than anything else. It is important, therefore, to define what some of the positive and negative aspects of minimum competency testing may be for teachers, in order to identify unresolved issues and to make useful recommendations about teachers' involvement with minimum competency testing of pupils.

Positive Aspects of Minimum Competency Testing for Teachers

For teachers, one possible positive consequence of minimum competency testing may be that some of the stress they experience because of pressures beyond their control will be alleviated. Relief of stress could occur in several ways.

There is evidence to suggest that anticipation of an event may be more stress-producing (anxiety-producing) than the event itself; that is, that there is a disposition to be anxious—to respond strongly to critical cues of threat (Keavney & Sinclair, 1978; Kourilsky, McNeil & Flannigan, 1974; Phillips, 1968). Although there undoubtedly are some disgruntled teachers in those systems and states that have already adopted competency testing, no discernible, let alone major teacher upheaval, is yet apparent in systems such as Denver, which has been administering competency measures for about 16 years, or in Omaha's Westside Community School District, which has been long enough in the business to have graduated at least two competency-based senior classes (Educational Testing Service, 1978).

So far, much of the concern about competency testing has taken place prior to the time it has been put into operation. The same phenomenon, with notable exceptions, of more stress during anticipation than during occurrence and operation, may be seen in communities in which school busing or mainstreaming of special education pupils have been mandated. The early reactions to proposals for accountability in the public schools also followed this pattern (Cooper, 1972; Pratte, 1972). This paper itself is an example of anticipated concern for the effects of the competency testing movement on teachers. The consideration of possible consequences, in the absence of firm data about actual consequences, arouses thoughtful concern in some and anxiety in others. Within several years, many of the issues raised at the conference on which this publication is based will not be issues at all. Reality is sometimes a salutary substitute for anticipation, even when reality is not all pleasant. At least one knows with what one is dealing.

Tension, stress, anxiety, or whatever it is called, may also be reduced when one perceives that a situation is under control and that the rules and consequences of behavior are clearly understood. Seligman's (1975) concept of learned helplessness suggests what may happen if one cannot control external stimuli at all, and the work of Janis and Mann (1976) on conflict, choice, and commitment supports the conclusion that people suffer when they cannot control their own behavior. For example, teachers did not create the system that has come to be known as social promotion or automatic promotion, but it greatly influences what happens in their classrooms. In our experience, when teachers are able to participate in individual decisions about which pupils should move ahead or stay back in grade (when pupil achievement is below expected level), the issue of social promotion is hardly an issue at all, at least for the teachers. When teachers have no choice in the matter but must accept pupils or pass along pupils who are not ready, in their opinion, for higher-level work, many teachers experience loss of control and diminished enthusiasm for teaching. As Gary Hart (1978), the educator-legislator responsible for drafting California's pupil proficiency law commented, "I have found that without standards and the accountability provided by a sanction students become contemptuous, teachers become demoralized, and schools increasingly lose credibility with taxpayers" (p. 594). It is possible that when competency testing is clearly related to classroom objectives and goals and when the relationship between the two are understood by teachers, pupils, and parents, realistic expectations about pupil performance can be established for individual pupils, thereby eliminating at least one source of pressure currently experienced by teachers (Fremer, 1978; Good & Brophy, 1973).

There are still other ways in which teachers may benefit from competency testing. Such testing may arouse student motivation or increase efforts to learn in order to receive a diploma, even if only to learn the minimal amount necessary to pass the tests. If so, some teachers with some children will have solved critical classroom problems, those of identifying and having available reinforcers that will serve to keep pupils manageable and attentive in the classroom. The problems of management and of sustaining the attention of some borderline pupils—those who have little interest in school and little respect for adult authority—is a serious matter to many teachers, especially in junior and senior high schools. It has been anticipated by some (American Friends Service Committee, 1978; Gentry, 1976) that competency testing will lead to increased pupil responsibility for learning. It is at least conceivable that more pupils will find reasons, not now present, to better use their time in school, thereby improving the lot of the teacher who is overburdened with pupils who heretofore have resisted involvement in their own education.

There has been criticism that competency testing can too easily lead to teaching "to the test" or "beating the test" (National Academy of Education, 1978; Reilly, 1978). However, for those who have been graduating from high school without basic knowledge or skills, whatever the various states may determine them to be, is teaching to the test really so bad? Within a competency-based educational approach, if one considers the test to be a measure of expected outcomes and behavioral objectives built into a curriculum concerned with life skills (Spady & Mitchell, 1977), it is appropriate to teach to the test. Should a student fail a test but pass it later, after further instruction, the testing program can provide a feedback or self-monitoring mechanism that has in other contexts been shown to be useful (Nelson, 1977). For these purposes, teaching "to the test" has potential for becoming a useful way to improve learning effectiveness. The teacher can be one of the beneficiaries if pupil improvement is perceived partly as an indication of teacher effectiveness as well as pupil outcome.

There are two other indirect benefits that may accrue to teachers from the minimum competency movement. The growing recognition that competency testing requires explicit attention to remedial efforts (Good & Brophy, 1973; Keefe & Georgiades, 1978; Pipho, 1978) improves the chances that remedial teaching positions will be created in the schools. In these days of diminishing school enrollments and lack of opportunity for teacher employment, any possibility of new positions is a welcome one.

Finally, proponents of competency testing have argued (Teaching Fads, 1978) that improved standards in the public schools may bring the schools in line with the public mood, as demonstrated by the greater prestige and significance given to the high school diploma. Teachers can only benefit if their activities are viewed more positively by the general public.

Negative Aspects of Minimum Competency Testing for Teachers

Unfortunately, the optimistic view of the effects of minimum competency testing must be counterbalanced by consideration of the harm the movement can do to teachers and to teaching. Any optimism is predicated on the assumptions that criterion scores that make educational sense can be established; and that competency testing will not be abused through gross misunderstanding, used for unrelated purposes, or for unwanted social and political side effects. The Committee on Testing and Basic Skills of the National Academy of Education in its report to the United States Assistant Secretary for Education (1978) was not optimistic about the future of competency testing. Nor are some of the national leaders in educational measurement (Glass, 1978; Jaeger, 1978), although others are more sanguine (Fremer, 1978).

The critical problems are the arbitrariness of any cutoff scores used to determine what constitutes minimum competency; the relationship of the subject matter of the tests to what is taught in schools; and the possibility that the use of standardized paper-and-pencil tests may be inimical to the life-skill competencies some states are attempting to measure (Nathan & Jennings, 1978).

All three of these problems affect teachers. If, in fact, test content and cutoff scores are arbitrary and educationally meaningless, there is a danger that their use will move teachers further in the direction of becoming educational bureaucrats, in the dictionary meaning of the term: "An official who follows and insists on an inflexible routine, proper forms, and rules" (*Webster's*, 1966, p. 194). When tests that are pseudostandards become the focus of teaching; when teachers are held accountable for teaching content that pupils can use to pass such tests; and when some or much of the content of the tests is not related to other aspects of the curriculum or must substitute for already existing parts of course content, then the tendency is increased for teachers to become persons who "sign-off" their pupils or carry out busywork. With much of the school curriculum already determined by legislation reflecting community values and variable public pressures, teaching tends to become cluttered and busy. Less and less time is being spent on more and more. From a teacher's point of view, the personal danger—translated into a serious educational problem for pupils—is that loss of curricular freedom reinforces the tendency for teaching to be less a profession and more a craft; that is, the carrying out of assigned tasks created by others in a routine and prescribed manner (Harris, 1975). Minimum competency testing will not create these conditions; they already exist. But it could further the demise of teaching as both a profession and an art.

If one accepts the pessimistic predictions about the benefits of minimum competency testing, teachers may be in a most awkward and difficult position. Should the movement fail and further public disillusionment occur, it can be predicted that teachers, perhaps more than others, will be held accountable for its failure, despite our lack of clear understanding of the relationship between teacher behavior and pupil achievement (Good & Brophy, 1973; Witkin, 1973) and despite our lack of precise understanding of how much of the variance in pupil achievement can be attributed to socioeconomic status, home conditions, or schooling (Shea, 1976). It would be tragic if the reputations of the vast majority of teachers, who are adequate to excellent teachers, are further tainted when, in truth, they are being used in large part as tools to carry out a policy created by public demand, legislated by state law, developed by measurement specialists, and administered by state departments of education and local educational administrators.

It may seem odd that we are arguing that failure of the competency testing movement, should it happen, cannot be attributed to any great extent to teachers, yet its success, should it prove to be seen as successful, should be attributed in significant measure to teacher behavior. Should the system fail, it will have failed before it reaches the classroom. The impact of regulations, test content, cutoff scores, procedures, funding, and nonschool variables, among other factors, will greatly influence the success of this system. Yet if the competency testing movement succeeds, it will do so because it will have become dependent on how it is carried out in the classroom (Thompson, 1974).

Another related factor that may result in negative consequences for teachers is an economic one. Minimum competency testing is expensive. It will increase the bill for public education (Anderson, 1975; Keefe & Georgiades, 1978; Wood, 1978). If it is to be done properly, teachers will need additional human resources and educational materials. It is immoral, if not illegal, for state legislatures to pass laws that require funding and then fail to appropriate sufficient funds to carry out the laws (Bennett & Bardon, 1975; National Center for Law and the Handicapped, 1978). If competency testing results in a heavier workload for teachers and increased pressure to produce, without additional support, we can expect negative reaction from teachers and increased militancy about teacher rights, roles, responsibilities, and salaries.

It is also a fallacy to think that minimum competency testing will somehow inspire poor teachers to be better ones. We know of no evidence to support the supposition that poor teaching is improved by the imposition of external standards. Perhaps sloppy or uninspired teachers will be more careful to mind their manners, but it is our belief that poor teachers—harmful teachers—are best eliminated by training programs, by careful recruitment, and by promotion and retention policies. Cosmetic changes are not necessarily real changes. No matter what else happens, it is our strongly held view that poor teachers will remain poor teachers.

Still another potential problem is the converse of what was stated previously about the positive aspects of teaching "to the test." Concentrating as we are on those pupils who do not meet some standard of minimum competence, we may sometimes forget that most pupils not only meet such standards but exceed them. The problem of minimum becoming maximum is a serious one (Keefe & Georgiades, 1978; National Academy of Education, 1978; Reilly, 1978). Some teachers under pressure to teach "to the test" may be inclined to pay less attention to those who can benefit from still higher standards.

Finally, we have already seen that the pupil competency testing movement is leading to the teacher competency testing movement (Pipho, 1978). The evaluation of teaching competency will likely include evaluation of pupil performance as one measure of teaching effectiveness (McClung, 1978; New Jersey State Department of Education, 1978). Unless pupil rate of learning, background factors influencing pupil performance, sex, community standards and conditions, and the host of other factors that may influence pupil learning (besides teacher performance) are

considered, we will have included a criterion in judging teacher performance that is at least as arbitrary as some say are the cutoff scores in pupil
competency testing. What evidence we have suggests that teacher effectiveness and student performance do not interact in a systematic way
(Good & Beckerman, 1978). What is good teaching for one student may
be poor teaching for another (Hunt, 1975; Witkin, 1973). Consistency in
teaching is still another variable. Most teachers are not consistently effective or ineffective even with pupils of similar attributes and attitudes
(Sherman et al., 1976). Arbitrary inclusion of pupil performance in the
evaluation of teachers is not likely to induce many teachers to be better
teachers.

Unresolved Issues

It is sad but true that the public, legislators, and many educators have
come to regard minimum competency testing in simple cause-and-effect
terms. You pass or you do not pass. If you do poorly at first, remedial
help will solve the problem. If you do not pass, it is either willful or the
result of poor teaching. If teachers know they will be held accountable,
they will "shape up." Perhaps it shall never be possible to convince those
who hold such clear views about what is correct and who is responsible,
that schooling does not work the way they think it does. As Arthur Wise
(1978) has pointed out, the theory of education underlying the development of minimum competency policy makes assumptions about child,
teacher, and learning that may not be warranted by our current state of
knowledge. Children are not infinitely pliable. We do not know why some
children fail to learn, and we do not know how to teach all children. We
are by no means certain what a good teacher is, except that the multiple
variables that determine even so direct a definition of teaching as the
production of academic results is extraordinarily complex and interactive
(Hunt, 1975; Good, Biddle & Brophy, 1975).

Moreover, teachers do not respond to legislation and orders to do better
by becoming better teachers. There is some evidence to suggest that
mandates to action may well produce increased defensiveness and en-
trenchment of formerly held positions (Fillos, 1978). The conditions for
the development of what has been termed "evaluation resistance" are
similar to the ways that teachers have been treated so far in many programs of minimum competency testing (Fillos, 1978). Loss of freedom or
threat of its loss often leads to valuing even more that which is threatened,
as psychological reactance theory and research indicate (Brehm, 1966).
When teachers believe they are losing organizational control of their own
classrooms; believe they are taken for granted when their pupils succeed

but punished when their pupils fail; and believe they are under pressure to produce but are not offered material, personnel, and moral support to get the job done—then we have no reason to expect improved teaching, much less adequate teaching.

As we well know, innovation in education has a way of being absorbed by the system so that changes appear to take place for awhile; yet nothing much happens (Rand Corporation, 1978; Sarason, 1971; Wood, 1978). Some of the signs of this "easy way out" have begun to appear. Commercial kits designed to teach the test appear to be in demand (Student aid, 1978). For high school teachers unfamiliar with basic skills (Taylor, 1978) the use of ready-made materials about which one does not have to think is attractive. But they do not address the problem of low achievement levels in schools. They help teachers get through the problem without dealing with it by offering them easy-to-use packaged programs that provide substitutes for teacher time, attention, concern, and involvement in the problems faced by low-achieving pupils.

We may begin to see some changes in grading practices as teachers at all grade levels at which competency testing is used receive feedback of pupil results. It is to be expected that teachers will seek congruence between test scores and classroom grades. Where effort and ability have been used as bases for grading, especially in the lower grades, as ways to reflect different aspects of classroom performance, these may give way to academic performance only. But attribution theory and research suggest that emphasis on effort and ability as promoters of success and emphasis on lack of effort as cause for failure may stimulate the academic performance of pupils (Bar-Tal, 1978). Grades have served many purposes, among which has been reporting on academic competence. We have not struggled all these years to develop multipurpose grading systems without cause. The use of academic performance on tests as the sole basis for grading may thus prove to be less helpful than it would seem.

Another issue to be faced is the specter of creating another category of special education. As special needs of children were identified and as laws provided funding to help meet educational needs, categorization proliferated (Reynolds & Birch, 1977). It is conceivable that pupils who fail competency tests will be separated out for special educational programming, as a convenient way to solve problems of spreading individual differences and instructional time in regular classes and as a way to concentrate teaching efforts on the specific tasks at hand. Let us remember that Public Law 94-142 was a reaction to the abuses of labeling and segregation, among other things, in the public schools. If teachers are told they can get rid of problem children by sending them to remedial classes—special classes—they will do so. However, if they know that they must continue to work with these children but have resources available, many of the stigmata until recently associated with special education may be avoided in remedial programs for failing or borderline pupils.

Conclusions and Recommendations

Minimum competency testing is here to stay, at least for a while. We have pointed out that it holds prospects of positive change for teachers, that it has negative aspects, and that it raises issues and problems that are unresolved. In fact, it is hardly a unitary educational practice or concept. It is an idea implemented idiosyncratically in the various states. It is intended to help correct a problem of standards that badly needs correcting. It is also a superficial approach to the improvement of teaching and of pupil learning, but it is a popular approach and its failure at this point will help no one. So, all should be done to make it work.

Teachers, we have said, are absolutely critical elements in its operation. Unless teacher reactions and needs are considered, minimum competency testing cannot accomplish its intended purposes. Therefore, we propose a number of not-very-startling recommendations in the hope that someone somewhere will pay attention to them. We applaud those states that have already given serious consideration to at least some of these recommendations in framing competency testing programs.

McClung (1978) has made suggestions to help states and schools avoid legal problems associated with competency programs. Interestingly enough, most of his good suggestions are among those we also want to make to help ensure that teachers can assist with the upgrading of standards in the schools and can teach those whose levels of competency can be raised. The recommendations we make are also in keeping with the spirit, if not the precise points, of the National Education Association Resolution 78-54 on Mandated Standards for Educational Programs (National Education Association, 1978).

First, develop competency objectives that are obtainable through regular instruction without massive overhaul of educational programs in the schools.

Second, insist on continuity between instruction and assessment objectives. Teachers must know what is expected of them.

Third, permit time for the reorganization of the curriculum. Do not ask teachers suddenly to change instructional approaches or add new material without time and thought given to how that can best be done.

Fourth, supply schools with materials, additional staff, and time during the school day or on some other acceptable basis to think through the planning of how competency objectives can best be achieved and how program changes and responsibilities can best be managed.

Fifth, perhaps most important of all, do not ignore teacher needs and morale as though they do not exist. Teacher involvement in creating the educational program to match competency requirements is essential. We do not mean superficial involvement, such as informing by bulletins and memos. We mean involvement in those decisions that determine how teachers will actually teach in their classrooms. At this time we know enough, from so many sources and areas of endeavor, about the importance of involvement for motivation, morale and the implementation of change, that it should not be necessary to mention this; but it is necessary.

More general recommendations may also be in order:

Sixth, follow the principles of parsimony and gradualness, if at all possible (Nance, 1977; Popham, 1978). The more complex, overpowering, different, and refined the system, the less likely it is to be used. Television has been accepted in the classroom when other educational innovations have not—perhaps because it is already known to teacher and pupil, requires only the click of a button, and offers the teacher a tool to use rather than another problem to solve. If multiple copies of forms, long computer printouts, difficult-to-interpret results, and elaborate reporting systems become part of the way minimum competency testing feedback and remediation efforts work, we predict the system will collapse under its own weight.

Seventh, do not be satisfied with single-system or token solutions to inservice education of teachers. For instance, feedback to teachers about pupil results is not sufficient to affect teacher behavior very much, even when the teacher is able to make changes. Neither is didactic instruction in measurement theory and terminology. Nor is inservice training on rules and regulations, the law, and teacher responsibility. Niedermeyer's (1977) study of the factors influencing the outcome of an inservice training program on teacher supervision is instructive in that it tells us that feedback or instructional strategies alone are not as efficient as the combination.

Eighth, to whatever extent possible, review and revise the use of teacher time in schools. As has been pointed out elsewhere, an inordinate amount of teacher time is spent in activities others can handle as well if not better (Goodlad & Klein, 1974).

Ninth, be clear about who is responsible for what. In the report *Improving Educational Achievement*, the National Academy of Education Committee on Testing and Basic Skills (1978) stated that, "The school district, or preferably, the school should be held responsible for what and how well students learn. It is that administrative level which should be held responsible for producing changes in educational achievement. It is important to hold responsible those who actually have the power to do something" (p. 19). Therefore, the teacher should be held responsible for that which the teacher can control; not that which the state, school board, or school administration has mandated regardless of its efficacy in the classroom. Teachers who are told what they are to teach, what results are to be achieved, and how they are to teach are hardly free agents in the teaching-learning interaction. The tighter the constraints, the less we can hold teachers responsible for results.

Minimum competency testing is policy. It involves broad and far-reaching views of what education should be. It involves technology and administration. But ultimately, minimum competency testing imposes conditions of learning on pupils and psychological burdens on teachers who must do something about all this in the classroom. This paper has tried to indicate at least some of the psychological implications of the competency movement for teachers and to point toward ways of increasing the chances that the movement will not become another passing innovation that adds to the public cynicism about the effectiveness of American public education.

References

American Friends Service Committee. *A citizen's introduction to minimum competency programs for students*. Columbia, S.C.: Author, April 1978.
American Personnel and Guidance Association. Teaching fads denounced. *Guideposts*, 13 July 1978, p. 7.
Anderson, E. N. Coping with Oregon's new competency-based graduation requirements: View from a practitioner. American Educational Research Association, 1975. (ERIC Document Reproduction Service no. ED 105 594).
Bar-Tal, D. Attributional analysis of achievement-related behavior. *Review of Educational Research* 48 (1978): 259-271.
Bennett, V. C., & Bardon, J. I. Law, professional practice and professional organizations: Where do we go from here? *Journal of School Psychology* 13 (1975): 97-104.
Brehm, J. W. *A theory of psychological reactance*. New York: Academic Press, 1966.
Chall, J. Minimum competency testing. *Harvard Graduate School of Education Bulletin* 22 (1978): 9-11.
Clark, K. Transcript of *Minimum competence: Part one: Program no. 123, options in education*. National Public Radio, 5 June 1978. 2025 M Street NW, Washington, D.C. 20036.
Cooper, L. G. Decision ability, not accountability. *Journal of Higher Education* 43 (1972): 655-660.
Educational Testing Service. Report of programs, in *Education Recaps* 17 (1978): 8.
Fillos, R. M. Evaluation resistance in elementary school teachers: A construct validation and description of the meaning of standardized achievement testing.

Paper presented at the meeting of the American Educational Research Association, Toronto, Canada, May 1978.

Fremer, J. In response to Gene Glass. *Phi Delta Kappan* 59 (1978): 605-606, 625.

Gentry, C. G. Will the real advantage of CBE please stand up? *Educational Technology* 16 (1976): 13-15.

Glass, G. V. Minimum competence and incompetence in Florida. *Phi Delta Kappan* 59 (1978): 602-605.

Good, T. L., & Beckerman, T. M. An examination of teachers' effects on high, middle, and low aptitude students' performance on a standardized achievement test. *American Educational Research Journal* 15 (1978): 477-482.

Good, T. L., Biddle, B. & Brophy, J. *Teachers make a difference*. New York: Holt, Rinehart & Winston, 1975.

Good, T. L., & Brophy, J. C. *Looking in classrooms*. New York: Harper & Row, 1973.

Goodlad, J. I., & Klein, M. F. *Looking behind the classroom door*. Belmont, Calif.: C. A. Jones, 1974.

Harris, B. H. Professionalism regained? *Educational Leadership* 33 (1975): 143-145.

Hart, G. K. The California pupil proficiency law as viewed by its author. *Phi Delta Kappan* 59 (1978): 592-595.

Hauserman, B. D. Power bases in inservice teacher education. In *Inservice*. Syracuse: National Council of States on Inservice Education, July 1978, pp. 6-11.

Hentoff, N. Transcript of *Minimum competence: Part one: Program no. 123, options in education*. National Public Radio, 5 June 1978. 2025 M Street NW, Washington, D.C. 20036.

Huff, M. A board member looks at requiring competencies for graduation. *Educational Leadership* 35 (1977): 108-113.

Hunt, D. E. Person-environment interaction: A challenge found wanting before it was tried. *Review of Educational Research* 45 (1975): 209-230.

Jackson, P. W. *Life in classrooms*. New York: Holt, Rinehart & Winston, 1968.

Jaeger, R. M. A proposal for setting a standard on the North Carolina High School Competency Test. Paper presented at the 1978 spring meeting of the North Carolina Association for Research in Education, Chapel Hill, April 1978.

Janis, I. L., & Mann, L. Coping with decisional conflict. *American Scientist* 64 (1976): 657-667.

Keavney, G., & Sinclair, K. E. Teacher concerns and teacher anxiety: A neglected topic of classroom research. *Review of Educational Research* 48 (1978): 273-290.

Keefe, J. W., & Georgiades, C. J. Competency-based education and the high school diploma. *NASSP Bulletin* 62 (1978): 94-108.

Kourilsky, M., McNeil, J., & Flannigan, G. Teacher evaluation by results: Its psychological effect on pupils. *Phi Delta Kappan* 55 (1974): 348-349.

McClung, M. S. Are competency testing programs fair? Legal? *Phi Delta Kappan* 59 (1978): 397-400.

McClung, M. S. Transcript of *Minimum competence: Part two: Program no. 124, options in education*. National Public Radio, 12 June 1978. 2025 M Street NW, Washington, D.C. 20036.

Nance, W. R. How fares competency development in Oregon? *Educational Leadership* 35 (1977): 102-107.

Nathan, J., & Jennings, W. Educational bait-and-switch. *Phi Delta Kappan* 59 (1978): 621-625.

National Academy of Education. *Improving educational achievement.* Report of the National Academy of Educational Committee on Testing and Basic Skills to the Assistant Secretary for Education, Washington, D.C., 23 February 1978.

National Center for Law and the Handicapped. State laws on special education may guide implementation of P.L. 94-142. *Amicus* 3, no. 4 (1978): 11-12.

National Education Association. Impact of minimum competency testing in Florida. *Today's Education* 67, no. 3 (1978): 30-36.

Nelson, R. Assessment and therapeutic functions of self-monitoring. In Herson, M., Eisler, R., & Miller, P. (eds.). *Progress in behavior modification,* vol. 5, pp. 263-308. New York: Academic Press, 1977.

New Jersey State Department of Education. Evaluation code remains unchanged. *Interact* 5, no. 2 (1978): 1.

Niedermeyer, F. C. The testing of a prototype system for outcome-based institutional supervision. *Educational Administration Quarterly* 13 (1977): 34-50.

Phillips, B. N. The nature of school anxiety and its relationship to children's school behavior. *Psychology in the Schools* 5 (1968): 195-204.

Pipho, C. Minimum competency testing in 1978: A look at state standards. *Phi Delta Kappan* 59 (1978): 585-588.

Popham, W. J. A competency-based high school completion program. *NASSP Bulletin* 62 (1978): 101-105.

Pratte, R. An uneasy inquiry into accountability. *Intellect* 101 (1972): 37-40.

Public Law 94-142, Part B. *Federal Register.* 23 August 1977.

Rand Corporation. *Federal programs supporting educational change, vol. 8: Implementing and sustaining innovations* (R-158918 HEW). Santa Monica, Calif.: Rand Corporation, 1978.

Reilly, W. Who benefits? Competency testing. *Compact* 12 (1978): 7.

Reynolds, M. C., & Birch, J. W. *Teaching exceptional children in all America's schools.* Reston, Va.: The Council for Exceptional Children, 1977.

Sarason, S. B. *The culture of the school and the problem of change.* Boston: Allyn & Bacon, 1971.

Seligman, M. E. P. *Helplessness.* San Francisco: W. H. Freeman & Co., 1975.

Shea, B. M. Schooling and its antecedents: Substantive and methodological issues in the status attainment process. *Review of Educational Research* 46 (1976): 463-526.

Sherman, G. J., Brophy, J. E., Evertson, C. M., & Crawford, W. J. Traditional attitudes and teacher consistency in producing student learning gains in the early elementary grades. *Journal of School Psychology* 14 (1976): 192-201.

Spady, W. G., & Mitchell, D. Competency based education: Organizational issues and implications. *Educational Researcher* 6 (1977): 9-15.

Student aid? *The Greensboro Record* (N.C.). 19 August 1978.

Taylor, R. The question of minimum competency as viewed from the schools. *The Mathematics Teacher* 71 (1978): 88-93.

Thompson, S. Competency-based education: Theory and practice. 1974 (ERIC Document Reproduction Service no. ED 149 413).

Utz, R. T., Leonard, L. D., Mertz, D. C., Baker, R. E., Johnene, S. M., & Nussel, E. J. A comparative analysis of two modes of implementing a competency based instructional system. Chicago: American Educational Research Association, 1974. (ERIC Document Reproduction Service no. ED 089 468).

Webster's new world dictionary of the American language, college edition. Cleveland: World Book Publishing Co., 1966.

Wise, A. E. Minimum competency testing: Another case of hyperrationalization. *Phi Delta Kappan* 59 (1978): 596-598.

Witkin, H. A. *The role of cognitive style in academic performance and in teacher-student relations.* Princeton, N.J.: Educational Testing Service Research Bulletin, February 1973.

Wood, D. F. Can we require students to learn? *The Mathematics Teacher* 71 (1978): 135-139.

8   Minimum Competency Testing: Psychological Implications for Students

Theodore H. Blau

Introduction

In the available literature concerning minimum competency testing there are rare references to the student (Buros, 1977; Competency test rapped, 1978; Ryan, 1971; Society for the Psychology Study of Social Issues, 1964; Student apathy, 1978). The focus seems to be on the process of developing another series of testing programs, and not on the individuals who are the "product" of the educational system. Certainly the issue of minimum competency testing is of great import to elected officials (Cabinet changes literacy test's name, 1978; Pipho, 1978; Literacy test hearings, 1978; New Dallas teachers fail, 1978). Some writers have even suggested that the entire issue reflects various ills and evils of modern society (Albee, 1978; Professor, 1978; Rickover et al., 1978).

Teachers, their unions, and educational administrators have generally taken a defensive view of the entire minimum competency movement (Adult performance level, 1975; Chicago school crackdown, 1978; Fisher, 1978; National Academy of Education, 1978; Miller, 1978; Pipho, 1978). On the other hand, some reports suggest that many parents of school-aged children are upset about the effects of minimum competency testing on their children (Blue ribbon panel fires salvos, 1978; Literacy test scoring called fairer, 1978; McCormack, 1978; The high illiteracy, 1978; The taught lesson, 1978). And there have been occasional efforts, primarily

172

by psychologists and educational researchers, to view the issue in a dispassionate manner (Cronbach, 1975; Gadway and Wilson, 1975; Glass, 1977). There are serious questions as to the criterion-validity of most tests, and there have been studied efforts to provide guidelines for the utilization of test instruments (American Psychological Association, 1974; Society for the Psychological Study of Social Issues, 1964; Wright and Isenstein, 1976). But there have been few efforts, even of limited perspective, to assess the situation realistically (Harris and Associates, 1970; Harris and Associates, 1971; Miller, 1978; Rosenthal, 1970).

The issue, in its intensity, may spawn a new kind of professional industry—"prepping" for the minimum competency tests (Student aid coming, 1978; Thompson, 1978). More fundamentally, there is no agreement as to the meaning of "minimum competency" (Miller, 1978). Data suggesting that students are learning less than ever before have been labeled by some researchers as deceptive (Fisher, 1978). We know that when scholars and researchers are caught up in public issues, composure, clarity, and judgment may suffer (Cronbach, 1975). One scholar has even suggested that any effort to determine minimum competency in relation to an absolute standard would tend to be capricious and authoritarian (Glass, 1977).

Why the Furor?

Anger, resentment, vituperation, and the other strong affects are usually products of threat or fear. There is considerable experimental evidence which is generally accepted to support this (Ryan, 1971; Society for the Psychological Study of Social Issues, 1964). As the concern for quality in public education developed sufficiently, legislation requiring minimum competency examinations for public school students resulted; rationale and justification of these procedures followed, together with angry opposition. The current proponents of minimum competency testing suggest the following: (1) the high school diploma is of questionable value since social promotions begin at the first grade and continue onward through all twelve grades; (2) the level of attainment by high school graduates is decelerating constantly; (3) students lack motivation and they require something to make them more concerned about school; (4) teachers are not as competent as they ought to be; and (5) the fabric of intellectual society is deteriorating, and the school system is helping to hide this by continuing to process students without concern about the pursuit of excellence.

Counterpositions by educators, administrators, and other behavioral specialists and scientists who oppose minimum competency assessment include: (1) test instruments used in minimum competency evaluations are of limited validity; (2) aside from technical considerations, tests are not a very fair way of assessing educational progress; (3) testing is anti-liberal and antiprogress; (4) tests label children and it is generally agreed that children should not be labeled; and (5) the use of minimum competency tests will force the schools to develop programs to "teach the test."

And so we have very large numbers of people who insist that we improve the quality of education. Part of this group says that we must not be unfair—to the teachers, to the school system, and (very occasionally) to the students. A growing number of legislators and political aspirants have hopped onto the bandwagon and insist that we must not upset the voters (unless perhaps, there can be political profit made from the distress).

The Composition of the Opposing Camps

It is difficult to identify the main groups to which leaders of the various camps belong. Those who favor minimum competency testing include educational researchers, parents, military officials, psychologists, employers, officials in universities, back-to-basics advocates, and legislators. The reasons they give range from one form or another of a desire to frighten (read "motivate") the students, to well-substantiated arguments about using high quality testing instruments as diagnostic tools to improve teaching methods and curricula.

The opponents to minimum competency testing make a series of cogent and powerful arguments. These arguments include the concept that such tests are unfair to minority groups, that tests are insufficiently valid and reliable, that the procedures will establish the pursuit of mediocrity, that the schools will be forced to "teach the test" instead of appropriate curricular content, that cheating will be encouraged, that children will be labeled, and in general that the schools will pursue mediocrity at a more rapid rate. The proponents of this position include members of the same professions and general groupings of parents, legislators, psychologists, educators, and so on. Both sides of the issue are backed by members of the same groups; this suggests that the issue is extremely complex.

Where Is the Student?

As was noted in the introduction, the available literature reveals almost no reference to the student and the student's needs. While there is considerable implication that the cause of the whole furor is the rapidly deteriorating competence of the student, the furor seems a classic case of "blaming the victim." Ryan (1971) points out that blaming the victim is an ideological process which occurs with a set of ideas and concepts derived from systematically motivated but unintended distortions of reality. In order to justify the status quo, it is necessary to find a victim of social problems who is identified as in some way disadvantaged, unhelped, or needful. Once such a victim is "discovered," a "cause" emerges with proponents who point out that the poor victim cannot be expected to do very well because of political conditions, economic conditions, cultural conditions, and any one of a variety of clever and articulate descriptions of the poor status of the individual who does not "make it." The educational system has been fertile ground for the discovery and blaming of victims.

In the issue of minimum competency testing, the student is again the "victim." Under the guise of "helping" the victim, it is necessary to examine the victim carefully, scientifically, objectively, mathematically, and so forth. The purpose is to confine the solution of the dilemma to manipulations of the victim. By concentrating all effort on the victim, it is possible to displace, ignore, and ultimately avoid the basic social causes of the problems being addressed. The most important subtle effect of this ideological process is that when one concentrates on the victim, one can avoid passing judgments on one's own adequacies. To concentrate on the inadequacies of our students in the school system is to sanctimoniously imply a "not guilty" verdict for ourselves. Genuine and pragmatic concern for the welfare of our students might better be demonstrated by carefully designed evaluation plans to answer questions about the relationship of schooling to quality of life and to personal success five, ten, and twenty-five years after graduation.

There is a minimum competency testing program currently operating in the state of Florida. It began in the mid-sixties, and included such highly desirable concepts as behavioral objectives, pupil progression plans, accountability, comprehensive planning, formative and summative evaluation, and criterion-referenced testing. The law was labeled "The Anti social-Promotion Bill." The system requires tests of basic skills to be administered in the 3rd, 5th, 8th, and 11th grades to "identify student needs" and to find out how various school districts are doing at meeting standards. In order to move on to the next level in school, a student will have to master specific objectives. The Functional Literacy Test, now called a student assessment test (Cabinet changes literacy test's name, 1978), is administered to high school juniors and seniors. Areas measured are reading, writing, and arithmetic. Several opportunities for passing the test are provided. The test has been the source of enormous controversy in Florida (Blue ribbon panel fires salvos, 1978; Leepson, 1978).

Where is the student in all this? During the past twenty-five years, while in full-time independent psychological practice in Tampa, Florida, I have had the opportunity to examine over two thousand school children. Most of them were not "doing well" in school. A small number were outstanding students. In each case, the parents or guardians, and frequently the teachers, were concerned about the student and sought professional psychological help. Each student was given a full Wechsler Intelligence Scale for Children, as well as a more informal intelligence scale such as the Peabody. A series of neuropsychological tests were administered to each child. Every student took an appropriate form of the Metropolitan Achievement Tests or the Stanford Achievement Tests. A reading survey such as the Gates-MacGinitie or the SRA Reading Survey was given to each student. A series of objective and projective tests of personality were administered. The parents were always interviewed, as was the student. Teachers and principals were consulted where appropriate. In each case, a very complete interpretation of results was given the parents, with children of thirteen or fourteen years and older present at this interpretation. During the past ten years, a tape recording of the interpretation session was given the family, to review, share with teachers, and so forth. Follow-up interviews to evaluate progress were scheduled with almost all families. These detailed assessments represent an extensive psychological study of school-aged children. In the course of these evaluations, there was an opportunity to share with students, parents and educators a considerable range and depth of views about education. These empirical observations included a series of direct questions to thirty-five recently-examined students about Florida's minimum competency testing program. If indeed the students are the victims, it would seem that we need to talk with the victims.

Thirty of the thirty-five students interviewed in depth were relatively distressed and disdainful about the whole testing business. They saw it as another burden developed by adults to make their progress through school more difficult. In most cases where the psychological assessment procedures were conducted as noted above, the greatest problem in working with the students was to convince them that the tests would be used for them rather than against them. As they were given immediate feedback about their performance we observed almost universally that the students became friendlier and more enthusiastic, curious, and active participants. Students seemed consistently "fed up" with adults—their parents, the teachers, administrators, and politicians. They felt that they had no part in any sort of needs-assessment to find out whether school would be of any value to them. The majority of students, including the very bright ones, simply do not care.

The students who failed the minimal competency test saw this result as another antagonistic "put down" from a society that does not like them very well. A number of bright students who will be admitted to college with advanced standing had almost identical views, except that they saw the tests as just another "piece of nonsense" that wastes time during high school and keeps them from productive learning. The poor students saw the tests as an additional barrier to success and esteem and not a help, while the good students saw them as a barrier to using their time effectively. Most students seemed to see the school system, their parents, politicians, and educational administrators as antagonists. Many students learn to manipulate the system. Not studying or performing is a way of fighting back or asserting oneself against authority figures. A "slave mentality" is created whereby students commit small sabotages to subvert a hostile system. These views are supported by a brief report of students' attitudes about these matters (Student Apathy, 1978), which was the only study of student attitudes found.

What Is Needed?

Educational institutions, government agencies, and politicians are geared up to implement minimum competency testing with only the data and experience we now have. Creative changes are not likely to be instituted. We all know how unwelcome new educational, research, or evaluation schemes tend to be. In order to make possible a reasoned, sensible, scientific, and humane approach, it would be necessary to declare a moratorium on penalties and pejoratives. This in itself may be impossible, in view of the historical tendency for educational institutions to maintain the status quo. If indeed it were possible, one way of potentially solving the current conflictive issues regarding minimum competency in favor of students might include the following procedures.

First, a proper needs assessment should be undertaken. This would have to include a broad-spectrum matrix of concerns. We have a lot of data about the concerns of legislators, school teachers, educational unions, educational administrators, and educational researchers. Competency involves more than preparing to meet the needs of industry and the bureaucracy (Albee, 1978). Particular attention will have to be given to the long-range goals of students, of their parents, and of the community in which the students intend to live. One would seek common factors and meaningful variance in these expectancies. The data would be most valuable in initial design plans for appropriate competency tests.

Given an adequate and agreed-upon needs assessment, the second step would be to develop a series of measures. Some may already be available, which could be reasonably associated with the goals developed by all interested parties. Long-range goals reflecting a variety of dimensions, variously described as "humanism," "quality of life," and "success," should be considered for significant periods of time past the student's educational experience, with the expectancy that test items can be developed to measure steps toward such goals.

Third, as the result of a broad-range standardization and validation experiment, it may be possible to identify academic content likely or unlikely to move the student toward a variety of goals. It would be important to design evaluation plans which clearly demonstrate the degree of confidence to be placed in how this curricular content is measured, and it would be desirable to establish fail-safe mechanisms to ensure that these measurement systems operate in a manner humane and helpful for the students and to society.

With continued emphasis on the student, the fourth step should include efforts to help the educational system present curricular content that is associated with long-range goals in a flexible manner, allowing for a broad range of individual differences, attainment lags, track crossings, and exchanges. Certainly such ideas are not new, but associating them with a respectable picture of student needs would be a considerable change in tactics.

Fifth, in order to ensure the continued viability of any system, it would be necessary to build an evaluation scheme which will allow formative and summative data to be available on an immediate (for the student), middle-range (for the teacher and the administrator), and long-range (for the politician, the administrator, and the curriculum builder) basis. The evaluation would determine the degree to which content and methods are helping students attain the previously determined, long-range goals. This information will perhaps be most useful in identifying the degree of success with which an individual student is attaining his or her goals. The importance of immediately and personally usable information cannot be overemphasized (Cronbach, 1975). It is of equal importance that the content of the curricula be attuned to meaningful long-range educational and survival goals (Buros, 1977).

The Student as Protagonist—A Psychological Model

As long as parents, legislators, teachers, and administrators see students as "problems," the student will serve as the blamed victim, and the antagonist role will be played by most parties. As a result, everyone will lose. Reversing this trend may mean opposing the status quo and may well be impossible. However, a psychological model of the student as protagonist is possible, and making such a model operational requires five conditions.

First, it requires an involvement of students in all decisions, including decisions about minimum competency testing, at all levels, but not in a merely token manner. Second, there must be some effort made to create or improve unstructured dialogue among all parties from the beginning to the end of schooling. Third, and critical to all of these steps, would be the establishment of feedback loops that place primary emphasis on communication between students at higher levels and students at lower levels. The enormously valuable information that can be passed from an 11th grader to a 9th grader, from a 7th grader to a 4th grader, and so forth, has never been carefully explored. One might pay particular attention to a concept about adolescents often voiced by the late Abraham Maslow. He frequently pointed out, in informal discussions, that if we could only harness the full-grown intellect, the idealism, and the energy of our age 12-18 population, we could accomplish great and humanistic goals. Fourth, some effort must be made to develop a system to give students some genuine control of their own education. This would mean their input to school boards, and their participation in curriculum committees and committees on hiring practices, credentialing efforts, budgeting, discipline, and evaluation. The fifth condition requires a study of how student leaders emerge. Sometimes selected by the authority figures in a school, and sometimes representing their fellow students, student leadership should be studied to develop ways and means to ensure that student leaders represent their fellow students. Student leaders should be responsive to long-range goals rather than the approbation of parents, teachers, and administrators.

This generalized, simplified psychological model is so idealistic that one might be tempted, with due apologies to both Thoreau and Skinner, to call it "Walden III." Nevertheless, concern for improving the quality of life should not be immediately denigrated because of practical matters. It is also an oversimplification to be pragmatic or hard-headed. Too often a shallow pragmatism prevails, and the human venture suffers accordingly.

An Epilogue

It seems apparent after one reads current literature on minimum competency testing that tests themselves are neither good nor bad. Certainly tests are used in ways that can be very good or very bad for students. Tests are currently not as well validated with respect to curriculum objectives as they should be. The proper application of test instruments, however, lags far behind technological development and the state of the art of instrumentation. Tests of any sort ought to be demonstrably useful in helping students achieve a higher quality of life and an improved pursuit of competence. The use of tests to label children and justify administrative decisions is deplorable. It is unlikely that we are going to see any major change in either the controversy about minimum competency testing or the educational conditions being questioned until we develop some ways to value, respect, trust, and better utilize the growing children who become the "outcome" of the system under consideration.

References

Adult Performance Level Project. *Adult functional competency: A summary.* Austin: Division of Extension, University of Texas, 1975.

Albee, G. W. A competency model must replace the defect model. Paper presented at the Ontario Institute for the Study of Education, Conference on Competency. Toronto, August 1978.

American Psychological Association. *Standards for educational and psychological tests.* Washington, D.C.: APA, 1974.

Blue ribbon panel fires salvos at state functional literacy test. *Tampa Tribune.* September 15, 1978.

Buros, O. K. Fifty years in testing. *Educational Researcher* 6, no. 7 (1977): 9-15.

Cabinet changes literacy test's name and scoring. *Tampa Tribune.* August 16, 1978.

Chicago school crackdown catches lagging readers. *Tampa Tribune.* July 14, 1978.

Competency test rapped as not fair. *Tampa Tribune.* July 3, 1978.

Cronbach, L. J. Five decades of public controversy over mental testing. *American Psychologist* 30, no. 1 (1975): 1-14.

Fisher, D. L. *Functional literacy and the schools.* Washington, D.C.: U.S. Dept. of HEW, NIE, U.S. Government Printing Office, 1978.

Gadway, C., & Wilson, H. A. *Functional literacy: Basic reading performance.* Denver: National Assessment of Educational Progress, 1975.

Glass, G. V. *Standards and criteria: An occasional paper.* Kalamazoo: Center for Evaluation, Western Michigan University, 1977.

Harris, L., & Associates. *Survival literacy.* New York: Louis Harris and Associates, 1970.

Harris, L., & Associates. *The 1971 national reading difficulty index.* New York: Louis Harris and Associates, 1971.

Leepson, M. Minimal competency testing is the most controversial issue in education today. *Tampa Tribune.* August 23, 1978.

Literacy test hearings planned. *Tampa Tribune.* September 2, 1978.

Literacy test scoring called fairer now. *Tampa Tribune.* August 17, 1978.

McCormack, P. Demystifying tests changes perspective. *Topeka Daily Capitol.* August 21, 1978.

Miller, B. S. (ed.). *Minimum competency testing: A report of four regional conferences.* St. Louis, Mo.: CEMREL, Inc., 1978.

National Academy of Education. *Improving educational achievement: Report of the National Academy of Education, Committee on Testing and Basic Skills* Washington, D.C.: Assistant Secretary for Education, February 23, 1978.

New Dallas teachers fail competency test. *Tampa Tribune/Times.* July 23, 1978.

Pipho, C. *Update VII: Minimal competency testing, report* #105. Denver: Education Commission of the States, 1978.

Professor: Test may encourage mediocrity. *Tampa Tribune.* September 14, 1978.

Rickover, H. G., et al. A principal debate: Do we really need a national competency test? *The National Elementary Principal* 57, no. 2 (1978): 47-70.

Rosenthal, J. Study finds 13% of U.S. adults fail elementary reading test. *New York Times.* September 12, 1970.

Ryan, W. *Blaming the victim.* New York: Pantheon Books (Random House), 1971.

Society for the Psychological Study of Social Issues. Guidelines for testing minority group children. *Journal of Social Issues* 20, no. 2 (1964): 127-145.

Student aid coming in math, English under Hillsborough remedial project. *Tampa Tribune.* June 25, 1978.

Student apathy. *Time.* April 17, 1978.

The high illiteracy. *Fresno Bee.* May 11, 1978.

The taught lesson. *Tampa Tribune.* June 20, 1978.

Thompson, T. (ed.). Functional literacy H. S. group. *Northside Community Health Center Bulletin,* July 1978.

Wright, B. J., & Isenstein, V. R. *Psychological tests and minorities.* Washington, D.C.: U.S. Dept. of HEW, PHS, Superintendent of Documents, 1976.

9 Competency Testing and the Handicapped: Some Legal Concerns for School Administrators

Kathleen S. Fenton

Competency testing programs potentially involve a morass of legal concerns with regard to the rights of handicapped students. Although local practices are a matter of local prerogative, the Supreme Court has made it clear that the behavior of educators must conform to fundamental constitutional safeguards and cannot conflict with basic constitutional rights.

Two constitutional rights set forth in the Fourteenth Amendment have special relevance for school administrators contemplating how they will deal with handicapped students in their competency testing programs. The first right is the guarantee of equal protection of the law, construed as equal opportunity when applied to education; the second right is to due process when state action may adversely affect an individual. Both these provisions have been embodied in Public Law 94-142, the Education of All Handicapped Children Act, and are elaborated on by this legislation and its regulations.

The purpose of this article is to raise questions concerning the application of these rights to the handicapped in the implementation of competency testing programs. These provisions require serious consideration. To facilitate discussion of the questions, the background of each provision will be presented, followed by an examination of the implications

This paper was prepared by Kathleen S. Fenton in her private capacity and the opinions herein should not be taken to represent the official position of the Bureau of Education for the Handicapped, U.S. Office of Education.

for the special education population and for school administrative practices.

Equal Opportunity

The thrust of the major, recent court decisions on the right of the handicapped to an education makes it clear that regardless of the nature or severity of handicap, the state educational authority is responsible for providing each child with an equal opportunity to receive an appropriate education according to her or his capacity. An appropriate education has been defined as instruction geared to a child's particular needs and aspirations (National Advisory Committee on the Handicapped, 1977). This right is derived from an application of the Fourteenth Amendment provision that forbids the state to deny any citizen the equal protection of the laws. And it is implemented through the Public Law 94-142 requirement of an individualized educational program (IEP) for each handicapped child. Public Law 94-142 defines the IEP as "a written statement . . . developed in any meeting by a representative of the local education agency who shall be qualified to provide or supervise the provision of . . . instruction, the teacher, the parent or guardian . . . and when appropriate the child. . . ." (Section 602 [19])

While Public Law 94-142 defines the IEP as a document, or a plan for the child's special education and related services, the IEP can be viewed as a comprehensive system for instructional service which includes planning, implementation, and periodic review and revision (Morrissey & Safer, 1977). The IEP also serves as a record of the education received, including the goals and objectives addressed, and the means by which the child's attainment of the goals were assessed.

The IEP is to include:

(a) A statement of the present level of educational performance of such child; (b) A statement of annual goals, including short term instructional objectives; (c) A statement of the specific special education and related services to be provided to the child, and the extent to which the child will be able to participate in regular education programs; (d) The projected dates for initiation of services and the anticipated duration of the services; and (e) Appropriate objective criteria and evaluation procedures and schedules for determining, on at least an annual basis, whether the short term objectives are being achieved. (45 CFR, 42 *Federal Register*, 1977, p. 42491)

Thus, the IEP is a documented plan which employs a competency-based curriculum approach—on an individualized basis rather than with a standard set of goals. Since objectives for a child's program are to be determined by the IEP planning team, several questions arise for administrative practices and the provision of equal opportunity for the child.

First, must the IEP goals and objectives reflect those of the regular educational program in so far as possible? The burden will probably be on the planning team to show cause for deleting goals and objectives known to be in the competency testing program. In the absence of an explicit rule, this interpretation follows the argument developed by Kotin (1978) which employs an extension of the principle underlying the least restrictive alternative. This principle suggests that the child's IEP should be comparable to the regular educational program unless there is a clear reason for other goals. Kotin cites the precedent established by sec. 88.34 of the regulations implementing sec. 504 of the Rehabilitation Act of 1973 which places the persuasion burden on the school in a dispute of the least restrictive environment (LRE). Moreover, he presents related guidelines issued by the Bureau of Education for the Handicapped (BEH) for states implementing LRE. These guidelines underscore the school's responsibility: "The burden of proof as to the appropriateness of any proposed placement, as to why more normalized placements could not adequately and appropriately serve the child's educational needs . . . will be upon the local agency" (Bureau of Education, 1974, p. 17). And finally, Kotin cites the fact that all recent court decisions bearing on the issue place the burden of proof on the school.[1]

Second, will schools have to develop a means to demonstrate that the child actually received the instructional program outlined in the IEP with regard to the competencies addressed in the testing program? The BEH has held that the IEP is not a contract binding on the implementing agency (the school), whereby educators can be made accountable for attainment of the goals and objectives listed. Nonetheless, it is clear that Congress intended for the IEP provision to bring an element of accountability into special education programming through the mandated annual planning and review process. At the very least, parents will be able to bring informal pressures on the school to show that the child's program was carried out. To meet these pressures, schools may be compelled to monitor the delivery and effectiveness of the prescribed services. But ultimately, formal pressure may be applied by parents through appeals and the judicial system if they see that instruction consistently fails to be delivered or fails to fulfill the goals of the IEP. If this situation arises, schools with self-monitoring procedures in place will avoid having such procedures imposed by judicial mandate.

The third question also concerns monitoring needs. Will the school need to ensure that instructional omission does not occur for mainstreamed children who participate in "pull-out" programs but who intend to participate in the regular competency testing program? L. C. Danielson (this volume) discusses the need to ensure content validity between the tests and the child's IEP. Thus the school has the obligation to develop or modify the curriculum so that it coincides with the district's chosen competencies. Students participating in pull-out programs dictate yet another administrative need: deliberate tracking as to when specific competencies are taught. Oregon provides an illustration of meeting this need.

The State Board of Education in Oregon requires local educational agencies to develop written course statements for the curricula in grades 9-12. Each course statement has to include, among other objectives, any required minimum competencies assigned to that course for purposes of verification. A benefit of such an approach is that instructional planning is more systematic and overall competency performance can be traced to particular staff and program areas. On the other hand, the time spent in record keeping and verification are of course an additional cost to the district.

It is apparent from this discussion that when competency testing programs are viewed in the light of the equal opportunity provision for the students involved, additional administrative procedures are required.

Due Process

In addition to establishing the right of every child to be educated according to the child's needs, the courts have determined that a child is entitled to the protection of due process whenever there may be a change in her or his educational status or program. This due process provision has its origins in the Fourteenth Amendment to the Constitution: "nor shall any state deprive any person of life, liberty, or property without due process of law." In applying this clause to education, the court held that the school is a proper agent of the state and that citizens (in this case, the handicapped child) must be protected from arbitrary and capricious action by the state (the school) whenever the consequences may jeopardize the child's life, liberty, or property.

The consequences of special education, both positive and negative, have been well documented (O'Neill, 1977). And the courts have found these consequences to be life-altering in nature. Thus, a working legal definition for the adequacy of any procedures adopted by schools in educational decision making is: when faced with a decision or potential decision affecting the educational environment, the individual has the opportunity to be heard as well as the right to impartial resolution of conflicting positions.

Public Law 94-142 requires that the development and review of a handicapped child's IEP be governed by due process procedures patterned after the judicial model. This model emphasizes the following elements: notice of pending action; informed consent; and the opportunity for resolution of conflicts through informal means and the right to formal appeal and an impartial hearing.

Thus, the questions pertaining to due process in any competency program address these elements. First, what provisions does the school make for informing parents and the child, when appropriate, that the contents of the IEP will determine the child's eligibility or preparation for the competency testing program? Furthermore, does the school make available to the parents (and the child) a list of the competencies included in the testing program so parents can judge the relationship between the program and their child's IEP? And third, are parents advised about the implications for their child's future educational opportunities and employment prospects if the IEP does not address the district's competencies? In 1972, by the Consent Decree in *Pennsylvania Association for Retarded Children* (PARC) v. *Commonwealth of Pennsylvania*, due process protection was extended to special education students. The decree stated that it is the right of the child and parents to be involved as interested parties in determining the evaluation, program, and placement of a child suspected of being educationally handicapped.

Prior to this directive, many educational agencies made efforts to inform parents of action taken involving their child's education and to secure parental support. However, informed consent was not insured. Moreover, provisions for active parental involvement and involvement of the child, where appropriate, were not found in general practice.

Exploratory research conducted by the BEH showed that existing provisions for consent generally consisted of a broad statement of intent with little specificity provided (Hoff et al., in press). Explanations in more detail were frequently delivered orally and by several different staff members. These practices result in vague parental understanding and inhibit the parents' ability to act prudently in behalf of their child.

Does the school have policies or procedures to promote informal resolution of conflicts when parents and schools disagree on which competencies are appropriate for a special education student? Is there a mechanism whereby parents or the child can appeal and receive an impartial hearing relative to participation in the competency testing?

The regulations for Public Law 94-142 (part 121a.226) now mandate a partnership between the parents of the child in question and the school whenever the status or program of a child may be altered. Parental consent is required and parents are to be advised of their right to appeal and an impartial hearing. Furthermore, Public Law 94-142 states that each meeting conducted for the purpose of developing, reviewing, and revising a handicapped child's individualized educational program should include one or both of the child's parents as participants and, where appropriate, the child under consideration. Thus, another question is: What are criteria for determining the appropriateness of including the child in the planning and for determining the appropriate degree of involvement if any?

Several additional questions should also be considered in conjunction with the policies regarding the role of the child. Does a parent or guardian have the right to waive a child's right to the opportunity to learn the material to be included in the competency tests? By what age and for what handicapping conditions should the child be given the opportunity to elect certain competency goals despite the parents' preferences? These issues have been left entirely to the discretion of local prerogative. But states and districts must realize their obligation to make these determinations on an individual basis. Otherwise situations will arise where districts face the prospects of having procedures defined through litigation.

Conclusion

The preceding discussion makes it clear that schools encounter a Pandora's box of individual rights when the results of competency testing determine an individual's educational status. The final question that follows is whether this use of competency testing is the best way to make schools accountable for preparing students to function in today's society.

The need to address the potential consequences of competency testing programs for the individual is eliminated if competency testing focuses on the system rather than the individual. That is, if schools or districts are used as the unit of analysis for test scores, the system's success at imparting minimum competencies to the students can be assessed. This is how standardized testing programs and the resulting achievement scores are frequently, albeit inappropriately, used today. Recall how the public report of declining test scores overall has given rise to the back-to-basics movement. The standardized tests, however, are not designed to assess minimum competencies but rather to discriminate levels of mastery. Moreover, they are not generally coordinated with the curriculum of a given school or district, so content validity is a serious problem. On the other hand, competency testing programs should be designed to coordinate the curriculum and criterion-referenced tests, based on state and local competency goals.

Assuming that standard test-development procedures are used to insure validity, competency testing could more accurately provide the public and educators alike with the accountability information they seek. But these accountability needs can and should be satisfied without a cost to individual students.

The "individual rights" problems rest with the application of the test results, not the testing program itself. Results are appropriately applied to the individual when used prescriptively during the development and review of a student's IEP. The legal restrictions governing the use of competency test scores in this manner are found in the protection-in-evaluation-procedures provision of Public Law 94-142. This provision requires that test information be considered along with other equally valid information about a student's needs and performance level. But little is gained and major problems arise when the test results are used to certify an individual for graduation.

Note

1. See *LeBanks* v. *Spears*, 60 F.R.D. 135 (E.D. La 1973); *Mills* v. *Board of Education of D.C.*, 348 F. Supp. 866 (D.D.C. 1972); *In re Downey*, 72 Misc. 2d772, 340 N.Y.S. 2d 687 (1972).

References

Bureau of Education for the Handicapped, "Implementation of new guidelines and regulations for part B, EHA, as Amended by PL 93-380." Guidelines distributed to chief state school officers. Washington, D.C., November 11, 1974.

Hoff, M.; Fenton, K.; Yoshida, R.; & Kaufman, M. Notice and consent: The school's responsibility to inform parents. *Journal of School Psychology*, in press.

Kotin, L. Recommended criteria and assessment techniques for the evaluation by LEAs of their compliance with the notice and consent requirements of PL 94-142. In *Developing criteria for evaluating the due process procedural safeguards provision of Public Law 94-142.* Washington, D.C.: Thomas Buffington and Associates, 1978.

Morrissey, P. & Safer, N. The individualized education program: Implications for special education. *Viewpoints: The Bulletin of the School of Education*, Indiana University, 1977, *53* (2): 31-38.

National Advisory Committee on the Handicapped. *The individualized education program: Key to an appropriate education for the handicapped child.* Annual Report. Washington, D.C.: U.S. Dept. of Health, Education, and Welfare, 1977.

O'Neill, D. M. "Discrimination against handicapped persons." Working report prepared for the Office for Civil Rights (DHEW) under orders #SA-4141-76 & #SA-2471-77. Mimeographed. Washington, D.C.: U.S. Dept. of Health, Education, and Welfare, May 4, 1977.

10   Test Scores and Individual Rights

Mary M. Kennedy

When Florida initiated its statewide minimum competency test, 45 percent of the Duval County juniors flunked math and 14 percent failed reading and grammar. According to Glass (1978), if a student fails Florida's test three times, he or she will receive a certificate of attendance rather than a diploma. This policy raises several questions. For example, is the state now responsible for correcting these test failures or are the individual students? Apparently, the State of Florida plans to assume some responsibility since the state legislature has appropriated funds for remedial programs. But how capable is a state of providing competencies to individuals? Are there any such competencies that can be guaranteed to all individuals?

Before considering the feasibility of state-assumed responsibility, however, some determination must be made regarding whether education itself is to be considered a right of the individual to be exercised at his or her discretion or whether instead society is responsible for assuring individual accomplishments. If we assume education is a right, we must realize that the right to an education is not like the constitutionally guaranteed rights such as freedom of speech or religious preference. Constitutional rights are unique in several respects. For example, they can be used and reused. That is, one can exercise one's right to free speech as often as one chooses and never exhaust the supply of this right (Okun, 1975). Not so for education: it must be exercised or acquired at specific times

The opinions expressed in this paper are solely those of the author, and should not be construed to represent those of the U.S. Office of Education.

and places and it must be acquired sequentially. Constitutional rights are also in infinite supply, unlike entities such as property or money whose supply can be exhausted. They, therefore, are free from the distributional constraints that arise with finite resources. They are universally available and equally available to any who wish to use them, and thus they can be guaranteed. If education is a right, it differs from constitutional rights in three important respects. First, education is supported with finite public resources. Though free to the individual, education is not free to society. And that means distributive decisions regarding social resources must be made—decisions which need not be made for rights such as free speech. This creates a dilemma: unlike other rights, the establishment of a universal right to education must necessarily include a method of distributing resources.

The second major difference between education and other rights is that the right to education cannot be exercised freely at any time or place. Rather, it must be acquired or obtained hierarchically, in a place and in a sequence prescribed by society; one must complete the requirements for one grade before one can attend the next. The use of minimum competency testing further structures the way in which an individual can exercise the right to education. By requiring passage of a minimum competency test before grade advancement or receipt of diploma, the test constrains individual rights of access to later educational opportunities.

Third, one cannot easily determine when an individual's right to education has been exercised or when it has been denied, though one can easily determine whether an individual was allowed to vote, for example, or to speak freely. But because of the structure of education and because it must be provided by society as well as "used" by the individual, there is considerable ambiguity over whether the right to education has in fact been granted. At one time, it was assumed that evidence of equal access to education constituted sufficient evidence that rights to education had been granted. But even more stringent criteria have been applied recently. Levine and Bane (1975), for example, argued that in *Brown* v. *the Board of Education* (1954), the concern was not merely for equality of opportunity, but instead it was for effective equality. That is, the evidence of equal rights to education must be found in the outcomes of education rather than simply in the provision of education. This point of view can also be found in at least one social scientist's attempt to measure equal opportunity, where the measure of equality has in fact been a measure of equality of educational outcomes, or at least equality of outcomes across major segments of our population (Coleman et al., 1966; Coleman, 1969; see also Mosteller and Moynihan, 1972).

But extending the measurement of equality to include the outcomes of education means that education as a right now has a considerably different status than constitutional rights. To redefine freedom of speech to mean effective free speech, for example, would mean that someone must listen to every individual's speech. Clearly no guarantee of effective free speech is possible. Equal opportunity for free speech, however, can be guaranteed by requirements such as equal time on public broadcasts.

How is the minimum competency testing movement related to the concept of effective equality? Wise (1978) described a court case in New Jersey which was originally "concerned with the equalization of educational expenditures, but in a bizarre turn of events resulted in a ruling to institute minimum competency testing" (p. 597). The turn of events is not so bizarre when viewed in the context of effective equality (equality of educational outcomes); the court apparently felt that the testing program would be more likely to promote equality of outcomes than would a change in the distribution of resources. If this is the court's view, then the use of minimum competency testing programs may be a necessary part of providing those educational rights that have been described here. These tests could become a measure of the extent to which society has provided equal outcomes of education. Thus, although Pipho (1978) has argued that the testing program places the burden of passing on the individual, the argument for effective equality suggests that it is society which must assure that an effective education has been acquired.

One characteristic of constitutional rights, however, which has been retained in the notion of equal outcomes of education, is that of universality. The concepts of equality of opportunity and of effective equality both imply that the right is universal. No group can be excluded. But can a set of competencies be defined that are universally requisite? Such a set must be defined if society is to assume responsibility for assuring educational outcomes.

It is one thing to give examples of how skills can be used in one's everyday life, and quite another to say that all individuals must have these skills in order to function in our society. The latter statement implies that the particular competencies that are required are known to be universally necessary for participation in society. Possession of these competencies gives the individual the right to pass from school to society.

But our society is complex and it is difficult to imagine competencies that are indeed universally requisite. For example, accountants can be hired to take care of individual finances, mechanics to maintain individual properties, and calculators purchased to balance checkbooks. Certainly not all individuals could afford to purchase all such services, but the fact that they are available means that individuals have the flexibility to choose which competencies they prefer to exercise for themselves and which they prefer to purchase. A complex society such as ours offers individuals a variety of means by which to function in the society.

Coupled with the diversity of ways of functioning is an equal diversity of individual strengths and weaknesses. This is best seen by considering handicapped individuals. For the individual who is visually impaired, the society provides Braille texts, seeing-eye dogs, dictaphones and reading machines. For the individual who is severely retarded, the society provides sheltered workshops in which the individual is capable of earning her or his own money and contributing to society as well. Thus, for those individuals who lack certain competencies, compensatory means of functioning are available. The diversity of our society permits diversity in the way individuals function, making it difficult to define a single set of competencies that are necessary to all members of society.

If the standards accompanying minimum competency tests are to become part of graduation requirements, other problems must also be resolved. Kirp (1969) interpreted recent court cases as expanding the protections of the Fourteenth Amendment to encompass those rights essential to the individual's "satisfactory life process." Does possession of a diploma influence the individual's satisfactory life process? It certifies that a student has completed those academic exercises that the school feels should be completed, regardless of whether the school employs competency tests as part of its requirement for graduation. Certification increases the graduate's access to employment and higher education. And educational credentials may be more important to an individual's future economic success than academic performance is (Jencks, et al., 1972). But credentials may influence other aspects of social status. For example, Weisskopf (1975) has argued that an important aspect of equality stems from feeling that one is a member of a community. To the extent that denial of certification denies one economic opportunities or a sense of membership in the community, then, it has influenced the individual's satisfactory life process. If one were to follow this line of reasoning, one could argue that any school which denies a diploma without providing the individual with due process may be violating the individual's rights.

If the Fourteenth Amendment protections encompass educational credentials, then schools must establish due process procedures before they can deny credentials to any individual. And if a minimum competency test were used as the basis for denial, the validity of the test would surely be questioned during the proceedings. The problems of determining which competencies are universally needed may become an issue in these proceedings. Ultimately, the courts may have to determine not only the extent of social responsibility for assuring educational outcomes, but also the extent of social responsibility for deferring credentials.

The difficulty of defining a set of universally needed minimum competencies has been recognized by others (for example, Glass, 1978; Haney and Madaus, 1978), but the fact of that difficulty does not mean that schools should use *no* standards for passing students from grade to grade or for graduating students. Nor does it necessarily mean that standards should be not be uniformly applied to all students. In fact, those minimum competency tests currently in use have apparently been developed judgmentally with criterion scores based on estimates of the proportion of students expected to pass the test. Thus the criterion is not entirely arbitrary for it is based on an estimate of the political feasibility of applying such standards. But this approach is not without its own set of problems. Brickell (1978) found that school teachers and principals felt they could only afford politically to deny graduation to around 3 percent of their students. Yet to guarantee that 97 percent of the students would pass, they estimated they could only require first or second grade-level competencies! Such a level of performance is sufficiently low to make the test lack utility as a vehicle for assuring effective equality: it would be designed to match the lowest levels of current student performance rather than to define a meaningful standard of performance. Thus the dilemma: higher standards of performance may result in denial of credentials to many more students than is politically feasible, whereas lower standards of performance may mean that the standards lack utility as a means of measuring effective equality of educational outcomes. How, then, can society assure effective educational equality?

Perhaps an analysis of the different reasons why students might fail a minimum competency test could be used to identify some students for whom society cannot take responsibility. There are a variety of reasons why children may not demonstrate the competencies required for graduation. They may be overanxious while taking the test; they may lack the motivation to perform well; or they may in fact lack those competencies precisely because the school failed to provide them with an appropriate education. Or they may not have been endowed with the ability needed to acquire these competencies. Of these several reasons, only the last one is truly outside the power of the school to change; it is these students for whom the school could argue that it cannot assure minimum competencies. Unfortunately, these students cannot be reliably identified in advance. Our knowledge of the relationship between education and the development of human skills is insufficient to determine which cases of test failure are caused by natural limitations and which by other reasons. Thus, the school cannot accurately identify those students for whom it cannot assume responsibility. In fact, our knowledge is so limited that schools can neither anticipate failure upon seeing evidence of one of these problems, nor accurately diagnose the cause of a failure once it does occur, so that it can be remediated. This lack of specific technology leaves the school in a difficult position: it (or the state) may be requiring competencies for graduation which it is not capable of providing to all students; yet it may not be able to distinguish those students for whom it can provide the skills from those for whom it cannot.

If we assume, nevertheless, that the school (and not the student) is responsible for assuring that these competencies are acquired, then what alternatives are available to a school which takes its responsibility seriously? It could impose a universal curriculum specifically to impart those competencies that are to be tested. (By universal, I mean that all children, including the handicapped and the gifted, would be provided the same curriculum.) Or the school could test students prior to graduation and put those who fail into such a specified curriculum. Under this second strategy, the same curriculum becomes a remediation curriculum rather than a universal curriculum. Or finally, it may determine a priori that certain segments of the student population are not a part of the school's responsibility and, by that decision, neither require the test nor provide the curriculum to those students.

Each of these alternatives has its own problems. If the school chooses the first, it unnecessarily imposes a curriculum on many students who do not need it. Though our common sense tells us such an approach is unnecessary, our sense of justice may tell us this is the most fair way to proceed, for it is the only solution that assures equal opportunities for graduation. One might argue that the second course also provides equal graduation rights since students are given a second chance to take the test and are offered a remedial course as well. But this approach may not assure equality, since some students might be so adversely affected by the negative results of their first test that they would give up and leave school without a diploma. If this happens, should the school take responsibility for these students' incomplete education? After all, it was the school's test imposed without the aid of curricular assistance that motivated the students to leave. McClung (1978) has argued that a fair test is one that is based on the school's curriculum, and although this second approach uses a test that is based on the school's curriculum, the students would not have been exposed to the curriculum at the time of assessment.

The school's third alternative amounts essentially to placing parameters on its responsibilities. If the technologies were available to precisely define that population for whom the school could not possibly instill certain competencies, the third approach would provide a reasonable solution to at least part of the problem of responsibility. Unfortunately, no error-free methodology exists. Thus, the third approach may lead to inappropriate and unjust denial of educational credentials to some students. Furthermore, the errors of prediction could occur in either direction so that while some capable students may be denied an opportunity, other less capable students may be placed in a curriculum designed to provide competencies which these students are not capable of acquiring. In these latter situations, the students would also be denied access to those special courses which would provide competencies they *were* capable of acquiring and may need, so that they would neither receive certification nor receive competencies they could use.

Furthermore, the competency assessment procedures themselves could also be discriminatory. Discrimination in assessment could occur in a number of ways and each could have different effects on the individual students involved. First, certain students (such as the handicapped) may be excused from taking the test. Second, certain children may take different tests than others do. Or third, all children may take the same test but the minimum criterion required of some children may be different than it is for others.

Consider the first alternative. If the notion behind a competency testing program is that the responsible school must be sure it has provided competencies to all its students, then exemptions make little sense. Klingstedt (1972) argues that a fundamental assumption behind the use of performance assessments for certification is that the competencies are universally required. If the exemption means that the competencies are not really needed by all citizens, then how can they be required of any? If it means that the school has denied its responsibility for some students, how can this be justified? We considered earlier the possibility that there are some students for whom the school cannot assume responsibility; however, a priori exemption implies not that the school has attempted to teach competencies to these students but rather that the school has abrogated responsibility for an arbitrarily specified group of students. And in so doing, the school has defined a class of students, usually handicapped students, who will be denied access to educational credentials that other students will receive. Such a practice not only violates one's sense of justice; it now also violates the law for most schools, since section 504 of the Rehabilitation Act of 1973 states that "no otherwise qualified handicapped individual . . . shall, solely by reason of his handicap, be excluded from the participation in, be denied benefits of, or be subjected to discrimination under any program or activity receiving federal financial assistance."

The second alternative is to test all students but to vary the tests. There are a variety of ways in which differential testing could be done. A school could, for example, require entirely different sets of competencies for different groups of students. Some students would be required to demonstrate skill in bathing, grooming, and dressing, while other students would have to demonstrate skill in reading, calculating, and writing. Or a school could require the same set of competencies for all students, but allow different students to demonstrate those competencies in different ways. Some might read Braille, while others would read printed material. This latter approach is in keeping with the regulations for both section 504 of the Rehabilitation Act and Public Law 94-142, the Education of All Handicapped Children Act. Both of these provisions require testing accommodations for handicapped individuals. But what about the former approach? Can different competencies be required of different students? Allowing different competency requirements for different students calls into question the assumption that there is a set of universally needed minimum competencies and thus requires redefining the purpose of the entire testing program, since it no longer is used as a means of assuring universal equality of outcomes.

The third alternative is to use one test but require different criterion scores for different students. This alternative presents the same philosophical problems as the use of different tests. It challenges the assumption that there are universal competencies that are needed. The procedure may be more stigmatizing, as well, since it makes explicit the school's assumption that some students are not capable of meeting standards which other students must meet. A variation of this procedure, proposed by Page (1978), is to offer "scaled certification," in which the student's score becomes a part of her or his high school graduation credentials. While this approach may solve the dilemma of defining a universal cutoff score, it still begs the issue of assuring some sort of standard for graduates and does not assist schools in their goal of assuring equality of outcomes.

These three methods of separating students are all fundamentally discriminatory. But whether the discrimination is considered a violation of individual rights or whether it is considered sound educational practice depends on how the discrimination is made. We expect teachers to discriminate among their students each day as they provide instruction. We assume that these discriminations enable the teacher to make each student's work challenging and interesting. Yet if we were to discover that teachers made distinctions among broad classes of students—for example, distinctions based on race, religion, or sex—we would be distressed. Whether the discrimination is considered a violation of rights depends on whether it is a valid and relevant distinction.

These same concerns hold for educational administrators, who are also capable of discriminating among students by either relevant or irrelevant factors. But relevance is difficult to determine when handicapped students are involved, since the range of handicapping conditions and their influence on children's educability is great. Some conditions influence thinking or learning, some influence sensing (hearing or seeing), and others influence movement. And the influences range from mild to severe. Clearly many of these conditions must influence a student's educational needs and influence the set of competencies the student is capable of acquiring while in school. In that sense, discriminations between these students and nonhandicapped students are educationally relevant distinctions. But a class distinction, that is, distinguishing the class of handicapped students for purposes of differential assessment and graduation, could be viewed as a violation of individual rights. Such a distinction ignores the variation in competencies within the class and may arbitrarily deny access to educational credentials to all members of that class of individuals.

The original dilemma remains. How can society, recognizing the variation among students as well as variation in society, reasonably satisfy its responsibility to assure universality of minimum competencies? Variation per se does not suggest that schools should not be concerned about the competencies their graduates have. Howe (1978) has contrasted the goals of educational equity and educational excellence, suggesting that the former is an egalitarian goal while the latter is an elitist goal. The more we emphasize one, the less we can emphasize the other. Since recent emphasis has been on the former, perhaps the testing of minimum competencies represents an attempt to move toward the latter again. Such an attempt may be appropriate, for according to Haney and Madaus (1978), the last thirty-five years of education have seen a growth in secondary school attendance from less than half of the population to roughly 90 percent of the population. Such a change in population certainly has implications for how education should occur, as well as for defining the value of educational credentials. The school, then, is faced with the multiple goals of maximizing competencies, equalizing competencies, and assuring that its certification decisions do not violate the rights of individual students.

Many educators see the use of minimum competency tests as a means of resolving this dilemma, since the tests provide the school with objective evidence that all graduates do in fact possess the minimum competencies. But the tests fail for three important reasons. First, these tests cannot accommodate legitimate variations among individual aspirations and abilities. Second, where these variations may lead to test failures, the extent of individual versus school responsibilities for failure has not been clearly defined. Third, tests for minimum competencies seem to be based on the assumption that education is an entity that can be "given" to individuals by society. In fact, education is a process; it occurs over time through the interaction between the individual and the educator.

The assumption behind the use of competency tests is that educational outcomes can be guaranteed. But since education is an interactive process, such guarantees may not be possible. In fact, it is even difficult to ascribe failures to either the educator or the individual, since their interaction is so complex. What is needed is a set of performance standards for society that can (a) assure that society is providing every opportunity to all individuals, yet (b) recognize that different individuals will graduate with different competencies, and (c) assure that individuals are not penalized for society's failures to meet its own standards.

There are competency test performance standards that can meet these criteria. One, suggested by Brickell (1978), involves setting standards for schools rather than for individuals. For example, a school might set a goal of passing 80 percent of its students. The following year, it may raise its goal to 85 percent. The advantage of this approach is that it establishes more clearly the school's responsibility and does not penalize students when the school fails to meet its goal. Brickell is unclear, however, as to what the school's responsibilities would be toward those students who fail the test. A second alternative is to reinforce the traditional criteria for graduation: an acceptable grade-point average. This alternative provides for a reasonable sharing of responsibility between the school and the individual student. Since the grade-point average accumulates, the student is at all times cognizant of his or her status and the school and student can work together to remedy inadequacies. In effect, this approach defines effective equality more realistically: it is not entirely a societal responsibility but is instead a shared responsibility.

A third option has been legislated for use with handicapped pupils—the establishment of individualized educational programs. These programs tailor educational goals to each student's unique educational needs. The goals are developed jointly by the school and the family. The school can thereby accommodate individual variation and still demonstrate that it is fulfilling its responsibilities to all students. Variation is not used to justify societal neglect. This approach redefines equality to mean an equality of opportunity such that each child receives the educational services needed to reach his or her maximum potential.

There are several advantages to these three approaches to graduation criteria: each protects individual rights to educational certification; each provides society with objective evidence of its efforts to provide educational opportunities to all students; and each accomplishes these two objectives without the unnecessary and unrealistic requirement of universality of educational outcomes. One reason why these approaches accomplish these diverse purposes is that they all recognize the interactive nature of the educational process and establish "working agreements" between the student and the school early in the student's education. Thus both parties are at all times aware of each party's obligations and expectations.

References

Brickell, H. M. Seven keynotes on minimum competency testing. *Phi Delta Kappan*, 1978, 59 (no. 9): 589-592.

Brown v. Board of Education, 347, U.S. 483-493 (1954).

Coleman, James S. The concept of equality of educational opportunity. In Harvard Educational Review (ed.), *Equal educational opportunity*, pp. 9-24. Cambridge, Mass.: Harvard University Press, 1969.

Coleman, James S., Campbell, E. Q., Hobson, C. J., McPartland, J., Mood, A. M., Weinfeld, F. D., and York, R. L. *Equality of educational opportunity: Summary*. Washington, D.C.: Government Printing Office, 1966.

Glass, Gene V. Minimum competence and incompetence in Florida. *Phi Delta Kappan*, 1978, 59 (no. 9): 602-605.

Haney, Walt, and Madaus, George. National consortium on testing staff circular no. 2: Making sense of the competency testing movement. Mimeo., the Huron Institute, 1978.

Howe, Harold. Tests and schooling. Address to the National Conference on Achievement Testing and the Basic Skills. Washington, D.C., March 1978.

Jencks, Christopher, Smith, M., Acland, H., Bane, M. J., Cohen, D., Gintis, H., Heyns, B., and Michelson, S. *Inequality: A reassessment of the effects of family and schooling in America*. New York: Harper Colophon, 1972.

Kirp, David L. The poor, the schools, and equal protection. In Harvard Educational Review (ed.), *Equal educational opportunity*, pp. 139-172. Cambridge, Mass.: Harvard University Press, 1969.

Klingstedt, Joe Lars. Philosophical basis for competency-based education. In Burnes, Richard W., and Klingstedt, Joe Lars (eds.), *Competency-based education: An introduction*, pp. 7-19. Englewood Cliffs, N.J.: Educational Technology Publications, 1972.

Levine, D. M., and Bane, M. J. (eds.). *The "inequality" controversy: Schooling and distributive justice*. New York: Basic Books, 1975.

McClung, Merle S. Are competency testing programs fair? Legal? *Phi Delta Kappan*, 1978, 59 (no. 2): 397-400.

McClung, Merle S., and Pullin, Diana. Competency testing and handicapped students. Mimeo., Center for Law and the Handicapped, 1978.

Mosteller, Frederick, and Moynihan, Daniel P. A pathbreaking report. In Mosteller, F., and Moynihan, D. P. (eds.), *On equality of educational opportunity*, pp. 3-66. New York: Vintage, 1972.

Okun, Arthur M. Equality and efficiency: The big tradeoff. Washington, D.C.: The Brookings Institution, 1975.

Page, E. B. Escaping the minimum competency dilemma: Scaled certification. Clearinghouse for Applied Performance Testing Newsletter, 1978, 3 (no. 5): 6-12.

Weisskopf, Walter A. The dialects of equality. In Levine, D. M., and Bane, M. J. (eds.), The "inequality" controversy: Schooling and distributive justice, pp. 214-227. New York: Basic Books, 1975.

Wise, Arthur E. Minimum competency testing: Another case of hyperrationalization. Phi Delta Kappan, 1978, 59 (no. 9): 596-598.

11   Educational Goals and Competency Testing for the Handicapped

Louis C. Danielson

In our diverse social environment, "minimum competency" does not have the same meaning for all people. For example, a retarded adult's survival in a halfway house may be an appropriate level of functional competency. The notion of minimum competency implies that there are basic skills and/or competencies which are necessary for any person to possess in order to function. But the term "to function" needs clarification, and schools must grapple with the fact that competencies are not absolute but are relative to the environment of the individual. Our society has long recognized that it contains many acceptable environments (subcultures). Should the testing domains follow from a child's educational goals or should a child's educational goals reflect the testing domains? How does each approach affect the utility of the testing programs for the schools and society? How does each approach affect the educational opportunities of students who need programs which differ from the regular curriculum?

To fully understand the relationship of educational goals to a competency testing program, it makes sense to evaluate a competency test in the same manner as any other achievement test. McClung (1978) pointed out that schools might be legally bound to demonstrate that tests have curricular and instructional validity. Curricular validity represents the

This paper was prepared by Louis C. Danielson in his private capacity and the opinions herein should not be taken to represent the official position of the Bureau of Education for the Handicapped, U.S.O.E.

match between the test and goals, while instructional validity indicates the match between the test and instruction. If instruction does not proceed from the goals upon which the test is based, the test may have curricular validity but lack instructional validity. Whether viewed legally or ethically, the content validity of these tests cannot be ignored. Competency tests should be based upon educational goals and the instruction which proceeds from those goals.

If the fundamental significance of educational goals in competency testing is acknowledged, then a number of critical issues must be raised. First, is there a common set of goals for all children which would lead to the development of one test with one standard? Second, are these goals stated in a manner that would make it clear to all concerned what the expectations are? Third, can we construct tests which assess student mastery of these goals?

I believe that there are both implicit and explicit goals which apply generally to education and for which a broad census exists. For example, most people agree that education should enable students to acquire skills necessary to function in society. The problem, however, is that broad functional goals do not adequately prescribe or define a domain from which test items can be selected. It is when we say that children should be able to take a square root, balance a checkbook, write a business letter, or compute income tax that arguments arise.

One such dilemma, concerning goals for the handicapped, is illustrated in the following hypothetical but realistic activity. Public Law 94-142, the Education for All Handicapped Children Act, requires that schools provide Individualized Education Programs (IEPs) for each handicapped child. The act requires that these IEPs be written statements which must include: a statement of the child's present level of educational performance; a statement of annual goals, including short-term instructional objectives; a statement of the specific, special education and related services to be provided to the child, and of the extent to which the child will be able to participate in regular educational programs; the projected dates for initiation of services and the anticipated duration of the services; and appropriate objective criteria, evaluation procedures, and schedules for determining, on at least an annual basis, whether the short-term instructional objectives are being achieved.

The IEP is developed in a meeting between parents and school personnel. The act provides for appeal procedures if the parent does not agree with the program the school provides. Now suppose that school personnel and parents agree on an IEP for an educable mentally retarded student at the secondary school level which contains the following: (1) the student will receive training in food preparation and actually work on a half-day basis at a local restaurant; (2) even though the child's basic skills are at the 4th or 5th-grade level, all agree that it is more productive to help the child become employable and to supplement this training with skills necessary for independent living.

Also, suppose this child resides in a state which has a basic skills competency test required for graduation. The child's current level of performance might not be sufficient to pass the test. Does the school modify the child's program? They cannot legally do so without revision of the IEP and without involving the parent. Suppose they meet with the parent. What should the parent do? Should the parent agree to a program that is perhaps less appropriate for the child's needs so the child can pass the test? This illustration makes explicit a decision that may be made unconsciously by educators for many children, both handicapped and nonhandicapped. Haney and Madaus (1978) have also pointed out this potential of competency testing to determine or at least to affect the curriculum.

This illustration emphasizes the need for predictive validity as well as for content validity. If tests are designed to assess the long-term goals of schooling, then the first steps toward achieving predictive validity are taken. However, this does not absolve competency testers from demonstrating a relation between test performance and post-school functioning.

In the above example, what if the competency test is not discussed during the IEP meeting? That is, what if the program for the handicapped child's unique needs is developed and provided, performance is assessed, and a decision is made that the child mastered the IEP objectives? Subsequently, suppose that the competency test is given and the child fails. If the child does not receive a diploma because he or she is judged to be incompetent, a dilemma is created. The IEP agreement between the schools and the parent was executed and the objectives were accomplished, yet this program may have no relationship with the student's performance on the competency test. This situation is not just; perhaps it is even illegal.

This hypothetical situation shows the need to construct a competency test which has both predictive and content validity. The task will be difficult. In fact, the notion of competency testing identified here is usually referred to as functional competency testing. To establish the predictive validity of a functional competency test includes defining what it means to be able to function in society. The difficulty is that society consists of many environments with very different functional demands. Presumably the pass-fail nature of competency tests predicts that a student who fails will be functionally incompetent in society. But society changes, as does the environment. The physically handicapped have had great difficulty functioning in many environments, frequently because of architectural barriers. With modification of the environment, however, functioning for many of the physically handicapped is possible. The limited availability of Braille materials for blind individuals has interfered with their functioning; yet technological developments like the Kurzweil Reading Machine eliminate the need for Braille. Greater modification of the environment may be necessary for other handicapped persons, such as the more severely retarded. Still, by reducing the complexity and the demands of the environment, *functioning* is certainly possible. Thus, minimal functional competency may be person-specific. If this is true, then the use of a single test or cutoff score is absurd.

Schools should have goals and standards, and they should assess learning outcomes. However, the appropriate model for assessing the handicapped is the IEP. In fact, the appropriate model for all children might eventually need to be individualization with a mechanism like the IEP. That is, goals and objectives based on individual needs are stated (keeping in mind the type of environment in which the child might function), instruction is based on these goals and objectives, and assessment of individual learning outcomes is made. Decisions related to student mastery are made from these assessments.

From our examination of the diverse levels of needs and environments faced by the handicapped, we see that decisions about individual children should not be made on the basis of statewide minimum competency tests. Recognition of and attention to the dilemmas of parents and educators of handicapped students is essential to any fair and valid statewide minimum competency assessment program.

References

Haney, W., and Madaus, G. Making sense of the competency testing movement. *Harvard Educational Review* 48 (1978): 462-484.

McClung, M. S. Are competency testing programs fair? Legal? *Phi Delta Kappan* 59 (1978): 397-400.

12   Adaptive Testing: How and
          When Should Handicapped
          Students Be Accommodated
          in Competency Testing
          Programs?

Patricia A. Morrissey

Introduction

In March 1978, I had the opportunity to conduct a seminar at the Educational Testing Service in Princeton, New Jersey. The seminar focused on recent education and civil rights laws for the handicapped and the implications of these laws for ETS testing programs. Many of the issues considered at ETS are of equal importance to local or state agencies when developing competency-based testing programs for deciding grade promotion or graduation from high school. The numerous unresolved technical, substantive, resource, sociopolitical, and individual rights issues associated with competency testing programs (Haney and Madaus, 1978) become compounded and confounded when an attempt is made to accommodate the handicapped reasonably and appropriately. Moreover, little information is available about competency testing programs and the handicapped. For example, Pipho (1978) has identified seventeen states which have high school graduation competency requirements. Florida has developed elaborate procedures for accommodating the handicapped. New York is just beginning to develop guidelines for accommodating the handicapped. Although interest and work in this area

The opinions and recommendations offered herein should not be construed as reflective of official U.S. Office of Education policy.

are likely to increase, a compilation of state and local efforts in test accommodation for handicapped students is not available at this time.

It is impractical in this paper to address the full range of issues associated with competency testing as it pertains to handicapped students. However, it is possible to identify areas of accommodation, to suggest tentative guidelines for accommodation, and to outline strategies for a comprehensive approach to accommodation in testing.

The remainder of this paper is composed of four sections: (1) a review of the concept of discrimination and the emergence of laws to protect the handicapped; (2) a consideration of the testing implications associated with such legislation; (3) a critique of various forms of test accommodation; and (4) recommendations for interim and long-range accommodation strategies. My comments apply primarily to those who must accommodate handicapped adolescents with average or better intellectual ability who have also been classified as deaf, blind, orthopedically impaired, or learning disabled. It is beyond the scope of this paper to describe the characteristics of these several impairments. In brief, these students often show performance deficits which cause the observer to assume erroneously that such deficits reflect concomitant deficiencies in competency. It is assumed here that although these students may require special accommodation, test content modifications would not be necessary.

Discrimination and Legislative Initiatives

Discrimination evokes contradictory responses. It may suggest denial of opportunities, yet its prevention or remediation may suggest excessive, special privileges. In remedying discrimination through judicial or legislative action, society must recognize and account for both of these attitudes. In seeking a reasonable balance, it identifies and sets apart special groups. This poses problems for individuals in such groups—they are viewed collectively, and they must accept the special status imposed by society in order to benefit.

Furthermore, when special attention is focused on a particular group, intragroup variance is frequently ignored. For example, if special, individualized accommodation were suddenly available to all handicapped students who must pass a competency test in order to graduate, five subgroups of handicapped students might be identified: (1) those students who passed a test before special accommodation was available and do not wish to be associated with a special status group post hoc; (2) those students who failed the test before special accommodation was available and resent not having had such an opportunity; (3) those students who want to take the test but fear that their competence will not be recognized if they accept special accommodation; (4) those students who take the test willing to accept the possible backlash associated with special accommodation; and (5) those students who misuse special accommodation.

Federal laws which foster responsiveness to handicapped individuals are now enforceable. Recent legislation, Public Law 94-142, the Education of All Handicapped Children Act of 1975, and section 504 of the Rehabilitation Act of 1973 mandate not only that each handicapped child receive a free appropriate public education, but also that the child be afforded specific protections when being evaluated.[1] As of September 1978, these laws apply to all handicapped children between 3 and 18 years, and by September 1980, they will apply to all handicapped 3 to 21 years. Also, section 504 mandates nondiscrimination on the basis of handicap in testing situations throughout a handicapped individual's life.[2]

These legislative initiatives are very important because they shift the emphasis from recognizing groups of handicapped persons to assuring services to the handicapped individual. Their procedural requirements endorse anticipatory and remedial efforts, and they require that educational decisions be made on an individual basis. And finally, these laws give the handicapped person or his or her representative a direct voice in judging public efforts to serve the handicapped.

Implications of Recent Legislation and Potential Problems

Section 504 is a pervasive legislative mandate. Whereas Public Law 94-142 emphasizes specific safeguards for handicapped individuals, section 504 not only mandates such safeguards but requires that "no otherwise qualified handicapped individual . . . shall, solely by reason of his handicap, be excluded from participation in, be denied the benefits of, or be subject to discrimination under any program or activity receiving federal financial assistance."[3] The Congressional intent was to assure equal opportunity for each handicapped individual to obtain the same result and achieve the same level of success as those designated nonhandicapped. Additionally, different or special accommodation is viewed as a viable means of meeting this intent.

The general 504 mandate is clarified in terms of specific contexts, one of which is testing to determine eligibility or placement. Tests used in these contexts must be valid. That is, they must reflect an individual's aptitude or achievement level rather than reflect a student's impaired sensory, manual, or speaking skills.

The implications of the section 504 mandate are clear. In a competency testing program a handicapped student must be individually accommodated.

The tests must be valid. The student must have an opportunity to qualify for promotion or a diploma equal to that of his or her nonhandicapped counterpart.

These blanket requirements ignore many of the technical problems associated with competency testing programs. They include the implicit assumptions that: first, ways exist or can be developed to neutralize or account for the effects of impairments on performance; and second, equal opportunity can be assured by determining how much handicapped individuals are alike rather than different from their normal competitors. Given the current state of affairs in competency testing, such assumptions are not valid. Interim guidelines are sorely needed to compensate for current technical limitations. Such guidelines would help to reduce inappropriate use and interpretation of tests, as well as decrease faulty decision making following testing.

Forms of Accommodation

Accommodation has taken several forms. Handicapped students have been excused from testing programs. Different criteria have been applied to the performance of these students. Special procedures have been developed. And finally, handicapped students have taken tests without any accommodation. Any one of these four alternatives may be an appropriate form of accommodation in a given case. In general, however, some basic differences can be identified.

Exemption is probably one of the most appealing options because there are no special resource commitments involved, and charges of discrimination are unlikely. The individualized education program (IEP) of Public Law 94-142, particularly the student evaluation component,[4] may serve in lieu of a competency test given to nonhandicapped students. But the exemption option suggests three problems. Will the handicapped student qualify for the same diploma? IEPs may be highly variable; will that result in a reverse discrimination charge—graduating is easier for handicapped than nonhandicapped students? Some handicapped students may not want to be exempted; what is the school's obligation if they fail?

Another alternative is the application of different criteria to handicapped students; for example, tolerance of lower scores. A second option would be to give increased weighting to other performance indices such as grades and teacher ratings, which then could be entered into a competency quotient with test scores. This particular option would put a new burden on administrative and evaluation personnel to develop, test, and apply special criteria. But there is, again, the possibility of a reverse discrimination complaint as an aftermath of the Bakke case and of the increased interest of the Supreme Court in the rights and protection of minors. Moreover, for this option to be successfully applied, state educational agency endorsement and monitoring of local compliance are necessary. The addition of a political element—state oversight of local districts—may increase competition among school districts, increase the need for inservice training, require the development of new forms of tests, and may eventually change the nature of instruction. Use of multiple criteria may have a significant impact on schools, and therefore may be more equitable if applied to all potential graduates.

The third option is perhaps not only the most equitable but the most challenging form of accommodation. Procedural modifications could occur in four general areas: environmental adaptations, format modifications, performance adjustments, or pacing flexibility. Environmental adaptations would include the location of testing, lighting, height of chair and/or table, and availability of prosthetic aids. Format modifications would include spacing, size of print, color, and cuing aids. Performance adjustments would include access and right to use tape recorders, typewriters, calculators, and computers and other modes of communicating answers. And finally, flexible pacing would include the option to vary the length of test taking, for example, one 15-minute break per hour of test time.

The underlying assumption here is that if a handicapped student is procedurally accommodated, then his or her performance will more closely approximate the true score for the student if the student were not handicapped. This particular option would place many resource demands on a state or local administrative unit. It would require materials development, experimentation, extensive time commitments, and a willingness to document efforts. To me it is the most equitable procedure, and therefore worth the investment.

In any testing program for handicapped students, the last option—no special accommodation—should be an alternative for those who wish to be treated as their nonhandicapped peers. Due process procedures, particularly notification of rights, could be included with this alternative to reduce misunderstanding.

Recommendations

We need interim and long-term strategies for accommodating handicapped students, particularly with the rapid expansion of competency testing programs. Four interim guidelines seem the most practicable. First, ask the handicapped individual before deciding on the nature and extent of accommodation. Second, decide any accommodations on a case-by-case basis. Third, do not use a test score as the sole criterion for deciding promotion or graduation. Fourth, document why and how accommodation occurred for each handicapped student.

If a comprehensive, systematic approach to competency testing is to emerge, several planning activities are needed: surveys of current practice; handicapped consumers' reactions to various forms of accommodation (questionnaires); review of incidence data to determine the level of effort and priorities for research and development activities; and dissemination of information from surveys, questionnaires, and priorities lists.

It is anticipated that systematic inquiry into forms of accommodation will lead to equal opportunity for the handicapped and fairer treatment of the nonhandicapped. And, in the long run, consideration of these accommodation issues may create a more flexible set of procedures for determining the minimum competencies of all students.

Notes

1. *Federal Register*, 1977, *42*, 163, 121a.530-534; *Federal Register*, 1977, *42*, 250, 121a.540-543.
2. Federal Register, 1977, *42*, 86, 84.11-14, 84.35, 84.41-46.
3. The Rehabilitation Act of 1973, 29 U.S.C. 706.
4. Each handicapped child, according to Public Law 94-142, is to have an IEP which includes procedures, criteria, and a timetable for evaluating performance on an annual basis.

References

Haney, W., and Madaus, G. Making sense of the competency testing movement. National Consortium on Testing Staff Circular no. 2. Cambridge, Mass.: Huron Institute, 1978.

Pipho, E. B. Update VII: Minimal competency testing. Denver: Education Commission of the States, November 15, 1977.

PART IV
Case Studies of
Minimum Competency Testing

This section presents descriptions of the implementation of minimum competency testing in a variety of settings. First, there are descriptions of programs in Florida, North Carolina, Oregon, and Virginia. These are followed by a discussion of present federal activities and by descriptions of a statewide minimum competency testing program in higher education. This section concludes with the presentation of two brief reports at the local school district level, one from the Los Angeles Unified School District and the other from the Portland, Oregon School District. The reader will find that the major issues examined in Parts I-III will repeatedly arise in these case studies. The issues are recurring themes in attempts to understand the pressure for accountability and to impose minimum competency standards through the medium of tests.

Thomas H. Fisher of the Florida State Department of Education traces the early events leading up to the adoption in 1977 of accountability laws, and particularly minimum competency performance standards. The results of the 1977 testing program are presented, along with an analysis of the support of legislators and the news media. Fisher also identifies some of the professional criticisms of the testing program presented in a report of an independent evaluation panel: *The Florida Accountability Program: An Evaluation of Its Educational Soundness and Implementation,* prepared by a committee under contract with the Florida teaching profession (NEA) and the National Education Association. Criticisms of the attempt to actually set standards are to be found in an article by Gene V. Glass, in a 1978 issue of the *Journal of Educational Measurement.*

James J. Gallagher describes the state of North Carolina's response to the movement to adopt minimum educational standards. His description is the only case study that specifically examines policy and practice for testing exceptional children, and the use of a state testing program in private schools. North Carolina will award a "Certificate of Accomplishment" instead of a diploma to students who fail to meet minimum competency standards. This is a controversial stand, as indicated by the specific rejection of this alternative in a recent decision by the Board of Regents in the state of New York (*New York Times*, February 11, 1979). Gallagher provides a detailed history of the test development and review process in North Carolina, and he also describes the use of teacher judgments and a procedure for achieving an advisory-committee consensus to set standards on statewide minimum competency tests in reading and mathematics.

Statewide graduation requirements in Oregon follow a very different pattern than the minimum competency testing programs described for Florida and North Carolina. Marshall D. Herron describes how the Oregon system arrived at its present status and some problems that he perceives in the present situation. He also anticipates the directions in which the Oregon system may evolve. Oregon diplomas are granted on the basis of fulfillment of all "credit, competency, and attendance requirements set by the state and local district." Local school boards are required to adopt their own competency statements within six areas prescribed by the state. Local staff are then expected to develop performance indicators (appropriate measures which the district will accept as evidence of competency) and record-keeping systems for documentation of competency attainment. The approach of using local communities to decide what levels of reading, computing, and other skills are needed by an individual to function in that community is very different from the state-centralized programs in Florida, North Carolina, and Virginia. Of particular interest is Herron's analysis of the role of a particular state superintendent of education, and the problems in moving from this one individual's vision of minimum competency and "survival skills" to less sophisticated definitions when performance requirements were actually developed. These definitional issues reflect the earlier debate between Jenne Britell and Maxine Greene on the nature of standards of excellence and competence. Also of interest in the Oregon case history is the continuing commitment to the concept of local control and the apparent disinclination to move in the direction of state-level proficiency tests for high school graduation.

James C. Impara, in his paper, *Virginia's Approach to Minimum Competency Testing*, describes a system which combines the centralized approaches in Florida and North Carolina with the local control described for Oregon. Virginia has a dual set of competency requirements for high school graduation, one set administered statewide and a second set administered by local educational agencies. Impara describes the activities undertaken to implement the statewide requirements. In this setting, again, the problem of setting performance standards is well described. School and community representatives were brought together and asked to recommend a standard of performance. Apparently, none of the major procedures for setting standards that are described in the measurement literature were used in the Virginia program. Impara also provides a useful comparison of the Virginia program with those of other states along a number of dimensions: whether or not the program is mandated by the state, the specific purposes of the program, the grade levels of the program, and subject areas tested.

Judith Sauls Shoemaker, in her paper, *Minimum Competency Testing: The View from Capitol Hill*, provides the reader with another perspective on the use of tests in the educational system. Recent federal testing activities range from congressional hearings and pending legislation to HEW's national conference on testing. Although there have been a number of suggestions for a national test of educational achievement, the HEW-sponsored conference on testing and basic skills in March 1978 was unanimous in recommending that such a test not be developed. There has been established, however, an Office of Testing, Assessment, and Evaluation within the National Institute of Education. The functions of this office are to provide information and referral services on achievement testing; to conduct regional conferences on the uses of educational tests; to assist in improving the skills of teachers, administrators, and parents in the use of tests; and to conduct research to improve testing.

Shoemaker describes the two major policies of the federal government in relation to achievement testing and basic competencies: one, there should be no national standards of performance or nationally developed tests; and two, no testing program may be used to deny equal educational opportunity. In her view, the most important contribution that the federal government might make to the minimum competency testing movement is the four-year, NIE-developed study of the long-term impact of minimum competency testing, now being conducted by National Evaluation Systems of Amherst, Massachusetts.

In contrast to the previous emphases on statewide assessment in the public elementary and secondary schools, the next three papers are concerned with a systemwide assessment of basic skills in higher education being conducted by the University System of Georgia. This series of papers is included because there is now a growing trend toward the assessment of basic skills, or minimum competencies, in higher education. The policy decision for an assessment program in higher education was made in 1969 by the chancellor of the University System of Georgia. Haskin R. Pounds describes this action in *The Development and Implementation of Policies for Assessing Basic Skills in Higher Education.* This assessment program is to determine if graduates of the state system of higher education can read and write. The policy was formulated in response to pressures similar to those giving rise to accountability programs at the secondary-school level. Policy questions that had to be answered by faculty committees were similar to those that arose at the secondary level: Who will be required to take the test and when? Will there be exemptions? Will passing the test be a graduation requirement? What will be the procedures for dealing with students failing the test? What about remediation? What about test content, security, and cutoff scores?

After a pilot testing program, the university system moved to a program of local test development and administration. Pounds's paper will be of interest to others in higher education who may be considering the development or operation of such a program. Additional papers by Susan E. Ridenour and R. Robert Rentz provide interesting contrasts to the handling of issues similar to those in elementary and secondary school programs. Susan E. Ridenour, in *Impacts of Proficiency Testing on Higher Education*, describes the impact of the Georgia Regents' Testing Program on curriculum, accessibility (admissions, retention, and graduation), as well as evaluation (further testing). It is interesting to note, in contrast to any published reports at the secondary-school level, that the standards in the Regents' Testing Program (passing requirements) have been raised as the program has been implemented in the past several years. In the area of curriculum, the Regents' Testing Program has brought about special remedial programs and more extensive testing for placement in beginning, basic-skills courses in English and mathematics. As one administrator aptly noted, "the power to test is indeed the power to determine curriculum" (quoted in Ridenour). Of particular interest to those administering secondary-level programs, however, may be the use of written essays. These essays are read and rated by faculty, with an apparently high degree of consensus and reliability. The procedures and results of the essay testing suggest that not all assessment programs need provide tests only in multiple-choice form.

R. Robert Rentz, in his paper, *Characteristics of Tests Used in a Minimum Competency Testing Program in Higher Education*, analyzes the reasoning that led to the local development of tests in the Georgia program and describes the procedures for establishing cutoff scores. He also describes Georgia's testing program, which uses a series of multiple, equated test forms, and he outlines the cutoff procedure used in the rating of essay examinations. Georgia's multiple-choice test (the reading test) is based on Rasch calibrations of items, a procedure similar to that used in a number of state programs, and also in one of the local programs described here, that of the Portland Public Schools.

Walter E. Hathaway describes *A School-District-Developed, Rasch-Based Approach to Minimum Competency Achievement Testing.* In his paper, Hathaway discusses the development of a large-scale item bank used in Portland, Oregon, as part of the district's procedures to implement the state graduation requirements described earlier. The paper includes the test plans for grades four through eight in the areas of mathematics, reading, and language usage. It also provides sample reports, which are prepared for individual teachers, identifying the students needing additional work on specific goals and showing the distribution of test results within individual classrooms. The paper presents an optimistic view of the implementation of the testing program and its use by principals and teachers. However, there is no specific evidence documenting the impact of the testing program in the local school district.

Robert Sallander provides a miniature case study, in the Los Angeles Unified School District, of the procedure for setting a cutoff score of minimum competence, in his paper, *Competency Tests: Decisions for Educators.* Sallander very candidly indicates the trade-off that formally or informally occurs in setting cutoff scores in many situations. As he boldly tells the reader, the bottom line was a consideration of how much the district could afford to spend for the remedial instructional program. That is, what was the trade-off between the money available for remediation and the school district's felt responsibility to provide remediation to those failing the tests? The arbitrary standard, or cutoff score, is the result.

As noted above, the papers in this section reflect many of the issues that were raised in the papers contained in earlier sections. The state-level case studies show that there is no consensus on the issue of local versus state control of testing programs, nor on the use of tests to measure a partial requirement for graduation, nor on the human and technical problems involved in determining general standards of minimum competency and cutoff scores for specific tests. Nor is the institutional responsibility to provide remedial education to those falling below cutoff scores clearly specified in many programs. It is clear that many programs operate in partial policy vacuums, and their consequences are barely understood. The dangers and implications of this ignorance are expressed in many of the other papers in this volume.

Cases in the States and the Federal Government

13   The Florida Competency Testing Program

Thomas H. Fisher

Background

The Florida competency testing program has evolved from thinking and planning over the last eight to ten years. These efforts began in the late 1960s when many states began moving toward systems management and educational accountability. Florida was one of the first states in this movement.

One of the first steps in Florida was the establishment of a research and development program in 1969 to facilitate the positive changes desired by the 1968 legislature (House of Representatives, 1976). This program was for activities which were "action research" oriented, and it later supported the initial development of the state assessment tests.

A second major step forward was accomplished in 1970 with the publication of *Goals for Education in Florida* (Department of Education, n.d.). This small booklet, typical of those produced in other states, set forth ten broad areas of intended accomplishment for Florida students and for the educational system itself. Significantly, one process goal in the booklet is that "teaching/learning strategies shall be directed toward achievement of the goals and objectives for student development established for the state system" (p. 10). And the following appears in the area of student learning: "All students shall acquire, to the extent of their individual physical, mental and emotional capacities, a mastery of the basic skills required in obtaining and expressing ideas through the effective use of words, numbers, and other symbols" (p. 6).

By March 1971 the Department of Education (DOE) had developed and printed a *Plan for Educational Assessment in Florida* (DOE, 1971). This booklet outlined an ambitious plan for product and process assessments and for analyses of educational costs. Importantly, the emphasis was on objective-referenced tests even at this early date. The plan did not stress individual student data, however, but instead proposed matrix-sampling procedures (DOE, 1971, pp. 7, 14-16).

The legislature enacted the 1971 Educational Accountability Act as its first formal attempt to define what it wanted done to make the schools more accountable. The act was brief and incorporated elements of the DOE plan for assessment. However, the original act merely called for testing students, which was a much more limited approach than was envisioned by the department (House of Representatives, 1976, pp. 19-20).

The Department of Education moved ahead, in January 1972, to introduce an assessment program based on sampling students at the second and fourth grades and assessing skills related to reading. This sampling approach was followed in 1973 and 1974 (although grades 3, 6, and 9 were also tested), and the tests included reading, writing, and math. Science was also tested in 1974 at grades 6 and 9 (House of Representatives, 1976, pp. 32-33).

The 1974 legislature altered the 1971 accountability act and specifically included an implementation schedule for the student tests. It mandated that all students in grades 3 and 6 would be tested in the three R's by 1974-75, and all students in grades 3 through 6 would be tested by 1975-76. No areas other than reading, writing, and arithmetic were to be tested until this was accomplished (DOE, 1974, p. 15). Thus, the legislature placed a priority on census testing in the basic skills. This effectively settled the question of what to test; there was no further argument about what was or was not important.

During the winter of 1975-76, the House Education Committee staff prepared an extensive review of the Department of Education's implementation of educational accountability. The report was comprehensive and critical, and it concluded that confusion had resulted from differences between what the legislature wanted and what the department provided. Secondly, it reported that accountability had not yet been implemented effectively in Florida (House of Representatives, 1976, pp. vii-xv).

The Florida legislature addressed this report and its recommendations during its spring 1976 session. The House of Representatives emphasized its desires for statewide data at both the elementary and secondary levels. The Senate, however, was interested in guaranteeing that each student would be at least minimally competent in the basic skills prior to promotion and graduation.

The compromise package, passed unanimously, provided for both interests. The 1976 Educational Accountability Act clarified several different legislative interests in things as diverse as pupil testing, implementation of a management information system, district comprehensive planning, and pupil progression plans. It sought to draw together and consolidate several elements of accountability appearing in other laws.

The assessment program was given a clear mandate to test at grades 3, 5, 8, and 11 in reading, writing, and arithmetic. Other subject areas could be tested as appropriate. The tests were to measure minimum performance standards adopted by the State Board of Education. Public reporting was guaranteed through reports by the Commission of Education and by reports of test results to local school authorities and citizens (DOE, 1976b, pp. 11-16).

Section 232.245 F.S. specified that each local school district would prepare a pupil progression plan by July 1977. Such plans were to address whether or not students had met both state and local standards. Furthermore, districts were to clearly articulate their high school graduation requirements. The specific wording was:

Beginning with the 1978-79 school year, each district school board shall establish standards for graduation from its secondary schools. Such standards shall include, but not be limited to, mastery of the basic skills and satisfactory performance in functional literacy as determined by the State Board of Education, and the completion of the minimum number of credits required by the district school board. Each district shall develop procedures for remediation of those students who are unable to meet such standards. Based on these standards each district shall provide for the awarding of certificates of attendance and may provide for differentiated diplomas to correspond with the varying achievement levels or competencies of its secondary students. (DOE, 1976b, p. 74)

The Department of Education interpreted its responsibilities to be the implementation of new assessment tests at four grade levels, all of which would measure new performance standards. Secondly, a test of functional literacy would be developed as part of the assessment program at grade eleven. The department moved immediately to discharge its responsibilities.

Development of Minimum Performance Standards (Objectives)

As previously stated, the Florida approach to educational accountability from the very start emphasized the articulation and measurement of specific student objectives. The first attempt to accomplish this was in late 1971 as the department contracted with certain state universities and local school districts to identify catalogs of objectives. These objectives were reviewed and revised as necessary by statewide committees and department curriculum consultants (DOE, 1976a, p. 3).

The objectives addressed many subject areas and were quite voluminous. Perhaps because of their volume and their highly specific nature, the objectives apparently never were used extensively either by local school districts or by the DOE.

For the first educational assessment to be conducted in 1972, the department contracted with the Center for the Study of Evaluation, University of California at Los Angeles (CSE), to identify certain objectives for grades two and four. Again, there was extensive involvement of local district teachers and curriculum consultants in the process of reviewing and setting priorities (DOE, 1976a, pp. 3-4).

From this point until the school year 1975-76 the statewide assessment used objectives which were based on the CSE set but were revised yearly. As time passed, there was considerable unhappiness with the specificity of the objectives. It was generally believed that they were too explicit to be of much help to teachers. During the winter of 1975, an effort was made to correct this situation. A consolidated set of minimum objectives was developed by consultants in the Department of Education and sent to each school district for review and revision. These objectives included two levels of specificity with the broadest category labeled "milestone" objectives. For example:

Milestone Objective: The student will add and subtract fractions.
Grade Level Objectives (8th): 1. The student will add two proper fractions having unlike denominators.
2. The student will add two mixed numbers having whole number components less than 10.

These objectives were adopted by the State Board of Education in May 1976 and formed the basis of the 1976-77 statewide assessment (DOE, 1976c).

In June 1976 the new Educational Accountability Act went into effect. This statute contained the following language:

229.565(1) The State Board of Education shall approve minimum student performance standards in the various program categories and chronological grade levels, expecially in reading, writing, and mathematics which the Commissioner of Education determines shall best indicate the status of the state system of public education. . . . [and]

229.57(2) (a) Establish, with the approval of the State Board, minimum performance standards related to the goals for education contained in the state's plan including, but not limited to, basic skills in reading, writing, and mathematics. The minimum performance standards shall be approved by April 1 in each year they are established for a period of no less than 3 nor more than 5 years. (DOE, 1976b, pp. 14-15)

Throughout the discussions which led to passage of this law, it was understood that a "minimum performance standard" was the same as a performance objective. The three to five year adoption period was desirable as a means of promoting some stability in the assessment program. This was an important consideration, as the assessment tests had been modified yearly to meet the constantly changing objectives and demands placed upon the program.

Because the 1976-77 minimum objectives had been accepted across Florida after their appearance on the statewide assessment tests, the new minimum performance standards were based upon them. Curriculum specialists from the Department of Education organized task forces of local district educators and lay persons to assist in reviewing the minimum objectives and revising them into performance standards.

All Florida districts were invited to form committees to review the proposed standards, and 46 of 67 did so. Additionally, three special panels consisting of teachers, principals, and lay citizens were created to review the standards. As a result of this process, some standards were revised, deleted, or added. They were adopted by the State Board of Education in April 1977 for a period of three years (DOE, 1976c, p. ii).

Most of the performance standards are subdivided into more discrete skills. In some cases, a standard will stand by itself. An example of a standard and its associated subskills is:

Grade 8 Mathematics Standard M
The student will multiply and divide decimals.
Skill 23: Multiply a whole number and a number having no more than two decimal places.
Skill 24: Multiply two decimal fractions, both named in tenths or hundredths.
Skill 25: Divide a decimal fraction named in tenths or hundredths by multiples of 10 less than 100. (DOE, 1976c, p. 21)

As will be seen in later sections of this paper, this organizational pattern had implications for the testing strategies to be designed.

The 1976 legislature did not attempt to define functional literacy as it was mentioned in 232.245 F.S. However, the State Board of Education adopted a definition of literacy in April 1977 when it approved the first set of minimum student performance standards: "For purposes of the 1977 Educational Assessment Program, functional literacy is defined as the application of the basic skills to problems of an everyday nature" (DOE, 1976c, p. iv). The essential element of the literacy test would be the application of basic skills. It should be made clear at this point that there is no evidence that the legislature intended anything further by its use of the term "functional literacy." Hence, the test can quite simply be regarded as an exit competency test comprised of application problems. No underlying psychological trait is necessarily implied.

In responding to this mandate for a functional literacy test, the department referred to the grade eleven minimal objectives adopted by the State Board of Education in May 1976, since these were, at that time, the only set of official objectives. From this set, department staff selected those which had a practical orientation (such as reading highway and city maps) or which could be adapted through the use of practical test problems (such as identifying an unstated opinion). This set of thirteen math and eleven communications objectives formed the basis for the functional literacy test.

Development of the Assessment Tests

The entire emphasis of the accountability program in Florida since the earliest days had been on the articulation of performance standards (objectives) and on determining the attainment of the standards. In the 1976 accountability act, the following language was not unexpected: "The Commissioner shall: (a) Establish . . . minimum performance standards . . . (b) Develop and administer in the public schools a uniform, statewide program of assessment to determine, periodically, educational status and progress, and the degree of achievement of approved minimum performance standards" (DOE, 1976b, p. 15). This language specifically implies that the statewide assessment tests should be designed along a criterion-referenced approach rather than a norm-referenced one.

This is not to say that the state assessment tests are not capable of producing normative information. Indeed, each year the program routinely calculates student, school, and district percentiles and uses these distributions in various ways. However, the emphasis is not on the norms as such. In fact, to further minimize use of normative data at the student level, the 1978 program did not offer percentiles even as an optional service.

The law itself does not specify whether the assessment program will be a census-level test. In the discussions following issuance of the House Education Committee staff report mentioned previously, there clearly was considerable sentiment in support of a statewide sampling program. This position was advocated by one or two of the larger local school districts which had a considerable investment in commercial norm-referenced test programs and did not want the bother, or competition, of a census-level state test. The counterargument was that school-level data were essential for certain requirements of the law and that sampling was not particularly efficient in producing school-level data. It seemed just as efficient to census test instead of using sampling to produce school-level data. The latter argument won the day, and sufficient funds were provided for a census-level testing effort.

Because the 1976 statute and its predecessors all specified the adoption of minimum performance standards for Florida schools, the DOE had to develop its own test items or obtain them through a lease agreement, assuming usable items could be found. The department had access to items used in previous assessments, but necessary new items were sought in two ways: searches of available item banks, and creation of items especially for the Florida standards.

Through a contract with Florida State University a massive search of available items was undertaken. The search team requested access to items from other states, large cities, and commercial item banks. Over twenty thousand items were screened, but only two usable items were found. (One of them had to be modified.)

The chief problems encountered in the search were (1) mismatches between the items and the intent of the minimum standards, (2) lack of any data on the quality of the items, and (3) mismatches between the items and the Florida test specifications. (Incidentally, it was quite disturbing to see how many items were in use for which there were no item statistics available.) Additionally, it was apparent that leasing items would be expensive and would also lead to problems, as test review panels would want to make revisions in the items in any event. Any normative data obtained with leased items would thus become of little use without further equating.

Therefore, the department decided to obtain its items for basic skills tests through contracts with state universities. The university teams would produce a test item, pilot test it, revise it if necessary, and provide camera-ready artwork. The cost varied from project to project but generally it was possible to obtain draft items for $30 each and field-tested items for $120 each.

When the 1976 accountability act was passed, many legislators and department officials thought that a single competency test would be developed and administered late in the senior year. Upon further reflection, they decided to make the test part of the eleventh-grade assessment, thus providing time for additional instruction and retesting of students who failed.

The Student Assessment Section of the DOE contracted with two state universities to produce the eleventh-grade test questions, many of which were to be "functional" (problems of application). These projects met with only limited success because the item writers had difficulty creating high-quality application problems.

Therefore, it was determined that the best course of action would be to develop two tests for grade eleven—one measuring the basic skills and one measuring the application of the basic skills. The latter test would be developed with the assistance of Educational Testing Service, Princeton, N.J. (ETS), using draft items the department had, plus others which would be created by ETS writers.

By February 1977, the items were ready, and they were field-tested in March with a small number of students in five counties. No attempt was made to draw a sample adequate to predict the exact statewide performance level, because its purpose was only to gain data for further revisions of the items. The final version of the test was ready by May 1977. It consisted of 117 items of which about a dozen were nationally normed items from the Adult Proficiency Level Test marketed by the American College Testing Company.

It is important to note that the department did not claim that the functional literacy test would be capable of determining whether a person who passed would be assured of employment, high wages, a college education, or a happy married life. It was all too obvious that some people would function in our society who could not pass the test. Instead, the department's position was that the test would be a high school test of competency to apply certain basic skills. No attempt was made to measure an underlying psychological trait known as "functional literacy." On the other hand, if such a construct could be revealed in the future, it would be an added bonus.

Because the emphasis of the 1976 accountability law was on mastery of selected performance standards, the assessment tests were criterion-referenced, as has been mentioned. To indicate mastery of a selected basic skill the department established the criteria in table 1. The number of items per skill varied, but most had five items each. As one might expect, vocabulary and spelling skills had the most items.

Much has been written about the development of criterion-referenced tests, but the literature is still fluid, showing great diversity of opinion about what approaches to take in developing cut-scores, creating test items, determining test reliability, and so forth. The department staff considered the current literature and made the best decisions it could, given the state of the art.

To determine cut-scores, the department established two classifications:

Table 1. Number of Items and Minimum Number Required for Mastery

Number of Items to Measure a Skill	Minimum Number of Correct Answers
2	2
3	3
4	3
5	4
6	5
7	5
8	6
9	7
10	7
11	8
12	9
13	10
14	10
15	11
16	12

mastery and nonmastery. Item specifications had been developed for each minimum performance skill, and items were generated according to these rules, although the system was not so sophisticated as to permit computer generation of item sets.

The department realized that decisions about mastery of a skill based on four, five, or six items would be imperfect, although nonmastery status could be more easily defended (Visco, 1977). For this reason, local districts were told to review the test results carefully. In some cases, more recent data may indicate mastery (or nonmastery) of a skill, controverting the classification provided by the test results.

More importantly, the law requires student mastery of minimum standards, not skills. Therefore, in many cases the number of items available to determine mastery of a standard was comfortably large, since two or three subskills may have been measured.

In the case of the literacy test at grade eleven, only two minimum standards were included—for math and communications. The former had 59 items while the latter had 58. A student passed the test if he or she correctly answered 70 percent of the items in each test and mastered at least half of the subskills on each test. (The second half of this criterion was removed by the State Board of Education on August 15, 1978. When the 1977 data were reprocessed, less than 400 students out of 120,000 had their status altered, 400 more passed the minimum standards.)

Much has been said about the "arbitrariness" of the scoring system used in Florida (Glass, 1978). However, the department does not believe that its decisions were based on whim, but that they were carefully reasoned. Ultimately, any scoring decisions are judgmental; no matter how much data are available, someone still has to make the final decisions. This does not make them arbitrary.

In this case of the eleventh-grade literacy test, the scoring system was first developed around the basic skills test. The criteria shown in table 1 represent a compromise between test length (and probable student fatigue and boredom) and accuracy of student classification to mastery or non-mastery status. The required number of correct responses provides a comfortable level of confidence, according to Millman's (1972) data on misclassifications. It represents a passing score which is considered reasonable by Florida school districts (verified by a department survey), and it is consistent with the system used for all the basic skills tests.

Not satisfied with these factors only, the Department of Education contracted with Florida State University to do a study of the construct validity of the literacy test. Literacy test data were gathered from adults of varying educational levels. Also, a cloze reading test was administered as an independent reading measure. The study reached the following conclusions, in part:

A substantial correlation was found between the communication total score on the *Literacy Test* and the independent measure of reading ability. The concurrent validity is about as high as can ordinarily be expected between two different instruments designed to measure the same thing. This is strong support for the statistical validity of the *Literacy Test* communications score. . . . We also found that the proportion passing the mathematics standard and the communications standard increased markedly from the group functioning at a low level in society . . . to the group functioning at a high level. . . . This is strong statistical support for the validity of the mathematics and communications scores. They are behaving precisely as one would expect them to if they were measuring a construct that reasonably could be required for high school graduation. . . . (Hills and King, 1978, pp. 43-44)

Given these statistics, the Department of Education is satisfied with the system at present. However, changes will inevitably come as more information is gathered and more experience is gained.

Results of the 1977 Statewide Assessment

The results of the 1977 statewide assessment in functional literacy received much more attention than did the basic skills results. "Florida Flunks," heralded *Time* magazine in an article which suggested that students were migrating en masse from Florida to Georgia to avoid the test (Florida Flunks, 1977). This was not true.

When the first test results were received for Duval County (Jacksonville) the results in the literacy test showed large percentages of failure in mathematics but very low failure rates in communications. This trend continued and when the statewide results were available, 36 percent of the students had failed math and 8 percent had failed communications.

Within the basic skills areas, the test results showed some variation across the grade levels. The minimum student performance standards are supposed to be achieved by all students, so one could theoretically consider anything less than 100 percent mastery as deficient. For now, it might be argued that 80 percent of the students should master at least three-fourths of the standards. Table 2 reveals the extent of student deficiencies under the latter criterion.

The test results were also summarized across each individual skill for each'of the four grade levels. The achievement rates demonstrate acceptably high performance in some areas and dismal performance in others. Table 3 illustrates a few skills as examples of both good and bad performance.

The literacy test scores revealed a pronounced trend of higher failure rates among minorities. The most serious problem was among black students. According to the final figures, 77 percent of the black students failed the math literacy test compared with 24 percent of the whites. In the communications area 26 percent of the blacks failed compared with 3 percent of the whites. The performance across the individual skills on the two tests varied somewhat, but there was a consistent difference in performance between the two groups. (The same trends were seen in the basic skills tests at all grade levels.)

Table 2. Percentage of Students in Four Grade Levels Mastering at Least Three-Fourths of the Minimum Standards in the Basic Skills Areas

Grade Level	Math	Reading	Writing
3	77	73	47
5	60	69	74
8	48	54	71
11	56	76	18

Table 3. Percentage of Achievement for Selected-Skills, Grade 8

Skill	Mastery Rate
Identify equivalent proper fractions	57%
Add three 4-digit numbers	95%
Identify a word's literal definition	43%
Find specific information in a selection	83%
Identify the plural forms of nouns	63%
Complete simple forms	94%

These results sparked charges of racial bias in the tests, but the department believes these charges are unwarranted. The test development activities included reviews of the items for potential bias, and bivariate scatterplots comparing black and white student data generally showed a consistent difference across the entire test. The department's official position was that the test results should be dealt with in a positive manner, not dismissed as the product of a faulty test.

Exceptional education students have generally been exempted from the assessment tests. They are not expected to meet the standards designed for regular students. However, since a standard diploma can be received only by passing the literacy test, some students have chosen to take it. The results demonstrated a large failure rate among such students.

Reactions to the Program

Often, a testing program within a local school district or a state rolls merrily along year after year without having any substantial impact. Data are collected, summary statistics are displayed (sometimes publicly), but little change actually takes place in individual schools and classrooms. This has not happened with Florida's minimum competency testing program, however.

Without trying to be exhaustive, several reasons may be cited. First, a traditional norm-referenced test may be used to generate impressive data with means, standard deviations, grade-equivalent scores, and student percentiles. Yet because there is no particular instructional linkage to the test, or the linkage is ill-defined, specific educational deficiencies cannot be easily discerned.

Second, testing programs designed on a sampling basis may have little impact because everyone has a potential "cop-out": the results are not specific. Releasing test data for individual schools and districts removes such anonymity. It is somewhat like the old story about hitting a mule with a two-by-four "just to get his attention."

Third, and most telling, is the fact that in Florida graduation is now tied directly to the state test results. There is no way for students or local educators to avoid this fact; the testing program stands between the student and graduation.

Under such circumstances, reactions to the program cannot help but be varied. The program affects newspaper editors, students, parents, Department of Education officials, teachers, and legislators differently. Their reactions are molded by their philosophies and perceptions of the way schools should be. It is likely, therefore, that people will get different impressions of what is happening in Florida; the impressions will depend on who speaks to whom.

Legislative Reactions

Ultimately, legislative reactions boil down to support—either it is there or it is not. Such support waxes and wanes for political reasons as much as for educational reasons.

In Michigan, where accountability found strong advocates during the early 1970s, legislative support is now reported to be less certain. On the surface, the decline of support appears to be an overall disenchantment with testing—but things may not be as they seem. For example, the Michigan Education Association (MEA) is a strong teacher association in a union-oriented state. The MEA has substantial influence on the State Board of Education and in the Legislature. Since the MEA opposes the state testing program, it is understandable that the Department of Education would have to struggle to keep its testing effort alive.

But in Florida, different circumstances prevail. The state is not very pro-union, there are a great number of retirees in the state, and the two prominent teacher organizations are locked in a struggle for dominance. Furthermore, the commissioner of education is elected, and the State Board of Education is composed of the heads of each of six governmental agencies, each an elected official in his or her own right.

Such a system means that the voice of the people is very strong and is reflected in the decisions of the legislators. As public disenchantment with the schools rose during the early and mid-1970s (as did enrollment in private schools in Florida), the legislature tightened its educational accountability programs. It also doubled (compared to 1974-75) the funding of the Student Assessment Section to about $1.3 million in 1978-79. Clearly, the legislature, reflecting the wishes of the people, wanted information about school achievement, and it wanted expeditious improvements.

The legislature also responded to the needs identified by the test results in 1976-77 with a State Compensatory Education Program funded at $10 million. The 1978 legislature raised the amount to $26.5 million and also overwhelmingly voted down several attempts to delay implementation of the graduation requirements previously mentioned. While the legislative posture may change in the future as public opinion shifts, the legislature to date can easily command an "A" grade for its support.

Support of the News Media

The news media in Florida played an influential role in building support for the 1976 Educational Accountability Act and continued to support the testing requirements as they were being implemented. This strong support was documented elsewhere (Fisher, 1978) and will not be repeated here.

The interest of the news media was intense during the period in which the tests were given and the results were being returned. "The test" was definitely the hottest educational news story of the year. Its controversial aspects were natural ingredients for such stories, but at the same time the news stories contributed greatly to public awareness of the program and created much public discussion of the issues.

The reporters' appetites had been whetted by their first-hand knowledge about the test, as thirty-seven of them had taken it earlier in the year. Further, they had been surprised when early predictions of a 30 percent failure rate had been made, based on field tests conducted by the department.

Reporters from one end of the state to the other waited anxiously for the first test results. One team of reporters even went so far as to trace a shipment of missing test results and volunteer to go get them for the district officials. (One shipment of results ended up in the storeroom of an Italian restaurant.)

Even after the large failure rates became known, the support of the newspaper and of radio and television stations was solid across the state. One editorial occurring during the peak of public discussion about the test results concluded:

It may be arbitrary to insist that Florida students should be taught to read, write and do arithmetic before we hand them a diploma and send them on their way. But any other educational goal would be equally arbitrary, and we don't think this one is unreasonable. Maybe the tests could be improved upon, but they shouldn't be abandoned or relaxed to the point that they have no real meaning. ("Why Dilute Tests?" 1978, no page)

Only one major newspaper in the state took a conservative stance regarding the literacy test—the *St. Petersburg Times*. The editorials primarily expressed concern over the large failure rate of minority students. Even so, the following editorial appeared in June 1978.

We still have some serious qualms about the way these tests are designed and administered. We are dubious also about the prospect that so many youngsters will be turned out of our schools with nothing to show for the effort but a certificate that says they attended.

But we don't think anybody doubts that functional literacy is a minimum educational goal, attainment of which can be reasonably demanded of high school graduates with any expectation of getting along well in the world. Far better to pass the test, kids, than to quibble. ("Back," 1978, no page)

As is typically the case, sooner or later some errors and half-truths appeared in print. One reporter made at least four telephone calls in the course of developing a story (one call to this writer all the way to Denver, Colorado). When the story appeared it was incorrect and had to be corrected through other wire-service stories. On other occasions, staff members of the Department of Education conveyed incorrect information resulting in stories which had to be corrected. But, in the vast majority of cases, the support of the press and other media was excellent and the stories were accurate.

Public Opinion

Public opinion supported the preliminary steps toward educational accountability in the late 1960s, and the support continues unabated in Florida. Every parent seems to have a personal story about the schools, which in some way aroused frustration. Perhaps there was a teacher of poor quality, a lack of supplies, an arbitrary discipline rule, and so on. In Florida, people wanted a tighter educational ship, and the testing program was a response to these desires.

When the news media began to focus national attention on Florida's competency test, letters started to pour into the Department of Education. They were uniformly supportive, and some examples are shown below.

From Florida:

I hope you can send me a copy of the Literacy Test so I can take it in my house just to see if I'm slipping or just holding my own.
Thank you.

From Louisiana:

I am very interested in obtaining a sample copy of your Functional Literacy Test. The paper stated it was top secret, but we.have four sons ages 16-22 and would like to have them take the test. . . .

From Ohio:

I would like to commend you for your action taken recently regarding your decision on testing in order for graduation before they receive their diploma. . . . Congratulations.

From New York:

Kudos to the person or persons who devised and are implementing the Functional Literacy Test. It sounds great! Hope it starts a nationwide trend. Best wishes.

While one can create a particular image by partially selecting from such letters, no attempt to do so was made for this paper. The truth is that few if any negative letters came to the Student Assessment Section office during the fall of 1977 as the literacy test was being administered and scores were being reported. Later, several letters were received in which the writers were concerned about the exceptional education students— particularly the Specific Learning Disability students. Still later, some letters were received from citizens concerned about the large failure rate among minorities.

A further indication of public support in Florida came from a public opinion survey conducted by Gannett Press. Approximately one thousand registered voters were asked whether they supported the graduation tests for high school students. Some 88 percent responded affirmatively, including 74 percent of the minority-group voters. The survey did not ask whether the respondents approved of the present Department of Education plans and procedures ("Voters," 1978).

Professional Criticism

Generally, the two professional organizations for teachers in the state were not happy about passage of the 1976 Educational Accountability Act. But the unions' political impact was only moderate during the legislative session.

Since that time, the FEA-United, an affiliate of the American Federation of Teachers, has adopted a policy requesting a delay in implementation of the graduation requirements. The Florida Teaching Profession, affiliated with the National Education Association (FTP-NEA), prefers that the whole program be dissolved or at least changed to a state-level sampling program.

The FTP-NEA financed an "evaluation" of the accountability program in Florida during early 1978 ("Expert Panel," 1978). The five-person committee was chaired by Dr. Ralph Tyler and the final report was issued at the NEA Convention in Texas in July 1978 (Tyler et al., 1978).

As with the House-Rivers-Stufflebeam study of the Michigan accountability system (1974), the NEA seems to have initiated the Florida study as a means of blasting achievement tests and state accountability systems in general. The Florida report was entirely predictable in its conclusions.

The Department of Education officially blasted right back, calling the report "unconvincing, intentionally contradictory and intellectually weak" (Turlington, 1978). The newspapers in the state supported this opinion with editorial statements such as:

It is natural to wonder how there could be so much ignorance displayed by a group associated with education as the National Education Association showed in its criticism of Florida's functional literacy test. The answer is, of course, the NEA is less of an educational group than it is a labor union . . . It is probable that NEA officials could pass the test with no trouble. But they could do with a little remedial work in social studies and logic. ("NEA Misinterprets," 1978, no page)

At this point, the FTP-NEA study seems to have had negligible impact in Florida, but perhaps it was really intended for use elsewhere.

Other professional reactions have been directed toward the general question of whether competency programs should exist at all. Two prominent statements along this line are those issued by the National Council of Teachers of English and by the Committee on Testing of the National Academy of Sciences (Suhor, 1978; National Academy of Education, 1978). Both organizations were opposed to competency programs. In the National Academy report, the conclusion was reached that such programs are "unworkable." These reports have not deterred Floridians yet, but, unfortunately, they do reflect the schism between citizens and educators on this important issue.

Legal Challenges

McClung (1978) has written about the legal bases for challenging competency-based testing programs. His paper presents a broad overview of attack points but does not give a full appreciation of what will happen when such legal actions are threatened.

In Florida, the first exploratory legal challenge was brought in February 1978. The president of the Dade County National Association for the Advancement of Colored People sought an injunction against the Department of Education to force its test-development meetings into the public arena. Florida government operates "in the sunshine," and plaintiffs demanded that these meetings between staff and technical advisers be opened to the public.

The judge refused the injunction on the basis that he had insufficient evidence to show that the department was acting improperly. The legislature later passed an act making it clear that the testing program was not included under the sunshine law, thus negating this avenue of attack (DOE, 1978, pp. 40-41).

A second challenge was brought by a citizen of Florida who claimed that the scoring procedures had been improperly adopted. Essentially, Florida has an Administrative Procedures Act (APA) which seeks to protect citizens from the "phantom legislature"—bureaucrats who adopt procedures without proper public input. The APA specifies steps to be taken to adopt "rules" which have the weight of law. This challenge sought to nullify the test scoring system on the basis that the department did not request approval of the State Board of Education before its use. The hearing officer ruled in favor of the plaintiff, and the department responded by appealing the ruling and approaching the state board for approval of the scoring system.

The State Board of Education was asked to adopt the scoring procedures on August 15, 1978, which it did after a lengthy public debate (some nine hours long). However, the same plaintiff again challenged the rule. This time the complaint was against the substance of the rule itself. The case was heard in September 1978, and the hearing officer later ruled in favor of the Department of Education.

From a test director's perspective, these cold, brief descriptions do not do justice to the drama of such legal challenges. Three thoughts immediately come to mind and may be useful to others facing the same situations.

First, attorneys speak their own language, and it is not easily understood by the untrained observer. Conversely, attorneys do not understand testing talk at all and cannot easily provide a good defense by themselves. The implication is that if you get sued, get very good lawyers and try very hard to communicate.

Second, our society today seems to be highly litigious as a way of solving problems. It is, therefore, highly likely that your competency program will be challenged and you, personally, may be included as a defendant. If this happens, try to keep in mind that no personal affront is necessarily intended, despite intense arguments in court which may indicate otherwise.

Third, the legal process permits various formal ways to reveal the "truth." One such device is, obviously, testimony and cross-examination. Another way is through discovery questions by which plaintiffs can gather information and data related to the legal issues. These questions are often difficult to answer either because of their breadth or because there may be no records on which to base an answer. One question to which Florida Department of Education staff had to respond was: "Identify any and all scholarly publications relating to setting minimum test scores that were used in the preparation or promulgation of the proposed rule or the mastery criteria contained therein" (*Brady et al.* v. *Turlington*). Such questions may seem like harrassment, but they must be answered. If the sheriff comes knocking on the door with such discovery papers, everything else must be dropped. It does not matter in the least whether a speech is being planned or a budget must be completed. The discovery question must be answered first.

The legal picture in Florida is not clear at this time, but it is anticipated that further actions will be taken by both sides. It probably will take two or three years for legal actions to run their course.

Impact on Education in Florida

The long-term impact of the competency testing program on education is unknown. So far, however, the testing program has had a very direct impact in terms of public discussion of the purpose and goals of education. "The test" has been the foremost educational news story of the year, and public interest shows no sign of weakening. The constant barrage of information has led to television and radio talk shows and many meetings of school authorities and parents. The 1978 election reflected the topic; several gubernatorial candidates made speeches on competency testing and at least one made testing of students and teachers a major platform plank.

On August 15, 1978, the State Board of Education addressed the adoption of scoring criteria for the state tests. In Florida, the Cabinet sits as the State Board of Education, and it is therefore extremely rare for the board to have prolonged and substantive debate on any issue. In this case, however, the board listened to almost nine hours of debate from citizens and professional educators. It was probably the longest period of time devoted to an educational issue in the last decade (or more). Clearly, such debate can only strengthen the public schools in the long run.

At the local school level, the impact of the test has been dramatic.

Testimony is heard time and time again to the effect that the students are working better now than in years previously. Discipline problems in classrooms are reported to be decreasing, and students are more willing to sit still and learn.

Testimony presented to the State Board of Education on August 15 by a highly placed official of the Hillsborough County (Tampa) schools revealed that their standardized test scores have increased dramatically over the last two to three years. Similar results are reported in Pinellas (St. Petersburg) and Dade (Miami) Counties (Pinellas, 1978; Grade School, 1978). Of course, there are many reasons why student performance could increase, but it appears that the increased attention to educational accountability given by teachers, administrators, and parents is showing signs of paying off for the students.

Most importantly, students who otherwise would have received a high school diploma without having minimum reading and math skills are now being given additional instruction. In some cases, students are being guided into secondary-level reading courses or are being required to take a second or third math course designed to bring their skills up to par. The general feeling is that students' achievements in these areas are going to increase as was intended by the 1976 legislature.

Summary

The Florida competency testing program is a natural outgrowth of the general educational accountability programs begun by legislators in the early 1970s. The 1976 Educational Accountability Act strengthened previous statutes and consolidated them into a single comprehensive act. The most visible parts of the act are those related to the specification of minimum student performance standards and the assessment of those standards for pupil promotion and graduation.

The Department of Education developed minimum standards and testing instruments for grades three, five, eight, and eleven. The tests are criterion-referenced and indicate student mastery of each of the various standards. At grade eleven, two tests are administered—a basic skills test and a test of functional literacy. For purposes of the 1976 act, literacy is defined as the application of the basic skills to practical problems. No particular claim is made that the test covers "life skills." All of the standards and tests were developed under the control of the Department of Education and with the wide involvement of Florida educators.

The results of the first administration of these new tests in October 1977 indicated a mixture of strengths and weaknesses. The literacy test results were the most highly publicized. They showed a 36 percent failure rate in mathematics and an 8 percent failure rate in communications. Minority students suffered a higher failure rate than white students.

The competency tests enjoy widespread support among Floridians; yet concerns are being expressed from several quarters about potential bias in the tests, the rights of exceptional education students, and the impact of the tests on the schools generally. Several legal skirmishes have already taken place, but the issues have not been definitely determined as yet. The legislature has strongly supported the program and has provided substantial amounts of money for an extensive remedial education effort.

The overall impact of the competency program in Florida has not yet been determined, although early indications are positive. Time will tell whether Florida's bold steps will contribute toward greater educational opportunities for all students or something quite the opposite.

References

Back to the Books. *St. Petersburg Times,* June 19, 1978.

Brady et al. v. *Turlington et al.* and *Blount et al.* v. *Turlington et al.* Florida Department of Administrative Hearings, Cases 78-136R and 78-1363R.

Department of Education. *Goals for Education in Florida.* Tallahassee: Author, n.d.

Department of Education. *Plan for Educational Assessment in Florida.* Tallahassee: Author, 1971.

Department of Education. *Florida School Laws, 1974 Edition.* Tallahassee: Author, 1974.

Department of Education. *Development of the Florida Statewide Assessment Program: A Chronology from 1971.* Tallahassee: Author, 1976a.

Department of Education. *Florida School Laws, 1976 Edition.* Tallahassee: Author, 1976b.

Department of Education. *1976-77 Statewide Minimal Objectives for Mathematics and Communication Skills.* Tallahassee: Author, 1976c.

Department of Education. *The 1978 Legislature in Review.* Tallahassee: Author, 1978.

Expert Panel to Examine Florida's Assessment Program. *FTP-NEA Advocate,* March 23, 1978.

Fisher, Thomas H. Florida's Approach to Competency Testing. *Phi Delta Kappan* 59 (1978): 599-602.

Florida Flunks. *Time,* December 12, 1977.

Glass, Gene V. Minimum Competence and Incompetence in Florida. *Phi Delta Kappan* 59 (1978): 602-605.

Grade School Students Gain in Reading, Math. *Miami Herald,* August 27, 1978.

Hills, John R.; and King, F. J. *Construct Validity of the Florida Functional Literacy Test.* Tallahassee: Department of Education, 1978.

House, Ernest R.; Rivers, Wendell; and Stufflebeam, Daniel L. An Assessment of the Michigan Accountability System. *Phi Delta Kappan*, 55 (1974): 663-670.

House of Representatives. *Florida Educational Accountability: A Program Review.* Tallahassee: Committee on Education, House of Representatives, 1976.

McClung, Merle. Are Competency Testing Programs Fair? Legal? *Phi Delta Kappan* 59 (1978): 397-400.

Millman, Jason. *Tables Needed for Determining Number of Items Needed on Domain-Referenced Tests and Number of Students to be Tested.* Los Angeles: Instructional Objectives Exchange, 1972.

National Academy of Education. *Improving Educational Achievement.* Washington, D.C.: Secretary of Health, Education, and Welfare, 1978.

NEA Misinterprets Literacy Test Goals. *Palm Beach Times*, July 6, 1978.

Pinellas Students Do Well in National Tests. *St. Petersburg Times*, August 22, 1978.

Suhor, Charles. A Resolution Passed by the National Council of Teachers of English at the Sixty-Seventh Annual Meeting, 1977. Private correspondence, July 5, 1978.

Turlington: Biased Panel Gave Biased Test Critique. *Tampa Tribune*, July 7, 1978.

Tyler, Ralph W.; Lapan, Stephen D.; Moore, Judith C.; Rivers, L. Wendell; and Skibo, Donna B. *The Florida Accountability Program: An Evaluation of Its Soundness and Implementation.* Washington, D.C.: National Education Association and Florida Teaching Profession—NEA, 1978.

Visco, Ronald L. The Classification of Students with Respect to Achievement, with Implications for Statewide Assessment (Doctoral dissertation, Florida State University, 1977).

Voters: Test Students and Teachers. *Brevard Today*, April 6, 1978.

Why Dilute the Tests? *Jacksonville Journal*, February 22, 1978.

14   Setting Educational Standards for Minimum Competency: A Case Study

James J. Gallagher

The public demand for some type of minimal educational standards has been one of the dominant forces impacting American education in the past few years. There has been legislative action in the majority of states, and no state has been unaffected by the movement (Pipho, 1977).

The source of this movement has been, clearly, public reaction to a variety of depressing news reports about the status and operation of public education. A recent summary of this "news" can give the flavor of the problem.

Scores on the Scholastic Aptitude Test (SAT) have fallen from a mean of 473 on the verbal section in 1965 to a mean of 434 in 1975; and from a mean of 496 on the mathematics section in 1965 to a mean of 472 in 1975.

The National Assessment of Educational Progress (NAEP) in 1975 reported a decline in science knowledge among American students between 1969 and 1973 equivalent to a half-year loss in learning.

Twenty-three million Americans are functionally illiterate, according to a study sponsored by the U.S. Office of Education.

Comparative surveys of writing skills in 1970 and 1974 show 13- and 17-year-old youth to be using a more limited vocabulary and writing in a shorter, more "primer-like" style in 1974 than in 1970.

The American College Testing (ACT) program also has reported a decline in the average scores of students applying for college admission.

The preparation of this manuscript was substantially aided by the work of Ms. Ann Ramsbotham.

The Association of American Publishers revised its textbook study guide for college freshmen in 1975, adjusting the reading level down to the ninth grade.

College officials, business firms, and public agencies are dismayed at the inability of younger persons to express themselves clearly in writing. (Clark and Thomson, 1976)

The purpose of this paper is to provide a case study of how one state responded to the movement to adopt minimum educational standards. The history of decisions on the development and implementation of a minimum competency testing program is also provided.

Legislation

In June 1977, the North Carolina General Assembly showed its deep interest and concern with the academic progress of North Carolina students by passing two laws, H.B. 204—the High School Graduation and Competency Program—and H.B. 205—the Annual Testing Program.

The basic purposes of this legislation were: to assure that high school graduates possess skills and knowledge necessary to function as members of society; to provide a means of identifying strengths and weaknesses in the educational process; and to establish additional means for making the educational system accountable to the public for results.

The following points reflect the essence of the competency testing legislation: (1) all eleventh-grade students were expected to take tests that would satisfy minimum competency requirements for graduation; (2) a trial testing of all eleventh-grade students was to be conducted in spring 1978; (3) full-scale testing was to begin in fall 1978 for all eleventh-grade students; (4) students who fail to pass any of the tests can retake the parts of the tests they failed. Any student can have as many as ten chances to pass the test; (5) the local schools are required to provide remediation to assist students who reveal less than minimum competency; (6) the legislation also called for the establishment of a Competency Test Commission to aid in carrying out the purposes of this bill.

There are a number of basic questions which must be answered in any statewide competency testing program: What competencies are to be measured, how are they to be measured, and what constitutes minimum competency? This case study outlines the steps taken by the Competency Test Commission, the State Board of Education, and the Department of Public Instruction in their efforts to address and resolve these issues.

What Competency Areas Should Be Addressed?

The commission invited comments and suggestions on the fields to be tested from a wide variety of persons, including experts from other communities and states that were more experienced in the development and operation of competency testing programs. As a result of this advice and discussion, the commission recommended that, for the trial phase and the school year beginning fall 1978, the competencies to be tested be limited to reading and mathematics, viewed as obvious academic survival skills and as fundamental to minimum educational attainment. The current focus of testing is upon the "functional" application of basic math and reading skills—that is, the ability to apply these skills to practical situations.

What Minimum Competency Objectives Should Be Measured?

The commission wished to ensure that the test instruments recommended for adoption would closely reflect educational objectives pursued in North Carolina schools. Thus, all local education agencies (LEAs) in North Carolina were sent a list of over 250 minimum competency objectives and were asked to arrange this extensive list of math and reading objectives in order of priority. Groups of math and reading teachers, who had previously rated and recommended instruments for the trial testing, were asked to cluster and compare the objectives rated by the LEAs with each of the field trial instruments. These clusters were used to determine how well the recommended tests reflected the curriculum objectives deemed most desirable. Major objectives in reading and mathematics identified by North Carolina school personnel are listed in table 1.

Who Should Take the Tests?

Exceptional Children

Many exceptional children in North Carolina have now been returned to regular classes. The goal for these students is full participation in regular school programs, to the degree possible. In keeping with this goal, the State Board of Education has adopted guidelines which state that all exceptional children, excluding the trainably retarded or severely retarded, shall take the tests. Testing modifications will be developed where needed, and parents may apply for exemption to their local school board for their exceptional child on the grounds that the test might be harmful. Exemption would not mean the granting of a regular diploma.

Table 1. North Carolina Minimum Competency Objectives as Judged by North Carolina School Personnel

Reading

1. To demonstrate word knowledge and to use contextual clues and abbreviations to determine word meaning
2. To follow written directions accurately
3. To select the main idea and related details from various passages
4. To classify information
5. To draw inferences from various materials
6. To draw conclusions
7. To compare and contrast various reading materials
8. To organize information
9. To locate and apply information
10. To interpret maps, charts, and pictures

Mathematics

1. To compute using whole numbers
2. To compute using fractions
3. To compute using decimals
4. To compute using percents
5. To solve problems involving money matters
6. To solve problems involving measurement
7. To use geometric ideas in solving everyday problems
8. To interpret and use maps, graphs, charts, and tables
9. To apply knowledge of probability and statistics to everyday situations
10. To estimate answers to problems

The Division of Exceptional Children has provided alternative procedures for testing handicapped students, including a Braille version of the tests for blind children, a large-print version of the tests for the partially sighted, specially signed directions for the deaf, and tape cassette instructions for those needing special help.

Private School Participation

The issue of private school involvement in the testing program has aroused some controversy. During the spring 1979 legislative session, the North Carolina General Assembly passed a law exempting students in private schools from the requirement to take the competency tests.

What Happens to Students Who Do Not Pass?

Students who fail to meet minimum competency standards as measured by the tests, but who meet other graduation standards, will be provided with a certificate instead of a diploma.

Each local educational agency is expected to provide a remedial program in basic skills for those who do not pass. Even after the student's class has graduated, he or she may return and take remedial programs and continue to take the competency test until age 21. If the student passes the competency test, he or she can replace the certificate with a standard diploma.

Spring 1978 Field Study

The General Assembly proposed a spring 1978 trial period that would require all eleventh-graders to take sample tests, thus allowing educators involved in the competency testing program to gain necessary technical information to help shape and choose the final instruments and procedures. This field test provided North Carolina with an opportunity unique among the fifty states to try out various techniques and methods before beginning the testing on a regular basis.

The commissioners reviewed more than 15 instruments in the two areas of reading and math. They asked all major test publishers to complete an extensive questionnaire and to testify in person before the commission. After receiving the counsel of math and reading teachers and consultants who also examined the tests, the commission chose three instruments in each subject area for administration in the spring 1978 trial testing. The tests used in reading were CTB/McGraw-Hill's SHARP, the reading test from Educational Testing Service's Basic Skills Assessment Program (BSAP), and a test developed by the American College Testing Program (ACT). In mathematics, the tests used were CTB's TOPICS, the Everyday Skills Test (EVDS) published by Educational Testing Service, and an ACT mathematics competency test.

The criteria used in selecting the tests were that they or their publishers show: an emphasis on functional application of basic skills; a match with the educational objectives of North Carolina's schools; a minimum competency emphasis; a commitment to further test development; attention to elimination of cultural bias; adequate technical information; and ease of test administration.

The strategy recommended and adopted for the field study was developed in consultation with a Technical Advisory Committee, composed of research and measurement specialists appointed by the commission. The plan for pilot testing required that all eleventh-grade students in the state be divided into three groups: First, a reading group (approximately 36,000 students, or half of those being tested) took three reading competency tests plus the ninth-grade reading comprehension achievement test from the California Test Battery previously chosen for use in the

Annual Test Program. Second, a math group (approximately 36,000 students) took three math competency tests along with the ninth-grade arithmetic computation test from the California Test Battery. Third, a mixed group (approximately 6,000 students) took one reading competency test (SHARP) and one math competency test (TOPICS) to allow estimation of the number of dual failures.

School districts which had one to three high schools were randomly selected to receive either the reading tests or the math tests. Large districts (those with four or more high schools) administered the math package in half the schools and the reading package in the other schools. North Carolina has a total of 145 school districts.

The Results of the Spring 1978 Field Trial

Analyses of the spring field trial data resulted in the selection of the SHARP (reading) and TOPICS (math) tests published by CTB/McGraw-Hill for use in the fall of 1978. The results displayed here illustrate the comparative performance of students on all of the field trial instruments, as well as more detailed information concerning student performance on SHARP and TOPICS.

Reading

The performance of over 36,000 North Carolina eleventh-graders on the three reading competency tests and the ninth-grade norm-referenced reading achievement test is depicted in figure 1. Reference points of 50, 60, 65, and 70 percent of items correct are used to illustrate passing rates associated with several possible cutoff scores. As was indicated by the high intercorrelations among the tests (.85-.92), similar skill and ability dimensions appeared to be tapped by all of the reading competency tests. It is clear that many North Carolina students performed very well on the tests and found them to be rather limited tests of their reading knowledge.

The performance of various types of students on the SHARP reading test and the TOPICS math test is shown in table 2. These data indicate the percent of students who answered less than 50, 60, 65, and 70 percent of the items correctly. Thus, the percent of students who would fail at each of those four reference points, and therefore require remediation, is shown. Results for the total group tested are shown, as are results for subgroups defined by sex, ethnic background, and level of parental education. As table 2 indicates, trends found in earlier statewide assessment programs are reflected in the results of North Carolina's competency testing: females performed better than males in reading; minority students scored significantly lower than did white students; and students' performance increased dramatically as parental level of education increased.

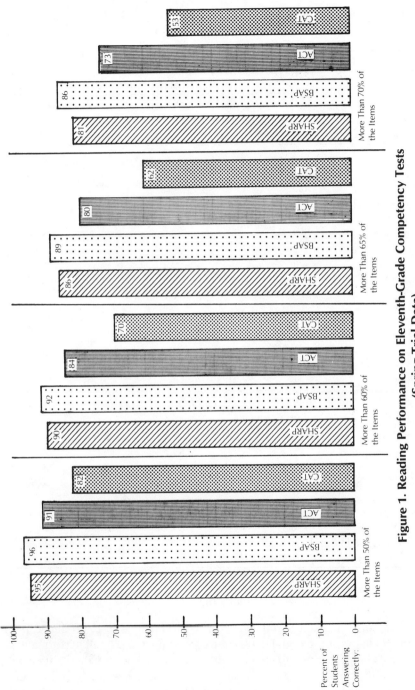

**Figure 1. Reading Performance on Eleventh-Grade Competency Tests
(Spring Trial Data)**

Table 2. Percent of Students Answering Correctly on SHARP (Reading) and TOPICS (Math) Test Items

		Spring Trial Data			
		Scores on SHARP (Reading)			
Group	N	Less Than 50% Correct (60 items)	Less Than 60% Correct (72 items)	Less Than 65% Correct (78 items)	Less Than 70% Correct (84 items)
Total	36,143	4.7	9.2	12.7	18.0
Males	17,463	6.6	12.2	16.5	22.3
Females	18,309	2.7	6.3	9.0	13.8
American Indian	367	8.7	17.7	25.6	34.3
Black	9,874	11.7	22.3	29.5	40.2
White	25,286	1.8	3.9	5.9	9.0
Parents' Education:					
Eighth or less	2,486	17.4	29.4	37.4	48.5
8-12	6,894	8.5	16.1	22.0	30.4
H. S. Graduate	13,928	2.7	6.2	9.0	13.8
Beyond H. S.	8,501	1.0	2.2	3.5	5.4
		Scores on TOPICS (Math)			
Group	N	Less Than 50% Correct (40 items)	Less Than 60% Correct (48 items)	Less Than 65% Correct (52 items)	Less Than 70% Correct (56 items)
Total	36,356	21.7	35.3	43.0	51.4
Males	17,756	22.6	35.6	42.9	50.9
Females	18,113	20.6	34.8	42.9	51.7
American Indian	314	35.4	55.7	65.0	75.8
Black	10,133	49.7	69.8	77.9	84.6
White	25,170	10.2	21.1	28.6	37.7
Parents' Education:					
Eighth or less	2,456	54.2	71.5	78.5	84.4
8-12	7,458	35.3	53.2	62.7	71.1
H. S. Graduate	13,364	16.8	30.7	39.0	48.4
Beyond H. S.	8,363	6.5	13.8	19.7	27.6

Mathematics

The performance of students on the mathematics tests produced patterns similar to those found in the area of reading, but overall performance, in terms of percent of items correct, was much lower. Comparative results on the three competency tests and the norm-referenced achievement test in mathematics are illustrated in figure 2. The results are somewhat more varied across tests than those found in reading. Differences might be due, in part, to content differences among the tests themselves; for

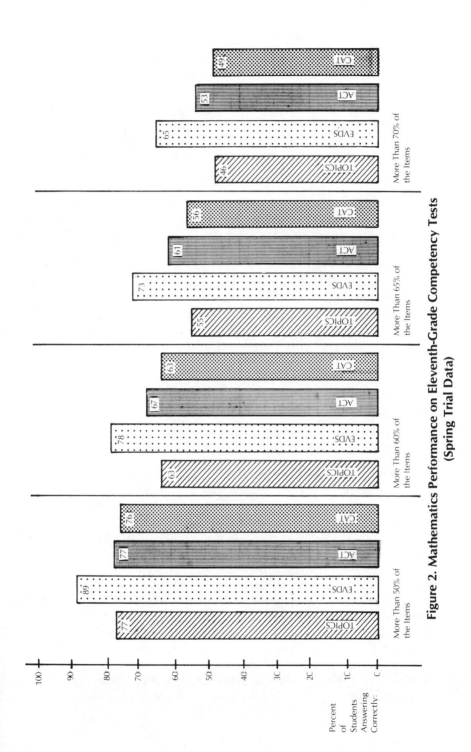

Figure 2. Mathematics Performance on Eleventh-Grade Competency Tests (Spring Trial Data)

example, both computation items and word problems are included in the Everyday Skills test, while the CAT involved only computation, and the TOPICS and ACT tests consisted only of word problems.

A number of factors must be considered in analyzing the performance of students in mathematics. Overall the mathematics test items appeared to be somewhat more difficult than the reading test items; many students in North Carolina take no mathematics after the ninth grade; and students were required to read and comprehend the problems, as well as do the necessary mathematical operations.

Problems dealing with percentages, fractions, and the interpretation of graphs and figures appeared to be particularly difficult for North Carolina students. One encouraging note is that all of these skills seem quite teachable.

Performance on the TOPICS is illustrated in table 2. These data indicate the percentage of students responding correctly to less than 50, 60, 65, and 70 percent of test items. The consequences of selecting each of these reference points as a cutoff score can be seen in results given for the total group tested, as well as for subgroupings by sex, race and parental educational level. The performance level of males and females was found to be much closer than was true for the reading tests. As in reading, the performance of minority students and of students whose parents' educational level was low, was substantially below the performance of white and economically more advantaged students.

Attempts to Eliminate Cultural Bias

A major concern of the commission has been to ensure that the tests recommended are as free of cultural bias as possible. For the spring trial, the commission chose tests which demonstrated some attention to that issue. In addition, the commission appointed a Cultural Bias Committee. As part of its work, this committee met with a consultant who had developed a subjective procedure to analyze test items for potential bias. All items on each test administered during the field trial were reviewed by the committee, and those items considered to be potentially biased were noted. In all statistical analyses, particular attention was paid to those items identified as possibly biased to determine whether the differential performance of various subgroups confirmed subjective analyses.

In detailed analyses of student performances on the individual items of the tests, the percentage of students passing each item was reviewed, as well as the point biserial correlation, which allows comparison of an individual item against the total test score to see if the item behaves as expected. Also, the performance of the highest-scoring 25 percent of students was compared with that of the lowest-scoring 25 percent, for each item on the test. Items that exhibited "bias" (that is, items that showed marked deviation from subgroup differences on total test scores, either in their subgroup "p" values or in their point biserial correlations) were modified or eliminated. The total number of items modified or removed for all reasons (to match state educational objectives or to reduce cultural bias) exceeded 40 percent on reading and 50 percent on math.

Setting Minimum Educational Standards

The establishment of minimum standards—that is, cutoff scores on SHARP and TOPICS—represented the last major task of the commission's first year. Many observers felt that this was a unique task and responsibility; they were unaware that educators have been deeply involved in similar processes since education began.

Although rarely discussed in public, the problem of setting educational standards has always been present. As Popham (1978) says:

There's no doubt that the enactment of minimum competency programs has forced into the open a problem about which educators have fretted over since prehistoric teachers of saber-toothed tiger trapping were faced with a pass-fail decision. Although educators have perennially been obliged to decide when a student "passed a test" or "passed a course," this obligation was discharged in private behind closed classroom (or cave) doors. (p. 4)

Generally speaking, educational standards have been established through a consensus of experienced persons in each special field of endeavor. As attested by a number of measurement experts (Conaway, 1977; Jaeger, 1976; Shepard, 1976), the establishment of a standard of minimum competency must eventually be a matter of human judgment.

Composite human judgment by experienced individuals forms the basis for practically all decision making in our society. Decisions, unvalidated by statistical or research evidence, are made every day in education; and few people suggest these should be stopped. For example, candidates for music schools are denied admittance, or accepted, based upon the judgments of two or three expert musicians who evaluate the students' playing; in Ph.D. oral examinations a candidate's entry into a profession is determined by the composite judgment of four or five professors; coaches routinely select students to participate on teams, based upon their estimate of a demonstrated level of skill; each teacher judges the competence of his or her students and determines whether a child should pass or fail a class.

Students have always been assessed at each step in their progress through school. The recent withholding of reasonable, negative judgment (manifested as social promotion) may be at the heart of the current public demand for a competency testing program.

The Competency Test Commissioners felt that they could best invoke the standard of informed human judgment by collecting as much relevant information and data as possible. Four specific studies were conducted for this purpose and are described briefly below.

Comparison of Competency Test and Norm-Referenced Test Results

Reading comprehension and mathematics subtests from the ninth-grade California Achievement Tests were administered during the spring 1978 trial testing period. These tests were also given as part of the Annual Testing Program to all ninth-graders in North Carolina. Figure 3 provides grade-equivalent scores on the reading comprehension and arithmetic computation subtests of the CAT that correspond to given percentages of items correct on SHARP and TOPICS. Equipercentile equating was used to establish percentile-rank correspondences, and the ninth-grade CAT norms were used to convert CAT percentile ranks to grade-equivalent scores. For this reason, care should be exercised in making too literal an interpretation of the grade-equivalent scores. The important information here involves the relative difficulties of the mathematics and reading competency tests.

On the SHARP reading test, a score of 70 percent correct falls just below an 8.0 grade-equivalent score on the CAT reading comprehension subtest, and a score of 65 percent correct on the SHARP corresponds to a CAT grade-equivalent score between 6.5 and 7. The percentage of students scoring only 50 percent correct on SHARP was similar to the percentage of students with a grade-equivalent score of 5.0 on the CAT subtest; this level is close to the chance score on the norm-referenced achievement test.

The TOPICS math test showed a different pattern. The same percentage of students who answered 70 percent of the items correctly on the TOPICS test received a grade-equivalent score of 10.5 on the CAT arithmetic computation subtest. Scores of 65 percent and 60 percent correct on the TOPICS test corresponded to grade-equivalent scores in the 9.0 to 9.5 range on the CAT subtest. Even at the 50 percent correct level on TOPICS, the corresponding grade-equivalent score was 8.0 on the norm-referenced CAT test.

There appears to be a marked difference in the level of difficulty of the two competency tests when measured against the benchmark of California Achievement Test grade-equivalent scores. These results

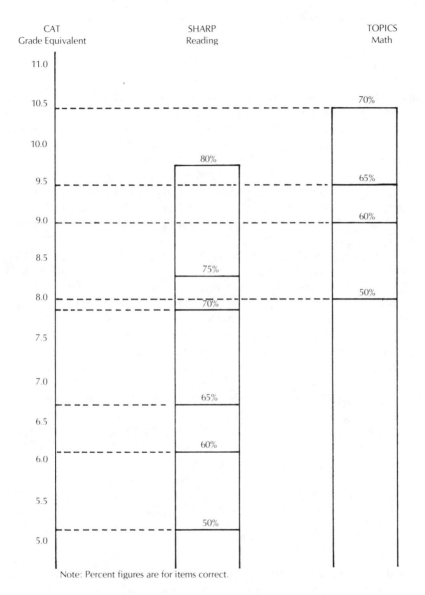

**Figure 3. A Comparison of North Carolina Competency Test Results
and CAT Grade Equivalent Scores
(Spring Trial Data)**

confirm the importance of establishing some comparable level of difficulty before one can set rational cutoff scores (Glass, 1977).

Teacher Judgment of Minimally Competent Students

A second study was conducted by Department of Public Instruction staff to aid in the establishment of cutoff scores on the competency tests. In this study, twenty schools across the state of North Carolina were randomly selected for use in identifying students who were marginally competent; that is, students who would have the ability to barely pass the competency test (Zieky and Livingston, 1976). Principals, teachers, and counselors in these schools were asked to identify five to eight students in their school whom they felt to be minimally competent, and similarly to identify students they felt to be incompetent. These judgments were then compared to the actual scores obtained by the students on the SHARP and TOPICS tests in the spring 1978 trial testing.

The results of that comparison may be seen in figure 4. In both mathematics and reading, students identified as "marginally competent" scored higher, on the average, than did students who were labeled as incompetent, although the difference between the two groups is more clearly seen in mathematics than in reading. Similar statistics were also calculated for the other competency tests used in the spring 1978 trial, and all showed a similar pattern. In each case, the students labeled "minimally competent" did better, on the average, than did those who were termed "incompetent."

On the SHARP reading test, the average percentage of items answered correctly by marginally competent students was around 67; these students scored an average of 51 percent correct on the TOPICS math test, suggesting a sharp difference in the difficulty levels of the two tests. Students judged to be incompetent scored an average of 65 percent correct on the SHARP test and 43 percent correct on the TOPICS test. These results are consistent with the establishment of different minimal performance standards (cutoff scores) on the math and reading tests.

Teacher Judgment on Cutoff Scores

The commission, in its previous discussions, had thought it important that the judgment of competent professionals be given a prominent place in the establishment of cutoff scores. Accordingly, a procedure was established by which groups of teachers who were specialists in the areas of reading or mathematics came together to provide their best judgments on what represented a minimum competency cutoff score on the North Carolina SHARP reading test and the North Carolina TOPICS mathematics test (Jaeger, 1978). A total of 45 reading and mathematics teachers completed the procedures that follow.

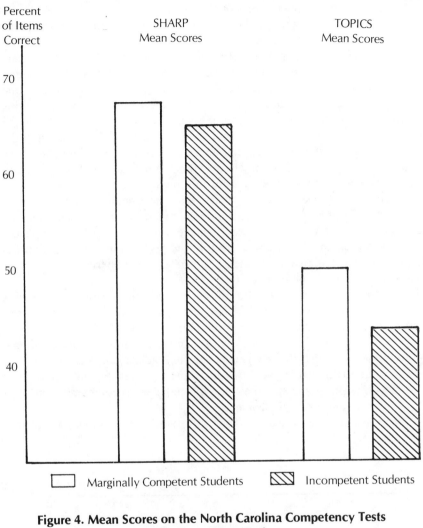

**Figure 4. Mean Scores on the North Carolina Competency Tests
for Students Identified as
Marginally Competent or Incompetent
(Spring Trial Data)**

Each teacher completed one of the competency tests with instructions to try to see the test through the eyes of a student whom they would judge to be competent, but not superior.

The teachers were then asked to make a judgment on an appropriate cutoff score for the particular instrument they completed. When aggregated across teachers, these data provided and represented the first judgment, shown in figure 5 as "I." As can be seen, there were striking differences in the percentage of items correct that were assumed to be appropriate for the reading test and the math test. Teachers' initial judgment for the reading test was that an appropriate cutoff score should be placed at 76 percent correct, whereas their initial judgment for the math test was that a proper cutoff score would be at 67 percent correct.

The teachers were then provided with information on the relative performance of North Carolina eleventh-graders on the two competency tests and on the norm-referenced achievement tests administered in the spring trial testing. They also were told the proportion of students in the spring testing that answered at least 50, 55, 60, and 70 percent of the items correctly on each competency test.

On the basis of that information and further discussion, the teachers were asked to provide a second judgment on appropriate cutoff scores. One option was to sustain their initial judgment. As can be seen in figure 5, the teachers' composite judgment for the reading test, given additional information (II), hardly changed at all. The additional information that the teachers received on the difficulty of the math test tended to influence their composite judgment; they now placed their recommendation on a cutoff score at 62 percent correct (II).

The teachers were next provided with the results of their own group's

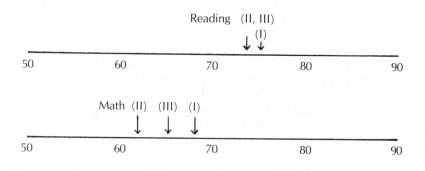

**Figure 5. Teacher Judgments on Appropriate Cutoff Scores
(Spring Trial Data)**

judgments and had further discussion about the test and the appropriate placement of a cutoff score. On the basis of that final discussion, a third judgment was made. The results are shown as "III" on figure 5. On the reading test, the cutoff score recommended at the third judgment was identical to that of the first judgment. In all three judgments for the reading test, the composite average of a suggested cutoff score remained at or around 75 percent correct.

The results of the discussion among math teachers caused their third and final judgment to be moved up somewhat, from 62 to 64 percent, but it still remained somewhat below the initial judgment they had made in the absence of students' test performance, their peers' judgments, and the relationship between scores on TOPICS and the ninth-grade CAT math subtest.

Omitted Items—Spring Trial

One of the statistical analyses completed with the spring trial data supported an investigation of the number of items omitted by students taking the test. Theoretically, on a multiple-choice test with no penalties for a wrong answer, a student wishing to maximize his or her performance should answer every item even if (s)he is not sure of the correct answer.

In the area of mathematics, the 80-item TOPICS test was combined with the 40-item CAT mathematics computation subtest, so as to resemble the revised math competency test used in the fall of 1978. Based on an analysis of omissions among the 120 items, it is clear that many students did not maximize their scores by answering every item; omission of items had a substantial effect on mathematics competency test scores.

Omissions did not materially affect scores on the SHARP reading test (table 3), with an average of less than one item omitted out of the 120-item test. In contrast, on the 80-item TOPICS test and the 40-item CAT, there was an average of over two items omitted by white students and almost eight items omitted by black students. The pattern of omissions clearly indicated that some students had trouble finishing the math tests. Subsequent liberalization of testing time limits and modification of

Table 3. Items Omitted by Race Spring Trial Data

		Black	White
Reading	Mean	.69	.19
N=(25,286)	σ	3.60	2.18
Math	Mean	7.72	2.18
N=24,931	σ	12.50	6.41

test administration instructions (Answer all the test items!) were adopted for the fall testing.

The Competency Test Commission's Decision

With the results of the four studies and the total spring trial analyses available to them, the commission followed a strategy of decision making patterned after the Jaeger (1978) model used in obtaining teachers' judgments on appropriate cutoff scores. After extensive discussion of the spring trial results and their meaning with consultants and advisors, the fourteen members of the commission went into executive session and determined preliminary cutoff scores through a secret ballot. The results of that ballot were then displayed to the commission, and members were urged to give further, overnight consideration to their decision.

On the next morning, the commission again went into executive session and followed a similar procedure of discussion and balloting. The results of the balloting were displayed and discussed further. The outcome of this procedure was a unanimous recommendation of a cutoff score of 72 percent correct on the reading test (SHARP) and 64 percent correct on the TOPICS math test.

Where Does the Program Go Next?

The development of a minimum competency testing program is a dynamic process, and many factors may have changed by the time this paper is in print. The case study presented above is not meant to suggest that the process of selecting measures and establishing cutoff scores used in North Carolina represents the right way. It is intended to encourage consideration of the kind of decision making that must be undertaken to develop and conduct such a program, and hopefully it will encourage more effective and efficient ways to make such decisions.

References

Clark, J., & Thomson, S. *Competency tests and graduation requirements*. Reston, Va.: National Association of Secondary School Principals, 1976.

Conaway, L. Setting standards in competency based education: Some current practices and concerns. Paper presented at the Symposium on Test Development Issues in Competency Based Measurement, April 1977.

Glass, G. *Standards and criteria*. Paper #10 in the occasional paper series, Kalamazoo, Mich. Evaluation Center, College of Education, Western Michigan University, November 1977.

Jaeger, R. M. Measurement consequences of selected standard setting models. *Florida Journal of Educational Research* 18 (1976): 22-27.

Jaeger, R. M. A proposal for setting a standard on the North Carolina High School Competency Test. Paper presented at the meetings of the North Carolina Association for Research in Education, Chapel Hill, N.C., spring 1978.

Pipho, C. *Minimal competency testing.* Denver: Education Commission of the States, 1977.

Popham, W. J. *Setting performance standards.* Los Angeles: Instructional Objectives Exchange, 1978.

Shepard, L. Setting standards and living with them. *Florida Journal of Educational Research* 18 (1976): 28-32.

Zieky, M., & Livingston, S. *Manual for setting standards on the basic skills assessment tests.* Princeton, N.J.: Educational Testing Service, 1976.

15   Graduation Requirements in the State of Oregon: A Case Study

Marshall D. Herron

Introduction

Demands from a variety of constituencies for accountability in education have coalesced into an idea that has spread at what can only be called an astounding rate. "Competency-based" education is an idea whose time has come—or so it would seem. Mandates for competency-based requirements, including competency (or proficiency) testing, continue to emanate from state legislatures and boards of education. To the general public, aroused by charges that schools teach skills and knowledge of little subsequent use, the rhetoric for competency-based education has strong intrinsic appeal. Who can argue with the proposition that we want our schools to produce graduates who are competent? And so the demand increases, to cut through the rhetoric and get on with the task of implementing competency-based education.

Ah, but there's the rub. First, the term "competency-based education" has little conceptual clarity. How can you respond to a concept when those who espouse it cannot even agree on what a "competency" is? Second, effective systems must have purposes—common goals to which those who run the system can aspire. But the various proponents of competency-based education come from positions that are not only varied, but often contradictory. As W. G. Spady notes, "Aside from universal beliefs in the desirability of school system accountability and student 'competence,' the adherents and practitioners of current elementary and secondary school CBE efforts are marching (or parading) in different uniforms to different drummers playing different tunes."[1] To some, "competency" seems to be equated with mastery of the basic skills of reading, writing, and computing. To others, "competency" denotes the ability to apply the things students learn in the classroom to life-role situations. To those who have been involved in an attempt to formulate competency-related graduation requirements, the issue of conceptual clarity has assumed critical importance. Without conceptual clarity, the road to implementation is hazardous indeed.

The first part of this paper describes the Oregon Graduation Requirements system as it is now. The second part describes how it got that way, some problems inherent in the present situation, and some directions in which the system may evolve.

Minimum Standards for Oregon Schools

In December 1974, the Oregon State Board of Education adopted the *Elementary-Secondary Guide for Oregon Schools*. This guide contains revised minimum standards for the public schools of the state. Although not directly rooted in legislation, these "administrative rules" have the effect of law, since the authority and responsibility to set such rules is delegated to the state board by Oregon Statute 326.051.

The major thrust of the new minimum standards is to establish a system of goal-based instructional planning and evaluation for all tax-supported school districts in the state. Notice that the term is goal-based, not competency-based. Oregon does not have a "competency-based educational system." The instructional planning standard (OAR 581-22-208) requires four steps. First, local school boards must adopt a system of local district goals in support of six recently-established statewide goals.[2] Local districts must establish sets of program goals for each of their instructional programs (such as language arts, mathematics, or music) which support the district goals, and they must also establish sets of course goals which support the program goals. The goals at all levels must be written in terms of student outcomes. Second, districts are required to assess, periodically, the extent to which students are attaining the outcomes defined by the program goals. The third required step in the cycle is a needs identification process by which assessed status and goals are compared. The fourth part of the cycle is program improvement, which in many cases may lead to further refinement of goal statements and hence a recycling of the instructional planning procedures.

One part of the standards (OAR 581-22-231) defines the graduation requirements of the system. According to these requirements, schools in Oregon are to grant diplomas on the basis of fulfillment of all "credit, competency, and attendance requirements set by the state and local district." Competencies in this context are special kinds of goal or outcome statements, related specifically to high school graduation. That is, in addition to traditionally expected time and course credit requirements, students are now expected to demonstrate competency in certain prescribed areas. The competencies referred to in the standards are defined in the Appendix.[3] The prescribed areas are subject to verification beginning with the graduating class of 1978. They relate to students' abilities to read, write, speak, listen, analyze, and compute. Seven additional competency areas are subject to verification beginning "not later than" the graduating class of 1981.[4] School districts must verify the competency attainment of their students in these areas before they may issue a diploma.

It is important to point out here that competency verification, based on the definition in the Appendix, becomes a kind of readiness certification. Just as schools routinely give readiness tests to determine if entering primary students are prepared to cope with the demands of the school curriculum, so competencies are here viewed as a kind of readiness to cope with the demands of the various life roles defined in the state board goals (the life roles are: individual, learner, producer, citizen, consumer, and family member). Local school boards are required to adopt their own competency statements within each of the prescribed areas. Each local staff is then expected to develop "performance indicators" and appropriate measures which the district is willing to accept as evidence that competency in each area has been attained. They are also expected to develop record-keeping systems for documentation of competency attainment.

The verification of competency in this system is no small task, since competency is defined in terms of the application of basic skills, knowledge, or understanding and is tied to the ability to function in some sort of "life role." Districts are encouraged to develop measures and performance standards for each performance indicator, several of which could relate to a specific competency statement. This simple generic assessment model is diagrammed in figure 1.

The intent of state requirements is to establish a verification system in which policy decisions as to where to set performance minimums are in the hands of local districts, but in such a way that these decisions must be negotiated with local communities. This leads to a measurement problem: establishing applied performance tests that are uniform and consistent across teachers within a school, from school to school within a district, and, to a certain extent, from one district to another.

Schools are not accustomed to measurement based on an "applied

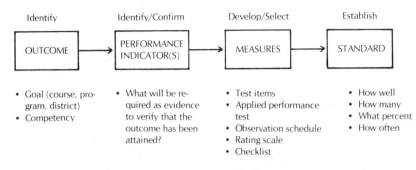

Figure 1. Components Necessary for Assessment

performance model." And the establishment of minimum performance standards is new and difficult to cope with. (In the next section we shall see how this problem interfered with statewide implementation of the new graduation requirements.) In spite of these problems, the Oregon Board of Education took the position that if the high school diploma is to indicate that its recipient can function effectively in applying basic skills in life-role-related situations, each local community must derive appropriate levels of proficiency from those life-role situations. What is "appropriate" in one context for one community may not be considered appropriate in other contexts and other communities. Local communities must decide what levels of reading or computing skills are needed by an individual to function as a consumer, producer, or citizen in that community. To what extent are individuals limited in a job or profession by their levels of proficiency in the basic skills? How important is it that an individual be able to read a newspaper, write a letter of application for a job, or balance a checkbook? How important is computing interest rates on a time-purchase contract, or locating some needed information in the local library? The state board felt that these questions are most appropriately answered by the local community.

In addition to deciding what levels of proficiency are appropriate within each competency area, local districts must determine what kinds of performance will be accepted as evidence that a given individual student has attained a specified minimum competency level. Local districts may alter performance indicators, or they may grant permission to substitute performance indicators that are appropriate to the unique needs and abilities of individual students (handicapped students, for example). Local boards may also grant certificates identifying which specific competencies students have acquired to those students who have met some, but not all, requirements for the diploma, and who choose to end their formal education. It is also within the authority of local districts to allow students to take more time (or less time) than usual to complete high school graduation requirements. This system does not change local prerogatives as to who does or does not receive a diploma; rather, it exposes the entire process to much more direct public scrutiny. The concept of local control is very strong in the state of Oregon.

The foregoing description applies to the standards as of October 1978. The next section describes some of the factors which affected the development of the new graduation requirements and explores some of the reasons why the competency systems implemented by many districts do not yet meet the intent of the standards. This description involves the interplay of two somewhat contradictory notions of the nature and function of a "competency." While the proponents of each of the two positions contributed significantly to the early momentum of the competency testing movement, their ideological differences are now pulling in entirely different directions. One attempts to change significantly the focus of schooling; the other to maintain the status quo, with new labels attached so as to identify with the competency "band wagon."

The conflict is between a view of competencies as minimal basic skills (Spady[5] calls them "capacities, or enablers"; Brickell[6] calls them "school skills.") and a view of competencies as applications of skills in life-related contexts (Brickell's "life skills"; Spady's meaning for competency).

Factors Influencing the Graduation Requirements

A number of events and activities of the late 1960s and early 1970s likely affected the development of new graduation requirements. These events do not fit into neat causal chains, and several must be viewed as simultaneous, interactive causes. Speculation regarding the timing and strength of these influences could be described completely only by former State Superintendent of Public Instruction Dale Parnell—a man whose role in the formation of the new graduation requirements will be considered in more detail later in this section.

One of the first events that appears to have had a direct bearing on the development of the new requirements was a "needs assessment" conducted by the Oregon Department of Education during the 1968-69 school year.[7] The study was conducted in response to an amendment to the Elementary and Secondary Education Act (ESEA) of 1965, which required each state to assess its educational needs before it could receive federal funds. The study was done in two phases. In the first, 120 in-depth interviews were conducted with members of the general public, educators, students, and high school dropouts concerning their perceptions of the needs of education in the state. Twenty-seven major concerns were identified through this process and were used to develop a questionnaire for phase two. The phase two questionnaire was completed by much larger numbers of people representing the same four groups. The intent was not only to identify needs, but to determine how well the four subgroups felt the needs were being met.

The needs assessment study was one of the first indicators that a sizable portion of the people in the state of Oregon felt that current student needs were not being met by the schools. Following are some of the needs that emerged from that study that appear to have a direct bearing on graduation requirements later developed: students need to learn to communicate effectively (number 4); students need to learn accepted health practices and physical effects of drugs and alcohol (number 5); students need to learn to become intelligent and economically literate consumers (number 9); students need to acquire early mastery of fundamental skills such as reading and arithmetic (number 11); students need to understand the economics of government financing and taxation (number 15); students need to learn the practical aspects and responsibilities of marriage and family living (number 16); students need to develop health and physical fitness (number 19).

One major result of the study was that the state board decided that no Title III, ESEA funds would be available to programs that did not "set forth objectives stated in performance terms against which the degree of attainment of the objectives can be measured, and the progress and outcomes of the project can be evaluated."[8] This was one of the first state board actions requiring the measurement of learner outcomes.

A second activity which occurred at about the same time was a series of "Town Hall Meetings" conducted by Superintendent Parnell and some members of the State Board of Education. Between October 1969 and January 1970, open meetings were held in fourteen cities, allowing over 2,000 citizens to express their opinions on the state board's proposed priorities for education within the state. By and large, the concerns expressed at the Town Hall Meetings were in agreement with the priority needs which resulted from the needs assessment study. Two new notes of concern emerged, however. One was the board's expressed intent to audit educational programs as a means of accountability. The other was its determination to review current high school graduation requirements in terms of their effectiveness in meeting individual student needs.[9] Concern for evaluation of the effectiveness of the whole educational system emerged from these meetings.

Almost simultaneously with the Town Hall Meetings, another very influential group was conducting a study. At Parnell's request, a subcommittee of the Oregon Association of Secondary School Principals spent six months examining current high school graduation requirements. The committee's final report, submitted in April 1970, supported the idea of change in the high school curriculum. The report was particularly critical of heavy reliance placed on the Carnegie Unit of credit, urging greater flexibility in graduation requirements. Other recommendations relevant to our present discussion included: minimum standards for high school graduation should include a passing score on the GED tests or their equivalent; minimum graduation standards should include 190 semester hours of high school work defined so that both in-class and out-of-class experiences can be included; the total resources of the community should be recognized and appropriately used as a proper extension of the school classroom; the standards of achievement must be variable and based on more than the identification of cognitive goals; there is a need to state objectives, to design activities by which objectives may be reached, and to develop accountability on the part of institutions charged with these tasks.

A fourth factor, although seldom mentioned among descriptions of the "steps" leading to Oregon's new graduation requirements, had a major impact nonetheless. This factor was legislative activity. At one point, the state of Oregon almost had a competency program, or a near facsimile, by legislative mandate. To understand the impact such a move would have had, one must realize that the Oregon legislature rarely takes a direct hand in the operation of the public schools. Although education is a constitutional responsibility of the legislature, it delegates this authority to the State Board of Education which administers by means of administrative rules. Failure of a local school district to abide by these rules can result in the loss of state support monies. For the legislature to intrude on the day-to-day business of running the public schools, it would have to circumvent its own operating system. In spite of this, in 1972 an Interim Committee on Education drafted two bills dealing with school goals and the curriculum of the public school system. The purpose of senate bill 1, as drafted, was to "assign and allocate responsibilities for achievement of educational goals among the State Board of Education, the local school districts, the community colleges, the State Board of Higher Education, the state colleges and universities, and the Education Coordinating Council." A variety of educational goals were proposed in the bill.

Senate bill 2 was more specifically relevant to the development of new graduation requirements. Its stated purpose was to "define and describe basic education for elementary and secondary education" and to "allocate responsibility between the state and local school districts in achieving the basic education of the student." Essentially, the bill was an attempt to determine how much of students' basic education the state should pay for. However, the language of the bill went so far as to list the specific abilities students should have upon completion of a given educational program. For example, the bill stated that:

Upon completion of the basic language arts and reading program, students will have demonstrated
—Ability to read with speed and comprehension;
—Ability to write legibly, to express thoughts clearly and effectively in writing, to think analytically, to spell and punctuate accurately, to use appropriate grammar, and to employ an adequate vocabulary;
—Ability to speak effectively and to listen with comprehension; and
—Knowledge of and ability to use information sources.

A total of twenty-one such statements were listed in the arts and humanities, language arts and reading, mathematics, science, citizenship, history, career opportunities, and health and physical education.

Although senate bills 1 and 2 were severely criticized by many educators as being overly prescriptive, and both died in the 1973 legislative session, they had the effect of accelerating the development of graduation requirements by the Department of Education and the state board.

Undoubtedly the most important factor of all was Dale Parnell, the chief architect of the new graduation requirements. Those who worked with Parnell still speak frequently of his remarkable ability to synthesize ideas from a variety of sources. It is enlightening to read through his speeches covering the period from 1968 to 1973, and trace the development of his ideas on the need for reform of high school graduation requirements. In these speeches he emphasized relevance to real life, measurable skills, and accountability. He came to this position by way of his strong commitment to the concept of career education.

Parnell's most cogent statement on high school graduation requirements is given in a September 1972 article on career education entitled "Survival Education."[10] This paper is an apparent expansion of a speech he gave in April of 1972 also entitled "Survival Education." He raised the question: "What competencies are required to survive during the last quarter of this century? What kind of competencies are required to successfully cope with life as a citizen, wage earner, consumer and learner?" (p. 5). His own answer to this question demonstrates that Parnell had in mind "life skills" or "application-type" competencies from the beginning:

. . . schooling can focus on the real life roles or careers of individuals and the competencies needed to cope with those careers and roles. (p. 5)
Successful performance in those roles requires more than knowledge, yet for some educators the main business of education is knowledge dissemination. (p. 6)

So much of traditional schooling is unrelated to the real world. The questions are asked, the right answers memorized, but unrelated to life. . . . While Americans are calling for universal education (every student has worth), schooling has given them the bell-shaped curve and a sorting system which says that unless a student receives an A or B grade in algebra, chemistry, or English, he doesn't amount to much. (p. 18)

In the April speech he quoted from James Coleman's experience-rich, information-poor paradigm and called for a school program that was to be both experience-rich and information-rich. He asked how students could be prepared to survive in a modern world by schools seeking to develop college preparatory students:

Students know about George Washington and the Incas of Peru; but do they know how their city council or school board works? How do you cope with a planning commission? . . . Fifty years ago when school requirements were basically established, there were no credit cards. Are young people being prepared to cope with today's installment buying, contracts, insurance and advertising tactics? (p. 3)

We are trying to equip students with the competencies to enable them to survive in today's society by basing our schooling methods and requirements on a current society. In essence, we are trying to pull schooling and life together into one experience. (p. 10)

In a recent Phi Delta Kappa monograph,[11] Parnell further clarifies his intent and the role he played in the development of new graduation requirements:

At its root, competency-based education is an emphasis on results. It calls for agreed-upon performance indicators that reflect successful functioning in life roles. . . . There is little direct relationship between the time-honored subject matter disciplines and the competencies required of an individual to cope with modern life. . . . Our daily lives do not compartmentalize neatly into math, social science, English, science. And therein lies one great problem for the modern public schools. (p. 18)

We . . . continue to insist on meeting the student at the point of subject-matter need rather than at the point of real-life needs. The schools have not kept in synchrony with the times and the real-life needs of a changing society. The needs have changed, but the schools and the school curriculum have not. (p. 22)

[The] hotly contested statewide battle to elect a superintendent of public instruction in 1968 brought much public attention to matters of education. During that campaign I outlined competency-based proposals, including a revision of the high school graduation requirements and career education emphasis in the schools. It was no secret that my election would mean that Oregon schools would move in the direction of competency-based education. My election, therefore, was interpreted to mean that Oregonians expected a modernization of the high school requirements and movement toward a performance-oriented curriculum. (p. 32)

Each civilization has its own artifacts, scrolls, tablets, coins and tools. It is very instructive to study other cultures. But it would be even more instructive to surround our students with the artifacts of our own society. These artifacts include credit cards, bank statements, ballots, rental agreements, checkbook stubs, loan contracts. Yet it is not only possible for most students to complete their formal education without ever seeing an installment contract, it is highly probable. Shouldn't we understand our own artifacts as well as those of the Romans and the Greeks? (p. 44)

Although Parnell's definition of "competency" is clear in these statements, his message did not come across to people in the public schools. This, as we shall see, was partially an implementation problem. In some respects, however, school people were misled by his use of the terms "minimal" and "survival."

In several places Parnell spoke of Maslow's hierarchy of human needs, "survival" being primary. But he went on to speak of survival in a society which is "highly technological, incessantly demanding, increasingly complex, and inexorably changing." When he accused traditional schooling of not meeting "survival" needs, he seemed to attach a more sophisticated meaning to the term than Maslow did. He criticized the schools for giving the self-actualization need the highest priority "even though survival was not assured." But in his use of the term "survival," he related competency to complex life roles. How many students can define the skills they are *going* to need in the kind of complex society Parnell is talking about? Surely Parnell's use of "survival need" is not equivalent to Maslow's primal kind of survival need. Unfortunately, it would appear that in borrowing a paradigm to make his point, Parnell's terms sidetracked many educators.

Drafting New Graduation Requirements

The first draft of the high school graduation requirements proposal was presented to the state board at its September 29, 1971, public hearing. This marked the first time that revision of graduation requirements had been considered separately from the larger issue of minimum standards for Oregon schools. The proposed new requirements were considered independently in the hope that the normal time between consideration of a change in the standards and implementation of a revision could be reduced. The board responded by approving a plan calling for the draft proposal to be given wide circulation to various organizations throughout the state.

The proposed new requirements were distributed between October and December 1971 to the Oregon Association of Secondary School Administrators (OASSA), the Parent-Teachers Association, and many other educational interest groups. Representatives of some of the groups continued to meet with Department of Education personnel during the winter months. A new draft was developed from the contributions of these groups. It was made public at the OASSA winter conference in January 1972. A third draft, completed in March 1972, took into consideration the comments and criticisms voiced at the OASSA conference. This draft was presented to the public in hearings held in Pendleton, Coos Bay, Salem, and Klamath Falls in the spring and summer of 1972. The response to the new graduation requirements at these hearings was generally supportive. The Board of Education approved the fourth and final draft of the proposed revisions in September 1972 and set an implementation date for no later than the graduating class of 1978.

A significant shift in the role of the state in setting competencies can be seen from the first to the final draft of the new requirements. While the concept of "minimum survival" level competencies is included in all of the drafts, the first draft listed specific survival skills that the department felt students would need. The final draft left decisions on specific competencies to require for graduation to individual local school districts.

Among the 44 competencies included in the first draft, but not present in the document adopted by the board, were statements to the effect that student must be able to: read a newspaper at a proficiency level; accurately compute the difference in cost per unit between small and large quantity purchases; describe the procedure for filing a permit to build a home; accurately balance a checkbook; demonstrate safe driving; and change an automobile wheel.

In the final draft, local school boards were asked to adopt locally defined minimum survival competencies in the area of "personal development" which would ensure that graduating students would be able to: read, listen, speak, analyze, write; compute using the basic processes; understand basic scientific and technological processes; develop and maintain a healthy mind and body; develop and maintain the role of a lifelong learner. In the area of "social responsibility," students were to be able to function effectively and responsibly as: citizens of the community, state, and nation; citizens in interaction with the environment; citizens on the streets and highways; consumers of goods and services. In the area of "career development," students were to be able to function effectively within a career cluster or within a broad range of occupations.

The final draft of the requirements, then, presented a very broad outline of mandated competency areas for graduating high school students. Local districts were expected to be more specific in stating locally adopted minimum competencies and in determining what would constitute a "survival level" of education in each of their communities. In this draft, districts were also asked to specify "performance indicators" which they would use as evidence of the attainment of specified competencies.

Over the course of development of these drafts, two key policy issues emerged. Although they were debated, they were never totally resolved. On the one hand, opponents of the first draft of requirements argued that the proposal would give the state too much control of the curriculum and educational programs of local school districts. Districts in Oregon have traditionally worked to maintain autonomy by defining programs to meet local needs. On the other hand, opponents of the final draft were primarily concerned with guaranteeing equal educational opportunity by imposing the same minimum requirements for all of the state's students. They believed that, by leaving the development of survival-level competencies to local districts, inequities in educational opportunity would likely result.

Although the issue of local autonomy was resolved in favor of strong local control, the question of equal educational opportunity continues to be a focus for debate in discussions of graduation requirements.

Implementating the Graduation Requirements

Early in the implementation phase, a decision was made to involve several local districts in the development of guidelines for implementing the new requirements. Six pilot writing projects were funded in November of 1972. These local districts were given responsibility for developing sample minimum competency statements and performance indicators in the areas of personal development, social responsibility, and career development. A task force was formed within the Department of Education to assist the six pilot projects. The target date for the guidelines was April 30, 1974. Task force members became the project managers, providing guidance and assistance to each of the pilot groups. These projects resulted in a major conceptual shift in the high school graduation requirements.

In May 1973, members of the six pilot projects met with task force members to synthesize their work. The results were released in four booklets. The first dealt with administrative requirements and timelines. The other three provided samples of program goals, minimum competencies, and performance indicators in the areas of personal development, social responsibility, and career education.

It is in these three booklets, thousands of which were distributed across the state, that a conceptual turnabout can be seen. It is evident from these documents that the local districts were totally unprepared to generate competency statements of the kind suggested by Parnell. The booklets' competency statements did not involve the application of basic skills to life-role functions. The notion of survival in a complex society, as Parnell so frequently expounded it, was largely ignored. Competencies were described as being equivalent to "course goals" written at a minimum performance level. They were defined as "possession of skills, knowledge and understandings to the degree they can be demonstrated." The orientation of the materials was toward school skills—Spady's "capacities," or "enablers." What emerged from the pilot projects was a number of sets of expanded behavioral objectives.

Parnell and his staff were fully aware of the implications of this shift in emphasis, but decided to proceed with planned implementation activities. They decided to take the districts "where they were" and try to add the application-to-life roles dimension as the project was subsequently expanded and modified. (The temptation may be strong here to "second guess" these implementation decisions. But the reader should bear in mind that this project was a first. A nationwide search had located no models to rely upon for such large-scale curriculum modification. An attempt was being made to bring about significant change within an entire state educational system in a relatively short period of time! The fact that the new requirements constituted a totally new educational approach meant that many of the answers had to be discovered along the way. There was simply no way, politically, that some courses of action could be reversed once they were undertaken.)

The written materials developed in the pilot projects were published with the stipulation that they were to be considered "models" that districts might use as guides in their own developmental efforts. In spite of this, there was a tendency for districts to simply copy and adopt these lists of competencies with few modifications.

One remaining implementation task was to integrate the graduation requirements with the broader minimum standards for public schools that were concurrently under development. This was thought to be the most reliable way of assuring compliance and also providing technical assistance to local districts via standardization team visits.[12] A task force from within the department—The Minimum Standards Steering Committee—was responsible for seeing that the graduation requirements became an integral part of the overall minimum standards.

The State Board of Education formally adopted the revised minimum standards in December of 1974. It had considered various drafts of proposed standards at eight official "readings" prior to adoption. Over the three years of development, twenty-nine public hearings and workshops were held throughout the state to obtain responses and suggestions from school administrators, teachers, board members, and other people interested in education. Draft copies had been distributed widely, for review by interested individuals and groups.

The revised standards were field tested in seven school districts during the 1975-76 school year. Following those field tests, further hearings throughout the state, and recommendations from an external review committee of educators, the state board, on June 23, 1976, adopted the standards, with minor modification, to become effective for the 1976-77 school year.

In the final version of the standards (excerpts may be found in Appendix A), the definition of competency that incorporated application of skills "assumed to contribute to success in life-role functions" was reinstated. The State Department of Education was thus left with a particularly awkward dilemma. Nearly all of the "model" competency statements contained in the pilot project reports that had been widely distributed around the state did not meet the "official" definition contained in the administrative rules published in the minimum standards. Even though the competency requirements were not to be imposed prior to the graduating class of 1978, many districts had begun to develop verification systems based upon the "models" contained in pilot project reports.

Despite numerous workshops, inservice sessions, standardization visits across the state, and circulation of a 1977 draft document entitled *Graduation Requirements Guidelines, Revised,* the dichotomy continues to plague Oregon educators. Some districts acknowledge that the major criticism from the consumers of many of our products—business and industry—is that too many of our graduates cannot apply to new situations the skills that they presumably have acquired in school. These districts are attempting to develop competency systems which verify students' abilities to apply their skills in life-role-related situations. Many other districts claim that basic skills have not been adequately mastered to begin with. They believe that if the basic skills are mastered, students will automatically be able to apply them whenever they are needed. These districts have implemented systems for verifying mastery of basic skills—some with district-level testing programs, others through teacher verification of performance indicators within the regular course structure.

Implementation Problems at the Local District Level

The verification and certification systems devised by most school districts in Oregon rely on the judgments of classroom teachers. Most competencies are assigned to specific basic-skills-related courses (such as English I, general math, personal finance) for verification. Some districts utilize a district-level testing program in some areas (such as reading, writing, computing) and teachers' judgments in others.

In those districts using pilot-project materials as models to generate "school skills" rather than "life skills," the tendency has been to produce large numbers of outcome statements at a behavioral-objective level of specificity. This has resulted in a number of problems. To begin with, the large number of outcomes to be certified necessitated massive and complex record-keeping systems and significant commitments of time from teachers. Many teachers, particularly at the high school level, resent having to take their time to verify what they consider to be elementary school skills. They feel that the process focuses attention on minimum performance, to the detriment of the more advanced "high school" material included in their courses. A related problem is their concern for liability. What if they certify (personally sign off on) the competence of a student who later forgets or otherwise fails to demonstrate continued "competence"?

Many districts used committees of teachers to generate their competency lists and performance indicators. In the early phases of implementation, these committees tended to set unrealistic performance requirements that many students could not reach as the school year progressed. The problem of providing remediation within the course structure of the typical high school quickly arose. Should students be required to repeat the first semester of English I, or should they add unverified competencies to those to be verified in the second semester? Should school districts create special competency sessions after school, or perhaps relax their standards for minimal performance?

As a result of these problems, some districts have imposed competency requirements and verification procedures in the lower grades. Other districts have begun to consolidate competencies into fewer, more general outcome statements.

Those districts that have been working with "life skill" competencies have encountered problems of a different genre. Record keeping is not as much of a problem, since fewer competency statements are involved. And since the "competencies" are application oriented, they are not as often criticized as too elementary for secondary school teachers to deal with. The major problem for these districts is how to implement a relatively unfamiliar measurement activity—applied performance testing. The districts typically provide a variety of sample performance indicators for teachers to use in verifying competencies. The problem inherent in this system is to assure that relatively uniform judgments on acceptable minimum performances are being made by all teachers within a school and, in the larger districts, by all schools.

Another problem brought into sharper focus by the latter districts was the wording of competency requirements to be in effect in 1981. It was difficult, but not impossible, for districts to deal with the application of skills such as reading, writing, computing, speaking, or listening. But knowing the "use of scientific and technological processes," or being "an informed citizen in the community, state, and nation" are outcome statements of a different nature. Is there any evidence that simulation measures are reliable indices of students' abilities to apply knowledge, skill, or understanding at a later date? Such outcome statements as these and others (for example, "be an informed citizen in interaction with environment," or "be an informed consumer of goods and services") relate to students' behavior outside the school environment. What authority or capacity do schools have to monitor students' behavior outside the classroom? How can the school certify that a student is able to "be an informed consumer of goods and services" if the actual consumption of goods and services cannot be observed? Does successful completion of a simulation activity guarantee that students will in fact "maintain a healthy mind and body"? What if they later choose not to follow generally accepted healthful practices? These questions of course remain unresolved. But they raise other questions concerning the limitations of the sphere of authority and accountability of public schooling.

Another problem that plagues local districts is evaluating the previous educational experience of transfer students. In the past, if a student's transcript showed satisfactory completion of a course in U.S. history, credit in U.S. history "or the equivalent" was granted, despite the fact that the content of the courses might have been quite different. Certain assumptions were made concerning the likely content of such a course. The wide variation in the competency verification systems developed in local districts across the state of Oregon now makes it difficult for schools to "place" transfer students, even from neighboring school districts. (The receiving school, for example, may assign a particular competency or set of competencies to English I. The transferring student may have already taken English I at the former high school, but may not have covered those particular competencies. Since certification is the responsibility of the graduating school district, the receiving school has the problem of verifying the competency of the transferring student by methods outside its regular procedures.) The problem is particularly acute if one school has competencies of the "school skills" variety and the other has competencies of the "life skills" variety.

Where Will We Go from Here?

When the state board adopted the minimum standards in 1976, it also resolved to reexamine their effectiveness every two years. That evaluation is currently under way. It is difficult to predict what may happen to the graduation requirements section of the standards. A legislative interim committee, hearing mostly from disgruntled teachers in districts utilizing teacher verification systems for "school skills" competencies, has recommended that the board take a hard look at systems which require massive record keeping at the secondary level.

Most districts utilizing "life skills" competencies seem satisfied with the results of their efforts, but are frustrated with the student transfer problem. In fact, many district administrators who argued vehemently for retention of local control of competency specifications are now asking the state board to have the Oregon Department of Education develop a synthesized list of competencies, to be adopted by every district in the state. This is not likely to occur.

One approach which looks promising would be to encourage local districts to track and verify "school skills" competencies at elementary and junior high levels. The tracking of these enabling skills could lead to the verification of related, higher-level, application-to-life-role competencies at the high school level. Teachers at each level would then verify the kinds of skills they view as most appropriate to their level of instruction. There would be fewer graduation requirements to verify, hence simpler record keeping, if the secondary teachers did not have to deal with behavioral-objective-level statements in the basic skills. And most elementary and junior high school teachers already view basic-skills development as their primary responsibility.

The beginnings of this kind of movement can be found in OAR 581-22-222 (see Appendix). This rule requires local districts to "insure instruction in any combination of grades K-8 to provide students with opportunities to acquire knowledge and skills applicable to minimum competencies required for graduation." (From Jim Impara's paper elsewhere in this volume, it seems that the state of Virginia may be headed in this direction as well.) However, some local districts are pressuring the board to modify definitions in the standards so that their existing secondary-level, basic-skills-proficiency testing programs will satisfy the simpler competency requirements. If this happens, no significant change will have occurred in the focus or function of the public schools as a result of the new graduation requirements.

It is not likely that Oregon will move in the direction of state-level proficiency tests for high school graduation. The state board has committed itself to strengthening the concept of local control. It will likely continue to ask local districts to set their own minimum performance levels, subject to the scrutiny and approval of their local communities. The board has specifically rejected the notion of using state-level cutoff scores, however impartial this may appear, in determining whether a given student may receive a high school diploma. The board's sentiment seems to be: judgments on the competency of *individual* students to function in post-schooling life roles should be kept as close to the classroom level as possible.

Notes

1. W. G. Spady, "Competency Based Education: A Bandwagon in Search of a Definition," *Educational Researcher* 6, no. 1 (January 1977): 9.

2. These six statewide goals are listed under OAR 581-22-201 in the Appendix.

3. Definitions are included under OAR 581-22-200 in the Appendix.

4. For additional competencies to be certified not later than the graduating class of 1981, see OAR 581-22-231 and 581-22-236 in the Appendix.

5. Spady, op. cit., p. 10.

6. H. M. Brickell, "Seven Key Notes on Minimal Competency Testing," a paper presented at four regional workshops for the Education Commission of the States and the National Institute of Education, October 1977.

7. R. B. Clemmer, "Assessing Educational Need: First Step to Accountability," *Oregon Education* 44, no. 16 (May 1970): 16.

8. Ibid.

9. M. Wright, *Oregonians Speak Out on Education: A Report on Town Meetings Conducted by the Oregon Board of Education* (Salem: Oregon Department of Education, 1970).

10. Dale Parnell, "Survival Education," a paper written on career education and circulated within the Department of Education in September 1972.

11. Dale Parnell, *The Case for Competency-Based Education*, (Bloomington: Phi Delta Kappa Education Foundation, 1978).

12. Any local district found not to be in compliance with requirements contained in the Oregon administrative rules (the mechanism of the minimum standards) faces loss of basic school support monies from the state. This is, on the average, approximately 40 percent of the budget of local districts.

Appendix: Excerpts from the Oregon Minimum Standards Adopted 23 June 1976

Definitions

Definitions

581-22-200 The following definitions apply to Oregon Administrative Rules 581-22-200 through 581-22-300, unless otherwise indicated by context:

(1) "Analyzing": mental processes by which individuals identify interrelationships within an entity and develop ability to make new applications;

(2) "Assessment": activities designed to secure and organize information describing student performance in specified subject matter at a given time;

(3) "Board": the State Board of Education;

(4) "Career Education": learning experiences enabling students to make career choices and develop attitudes, knowledge and skills needed for the producer (occupational) life role and for related aspects of other life roles. It includes awareness and exploration of work, preparation for occupations and specialization in a specific occupation;

(5) "Citizenship/Government Education": study of structures and functions of government and the human relations skills and understandings necessary for individuals to work productively with each other;

(6) "Competency(ies)": a statement(s) of desired student performance representing demonstrable ability to apply knowledge, understanding, and/or skills assumed to contribute to success in life role functions. (Each statement usually covers related tasks, contains a performance (action) verb and describes an outcome from which verifiable standards of achievement may be determined. The statement may relate to several goals);

(7) "Computing": manipulation of math symbols through fundamental processes of addition, subtraction, multiplication, and division;

(8) "Conditionally Standard School": a school having failed to meet provisions of the minimum standards but for which the local board has adopted and submitted a plan, subsequently approved by the Superintendent, for correcting deficiencies;

(9) "Consumer Education/Economics/Personal Finance": instructional activities to help students cope with consumer concerns in our economic system, including money management, credit, purchasing goods and services, and rights and responsibilities in the marketplace;

(10) "Course Goals": statements of desired learner outcomes for each course or unit of study in grades 9 through 12;

(11) "Credit by Examination": ascertaining student achievement for waiving course requirements and, if appropriate, granting credit;

(12) "Department": the Department of Education;

(13) "Diploma": the document a local unified or union high school district issues attesting to the holder's having:

(a) Demonstrated minimum competencies the local board has adopted for graduation,

(b) Completed requirements for earning the Board's 21 units of credit (OAR 581-22-226) and any additional units of credit the local board specifies,

(c) Completed 12 school years of educational experience, or the equivalent, as authorized by local board policies adopted in conformance with these rules;

(14) "District Goals": statements of broad, general learner outcomes a local district and its community see as desirable consequences of instruction and relevant to attaining Board Goals for Elementary and Secondary Education (OAR 581-22-201);

(15) "Elementary School": an organizational unit of any combination of grades kindergarten through 8;

(16) "Goals": statements of desired learner outcomes at various instructional levels (district, program, course);

(17) "High School": an organizational unit composed of any combination of grades 10 through 12 in districts providing a junior high school containing grade 9;

any combination of grades 9 through 12 organized in a separate unit; grades 9 through 12 housed with grades kindergarten through 12; grades 7 or 8 through 12 if Department approved;

(18) "Junior High School": an organizational secondary school unit composed of any combination of grades 7, 8, and 9 organized separately from other grades in the system and Department approved;

(19) "Language Arts/English": communication disciplines contributing to skills in reading, writing, speaking and listening;

(20) "Middle School": an organizational elementary school unit composed of any combination of grades 5, 6, 7 and 8 organized separately from other elementary grades in the system and identified as a middle school with the Department;

(21) "Minimum Standards": rules for public elementary and secondary schools found in Division 22 of the Board's administrative rules;

(22) "Nonstandard School": a school having failed to meet provisions of the minimum standards and within ninety days of the Superintendent's notification of deficiencies not having submitted a plan of correction or adhered to the plan of correction the Superintendent received and approved. A nonstandard school is deficient for purposes of ORS 327.103;

(23) "Performance Indicator": an established measure to judge student competency achievement;

(24) "Planned Course Statement": a course title, a course overview, course goals and, where appropriate, minimum competencies;

(25) "Procedure": a specified routine method to be followed in complying with requirements of administrative rules and in implementing board-adopted policies;

(26) "Process": specified actions which insure validity of the results of a procedure;

(27) "Program": a planned series of interdependent activities or services contributing to the attainment of a common goal or set of goals;

(28) "Program Goals" (Instructional): statements of desired learner outcomes for each district instructional program in any combination of grades kindergarten through 12;

(29) "Program Goals" (Support): outcomes of a program in a school system to support the entire system or one or more of its components, usually stated in terms of service to be performed;

(30) "Program Improvement": using assessment and needs identification information in making program revisions that reduce needs identified;

(31) "Program Needs Identification": development and application of procedures for specifying and prioritizing differences between actual learner outcomes and desired outcomes of program instruction sufficient to warrant considering program revision;

(32) "Reading": purposeful thinking processes by which an individual interprets written symbols as meaningful words and ideas;

(33) "Required Courses of Study": instructional programs under OAR 581-22-218 through OAR 581-22-236 prescribed by ORS 326.051(d). Guides the Department develops and issues shall provide further definition of assistance for local program implementation;

(34) "Social Studies/History": systematic study of societies and their activities.

(35) "Standard School": a school having met provisions of the minimum standards.

(36) "Superintendent": the State Superintendent of Public Instruction;

(37) "Unit of Credit": successful completion of a minimum 130 clock hours of classroom or equivalent work identified as part of a planned course. Equivalent work may include independent study, work experience, and research time;

(38) "Writing": written representation of a language following a systematic order designed to clarify and express thought.

Goals

Goals for Elementary & Secondary Education

581-22-201 (1) The Board, in response to the changing needs of Oregon learners, sets forth six goals for the public schools.

(2) Conceived and endorsed by Oregon citizens, the statewide goals are designed to assure that every student in the elementary and secondary schools shall have the opportunity to learn to function effectively in six life roles: INDIVIDUAL, LEARNER, PRODUCER, CITIZEN, CONSUMER, and FAMILY MEMBER. Each goal suggests the knowledge, skills, and attitudes needed to function in these life roles.

(3) The statewide goals shall be implemented through the district, program and course goals of each local school district. These local goals are set by schools and communities together to fulfill a mutual responsibility for the education of every student. Because most of the knowledge and skills needed to function effectively in the role of LEARNER are acquired in school, the school has primary responsibility for helping students achieve this goal.

(4) Each school and its community should establish priorities among the goals to meet local needs, and allocate their resources accordingly. This process should provide each student with the opportunity to achieve the requirements for graduation from high school, and as much additional schooling as school and community resources can provide.

(5) Each individual will have the opportunity to develop to the best of his or her ability the knowledge, skills, and attitudes necessary to function as a(an):

(a) "Individual": to develop the skills necessary for achieving fulfillment as a self-directed person; to acquire the knowledge necessary for achieving and maintaining physical and mental health and to develop the capacity for coping with change through an understanding of the arts, humanities, scientific processes, and the principles involved in making moral and ethical choices;

(b) "Learner": to develop the basic skills of reading, writing, computing, spelling, speaking, listening, and problem-solving; and to develop a postiive attitude toward learning as a lifelong endeavor;

(c) "Producer": to learn of the variety of occupations; to learn to appreciate the dignity and value of work and the mutual responsibilities of employees and employers; and to learn to identify personal talents and interests, to make appropriate career choices, and to develop career skills;

(d) "Citizen": to learn to act in a responsible manner; to learn of the rights and responsibilities of citizens of the community, state, nation, and world; and to learn to understand, respect and interact with people of different cultures, generations and races;

(e) "Consumer": to acquire knowledge and to develop skills in the management of personal resources necessary for meeting obligations to self, family, and society;

(f) "Family Member": to learn of the rights and responsibilities of family members, and to acquire the skills and knowledge to strengthen and enjoy family life.

Accreditation

Administration of the Standardization Program

581-22-202 (1) The Board develops and issues minimum standards for Oregon public schools under authority of ORS 326.051. All public schools must comply with these minimum standards and Board administrative rules. These standards are not applicable to community colleges defined in ORS 341, except for program requirements for granting adult high school diplomas.

(2) The Superintendent initiates standardization visits to public elementary and secondary schools on a regularly scheduled basis and at other times as necessary. A public school desiring an official standardization appraisal at other than scheduled times shall present a written request to the Superintendent. The school will be classified after an official standardization visit.

Assignment of Standardization Classification

581-22-204 (1) An official standardization classification is assigned to each school in a district after Department personnel supervise an on-site appraisal.

(2) Classifications shall be:

(a) Standard school;

(b) Nonstandard school;

(c) Conditionally standard school.

(3) A local district with one or more nonstandard schools shall be found deficient and classified nonstandard and must submit a plan of correction to the Superintendent pursuant to ORS 327.103(3). The plan of correction shall provide specific steps to correct each deficiency, a completion date for correcting each deficiency and the date the local board approved the plan. When the Superintendent approves the plan of correction, the classification of the local district will become conditionally standard.

(4) A conditionally standard classification indicates a temporary status. Failure of the local district to meet terms of the correction plan shall cause the classification of the district to revert to nonstandard, until such time as it adheres to the plan or it amends and the Superintendent approves the plan.

(5) When a local district classified as conditionally standard has completed its plan of correction and district officials certify the district is meeting all provisions of these minimum standards, the Superintendent may change the classification of the district to standard.

Waiver Provisions

581-22-206 (1) In administering the standardization program, the Department shall encourage school districts to develop instructional programs exceeding minimum standards as well as carefully planned pilot or experimental programs. When a special program or independent textbook adoption necessitates deviation from the standards, a school district shall submit a description of its proposal and secure approval prior to implementing the change. Approval, if granted, will be for a specified time and may be followed by a Department evaluation of the program.

(2) When local district officials believe it not feasible to comply with a specific standard in a school or schools, they may petition the Superintendent for a waiver.

(3) The petition for waiver shall:

(a) Identify the specific standard for which the waiver is requested;

(b) Specify why the district cannot reasonably comply with the standard;

(c) Specify how the district is compensating to provide for the education, health and/or safety of the children affected;

(d) Identify a maximum time for which the waiver is requested.

(4) The Superintendent shall recommend to the Board approval of such waivers and deviations when the local superintendent provides satisfactory written assurance that district needs and intent of minimum standards are being met. The Superintendent shall specify the time any approval shall be in effect.

(5) Petitions for waivers and deviations modifying requirements specified in the "Oregon Revised Statutes" shall not be approved.

Instructional Planning

Instructional Planning

581-22-208 Each local district shall adopt and implement a system of instructional program planning and assessment to provide for:

(1) Sets of goals including:

(a) District goals, adopted by the local board, by 9-1-76,

(b) Program goals contributing to achievement of district goals by 9-1-76,

(c) Course goals contributing to achievement of program goals by 9-1-77;

(2) Assessment in reading, writing and/or computing within three instructional programs by 9-1-79 and six by 9-1-81 and reporting results to the local community. Such assessment shall:

(a) Occur after determining if reading, writing and/or computing skills must be developed or applied for students to achieve program goals, and

(b) Use valid measurement procedures;

(3) Needs identification related at least to reading, writing and computing for programs assessed and setting priorities for addressing such needs by 9-1-80. This process shall include local board review of needs identified and priorities set;

(4) Policies and procedures for making program improvements by 9-1-80 at least in reading, writing and computing in programs selected for assessment.

Instructional Program

Educational Program

581-22-218 To provide all students opportunity to achieve district-adopted learner outcomes, requirements for graduation and personal goals through participation in educational programs relevant to their needs, interests and abilities, each local district shall by 9-1-79 adopt procedures to:

(1) Identify individuals' learning strengths and weaknesses;

(2) Provide learning opportunities for students responsive to their needs;

(3) Determine progress students make in their educational program;

(4) Maintain student progress records and report the information to parents and students.

Elementary Instructional Programs

581-22-221 Students in local districts having any combination of grades kindergarten through eight shall by 9-1-76 receive instruction in language arts, mathematics, science, social studies, health education, physical education, music education and art education. Local boards may grant exemptions when required by students' religious or cultural beliefs, or for students with special physical, sensory, or other handicaps.

Elementary Instruction Applicable to Required Competencies

581-22-222 Local districts shall by 9-1-77 establish procedures to insure instruction in any combination of grades kindergarten through eight to provide students with opportunities to acquire knowledge and skills applicable to minimum competencies required for graduation adopted for receiving schools.

Graduation Requirements (Class of 1977)

581-22-224 Each local district enrolling students in grades 9 through 12 shall offer subjects to enable students to meet the following graduation requirements for the graduating class of 1977:

(1) Three units (30 semester hours) in language arts/English;

(2) Two units (20 semester hours) in social studies. The social studies series requires courses in United States history/government and modern problems, or equivalent Board-approved work;

(3) Two units (20 semester hours) in health education and physical education;

(4) One unit (10 semester hours) in science;

(5) One unit (10 semester hours) in mathematics;

(6) Ten units (100 semester hours) in elective subjects unless local board policy prescribes additional work in certain subjects.

Graduation Requirements

581-22-226 (1) Each local district enrolling students in grades 9 through 12 shall implement Board-adopted high school graduation requirements beginning with the graduating class of 1978.

(2) Credit Requirements for high school program completion:

(a) Each student shall earn a minimum 21 units of credit in grades 9 through 12;

(b) Units of credit shall be earned in the following areas of study:

(A) Language Arts/English—3

(B) Mathematics—1

(C) Social Studies/History—1

(D) Citizenship/Government—1

(E) Science—1

(F) Health Education—1

(G) Physical Education—1

(H) Consumer Education/Economics/Personal Finance—1

(I) Career Education—1

(J) Electives—10

(c) Local boards may alter the number of units of elective credits;

(d) Local boards may establish additional credit requirements beyond the minimum number.

(3) Planned course statements shall be written for courses in grades 9 through 11 by 9-1-76 and in grade 12 by 9-1-77 and shall be available to students, staff, parents, local board, and interested citizens.

Diplomas and Certificates of Competency

581-22-228 (1) The local board shall award a diploma upon fulfillment of all state and local district credit, competency and attendance requirements.

(2) The local board may grant a certificate identifying acquired minimum competencies to students having met some but not all requirements for the diploma and having chosen to end their formal school experiences.

Performace Requirements for Program Completion

581-22-231 (1) Student transcripts shall record demonstration of minimum competencies necessary to:

(a) Read, write, speak, listen;

(b) Analyze;

(c) Compute;

(d) Use basic scientific and technological processes;

(e) Develop and maintain a healthy mind and body;

(f) Be an informed citizen in the community, state, and nation;

(g) Be an informed citizen in interaction with environment;

(h) Be an informed citizen on streets and highways;

(i) Be an informed consumer of goods and services;

(j) Function within an occupation or continue education leading to a career.

(2) The local board shall by 9-1-76 adopt and make available to the community minimum competencies it is willing to accept as evidence students are equipped to function in the society in which they live. Students need not develop all competencies within the formal schooling process. Schools shall provide necessary instruction for those who need it. The local district shall identify performance indicators used for competency verification.

(3) The local district may alter performance indicators for competencies or the local board may declare a policy for granting waivers to substitute competencies appropriate to unique needs and abilities of individual students.

Attendance

581-22-232 (1) Twelve school years, beginning with grade one, of planned educational experience shall be required, except as local boards adopt policies providing early or delayed completion of all state and local program, credit and performance requirements.

(2) Local boards may adopt policies to allow credit by examination or allow credit for off-campus experiences.

(3) Local boards are encouraged to adopt policies allowing individual program completion in more or less than twelve school years.

(4) In any modification of the attendance requirements for graduation, the administrator shall consider age and maturity of students, access to alternative learning experiences, performance levels, desires of parents or guardians, and local board guidelines.

Developing Appropriate Electives and Additional Course Offerings Beyond State Minimums

581-22-234 Local districts are encouraged to develop elective offerings providing students opportunities to earn a minimum ten elective units of high school credit. As indicated in OAR 581-22-226(2), however, the minimum number of elective units of credit may be altered if the local district increases the number of required units of credit. These electives shall be structured in terms of identified student needs for diverse experiences in vocational, scientific, fine arts, modern language and humanities education.

Local District Responsibility for Implementation

581-22-236 Each local district enrolling students in grades 9 through 12 shall implement the competency component of its graduation requirements as follows:

(1) Establish minimum competencies and performance indicators beginning with the graduating class of 1978;

(2) Certify attainment of competencies necessary to read, write, speak, listen, analyze and compute beginning with the graduating class of 1978;

(3) Certify attainment of all competencies beginning not later than with the graduating class of 1981.

16 Virginia's Approach to Minimum Competency Testing

James C. Impara

This paper describes Virginia's minimum competency testing programs and the significant events which led up to and influenced the programs' development. Virginia's programs are then compared to those of other states.

At this writing 35 states have some form of minimum competency testing program planned or instituted (Pipho, 1978). Virginia became an initiate in the minimum competency movement in 1976, when two actions were begun almost simultaneously: one by the state legislature and the second by the Board of Education. The legislative action was the passage of the Standards of Quality and Objectives for Public Schools in Virginia 1976-78 (76-78 SOQ). This legislation contained a standard (standard 1 B) requiring the Board of Education to set minimum educational objectives in reading, communication, and mathematics skills that should be achieved in the primary and intermediate grades. The 76-78 SOQ also required (standard 7) each local education agency— called a school division in Virginia—to administer tests primarily to provide information to classroom teachers on the progress of each child toward the minimum educational objectives. The tests were to be developed or approved by the Department of Education. The testing was scheduled to begin in fall 1978.

I am extremely grateful to Drs. Gerald Bracey, Paul Williams, and Claude Sandy for their willingness to provide factual input and details about Virginia's programs. Any errors of fact and all editorial comments are attributable only to the author.

The second action was the adoption by the Board of Education of a revised version of the Standards for Accrediting Secondary Schools in Virginia. Of the two, this action received the most publicity because it changed the rules under which students would be permitted to graduate from high school. While retaining a slightly modified set of credit requirements (Carnegie type units), the new rules imposed the additional requirement that students who were to graduate in 1981 demonstrate, to the satisfaction of local school officials, attainment of minimum competencies in four areas: communications, computation, citizenship/social studies, and postsecondary readiness.

In spite of the obvious differences in these two actions, there was considerable confusion about them at the beginning of the 1976-77 school year. During the period from November 1976 through June 1977, I visited several school divisions to discuss these new requirements and their implications for schools. Many central office staff and even more teachers expressed their confusion either directly or through questions about one or both programs. In order to avoid confusion, each program is discussed here independently.

Basic Learning Skills (BLS) Program

The Basic Learning Skills (BLS) program, as the elementary school minimum competency program is called, began with the passage of the 76-78 SOQ (Virginia Board of Education, 1976b). In December 1976, the Department of Education staff began intensive planning for the fall 1978 testing. Even earlier the staff realized the magnitude of the task of assembling or developing objective-referenced tests in reading, communications (including writing, listening, and speaking), and mathematics for all students in grades one through six. The task was further complicated because no set of minimum educational objectives had been approved by the board as of December 1976. At that time the testing and evaluation staff consisted of two professionals who operated statewide standardized testing programs, which were to continue.

From December 1976 to May 1977, the testing and evaluation staff, other staff of the Department of Education, and several outside consultants were involved in numerous concurrent activities. Among these activities were: (1) obtaining additional funding and additional staff; (2) developing and obtaining board approval of a set of minimum educational objectives appropriate for all students in kindergarten and grades one through six; (3) appealing to the 1977 legislature to modify the 76-78 SOQ to a more reasonable level of effort (reducing either the number of grades or subjects to be tested); and (4) developing plans and alternative strategies for test acquisition or development, test administration, scoring, and reporting.

The efforts were all successful to some degree. Several new staff positions were authorized and a vacant position was filled—director of program evaluation and testing (now called director of research, evaluation and testing). Some additional funding was secured by redirecting existing funds. Objectives in each of the three curricular areas were developed and distributed for criticism to all school divisions and prepared for board approval. The legislature was persuaded to modify the standards; however, the new modifications were not as favorable to the Department of Education as they could have been. The modifications reduced the grades from one through six to one through three—levels where fewer materials were available and which would require hand scoring. Plans for test development and administration were formulated and began moving through the various review and approval mechanisms.

Increasing Staff

By May 1977, the department had recruited Dr. Gerald Bracey to fill the vacant director of testing and evaluation position. Two additional positions were also authorized, and one of the existing positions was upgraded from assistant supervisor to supervisor. Although this seemed to increase the number of professional staff from two to five, a reorganization of the department assigned additional responsibilities to the director, whose title was changed to include research in addition to testing and evaluation. Consequently, only two additional full-time positions were added, and the four professionals had one ongoing and one new testing program to administer. (Another new program—the statewide graduate requirements test—was added in June 1978 without an increase in staffing.)

Determining BLS Objectives

The substantive activities leading up to the 1977-78 BLS program began with the development of objectives (Virginia Board of Education, 1977). This activity was assigned to the Division of Curriculum and Instruction; testing and evaluation staff served in a consulting capacity only. The Department of Education felt that the objectives should not be written to comply with testing needs; rather, instructional concerns should take precedence. Three committees of local educators—one each in reading, communications, and mathematics—were appointed to develop first drafts of the objectives.

The committees began their work by identifying broad objectives for end-of-sixth-grade performance. A set of specific minimum objectives thought to contribute to the attainment of each broad objective was then developed, and estimates of grade-level appropriateness were assigned to these minimum objectives. Grade-level appropriateness was defined as the highest grade in which a student is expected to have achieved the objective. A field review was undertaken to obtain the opinions of Virginia educators regarding the appropriateness of the minimum and terminal objectives and the accuracy of grade-level assignment. Over 20,000 responses were received (this is a duplicated count, as some local committees reacted to all three curriculum areas). Some revisions were made, based on the field review, and the objectives were submitted to and adopted by the Board of Education in May 1977.

The adopted objectives varied in their degree of specificity within and across subject areas. For example, one first-grade objective in mathematics required students to subtract a one-place number from a two-place number less than 20 without regrouping; another first-grade objective required the student to draw open and closed figures. The reading objectives included decoding, comprehension, and study skills across a wide array of specificity.

Revision Legislation

The revised 76-78 SOQ still required school divisions to use the statewide minimum educational objectives in the primary and intermediate grades (1-6), but it revised the testing schedule as follows: beginning 1978-79, reading and mathematics objectives, grades 1-3; beginning 1979-80, reading and mathematics objectives, grade 4; beginning 1980-81, reading and mathematics objectives, grades 5 and 6, and communications objectives, grades 1-6 (Virginia Board of Education, 1977).

Developing BLS Tests

National Evaluation Systems, Inc., won a competitively bid contract to meet these revised standards. The specifications of the contract required development of the BLS items, review of the items by Virginia educators, assembly of the items into one or more test forms, field testing the items, and item revision based on field test results. The time allotted for these activities was extremely short. The contract period began in early fall 1977, and field testing was scheduled for April 1978.

As a result of this contract there exists a pool of over 900 objective-referenced test items related to the 83 minimum BLS objectives. These items were developed cooperatively by the contractor, department staff, and two review committees composed mostly of local, school-division personnel. The development process entailed producing prototype items which were subjected to an extensive field review by school-division and higher education personnel. These prototypes served as models for item development. There were initially twelve items for each reading and math minimum objective, and each objective was keyed to grades one, two, or three. The number of items was reduced slightly for some objectives after the field test.

Approximately 12,000 students participated in the mid-April, 1978 field test. The field test was designed to obtain responses on each of the 996 items from about 400 students at the targeted grade level. A multiple-matrix sampling approach was used: classrooms represented one dimension and the 996-item pool, organized by objective, represented the other. The items were assigned to 129 field-test forms and data were summarized only at state level, because the major intent of the field test was quality control of items rather than instructional feedback to teachers. In addition to the data on student performance at the item's targeted grade level, grade-level bracketing of each item was accomplished by testing about 200 students in the next lower grade and also in the next higher grade. All tests were administered and scored by teachers who completed a questionnaire related to the usefulness of the tests and testing procedures. These questionnaires have not yet been analyzed systematically. The bracketing of each item, while serving a quality-control function, also helped to verify the grade-level appropriateness of items (and by inference the objectives).

Item quality and appropriateness decisions were made on the basis of both standard item-analysis techniques and latent-trait methodology. Item difficulties and discrimination indices (point biserial correlation with the total score per objective) were computed, and, based on estimated total scores, each item was "Rasch calibrated." These two strategies were combined to improve the tests' instructional feedback to teachers.

Instituting the BLS Program

At its annual summer conference for local test directors the department presented its plans for the BLS program. The department views the BLS program as more than just testing. It is an instructional program which incorporates testing as part of instructional management. Potentially the testing may also serve as a means for reporting to the public the status of educational attainment in the primary and intermediate grades.

In order to accomplish its major purpose—instructional feedback— and a possible second purpose—public reporting—two test forms have been developed at each grade level. There is also a User's Guide to aid the teacher in administering, scoring, and interpreting the tests.

There are six versions each of Forms A and B (reading and mathematics by three levels). Each Form A includes four test items for each objective at the specified level. This form is designed to serve as either a screening or summative measure with screening as the recommended use. The interpretation of the results recommended in the User's

Guide (Williams, 1978) relies on a mixture of latent-trait methodology and judgment. In order to use the results diagnostically, teachers must obtain a total raw score and a raw score for each specific objective for each student. The total raw score is converted to a Rasch ability score (on a scale of 160 to 240). Based on field test data each objective has been ordered in difficulty within its grade level from 160 to 240. Thus, the probability that a student has attained mastery of an objective is known. The teacher then examines a student's score for each objective to determine if there are "surprises,"—for example, has the student failed to master (answer correctly at least three of four items) an objective below the ability level, or has the student mastered an objective at a higher ability level. Strategies for dealing with both false positives and false negatives are also suggested.

The versions of Form B are quite different from Form A in structure and use. Form B is a set of booklets, each containing six items. Each booklet corresponds to one minimum objective. A booklet may be used to verify a false positive or false negative detected on Form A or with direct instruction on the objective. Any form or booklet may be used with individual students or groups at the teacher's option.

This testing program is required by the state, but as yet, the decision to collect and report data publicly has not been made. School divisions may request permission to substitute their own tests in lieu of the BLS tests. The criteria for approval of local tests (Campbell and Boyer, 1978) are not being rigidly applied during the initial year of the program (Sandy, 1978). The criteria include demonstrated correspondence to the BLS minimum objectives, utility for providing instructional feedback, and acceptable psychometric properties. The Division of Research, Evaluation and Testing has approval authority.

The BLS is being implemented as this is written. The department has received little feedback beyond the teacher questionnaires obtained during the field test. Some negative feedback is expected because of the burden being placed on teachers to score and interpret at least one administration of Form A (or an approved alternate) for each student.

School divisions and teachers need not administer Form B, but Form A or an equivalent must be administered at some time during the school year. School divisions ordered their copies of the two test forms in late summer 1978, and distribution to the divisions is now completed.

Graduation Requirements Program

In Virginia, as in many states, the general specifications for school quality are described in standards for accreditation. Among these specifications for quality are the requirements students must meet in order to be graduated from high school. Until 1976, high school graduation indicated that a student had received a certain number of units of credit which were based on contact hours. During the years prior to 1976 the school subjects and number of units of credit in certain subjects varied, but no other requirements were imposed. In May 1976, the Board of Education requested that the department recommend a competency-based graduation requirements program. Based on the board's request, a recommendation was made, and in July 1976, Virginia joined those states and localities which were adopting a demonstration of competency as an additional graduation requirement (Karlen, 1977). This rather sudden and dramatic action elicited positive reactions from the press and other media, but spread anxiety and confusion among many educators. Much of the anxiety in the educational community was due more to several ambiguities in the board's ruling than to the intent of the new requirements.

The 1976 accreditation standards for graduation eligibility are reiterated below:

*In order to graduate from an accredited secondary school and receive a high school diploma in Virginia, students shall earn the number of units of credit prescribed by the Board of Education and be able to demonstrate to the satisfaction of local school officials attainment of the following minimum competencies:
1. Functional literacy in communicative skills including the ability to read, write, and speak: (SIC)
2. Computational skills including the ability to work with decimals and percentages to the extent that they can effectively participate in society as consumers;
3. A basic knowledge and understanding of the history and cultures of the United States, including concepts and processes of democratic governance and our economic system;
4. The ability to pursue higher education in post secondary schools or gain employment as a result of having gained a job-entry skill.

---

*Change to become effective July 1, 1978 (Virginia Board of Education, 1976a)

Between July 1976 and January 1977, the board made several clarifications, and the department began several technical assistance efforts. The board clarified the effective date by specifying that these requirements would apply to the graduating class of 1981. Although not specified, the means by which competency was to be demonstrated was through testing. (I have no documentation of this assumption; however Mr. Bradner, Dr. Bracey, and other department staff, in addition to Mr. Tulloch, a board member, have indicated in several conversations with me that this was the assumption.)

The department's technical assistance followed two alternate tracks: first, the formation of committees in each of the four competency areas to develop sample competencies, performance indicators, and test items, and the appointment of an external advisory committee to review the sample materials and to suggest general guidelines to accompany the sample materials; and second, the funding of a consortium of school divisions to develop model procedures and materials useful in their divisions. These two efforts were to provide school divisions with alternative models and materials which could be adopted, modified, or ignored.

Even with these efforts under way, resistance within the educational community was building. The timelines were short, and the problems of competency-based graduation loomed large in the eyes of many local superintendents. Some of the recognized problems were: inconsistency of competency certification across divisions (the board has not yet clarified how transfer of credit is to be accomplished); costs and other difficulties associated with test development; setting performance standards; and threats of legal actions if competency certification was viewed as discriminatory. Neither the department nor the board offered much direct help in solving these and other specific problems. In mid-1977, several superintendents began to pressure the state superintendent and the board to modify the graduation requirements. This movement by the local superintendents occurred through individual communication and through the Virginia Association of School Administrators and the Virginia School Board's Association.

While the department and the board were being pressured by the superintendents to change the graduation requirements, the legislature was moving toward requiring competency demonstration as a high school graduation requirement. In its 1978 session, the legislature had to update the standards of quality. One of the revisions of the SOQ related to graduation requirements and added fuel to the fire begun earlier by the superintendents. The new 78-80 SOQ included the following standard (standard 9 C):

It is the policy of the Commonwealth that the awarding of a high school diploma shall be based upon achievement. In order to receive a high school diploma from an accredited secondary school after January 1, 1981, students shall earn the number of units of credit prescribed by the Board of Education and attain minimum competencies prescribed by the Board of Education. Attainment of such competencies shall be demonstrated by means of a test prescribed by the Board of Education. (Virginia Board of Education, 1978)

While this legislation was pending, a set of recommendations was presented to the board on February 29, 1978, by State Superintendent W. E.

Campbell (Campbell, 1978). Dr. Campbell recommended that: the board adopt a statewide program to certify reading, writing, speaking, and computational skills; commercially produced tests be used having two or more forms to provide for retesting of a student if necessary; a ninth-grade diagnostic test, compatible with the graduation test, be used for determining which individual students need remedial instruction; and considerable thought be given to awarding differentiated diplomas.

These recommendations were distributed to school divisions and responses were made to Campbell directly and through his Superintendent's Advisory Council (a group of local superintendents). Most respondents supported the concept of state testing (any other reaction was doomed politically), but many questions were raised in an attempt to clarify the recommendations. The minutes from a meeting of a consortium of school divisions included three pages of questions (Impara, 1978). These questions and others (Flanagan, 1978) were sent to members of the Superintendent's Advisory Council, Department of Education staff, and members of the Board of Education.

In response to the legislation and to the recommendations by Superintendent Campbell, the accreditation standards were revised at the March 1978 meeting of the board. The new standards specify:

*In addition to the units of credit specified in these standards, an accredited school shall require as a condition of graduation that students demonstrate mastery of minimum competency in the areas of reading and mathematics on tests prescribed by the Board of Education. Local authorities shall also require evidence, through performance related assessment tasks as part of the instructional program and/or through a test if preferred by a locality, that graduates have attained minimum competencies in the following:
1. Essential citizenship skills, concepts, and knowledge of history and government necessary for responsible participation in American society.
2. The skills to qualify for further education or employment.

---

*Effective no later than with graduating class of 1981 (Virginia Board of Education, 1978).

In addition to revising the accreditation standards, the board approved several of Campbell's other recommendations. Specifically, the department was charged with testing tenth graders in the fall of 1978 using commercially available tests.

These new graduation requirements made Virginia unique among the states by having a dual set of competency requirements—one set administered statewide and a second set administered by local agencies. The remainder of this section will emphasize the activities undertaken to implement the statewide requirements.

Selecting Graduation Requirements Tests

To institute the accreditation standards, the department built upon work it had already done and also upon work by other agencies within the state. A new committee was formed and verbally instructed to recommend specific competencies and tests in reading and mathematics. The committee members, some appointed by Superintendent Campbell and some selected from each of the seven regions and special interest groups, represented a variety of affiliations throughout the state: teachers' organizations, teachers and central office staff with training and experience in communications and mathematics, and Department of Education specialists in testing and curriculum. Because time was short the department personnel also performed much of the necessary staff work, such as assembling copies of tests and arranging meeting space. The department also began preparing for a pilot administration of the selected tests and investigating means by which performance standards would be established.

One of the first problems (aside from time) the committee faced was the identification of the competencies to be tested. The department had formed, as part of its earlier technical assistance, various committees which developed, either independently or through a consortium, sets of competencies and performance indicators. The committee obtained copies of all these materials and compared those developed by school divisions with those developed as part of the department's guidelines. Because the department's materials seemed to be the most widely distributed and acceptable statewide, the committee compared the tests it examined to the department's set of competencies and performance indicators.

These competencies ranged considerably in their level of specificity. One reading competency, for example, requires students to be able to interpret information contained in print. These competencies were operationally defined by giving examples of specific performance indicators. One such performance indicator for the above competency was: given a bank statement, the student will interpret the code for deposit, withdrawal, interest, charges, and balance. The computational competencies were usually expressed more specifically than those in reading (for example, find a given percent of a number), so fewer performance indicators were needed for definition.

After examining many tests, the committee selected for reading the IOX Basic Skills Test: Secondary Level (1978), and it selected a modified version of a mathematics test developed by STS (a test publishing company) for Virginia Beach public schools. The selection of the math test was due largely to the fact that Virginia Beach had adopted, with minor modification, the department's competencies and performance indicators. Upon selection of these tests, the committee recommended their adoption to the board. This recommendation was accepted at the June 1978 board meeting.

The committee also recommended that these two tests be used only for the graduating classes of 1981 and 1982. The board approved these and other committee recommendations (Campbell, 1978b). Most of the other recommendations were related to the management of the program—such as the number of times a student must pass the test, the number of chances a student should have if unsuccessful, who scores the test, the nature of reporting results, the mechanics for revision, and that the passing score should be set using student performance data as input.

Only one recommendation was not approved by the board at the June meeting—the recommendation that "the competency testing program be a one-tiered program; once the student has passed the test the student should not be required to take the test again" (Campbell, 1978b). This recommendation generated substantial debate at the June meeting and again at the October meeting, at which time it was finally approved for the 1981 and 1982 graduating classes.

Piloting the Graduation Requirements Test

The selected tests did not fully meet Dr. Campbell's recommendations that each test have two or more forms and that they be "off the shelf" commercial tests. Prior to the adoption of these tests, the department had determined that STS would be able to produce additional mathematics items and that a second form of the secondary reading tests was scheduled for completion in the near future. Because some of the mathematics items had not previously been administered in the state, although some had been given to Virginia Beach students, a pilot test was planned prior to the fall test administration.

The lack of time demanded conducting the pilot test during the summer of 1978. This was accomplished without some of the problems which might have been expected because of the nature of the typical summer-school population. Ninth-grade students in Prince William County, which operates a year-round school system, participated in the pilot test. There is no assurance that the Prince William County summer students are comparable with students of the regular school year, but they are more typical of all students than other summer students who attend for either enrichment or remediation.

To accommodate the differences between the Prince William County students and a statewide population, a latent-trait analysis (Rasch) was performed on the items, in addition to standard item-analysis techniques. These analyses resulted in the replacement of some items on the mathematics test. The new items had not been previously used in Virginia or elsewhere. The final version of the mathematics test contains 99 items.

The reading test was not piloted even though it had not been administered previously in Virginia. The original IOX test consisted of two parallel forms of approximately 30 items each. The advisory committee felt that while the topical coverage of the test was adequate, it was too short, so the two forms were combined into a single test of about 60 items.

As a result of using untried mathematics items and combining forms to construct the reading test, the psychometric properties of both tests can only be guessed at until data on Virginia students are collected. Despite this lack of knowledge, the board has set a performance standard and has approved making final decisions about a graduation eligibility, based upon the results of the fall testing of tenth graders. The board took these steps contrary to the advice of department staff.

Setting Performance Standards

At its October 1978 meeting the board set a minimum performance standard requiring students to answer correctly 70 percent of the items on both the mathematics and the reading tests in order to be eligible to graduate. This level was set amid some controversy and in a different manner than had been approved by the board in its June meeting.

The original plan for establishing cutoff scores for high school graduation called for a normative/judgmental approach similar to the method proposed by Jaeger (1978) for use in North Carolina. The tests were to be administered statewide to all tenth graders during October 1978. The results of this administration were to be used in the standard-setting process. This approach met hostility from the press, because it was perceived as a means for artificially minimizing the failure rate by manipulating the cutoff scores (Brown, 1978a). This and other media criticism had an impact on an already anxious board.

In its September 1978 meeting the board approved a delay of several weeks in the planned tenth grade statewide testing and insisted that the performance standard be set prior to administration of the test. This decision followed a lengthy discussion between several board members, particularly the board president, Mr. Henry Tulloch, and department staff who advocated test administration prior to standard setting. After the board meeting, the responsibility for setting the standards was assumed by the assistant superintendent for program development rather than being assigned to the Division of Research, Evaluation and Testing, as was expected.

The process selected for setting the performance standard involved finding several school divisions willing to bring together some of their personnel and local citizens. These nonrandom, nonrepresentative samples of individuals took the tests and undertook to recommend a standard of performance.

The recommendations were sent directly to the assistant superintendent for program development, who presented them to the board at its October meeting. The data were presented in the form of the number of individuals whose recommendation fell within specified intervals. The intervals were "50 and below, 51-55, 56-60, . . . 81-85, 86 and above" (Brown, 1978b). Based on this presentation, the majority of the 90 people who participated (60 educators, 30 noneducators) selected a cutoff score at or below 70 percent. I suspect that had the intervals been displayed differently, such as 50-54, 55-59 . . . 80-84, the majority would have selected a cutoff score at or above 70 percent and the board might have set the cutoff score at 75 percent rather than at 70.

Administering the Graduation Competencies Test

As of October 1978, the only test administration has been the pilot test during the summer of 1978. Prior to September 1978, the test was to be administered to tenth graders as a diagnostic measure (identification of students needing more instruction in reading and mathematics). A spring 1979 administration to ninth graders was also planned for the same purpose (diagnostic) as the fall 1978 administration. As a result of the board's October 1978 meeting, the one-tiered recommendation of the advisory committee was adopted for 1981 and 1982 graduates. Hence, students who achieve scores of 70 percent or higher will not have to be retested prior to graduation.

When administered, the graduation competency tests will apply to all students graduating from an accredited school. The ninth and tenth grade administration will take place in all public schools. Private schools may participate if they wish. Because some private schools are accredited by the state, their students who wish to graduate must pass the statewide test at some point. No determination of how the locally administered requirements in citizenship and postsecondary readiness will be accomplished in private schools has been made.

Because some school divisions moved more rapidly than others to institute testing programs for graduation, the state has made provisions for using locally approved tests in lieu of the state's tests for the 1981 and 1982 graduating classes. The major criteria for approval of local tests are that they had been administered prior to the state's tests and that students had been told that the local tests would be used to decide on the competency-based component of graduation eligibility.

Locally Administered Graduation Requirements

Many school divisions are continuing their earlier efforts in the two areas for which they have primary responsibility. The two consortia are still working toward the development of measures in citizenship and social studies and in postsecondary readiness. Some divisions, however, have ceased their efforts because it is not clear that testing is required. The accreditation standards require "evidence, through performance related assessment tasks as part of the instructional program and/or through a test" (Virginia Board of Education, 1978). This statement is sufficiently open so that some divisions may undertake a curriculum analysis, revise to assure the inclusion of instruction on the competencies, and use passing marks in required courses as evidence.

In a conversation with a board member and a legislator, I was informed that this strategy was not the intent of the legislature when they enacted standard 9 of 78-80 SOQ. As yet there has been no reconciliation between the accreditation standard, allowing local discretion, and standard 9, which requires the use of a test prescribed by the board. The resolution of this conflict is only one of many conflicts and ambiguities which needs to be settled before the class of 1981 has graduated.

Comparing Virginia to Other States

The task of comparing minimum competency testing programs is complicated. Many states are still in the planning and development stages, and several states, like Virginia, Florida, and California, have more than one type of program. Even states with only one program are not similar. In an effort to classify planned or extant programs, a framework for comparison has been developed. The framework includes a number of dimensions along which minimum competency testing programs may be classified. The framework is described briefly, and then Virginia is compared to other states along the dimensions of the framework.

The first dimension is whether the program is or is not mandated by the state. It includes the agency or jurisdiction responsible for setting standards and for developing or prescribing the instruments for measuring performance. In many states, participation in the minimum competency testing program is required, the standards are set by an agency at the state level, and the measures are developed or prescribed by a state-level agency. Florida's functional literacy test is an example of this combination. In other states, participation in the program is required, but only broad areas of competency are prescribed by a state level agency, while the specific standards and measures are the responsibility of local agencies, as in Oregon. Other states which require participation use a combination of approaches by setting standards and prescribing measures in certain competencies, but in other competencies assigning responsibility for standard setting and measuring to local agencies, as does Virginia. Other combinations include states like Colorado, where participation by local education agencies is voluntary, but if the option is taken, certain rules apply.

The second dimension is the category of use. Most extant programs have been planned around one or more specific purposes: certification (grade-to-grade promotion or high school graduation); student diagnosis or placement in instructional activities; or assessment both to report publicly on the achievement status of students in the state or district and to assist in broad-based instructional planning. Similar uses have been combined in the framework: graduation and promotion, because graduation is a special case of promotion to the next higher grade, and placement and diagnosis. Although diagnosis is a desired use of the test results, the nature of the testing activity is often screening or placement rather than diagnosis and remediation.

At the outset of the minimum competency testing movement substantial emphasis was placed on competencies related to survival or success in adult roles. Spady's (1977) distinction between competencies (corresponding to life roles) and capacities (corresponding to enablers) on which the competencies depend was an important concept in competency-based education and minimum competency testing. Similar concepts were described by Brickell (1978) as life skills, school skills, and basic skills. Many current programs specify or imply a competency, or life-skills approach (such as Florida's functional literacy test), while other programs are expressly directed toward capacities or school or basic skills (such as Virginia's basic learning skills program). Still other states are not clear about the nature of their program, and the test may include measures of both competencies and capacities (such as Maryland's Project Basic). These differences compose the third dimension of the framework.

Grade level represents another dimension of the framework. Even though the impetus for minimum competency testing was high school graduation, the implications for elementary and early secondary grades quickly became apparent. Many states have added, and more recent initiates have incorporated, minimum competency testing for grades below 11 or 12. Policies also vary on the inclusion or exclusion of special education students.

Another dimension includes subject area tested. Most programs include reading and mathematics; many programs include other topics such as citizenship, job entry skills, leisure activities, science, and writing.

How do Virginia's minimum competency testing programs compare with other states on these dimensions? Each of Virginia's programs is compared with other states based partly on personal contacts with states and mostly on Pipho's (1978) description of state minimum competency testing programs. Some information about other states is missing or awaiting a decision. These unknowns may be filled in as work is completed on a recent National Institute for Education procurement to survey the states with programs.

In comparison to Virginia, none of the other states have legislatively mandated programs for grades one through three in which the state provides the test and local districts set the standards. Kentucky's program is close to Virginia's, but the source of the test (state or local) is not known and the use of the test is not specified (although a 1977 State Board of Education program specified the tests were to be used for grade promotion). Only eight other states have minimum competency testing programs which include one or more of grades one, two, or three.

Comparisons between Virginia's minimum competencies programs for high school graduation and those of other states indicate that no state has programs similar to both of Virginia's. Each separate program—the statewide program and the local certification—has counterparts, however. Delaware, Florida, Kentucky, Maryland (Project Basic), Nevada, New York, North Carolina, Tennessee, and Vermont have programs very similar to Virginia's statewide program. Other states: California (AB 3405), Oregon, and Utah have programs very similar to Virginia's local certification program.

One might well question why Virginia has decided to be so eclectic in its approach to minimum competency testing. Perhaps the answer lies in the comments of Mr. Henry Tulloch, president of Virginia's Board of Education.

In Virginia, we are into competencies K-12, not just in high school. Competency-based education is part of the Standards of Quality which began in 1968. Standard 9C is the crux of Virginia's high school graduation requirements. Standard 9C was not recommended by the Board, it was brought in by the legislature presumably in response to public pressure. The Board had to determine if 9C could be instituted statewide by the state or locally. In 1976, the Board had decided that the certification of competencies was a local prerogative, that is, tests would be developed and administered locally. The local superintendents changed their position and the Board responded to this pressure and made reading and math a statewide effort (Tulloch, 1978).

In these comments one can see that many groups—the legislature, the board, local superintendents, and others not mentioned—assume leadership in education in Virginia. Some of these groups—the legislature and board—have the authority to act somewhat independently, and each responds to different pressure groups, resulting in simultaneous activities.

Table 1. Other State Programs Compared to Basic Learning Skills Program in Virginia

	Grade Level	Mandate/Standards/Measure			Use	Type of Competency	Subject Areas
	Elementary 1-3	State Mandate (legislature)	Local Standards	State Measure	Diagnosis/ Placement	Basic School Skills	Reading Computing
Alabama	-	-	-	x	-	x	?
Arizona	-	-	-	-	-	x	x
California (AB65)	-	x	x	-	-	x	x
Colorado	-	-	x	-	x	optional	optional
Connecticut	-	-	-	x	-	optional	x
Delaware	-	-	-	x	-	-	x
Florida	grade 3	x	x	x	-	-	x
Georgia	-	-	-	x	?	x	x
Idaho	-	-	-	x	-	x	x
Indiana	grade 3	-	x	?	x	?	reading
Kansas (HB3115)	grade 2	x	-	x	?	x	x
Kentucky (HB579)	grade 3	x	x	?	-	x	x
Louisiana	-	x	-	x	?	x	x
Maine	-	x	-	x	-	x	?
Maryland	grade 3	x	-	x	-	x	reading

Massachusetts	-	-	-	-	?	x
Michigan	-	-	x	?	x	x
Missouri	-	-	x	?	-	x
Nebraska	-	x	optional	x	x	x
Nevada	x	-	x	-	?	x
New Hampshire	-	-	x	?	x	x
New Jersey	grade 3	-	x	x	x	x
New Mexico	optional	-	x	optional	optional	optional
New York	-	-	x	-	x	x
North Carolina (HB205)	grades 1, 2	x	x	?	?	?
Oregon	optional	-	x	-	-	x
Oklahoma	grade 3	-	x	?	x	reading
Rhode Island	-	-	x	?	-	?
South Carolina	?	?	?	?	?	?
Tennessee	-	x	-	x	optional	optional
Utah	optional	x	-	-	optional	x
Vermont	optional	-	x	-	x	optional
Washington	-	x	x	optional	x	x
Wyoming	-	x	?	-	?	x

Legend: - different, x same, ? unknown or undecided

Data for this table from Pipho (1978) and personal communications. For states with more than one program, only the most comparable program is shown (as is the legislative reference where known).

Table 2. Other State Programs Compared to Statewide High School Graduation Program in Virginia

	Grade Level	Mandate/Standards/Measure			Use	Type of Competencies	Subject Areas
	Grade 11 or 12	State Mandate (Board)	State Standards	State Test	High School Graduation	Mixed	Reading
Alabama	x	x	x	x	x	?	?
Arizona	x	x	x	-	x	-	x
California (AB3408)	x	x	-	-	x	?	x
Colorado	x	-	-	-	optional	optional	optional
Connecticut (Early Exit)	age 16	-	x	x	optional	optional	x
Delaware	x	x	x	x	x	-	x
Florida	x	-	x	x	x	x	x
Georgia	x	x	x	x	?	?	?
Idaho	x	x	x	x	optional	?	x
Indiana	grade 10	x	-	-	-	?	reading
Kansas	x	-	x	x	?	?	x
Kentucky (Board)	x	x	x	x	x	?	x
Louisiana	x	-	x	x	?	-	x
Maine	x	-	x	x	x	?	?
Maryland (Project Basic)	x	-	x	x	x	x	x

Massachusetts	x	x	-	x	-	x
Michigan	grade 10	x	x	x	-	x
Missouri	-	x	x	x	-	x
Nebraska	-	x	-	optional	-	x
Nevada	x	-	x	x	x	x
New Hampshire	-	x	x	x	-	x
New Jersey (A1776)	?	-	x	x	-	x
New Mexico	-	x	x	x	-	x
New York	x	x	x	x	x	x
North Carolina	x	x	x	x	x	?
Oregon	optional	x	-	-	x	x
Oklahoma	x	x	?	x	?	reading
Rhode Island	x	x	?	x	?	x
South Carolina	?	?	?	?	?	?
Tennessee	x	x	x	x	x	x
Utah	x	x	-	-	x	x
Vermont	x	x	x	x	x	x
Washington	-	-	-	x	-	x
Wyoming	?	x	-	?	x	x

Legend: - different, x same, ? unknown or undecided
Data for this table from Pipho (1978) and personal communications.

Table 3. Other State Programs Compared to Local High School Graduation Program in Virginia

	Grade Level	Mandated/Standards/Measure			Use	Type of Competencies	Subject Areas
	Optional 8-12	State Mandate (Board)	Local Standards	Local Measures	High School Graduation	Life Skills	Citizenship/ Post. Second.
Alabama	x	x	-	-	x	?	?
Arizona	grades 8 & 12	x	-	x	x	-	-
California (AB3408)	x	x	x	x	x	?	-
Colorado		x	x	x	optional	optional	optional
Connecticut (Early Exit)	age 16	-	-	-	optional	optional	optional
Delaware	grade 11	x	-	-	x	x	-
Florida	grade 11	-	-	-	x	x	-
Georgia	grade 11	x	-	-	?	?	?
Idaho	x	x	-	-	optional	?	-
Indiana	grade 10	x	x	x	-	?	-
Kansas	grade 11	-	-	-	?	?	-
Kentucky (HB579)	grade 10	-	x	x	?	?	-
Louisiana	grade 11	-	-	-	?	?	-
Maine	grade 11	-	-	-	x	?	?
Maryland	grade 11	-	-	-	x	-	x

							government
Massachusetts	x	x	-	-	-	-	-
Michigan	x	grade 10	-	-	-	-	-
Missouri	x	grade 8	-	-	-	x	-
Nebraska	x	-	x	optional	-	-	-
Nevada	-	grades 9 & 12	-	-	x	?	-
New Hampshire	x	-	-	-	-	?	-
New Jersey (A1176)	-	?	-	-	-	?	-
New Mexico	-	grade 10	-	-	-	-	-
New York	x	x	-	-	x	x	x
North Carolina	x	grade 11	-	-	x	x	x
Oregon	x	x	x	x	x	x	x
Oklahoma	x	grades 9 & 12	-	-	?	x	?
Rhode Island	x	late sec.	?	-	?	x	?
South Carolina	?	?	-	?	?	?	?
Tennessee	x	grades 11 & 12	x	-	x	?	-
Utah	x	x	-	x	x	x	x
Vermont	x	x	-	-	x	x	-
Washington	-	-	x	-	-	-	-
Wyoming	x	?	x	?	x	?	x

Legend: - different, x same, ? unknown or undecided
Data for this table from Pipho (1978) and personal communications.

Summary

Virginia has two minimum competency testing programs, each intended to meet different goals. The first is the basic learning skills (BLS) program. It is a legislatively mandated program intended to provide instructional feedback directly to elementary school teachers. The second is the graduation requirements program that has two parts, both intended to insure that high school graduates have accumulated knowledge and skills necessary in their postsecondary experience. One part of the graduation requirements program is a statewide test in reading and mathematics. The second part requires local school officials to obtain evidence of competency in the broad areas of citizenship and postsecondary readiness.

Basic learning skills were defined in legislation passed initially by the 1976 Legislative Assembly. These skills include reading, communications, and mathematics. In response to this legislation, BLS objectives were developed by several subject-area committees appointed by the Department of Education. The objectives were distributed statewide to obtain reviews and reactions from local educators. Upon completion of the review and reaction process, the modified objectives were adopted by the Board of Education as required by the 76-78 SOQ. A testing program is to be phased in over the next several years. It will begin this year (1978-79) in reading and mathematics at the primary grades—grades one through three. The 1978-79 tests are constructed from item pools which contain about twelve items for each of the 83 minimum, or specific, objectives; thus, the item pool contains almost 1,000 items. These items were pilot tested in spring 1978 and were Rasch calibrated. In each subject-area two test forms were constructed. Form A has fewer items per objective and is intended to be used as either a beginning-of-the-year screening test or a summary, end-of-year test. Form B is a series of subtests on each of the minimum objectives and is intended to provide direct feedback to teachers on student mastery of each objective.

No performance standard has been set by the state, but, based on field-test results and through the use of Rasch calibration, teachers may estimate the extent to which students are working at their ability level. A dual index of ability based on Rasch technology and standard techniques is suggested.

Both forms of the test are hand scored by teachers. It has been proposed that each year the department will receive from local education agencies a report on the percentage of students, by grade and age, who have mastered each objective. These data, if they are collected, may be used by the Department to report to the board on the achievement status of elementary school students.

Local education agencies may make a request to substitute tests of their choice for the department's BLS test. Some agencies have made such a request and some requests have been approved on a temporary basis as of October 1978.

The BLS program is just beginning, and many components will undoubtedly change in the future. Given the legislative mandate and the time frame for development, the program has started well because the staff of the Division of Research, Evaluation and Testing has worked hard to produce a well-conceptualized design. This has been accomplished within constraints which at times yielded less than ideal results—for example, the objectives were developed with minimum input from testing specialists and without benefit of any explicit theory of learning or even domain specification. However, given adequate financial and administrative support the BLS program can benefit education in Virginia.

The graduation requirements program began in July 1976 with the adoption, by the Board of Education, of revised accreditation standards for secondary schools. These standards included the requirement that in order to graduate from an accredited high school, students must demonstrate competencies in functional literacy, computation, citizenship/social studies, and postsecondary readiness. The board initially chose to follow Oregon's lead and made local school officials responsible for certifying student competencies in these four areas.

This new mandate aroused confusion and controversy. In March 1978 the graduation requirements portion of the accreditation standards was modified by the board. The modifications were brought about in part by pressure from local school superintendents and in part by new legislation which mandated a test previously prescribed by the board. The changes resulted in the establishment of statewide testing in reading and mathematics. Retained, however, was local responsibility to certify competencies in citizenship and post secondary readiness. These graduation requirements apply to high school graduates beginning in 1981 (1978-79 tenth graders).

The intent of the board was to have an early test (ninth or tenth grade) for identifying students with weaknesses and for implementing a twelfth-grade test for graduation. The short time span between adopting the requirement and instituting the program did not permit the wide involvement of school personnel in the development of competencies and tests. A committee of educators was empaneled by the department to review and select competencies, performance indicators, and tests to be used for at least the first few years of this program. The committee completed its work in two months and recommended a reading test (IOX Basic Skills Test: Secondary Reading) and a math test (developed by STS for the

Virginia Beach Public Schools). Both tests matched fairly well a set of competencies and performance indicators that were developed prior to the modified standards, as part of the department's technical assistance program. The committee also recommended a one-tiered test; that is, the same test should be used at both ninth and twelfth grades and students should only have to pass once.

Because the math test had relatively few items, additional math items were supplied by STS and were piloted in Prince William County, Virginia, public schools in summer 1978. A full-scale administration of the tests to tenth graders had been planned for October 16-20, 1978, but controversy over the schedule and method for setting performance standards delayed administration until October 31-November 2. The original plan for setting performance standards would have modified Jaeger's (1978) proposed method, which incorporates a statewide sample of the public and of educators who would have had access to both the test and the results of the October testing. Although approved by the board in June, this plan was dropped after being criticized in the press. Standard setting was instead undertaken in a few selected school divisions. Only those individuals involved in standard setting took the test, and a performance standard of 70 percent on each test was approved by the board at its October 1978 meeting.

Much controversy still surrounds the graduation requirements program. Some local agencies resent being burdened with the responsibility for certifying students in citizenship and postsecondary readiness. This resentment is due in part to the fact that these are the most difficult areas to assess (little help is forthcoming from the department), and in part to the language of the standard, which is unclear as to how the local school officials must comply—with a test or through normal classroom activities.

The combination of a state administered Basic Learning Skills program and a state required, locally administered graduation requirements program is unique among the several states in which competency tests are required for high school graduation. The elementary school BLS program is different from other states primarily because it extends downward to include each of the first three grades.

The comprehensiveness of Virginia's competency-based testing programs, combined with the intent of these programs, could have made Virginia an exemplary state. In reality, Virginia is exemplary, but in a negative sense. The various actors—the State Board of Education, the superintendent of public instruction, the state legislature, local school superintendents—have too often worked at cross-purposes, and thus the competency programs (particularly the high school graduation requirements) will not, in the near term, achieve their intended, but implicit, goals of improved delivery of educational services and accountability.

References

Brickell, H. M. Seven key notes on minimal competency testing. *Phi Delta Kappan* 59 (May 1978): 589-592.

Brown, Jeff. Competency-test cutoffs may tempt manipulation. *Virginian-Pilot.* September 10, 1978a.

———. Most on panel set test score at under 70%. *Virginian-Pilot.* October 26, 1978b.

Campbell, W. E. Competencies for graduation from high school. Superintendent's memorandum number 54. Department of Education. Richmond, Va. March 3, 1978a.

———. Recommendations of the advisory committee for selecting competency tests. Attachment 1 to Superintendent's Memorandum Number 22, Department of Education. Richmond, Va. July 1978b.

Campbell, W. E. and Boyer, R. L. Guidelines and criteria for approval of tests in lieu of Department of Education's basic learning skills tests. Attachment to superintendent's memorandum number 34. Department of Education. Richmond, Va. April 1978.

Flanagan, S. Unpublished letter to the Board of Education. April 1978.

Impara, J. C. Attachment to the March 7, 1978-March 9, 1978 meeting summary of the competency-based graduation requirements - pilot project reactions to superintendent's memorandum #54. Unpublished minutes. March 1978.

Instructional Objective Exchange. *IOX basic skills test: secondary level reading.* The Instructional Objectives Exchange. Los Angeles. 1978.

Jaeger, Richard M. A proposal for setting a standard on the North Carolina high school competencies test. Paper presented at the meeting of the North Carolina Association for Research on Education. Spring 1978.

Karlan, B. The role of the Virginia State Board of Education in policy making. Doctoral Dissertation, College of Education, Virginia Polytechnic Institute and State University. May 1977.

Pipho, C. State activity: minimum competency testing. Mimeo. Educational Commission of the States. Denver, Colo. July 10, 1978.

Sandy, C. Personal communication. October 1978.

Spady, William. Competency-based education—a bandwagon in search of a definition. *Educational Researcher 6* (1977): 9-14.

Tulloch, H. Presentation to graduate students and faculty at Virginia Polytechnic Institute and State University. July 31, 1978.

Virginia Board of Education. *Standards for accrediting secondary schools in Virginia.* Available from Department of Education. Richmond, Va. July 1976a.

———. *Standards of quality and objectives for public schools in Virginia 1976-78.* Available from Department of Education, Richmond, Va. 1976b.

———. Virginia basic learning skills (BLS) testing program 1978-79. Brochure. Testing Service, Division of Research, Evaluation and Testing, Richmond, Va. 1977.

———. *Standards of quality and objectives for public schools in Virginia 1978-80.* Available from Department of Education, Richmond, Va. 1978.

Williams, Paul. Intergrating latent-trait analysis with criterion-referenced testing. Paper presented to 27th Annual Conference of the Directors of State Testing Programs. October 1978.

17 Minimum Competency Testing: The View from Capitol Hill

Judith Sauls Shoemaker

Political Context

The forces that have led to minimum competency testing at the state and local levels also operate at the federal level. There seems to be growing public disenchantment with education in general, especially in the wake of test score declines and growing costs of schooling. Among the issues most often cited are: the highly publicized decline in college entrance examination scores; declines in performance on items administered through the National Assessment of Educational Progress; the rising costs of schooling, and a growing mood of "taxpayer revolt" associated with California's Proposition 13; complaints by employers and labor union officials about the lack of entry-level job skills of young employees, and about the difficulty young employees have in reading job manuals and in performing simple business arithmetic; the need to provide remedial coursework for college freshmen in writing and mathematics; the concern expressed by parents that their children are unprepared for jobs or college.

At state and local levels, as indicated by other papers in this book and in this section particularly, the response to the issues cited above has been to establish minimum competency testing programs. At this writing, according to the Education Commission of the States (ECS), 37 states have mandated minimum competency testing programs. The movement

This article was written by the author in her private capacity. The views expressed herein are those of the author only and do not necessarily represent the position or policy of the National Institute of Education or the Department of Health, Education and Welfare.

has been so rapid at the state level that within a span of 18 months (April 1976 - November 1977), ECS published seven legislative updates on minimum competency testing. A considerable number of local districts have also instituted such testing programs, some of which are mandated or otherwise encouraged by state legislation; other districts have authorization from local school boards.

Although they vary considerably, all minimum competency testing programs assess student performance in relation to desired performance levels, or minimum performance standards, in specific skill areas. The skill areas which are assessed also vary widely, but usually include reading, mathematics, and writing. The consequences of failing to meet desired levels of performance also vary from program to program. In some programs, test performance is used to control high school graduation or promotion from grade to grade. Some programs use test performance to permit "early exit" from high school. Still other programs prohibit the use of test results for such purposes and allow their use only to identify groups of students who should receive special instruction. Most programs assess student performance periodically, at various checkpoints in their educational careers, but most often this occurs at the school exit level, or just before high school graduation.

It should be noted that these programs are dynamic, constantly reassessing their procedures and reevaluating their impact. Most have just begun, with enforcement of test-related high school graduation requirements not scheduled until 1979 or later. To date, we have had only modest experience with, and little evidence of the effects of, such programs.

However, this lack of evidence has not deterred the public and educators from debating the merits and faults of competency testing. Proponents see these programs as one way to raise achievement test scores. They claim that, by requiring every student to pass a competency test, performance levels (at a certain minimum level) will be guaranteed. Those in favor of competency testing generally support the associated curricular emphasis on the basic skills of reading, writing, and mathematics. In addition, these programs are seen as powerful tools for making the schools more accountable for the achievement levels of their students. Proponents also claim that these programs have caused administrators, teachers, and parents to reexamine the goals and objectives of schooling.

Proponents have also welcomed the application of a uniform standard of performance for all students. Minimum competency testing is seen as a way to raise the expectations of groups which typically perform at low levels, and to ensure that these groups receive the instruction they need to attain desired performance levels.

On the negative side, opponents often remind us that requiring "minimum competence" or "legislating literacy" does not really address the fundamental problems of education. In fact, there is some fear that the minimums will become the maximum level of performance, resulting in a general lowering of performance. Legal experts have questioned the legality of the use of tests to deny graduation, especially if the school did not teach the areas tested (which may occur if so-called life skills, like filling out an income tax form, were not taught by the school), or if there were not multiple opportunities to pass the test.

Technical questions have also been raised concerning the setting of desired performance levels—a critical factor in establishing these programs. Many programs employ a judgmental approach, using the opinions and judgments of many people who know and understand the capabilities of the students to be tested. However, this approach has been criticized by measurement experts as being psychometrically or statistically indefensible.

The potential impact on minority students and the handicapped has also been debated. There is some concern that these students may effectively be isolated from many learning opportunities on the basis of their test scores.

Recent Federal Activities in Testing

During the last year, the federal government has shown increasing interest in educational testing. There have been a variety of federal activities in this area, ranging from Congressional hearings and pending legislation to the Department of Health, Education and Welfare (HEW) National Conference on Testing.

The beginnings of this increased interest in educational testing occurred in fall 1977, when Senator Claiborne Pell from Rhode Island held hearings on possible legislation to establish national standards of educational proficiency. At that time, Pell received comments on his recommendation that the federal government establish a voluntary national test of basic skills in reading, writing, and mathematics. The federal government would sponsor the development of the tests and would create a panel to establish national standards of performance for use in local-national comparisons. Participation in the testing program would be voluntary.

In testimony provided at the hearings, Admiral Hyman Rickover was quite supportive of Pell's recommendations, but felt that they did not go far enough. He suggested that such testing should be mandatory nationwide. Speaking against Pell's plan were Assistant Secretary for Education Mary Berry, National Assessment Director Roy Forbes, and National Institute of Education (NIE) Director Patricia Albjerg Graham. Their testimony suggested that, although it is technically possible to develop and administer a national test, it would not be politic to do so. They claimed that the setting of national standards would inevitably raise questions over local control of schools. If all students were expected to reach national standards of performance, then schools would necessarily have to teach the skills tested. This process would ultimately lead to the development of nationally determined curricula, in direct conflict with local control of schools.

As a result of the hearings and their largely negative response, Senator Pell did not introduce any legislation of this topic, concluding that this was not the time to introduce a national testing program.

Meanwhile, in the U.S. House of Representatives, Representative Ronald Mottl (Ohio) introduced a series of bills to establish basic standards of educational proficiency. He initially introduced a bill which would establish a national commission to identify educational proficiency standards and would require examination of all students according to such standards before graduating from high school, thus making high school graduation contingent upon passing the proficiency exam. However, Representative Mottl also received negative comments on the idea, and successive versions of the bill proposed voluntary state participation with no national commission to set standards. The last draft of the bill was included in the House's final version of the Elementary and Secondary Education Act Amendments of 1978 (HR15). It provided for grants to states to implement their own plans to establish educational proficiency standards and for technical assistance to states to implement such plans. This section was retained by both the House and Senate conference committee, and it is now part of the Education Amendments of 1978 (Public Law 95-561). This law will be described in more detail in the third section of this paper.

Another House bill which received much publicity last year was Representative Michael Harrington's (Massachusetts) Truth in Testing Bill, which had the following provisions: (1) copies of tests used by any education agency and copies of the answers must be made available to any examinee upon written request after the test is administered; (2) the standard error of measurement must be reported with each test score; (3) test takers must be informed of the content of the test, the scoring procedures to be used, and the accuracy and significance of the test score; and, (4) no higher education institution may deny admission on the basis of a test score alone. This bill received many negative reactions, especially from the test publishing industry, which argued that such action would make test development prohibitively expensive. Others welcomed the bill as an assertion of the basic rights of test takers. However, the bill was not reported out of committee. With Harrington leaving office this term, is not likely that this bill will be reintroduced in the next session of Congress.

Congressional leaders remain interested in some sort of program to develop national competency standards. Like many state and local leaders, they see such a program as one way to ensure basic levels of achievement for our nation's youth. Speaking at the HEW National Conference on Testing (described below), Senator S. I. Hayakawa (California) called for a "nationally calibrated thermometer of education achievement." Stating that he is generally opposed to federal involvement unless all else fails, he claimed that in education, "It seems all else has failed."

Additional activities in educational testing have been conducted by HEW. In March 1978, HEW sponsored a National Conference on Testing and Basic Skills to determine how tests can be used more effectively and to obtain recommendations on what should be the federal government's role in educational testing. The invitational meeting was attended by 300 educators, testing experts, government officials, and representatives of parents' and teachers' organizations. Based on the recommendations of the conference, HEW Secretary Joseph Califano agreed to: provide information and referral services on achievement testing; conduct regional conferences on the uses of achievement tests; work to improve the skills of teachers, administrators and parents in the use of tests; and conduct research to improve testing. Largely in response to these commitments from Secretary Califano, and partly as a result of an internal reorganization, NIE established an Office of Testing, Assessment and Evaluation in June 1978, which has major responsibility for implementing the recommendations of the national conference. This office is also responsible for improving the practice of testing and evaluation through research, development, and dissemination.

The testing program within the Office of Testing, Assessment and Evaluation sponsors activities in three areas. Examples of activities for each area are described below. First, in the area of improving testing practices, the program sponsors development and dissemination of easily understood materials on testing, such as "A Parents' Guide to Testing." It also sponsors regional conferences on critical issues in testing, beginning with eight regional conferences for teachers to be held in spring and summer, 1979. Second, in the area of studying the role and impact of testing, including a study of the impact of introducing nationwide standardized testing in Ireland, and a study of the effect of minimum competency testing programs here in the United States. Third, in the area of integrating testing with the instructional process, the program investigates alternative forms of testing that capitalize on recent advances in computer technology and on research in cognitive processes. It also examines the instructional value of content-referenced tests.

Federal Policies

This sketch of recent federal activities related to educational testing makes it clear that the federal government is aware of the debate on competency testing and has responded in several different ways. In keeping with state and local actions, the federal government has considered the possibility of using tests to ensure that all students attain basic, minimum levels of achievement. President Jimmy Carter's greeting to the National Conference on Achievement Testing, delivered by Secretary Califano, indicated "there is no greater challenge than the one facing our educational system—to ensure that all children learn, at the very least, to read, to write, and to compute. . . . I believe that achievement testing can and should play an important and constructive role in the educational system."

The federal government's activities in testing have been shaped by two overriding policies. First, there shall be no national standards of performance or nationally developed tests. Establishing expected standards of performance is the responsibility of state and local educational agencies. Second, every educational program of an education agency that receives federal funds must ensure equal educational opportunity. Thus, no testing program may be used to deny equal educational opportunity. These two policies have had, and will continue to have, an instrumental role in shaping the federal government's response to minimum competency testing.

No Federal Test

Four events have shaped the federal government's position on the development of national tests and national standards of performance. The first event was a major address on educational testing given by Secretary Califano at the twenty-fifth anniversary of the College Entrance Examination Board (October 24, 1977). In that presentation, Secretary Califano carefully outlined what he saw as the appropriate uses of tests: "In short, basic competency tests, used skillfully and sensitively, are useful and necessary—they are a limited, but very important tool for charting and improving the process of education. We need to do more testing and we need to do better testing."

Did this mean that he was in favor of a program of national tests or national standards of academic performance? "Absolutely not," was the reply. He went on to say, "I believe that proposals for federal testing programs, however well-intentioned, are misguided; that even a wholly voluntary national test or set of standards would be a step in precisely the wrong direction."

Secretary Califano gave four reasons why he opposed "so strongly the idea of tests and standards imposed from Washington." First is the potential lack of local commitment to a program developed in Washington. "The tests may end up as little more than a distracting waste of time and money, rather than part of an enthusiastic effort to spur individual educational achievement." Second, no single test is appropriate for every school in the country. Based on population needs, local priorities for education vary from city to city. Even within basic academic subjects such as reading and mathematics there are differences of opinion concerning what should be taught and tested. Third, there are technical questions such as reliability and validity concerning the appropriate design of competency tests. Such questions normally arise in any test development process and would certainly have to be addressed for a national test. Fourth and "most important" is the issue of local control of education. The development of a national test and national standards of performance would be perceived by state and local educational agencies as the first step toward federal control of curriculum. If teachers were responsible for making sure their students passed such a test, then local curricula would reflect what was to be tested and the result might be a national curriculum. This result would be contrary to the historical prerogative of local schools to select and administer their own instructional program.

On this last, "most important" issue, Secretary Califano stated that "in its most extreme form, national control of curriculum is a form of national control of ideas. We should be very wary of heading in that direction; the traditional role of federal support for education has been to encourage diversity—not rigid uniformity."

In defining what should be the appropriate federal role in competency testing, Secretary Califano stated:

It is one of the chief virtues of our Federal system that we have fifty potential laboratories for innovation in education; fifty different centers for developing ideas and programs. I believe that every state should have a program for developing and measuring basic skills that include competency testing; but I think each of the fifty states—and each of the school districts within those states—should decide how it can make most effective use of competency testing in its program. The Federal government should support, but not direct, their efforts.

The second event which helped to consolidate the administration's position on national competency tests was the oversight hearings of the Senate Education Subcommittee on the Quality of Education, chaired by Senator Claiborne Pell. As indicated earlier, Pell's idea was to establish a voluntary, standardized national minimum competency test which would measure performance in reading, writing, and arithmetic. It would be federally developed and sponsored, but its use by states would be voluntary.

Testimony on the idea was heard from Assistant Secretary for Education Mary Berry, Admiral Hyman Rickover, Educational Testing Service President William Turnbull, National Assessment Director Roy Forbes, and NIE Director Patricia Graham.

Rickover, who for years has advocated a national test, argued in favor of a mandatory national test to measure specific skills for various grade levels, starting in the early elementary grades and extending through high school. As he said in his testimony, "Thus a yardstick would be provided to measure academic performance—a means of assessing achievement of individual students, effectiveness of teachers, and over-all academic attainment of schools. . . . For the first time, parents would have a means to hold teachers and schools accountable for the quality of their work."

Berry, Forbes, Turnbull, and Graham spoke against the idea of a national test, mandatory or voluntary. Berry indicated that she shared Rickover's concern that schools were not providing a good education, but she noted several problems with using a national test to improve schooling. First, there is "no consensus in the country" on what every student should learn; second, national testing "may run counter to local control and local agreement"; and third, "Until we're sure of what we're testing, it's difficult to develop a fair test." She stressed that the federal role should be restricted to offering advice and technical assistance to states wanting to develop minimum competency tests.

The idea of a national competency test drew guarded reactions from Turnbull and Forbes. Turnbull noted that most states are in the process of developing minimum competency tests and, "If I believed that the states had no intention of doing the job, I might be making arguments for Federal development of a standardized test." He added that, if a national test is sponsored by the federal government, states and school districts might feel compelled to use it, even if the test were not tailored to state or local educational agency needs. With state efforts already under way, Turnbull said that "the principal need at the Federal level is educational leadership in delineating constructive alternative solutions: models of what can be done and how. The second need is to do some of the research and develop some of the techniques that will be needed for effective action. The third need is the channeling of some funds, new or already appropriated, toward this set of problems." Echoing Turnbull, Forbes said that "standards should essentially be the prerogative of the state and local educational agencies" and that the appropriate role of the federal government is to provide technical assistance.

Graham told Senator Pell that while it is "relatively simple . . . to develop traditional, standardized tests which discriminate among children and which provide at least a rough indication of what children have learned, it is extremely difficult to envision an effective and equitable test by which national standards for reading, writing and arithmetic for various grade levels could be established and administered." Graham stated that, since education has been significantly reserved to state and local educational agencies, the federal government is under "legitimate and vigorous scrutiny" if it attempts to set a national educational standard. "While testing is not identical with curriculum, many teachers and administrators would recognize that testing requirements, particularly if they are regarded as important, have a profound influence on what is taught in schools. Thus, a national test might incline use toward an indirectly determined national curriculum. I believe that, if we wish to change the assumption that education is principally a local and state matter, we should address the issue directly, not indirectly through the question of national tests."

Graham also told Senator Pell that his objectives could be achieved best through a "national effort aimed at assuring that we have a variety of tests appropriate to specific curricula and educational objectives of parents, communities, states, etc. Most nationally administered tests of reading and mathematics, for example, are not now closely tied to specific educational objectives. Cross-referencing of tests would enable State and local educational authorities to make appropriate comparisons while preserving autonomy in choosing goals and educational programs."

The third event to shape the Federal testing policy was the report of a special panel of the National Academy of Education. HEW Secretary Califano and Assistant Secretary for Education Berry asked the academy panel to respond to a series of policy questions on education. The panel, composed of Stephen Bailey, John B. Carroll, Jeanne Chall, Robert Glaser, John Goodlad, Diane Ravitch, Lauren Resnick, Ralph Tyler, and Robert Thorndike, released its report in February 1978. On the general issue of minimum competency testing, the panel reported:

. . . any setting of statewide minimum competency standards for awarding the high school diploma—however understandable the public clamor which has produced the current movement and expectation—is basically unworkable, exceeds the present measurement arts of the teaching profession, and will create more social problems than it can conceivably solve. . . . However, the Panel is in agreement that a series of standardized tests at the lower grade levels used for diagnosing individual student weaknesses, pinpointing remediation needs, and building public pressures if school-wide performances in basic skills continue over time to be consistently low could be positive influences on student learning.

The panel also responded directly to the question of the development and administration of "voluntary national tests." Although the panel acknowledged the role of the federal government, in partnership with state and local agencies, in improving educational opportunity and quality, the Academy "strongly recommends against the creation of 'national tests'—mandatory or voluntary." In explaining its position, the panel noted, "The logic is clear. Those who make up tests that confer educational status on individuals determine what is taught in the local classroom. The Federal government should not be thrust into the position of fostering a national curriculum by inadvertence." The appropriate role for the federal government is to "support research designed to improve the quality of tests and programs to increase public understanding about their use."

The panel's report was distributed at the fourth event influencing federal testing policy: the National Conference on Testing and the Basic Skills, held in March 1978, which was described earlier in this paper. Participants at this conference discussed how state and local educational agencies could use testing more effectively, the nature of an appropriate federal role in testing. There was general agreement among participants that (a) educational accountability is necessary and inevitable, and that achievement tests are necessary but imperfect tools for any purpose and (b) testing is not the fundamental issue—the critical issue is establishing basic, understandable, and attainable goals in such areas as literacy and basic skills. Additionally, there was overwhelming opposition to a national test of educational achievement.

Senators Hayakawa and Pell, together with Representative Harrington, shared their views on testing with the participants. When Senator Pell asked the audience how many would support a national competency test, only three raised their hands. Pell then admitted that a national test was an idea whose time had not yet come.

The proceedings of the conference summarized the recommendations in this manner:

About testing, it was widely agreed among conferees that the minimum competency movement is a manifestation of an age of consumerism and accountability in the society at large; that tests are social dynamite and can do irreparable harm as well as good; that the issue should not be more testing or less testing but better testing and better test usage; and, most important, educational goals should set the agenda for testing, not the other way around.

These four events, then, helped to shape the policy of no national competency tests, which continues to be a major theme throughout the NIE program plans for the Office of Testing, Assessment and Evaluation; for the Assistant Secretary's Office; and for agencies elsewhere in HEW.

Equity Concerns

The second overriding issue shaping the federal government's response to minimum competency testing is a concern for equal educational opportunity. The federal government has responsibility for ensuring that educational opportunities are not denied on the basis of sex, race, ethnicity, or other characteristics; that is, no student should be excluded from an opportunity to learn on the basis of group membership.

There are two equity issues related to educational testing. First, there are concerns about the test items themselves. Ideally, items should be written to discriminate only between "masters" and "nonmasters" of the skill being tested. If the skill tested is to solve a word problem in mathematics using an algebraic equation, then, to the extent that the item also taps other skills (reading skills, ability to visualize the situation described, and so on), the item may actually differentiate several groups of students, such as readers and nonreaders.

Test items have been analyzed for evidence which might favor one sex of students or one cultural group over another. Persons and situations represented in test questions are often balanced according to sex and race, in an attempt to overcome any possible interference with the performance of one or another group. The structured language used to phrase test questions can also be unfamiliar to some groups of students, thus lowering their performance. These cultural and linguistic demands of tests may unfairly affect student performance; discrimination between groups on dimensions other than what is supposed to be measured may be construed as evidence of bias.

The second equity issue is the impact of the testing program on special populations, such as minorities, special educational students and the handicapped, and gifted and talented students. If scores are used to place students into remedial programs, and if the tests are racially or sexually biased, there is a danger that some minority groups may be unfairly overrepresented in remedial programs. Some minority leaders have stated that these remediation programs may have the effect of resegregating the schools. Others have welcomed the application of uniform performance standards and see the minimum competency testing movement as one way to obtain special help for the students who need it most. They also see competency testing as a powerful way to raise expectations concerning the achievement of minorities.

When test results are used to place students in instructional programs, there could be several harmful effects. First, a high percentage of certain groups of students could be termed "remedial," which is a potentially pejorative label that carries lowered expectations for achievement. Second, two separate instructional systems could be created, resulting in resegregation within schools. Two separate curricula would inevitably lead to questions concerning equal educational opportunity. Would both systems be "equal" in terms of educational effectiveness? For handicapped students, would both qualify as a "least restrictive educational environment," as required by Public Law 94-142? Although the gifted and talented probably wouldn't be placed in remedial programs, there is a danger that resources, including teacher time, formerly used for accelerated classes would be diverted to remedial classes, thus denying gifted students an opportunity to achieve their potential. This may also be true for others not receiving special help in remedial programs.

The impact of minimum competency testing on equal educational opportunity is not clear. Each program is different and provides different consequences for not passing the test. Achieving equal educational opportunity is also difficult. It is clear that the federal government, which has major responsibility in this area, is watching the movement closely.

Federal Activities in Minimum Competency Testing

Given these two overriding policy concerns, what activities in minimum competency testing is the federal government sponsoring? Current federal activities fall into three areas: support for programs; technical assistance; and, research and evaluation.

Support for Programs

Although the federal government does not currently support or provide assistance for any minimum competency testing program, the new Elementary and Secondary Education Act Amendments of 1978 (Public Law 95-561) authorize support for both state and local competency testing programs. The law calls these programs "plans to implement educational proficiency standards." The section passed into law was the final version of Representative Ronald Mottl's legislation, described earlier in this paper.

The section on "Educational Proficiency Standards" provides grants to state, and in some cases local, education agencies to carry out an approved plan to assist students in achieving levels of educational proficiency. These levels, or standards, are to be established by the education agency. The plan must have the following four provisions. First, the plan shall contain a description of the educational proficiency standards, as defined by the agency, for reading, writing, mathematics, and "any other subject for which the Commissioner [of Education] may require such standards." Second, the plan shall describe the programs designed to assist students in achieving levels of proficiency compatible with the standards. Third, the plan may provide for examinations or tests for students at specified intervals or grade levels to measure levels of proficiency. Fourth, the plan shall contain assurances that any student who fails such an examination shall be offered supplementary instruction.

This section also indicates that "Nothing in this section authorizes the Commissioner to impose tests on State and local education agencies and no such agency shall be compelled in any way to apply for funds under this section."

Technical Assistance

The section on "Educational Proficiency Standards" also contains a section on "Achievement Testing Assistance" which authorizes the HEW secretary to assist state and local educational agencies to develop their capacity to test the achievement of basic skills. This section indicates that it would support activities such as: dissemination of information on availability and uses of achievement tests; training in the use of tests and test results; and, research and evaluation for the improvement of basic skills. This section also adds a caveat: "Nothing in this section shall authorize the Secretary to develop specific tests or test questions."

As with the first section, it is too early to know how these programs will be designed and implemented. But the message is clear: the goal is to improve students' achievement in reading, writing, and mathematics. The strategy is to establish desired levels of performance, or performance standards, and to provide instruction to enable students to meet those standards. Although testing is not required, it seems to be an integral part of this strategy. Testing as a means of increasing achievement is further emphasized in the second section, which provides technical assistance for achievement testing. Throughout both sections run the policies of "no national test," and voluntary state and local participation.

The National Institute of Education is also providing technical assistance in the form of a series of resource booklets which are being developed as part of a larger study of the impact of minimum competency testing programs. The booklets will describe the steps used in developing minimum competency testing programs, present options for implementation, and make liberal use of examples from current state and local programs. They will also draw from the best of the measurement art and will include analyses of issues affecting competency testing. These booklets will be widely disseminated to state and local education agencies by January 1980. The booklets are being developed by National Evaluation Systems, Inc., of Amherst, Massachusetts.

Research and Evaluation

The National Advisory Council on Women's Education Programs is supporting a study to analyze various minimum competency tests for evidence of race and sex bias. This study, being conducted by the Educational Policy Research Institute, involves a thorough investigation of the items in the minimum competency tests themselves, plus an analysis of test results by race and sex. The advisory council has a special interest in the effects of educational programs on women and on minority racial groups.

The last activity to be described represents what is potentially the most important contribution the federal government can make to the minimum competency testing movement. This activity is a four-year, NIE-developed study of the long-term impact of minimum competency testing programs. The study was begun in December 1978, and will involve review and analysis of the minimum competency testing programs in over 30 states and numerous local school districts. The study will include an impact analysis of a sample of these programs. Phase I of the study will last one year and will focus on four major tasks: (1) description of all state-mandated competency testing programs, including a sample of twenty locally mandated programs; (2) creation of a typology describing the chief features of these programs; and, (3) production of a series of practical guides for educators to assist in planning or modifying their own minimum competency programs. Phase II of the study will explore the impact of minimum competency testing programs on students, teachers, and curricula.

As indicated in papers in this volume and elsewhere, educators continue to argue the merits of minimum competency testing programs. Detailed, reflective information about the impact of minimum competency testing is currently unavailable, yet educational decision-makers are being charged with designing or refining minimum competency programs in their states and local districts. This NIE-directed study of the impact of minimum competency testing programs was developed in response to the pressing need for information about the outcomes of such programs and the need for technical assistance in their implementation.

A Case in Higher Education

18   Development and Implementation
of Policies for Assessing Basic
Skills in Higher Education

Haskin R. Pounds

Introduction

When personnel in an educational institution begin to develop a plan for assessing basic educational skills, they will discover they are entering a maze of conflicting philosophies, desires, and ambitions. They can expect to encounter resistance from faculty, who will charge interference with academic freedom and faculty rights. They may find resistance from students, who will charge harassment, discrimination, and double jeopardy. Administrators will express concerns that the results of assessment may damage the school's reputation. The assessment planners may find some parental support, however, and they are likely to find legislators the most supportive of all. All of these responses occurred when the University System of Georgia began developing a plan for assessing basic skills in its thirty-two state-operated colleges and universities.

It is ironic but true that most impetus for educational change comes from outside the individual educational institution. This will be especially true in the establishment of programs for assessing basic skills in higher education. In Georgia, Chancellor George L. Simpson, Jr., took a strong and controversial stand in 1969 when he established the policy of determining whether graduates of the state system of higher education could read and write. The product of this policy is generally referred to as the Regents' Test. The purpose of this paper is to discuss the problems and issues associated with the development and implementation of such policies for assessing basic skills in higher education.

Policy Development at the College Level

The first and most important step is to have administrative and faculty leaders recognize the need for a program to assess basic skills. In Georgia, the need for assessment was demonstrated by an examination of information about entering students, by reports from employers about the poor performance of graduates, and by evidence indicating a low rate of success on professional exams and admission to graduate school. While not much was being written on the subject at that time, today an examination of the literature about the problem of declining academic skills may be used to support the need for assessing basic skills (College Board, 1977). Expressions of concern from Georgia's legislators and governmental officials were also influential in causing the state university system to examine the need for assessing basic skills. Recent experience in other states indicates that a more effective program can be developed if educational institutions initiate their own assessment program, thus preempting the usual rigidity of legislative mandates.

While walking the fine line between academic freedom and faculty rights and responsibilities on the one hand, and the public's demand for educational accountability on the other, leaders of the institution must attempt to persuade the faculty that an assessment program is needed. Once the need for assessment is accepted, however reluctantly, the next step is to involve representatives of the faculty in the development of the policies and the program.

The University System of Georgia has for years had an Advisory Council of institutional presidents with a number of standing administrative and academic committees. The Academic Committee on English was selected to guide the development of the Regents' Testing Program. Committee membership consists of the English department heads in the thirty-two institutions in the university system (Statutes of the University System Advisory Council, 1979).

An institution can use an established faculty committee as the advisory group for the assessment program, or the institution's president may appoint a special faculty committee with the responsibility to develop and oversee the program. Because the assessment program requires a great deal of time, members of the advisory committee will need to make a major time commitment, especially in the early stages of program development.

In the University System of Georgia, the Academic Committee on

English not only recommends policy but reviews and makes recommendations concerning the technical aspects of the Regents' Testing Program, such as tests to be selected or developed, cutoff scores, and administrative procedures. It has always been stressed that the governing Board of Regents has the final authority in establishing policy and approving policy revisions.

Several versions of policies should be developed by taking policy recommendations from the committee to the entire faculty for suggestions and then returning them to the committee. A policy statement should contain a preamble stating the purpose of the program. Initially, it is important to establish general policies rather than attempting to develop a finished program that anticipates every eventuality. For example, it has been necessary to amend the policies governing the Georgia program three times since their implementation (Policies, 1979).

After the purpose of the assessment program has been stated, the faculty committee can consider specific questions, which will fall into three broad categories. First, who will be required to take the test and when? Will there be exemptions? Will passing the test be a graduation requirement? Second, what will be the procedures for dealing with students failing the test? How many times may a student repeat the exam? Will remediation be provided and/or required? Third, what will be the test content? How will such matters as test security, costs, score reporting, and cutoff scores be established and administered?

At this stage of the planning, it is important for the committee to recommend actions that will assist students and faculty to understand the program. There should be an awareness of the potentially disproportionate impact of the assessment program on minorities, possible challenges to the program because of such impact, and ways to assess and evaluate the validity of such impact.

One of the early decisions to be made will be whether to use published tests or develop tests locally. There are advantages and disadvantages either way. The initial effort in Georgia was to use standardized tests: the College-Level Examination Program published by Educational Testing Service. However, after several trials it was apparent that these tests were not satisfactory, and the university system instead decided to develop tests specifically designed for assessing the basic skills of reading and writing. If an established test is used, expensive and time-consuming test development is already done. Local development of tests takes time and thus delays implementation, but it gains more faculty and student support through their involvement and their belief that the tests are designed for local needs. A less desirable option to consider, if implementation time is critical, is to start with established tests and then take the necessary time to develop tests locally. Cost must be considered in deciding to develop tests locally, since the initial test development will be expensive. However, an institution should consider that long-term savings may offset the initial expense of developing a test locally.

In Georgia, since the decision had been made to develop tests locally, a trained and experienced measurement specialist was selected to direct the program. If there is any one factor that will contribute to the success or failure of a program, it is the presence of a qualified and experienced measurement person as director. Dr. Robert Rentz directs the Georgia program and also holds a faculty position at Georgia State University. This unique arrangement has worked well in that Dr. Rentz has access to all necessary supporting services to implement the Regents' Testing Program and can at the same time maintain the scholarly pursuits necessary for advancement in his profession.

Since a new test was developed, it was necessary to document its reliability and validity. There have been more than ten studies of reliability, validity, bias, and various performance factors relating to the Georgia Regents' Testing Program. Results of these studies have been used by the University System of Georgia to further improve the program (Roberts & Rentz, 1978).

It is also desirable to conduct experiments to solve procedural problems prior to making the testing policies effective. There were trial administrations of the Regents' Test in 1971 that provided information for item analysis as well as for administrative procedures. This information was studied by the Academic Committee on English as it completed many aspects of the testing policy. Not only must tests be proven reliable and valid; the administration of the assessment program must also be proven workable. Because of the importance of administration, it would have been useful to have administrators such as registrars, testing center directors, and others as members of the advisory committee.

Although development of the program and policies proceeded piecemeal, a single, coordinated program for the entire institution was the long-range goal. Since establishment of the Regents' Test, the University System of Georgia has developed an entrance assessment of basic skills, the Basic Skills Examination. Currently being developed is a program of major area exams to be passed by each candidate for the baccalaureate degree.

Policy Implementation

If the policies to be developed are applied to several types of institutions, there is more need for flexibility. Since the University System of

Georgia is composed of 4 universities, 13 senior colleges, and 15 junior colleges, the maximum amount of flexibility was desired. As policies were implemented, experience indicated the need for certain policy changes. Suggestions for such changes were directed to the committee, which considered them and made recommendations.

There is always the problem of interpreting policy. To meet this need, responsible officials were designated to deal with questions concerning interpretation; each institution in the University System of Georgia was asked to designate a Regents' Test coordinator. The test coordinators interpret policy and are also called together from time to time to give advice on the operation of the program. In a like manner, persons should be specified who will be responsible for various administrative aspects of the program—for example, who will notify the student as to the time for testing, who will provide remediation, who will answer inquiries from the public, and so on.

Policies should be thoroughly circulated on the campus and published in such college publications as the catalog, student handbook, faculty bulletin, and student newspaper. A brochure should be prepared and widely distributed describing in some detail the basic skills assessment program, its rationale, its policies, and its procedures. All university system college catalogs contain a statement of the Regents' Test requirement, and most institutions have prepared brochures giving further information about the test.

Ample advance notice to all concerned, especially students and parents, is an important legal, educational, and public relations concern. The more advance notice, the smoother the policy implementation. Students and faculty need time to think and prepare. Students need written notice of a test requirement very soon after their first contact with the institution, and the requirement should also be stated in the catalog seen by students when they first enter the institution. Registrars in the University System of Georgia have developed procedures for automatically notifying students when they must take the exam, either by using grade reports or by special letter. While the catalog is not considered a legal contract and is sometimes changed during a student's time in college, many students and parents believe the graduation requirements in the initial entry catalog should remain the same during the entire college stay. The adverse effects of changes in degree requirements, such as adding a basic-skills exam, can be avoided when time permits giving adequate advance notice.

Due to the numerous problems that arise when students finally are confronted with the requirement that they must pass a basic-skills exam, the initial phase of implementation is a trying one. No matter how well the students, faculty, and parents are informed, it takes time for reality to permeate not only the institution, but the entire community it serves.

Administrators and faculty must be prepared to spend considerable time discussing the purpose and technical aspects of the program with students and parents. In the University System of Georgia the willingness of faculty and administrators to talk with students and parents in a knowledgeable and supporting manner did more than anything else to ease tensions and solve most implementation problems. Students wanted to know what, how, when, and where about virtually every aspect of the program and expected immediate assistance in completing each phase of the program.

Legal challenges can be anticipated. From the very first, efforts should be made to insure that the assessment program meets the appropriate judicial requirements of recent court decisions. Legal decisions were studied and legal advice was taken on how to accomplish this compliance. Advice focused on the test validation prior to its implementation. If the validation is sound and continuous, most litigation will be terminated at an early stage.

The instructional impact of the assessment program is one of its most important aspects. In order for the assessment to contribute to the improvement of instruction, it must provide adequate information about student performance to faculty and administrators. They continuously receive reliable information in the Georgia program and, when necessary, have assistance in interpreting its meaning for instructional improvement. (This aspect of the University System of Georgia's program is discussed in some detail by Susan E. Ridenour in the following chapter.)

Summary

Most institutions of higher education are quickly passing the point where they can question whether there will be an assessment of basic skills; now they must ask who will do it. While assessment is best done internally, by educational personnel, a failure there may lead to a requirement by an external agency, possibly with less concern for educational effectiveness. The University System of Georgia has been fortunate in initiating its program to assess basic skills prior to legislative mandates and societal pressures.

After the need for a program to assess basic skills was generally recognized, a faculty and staff committee was designated to develop and monitor its implementation. It should be understood, however, that the governing Board of Regents has the final authority. The committee considered as many questions as possible, but its initial policies needed modification and expansion as the testing program was implemented. It was crucial that the director of the program was an experienced measurement professional. This insured that its technical aspects, including the necessary reliability and validity studies, were conducted according to acceptable standards.

In implementing the program, it was important that adequate advance notice was given to students, faculty, and parents. A great deal of time was spent in explaining the program and assisting students in completing the requirement. After testing began, information about the results was made available to faculty and staff so that the assessment program could contribute to instructional improvement.

The development and implementation of a sound assessment program, while difficult, can have a tremendous impact on improving elementary, secondary, and college education. In Georgia, we look forward to the return of public confidence in the quality of education at all levels and to the lessening, perhaps, of the need for such a program to assess basic skills.

References

College Board. *On Further Examination: Report of the Advisory Panel on the Scholastic Aptitude Test Score Decline.* New York: College Entrance Examination Board, 1977.

Policies, Board of Regents, University System of Georgia. Atlanta: University System of Georgia, 1979.

Rentz, R. Robert, and Steller, Nancy A. *Documentation Related to the Regents' Testing Program.* Atlanta: University System of Georgia, 1976.

Roberts, David M., and Rentz, R. Robert. *Research Related to the Reliability and Validity of the Language Skills Examination.* Atlanta: University System of Georgia, 1978.

Statutes of the University System Advisory Council. Atlanta: University System of Georgia, 1979.

19 Impacts of Proficiency Testing on Higher Education

Susan E. Ridenour

Basic skills assessment is spreading through public school systems nationwide. Can assessment in higher education be far behind? What are the effects when proficiency testing is instituted in higher education?

For the past seven years, the University System of Georgia has operated the Regents' Testing Program, a proficiency testing program, in all thirty-three state-supported colleges and universities. (This program is discussed by R. Robert Rentz in the following chapter.) This common base for assessment, when administered across classes and institutions, provides a means to investigate areas beyond individual student performance, areas such as: program effectiveness, student placement or certification, teacher evaluation, and institutional comparison. Also, systemwide testing provides insight into areas where impacts can be expected. These areas of impact include: educational content (curriculum), accessibility (admissions, retention, and graduation), as well as evaluation (further testing). Finally, the demand for accountability requires analysis of assessment results to confirm effective teaching methods or to initiate better approaches.

In the Georgia system, accountability has been addressed through test results. In the late 1960s, the chancellor of Georgia's university system asked for ". . . some sort of proof . . . [to be] developed to refute . . . charges . . . of laymen that college graduates could not read and write" (Simpson, 1978). Soon system officials, legislators, and the public at large were demanding to have additional validation of basic competencies.

The demand for accountability reflects a desire for resolution of the conflicting reports on levels of learning.

Since the decision was reached to test reading and writing proficiency in the University System of Georgia, educational priorities have influenced subsequent decisions. This paper outlines the growth and refinement of minimum competency assessment, presents faculty and administration perceptions of the consequences of this assessment, and notes the resulting modifications in priorities and methods which have occurred in the university system.

Refinement of Minimum Competency Assessment

There can be a relationship between test performance and instructional practices,—that is, if students do poorly on a test, either the test (or testing program) may be changed, or instructional procedures may be changed, or a combination of both changes may occur. In Georgia, a combination of both approaches is evident. Even though 30 to 35 percent of students tested have failed the Regents' Testing Program's Language Skills Examination (LSE), that test now has higher passing requirements. In addition to changes in the testing program, instruction in basic skills has also received considerable attention as a result of the Regents' policies. The Board of Regents (the governing board for the University System of Georgia) has recently adopted more stringent policies regarding remediation for those who fail the LSE. The class size for English courses has been limited, writing assignments in all departments are increasing, and course content in first-year English classes has become more standardized throughout the system.

Further, conditions revealed by the initial administration of the LSE influenced the systemwide creation of special remedial programs for first-year students. The remediation includes extensive testing for placement and for exit certification using the Basic Skills Examination (BSE), which was developed by university system personnel. New departments have been established in all institutions to provide basic skills instruction for students who need this additional preparation before attempting college-level courses. New courses that emphasize composition have been instituted in a number of departments of English, and existing courses in other departments in several institutions have been modified to include more instruction in communication skills. An evaluative cycle—performance appraisal, program modification, performance appraisal—has been developed from the systemwide assessment in basic skills. The cycle continues in an iterative approach toward improved student performance.

Perceptions of Consequences of the LSE

The BSE and LSE have affected instruction and curricula throughout the university system. To gather evidence on these changes, the deans, vice-presidents, and heads of English departments were surveyed for their perceptions of the effects of the Regents' Test (LSE) on curricula.[1] The responses include the following samples:

> . . . the power to test is indeed the power to determine curriculum.
> Curricula are shaped by the sensitivity and validity of the measures used.
> . . . the result [of realizing] the serious nature of the problem . . . has been an improvement in the focus of [English] courses with a return to the realization that 'basics' must be achieved before more sophisticated material can be mastered.
> [A]lthough much of the motivation for improving . . . has been negative, the critical need . . . has had somewhat of a halo effect and has caused many students and faculty to experience a renaissance of awareness concerning the importance of communicative skills in the educational process. The weak performance of our students . . . has galvanized the faculty and [to a lesser extent] students into . . . action focused on improvement.[2]

One vice-president summarily stated that changes seem to "be in two directions: first, more attention in non-writing courses toward written expression; and, second, in writing courses more attention toward practical symptoms of basic composition as opposed to theories . . . ."[3]

Although the detail and depth of responses to this open invitation for perceptions of impact varied, several general conclusions can be drawn. First, the basic college-level English courses now have an increased emphasis on composition and communication skills. Comments regarding this change were both positive and negative. Some respondents thought the return to basics was correct; others reported the loss of academic excellence and depth for students who do not need the basic skills remediation. Writing assignments in basic English courses are more frequently argumentative essays on topics of general interest (similar to LSE essays), rather than critical reviews of literature. To avoid restricting college-level course content to such basics, some faculties elected to increase entrance standards for regular English courses.

Second, students are exposed to simulated test situations in preparation for LSE testing. Numerous essays are written under the conditions of the LSE (unannounced topic with time limitations and no assistance from class discussion or references). Students seek assistance in the practice of writing essays through workshops, writing labs, and so forth. Frequently, LSE-like essays, used as department exams, are graded by three raters, as are the LSE essays.

Third, remediation is tailored to deficiencies identified through failures on both the LSE and BSE. The writing deficiencies identified by the LSE essay include problems of organization, rhetoric, and mechanics. The LSE reading test and the BSE reading and English tests incorporate questions to measure competence in the areas of diction, point of view, vocabulary, reproducing ideas, making inferences, analyzing motivation and presentation, and criticizing a passage used for reading comprehension. The BSE math test covers both arithmetic and algebraic applications. Review is also provided for students who request assistance before attempting the LSE. Most institutions' remediation emphasizes essay writing. Now that the minimum score on the reading component of the LSE has been raised, more remediation in this area is expected to be necessary. One-to-one tutoring is frequently used to meet diverse remedial needs. However, one institution has abandoned remediation attempts for the LSE essays owing to a lack of positive results in subsequent testing.

Fourth, faculties outside the English departments are asked to emphasize correct writing. This request is not always followed. When it is, the practice usually takes the form of term papers, reports, and responses to essay questions. Professors throughout the colleges are also asked to promote the development of reading skills.

Fifth, cooperation and responsibility for basic skills improvement is increasing throughout each institution and, occasionally, between different campuses. Some English faculty members have worked with high school teachers to involve them in addressing basic skills deficiencies. Institutionwide, inservice workshops are offered to assist faculty in coping with this increased responsibility for reading and writing skill development.

Sixth, administrative decisions reflect increased emphasis on basic skills. (These policies are discussed by Haskin R. Pounds in the preceding chapter.)

Changes in Procedures and Priorities

Basic skills assessment has influenced admission decisions as well as retention and graduation requirements. After a period of open admissions, the University System of Georgia's Board of Regents has set a standard below which high school graduates will be denied admission to any state institution. Fully 23.3 percent of 41,839 fall, 1978 freshmen in the university system were required, by result of competency test scores (BSE), to take one or more noncredit remedial courses before attempting college-level work. This remediation policy has influenced admissions and retention because some students elect to enroll in institutions outside the state system to avoid remedial work and the various proficiency tests which are an integral part of public higher education in Georgia. As one department chairman expressed it, "quality controls on one hand and attrition rates on the other have placed faculty . . . [who teach composition] . . . in an uncomfortable posture. . . . Notable numbers of students are leaving the University System of Georgia because they cannot pass the Regents' Testing Program or they don't want the 'hassle.'"[4] In Georgia, the system's chancellor responded to this issue with, "none of us must let the prospect of enrollment *loss* interfere with our educational judgment. This is especially important as we approach hard decisions on entrance levels and levels of performance in classwork" (Simpson, 1978).

The Basic Skills Examination (BSE) is used for several purposes in the Georgia system. It regulates placement within and exit from remedial work discussed earlier. Passing the BSE is an entrance requirement to regular college coursework, so this test also serves as an admissions instrument. Students who do not successfully complete the remedial programs (called Special Studies) within one year are refused admission to college-credit courses.

Passing the Language Skills Examination (LSE) also influences admission, retention, and graduation. Recent policy changes made the LSE the selection device for upper-division work, as well as part of the requirements for awarding an associate degree. Shortly, the LSE will affect transfers from outside the state system. Students who enter with more than 105 quarter credit-hours will be required to pass the LSE before continuing credit work toward a degree. Students who fail the test will be limited to remedial courses until successful completion of test requirements. All students seeking a baccalaureate or associate degree must have passed the LSE.

University system officials continue to experiment with and plan for other proficiency tests. For example, four institutions are currently investigating the feasibility of a sophomore comprehensive examination to cover general courses taken in the first two years of college. The problem reported thus far is the inability to identify broad, substantive areas in general courses which all students should be expected to have mastered.

All institutions currently administer senior examinations in each major area of study; these data are used at each institution for independent studies and program evaluation. Some institutions administer locally developed senior exams, while others employ the Graduate Record Examination, the National Teacher Examination, and other nationally available instruments.

Academic deans were surveyed in 1976 about the impact of these major-area examination results (Collins, 1977). Because senior tests had been in effect only two years, most administrators said that generalizations and conclusions would be premature. However, several deans commented that weaknesses as well as strengths in various academic disciplines had been demonstrated by students' performances. Responses at campuses included test revisions, adoption of alternative tests, and curriculum and instructional revisions. It should be noted, however, that interpretation of these major-area test results at the institutional level is difficult owing to low student motivation, since results do not affect individual students. At the system level, interpretation problems involve the equating of results based on various instruments. Yet, the senior tests are another example of an external evaluation that is being accepted as another checkpoint of educational progress in the state system of higher education.

In the future, educational goals, curriculum, and student selection will continue to be determined to some extent by the results of external tests. The test results will help explain what a college degree means. One dean in Georgia stated, "I [am] glad that a degree from a University System institution carries with it at least that guarantee—that students who graduate can demonstrate on a test their ability to write some level of basic English. The Regents' Testing Program is one of the boldest experiments I know of in higher education."[5]

This praise and the cooperation of faculties and students were hard won (to the extent that they have been won). Groups with vested interests initially resisted the systemwide testing procedures. English teachers resented the implication that they were the only faculty members who were accountable. Minority students questioned the test's validity, and other students questioned the content relevance of the test. College officials resisted the comparison of their school with other schools on the basis of test results. Parents found it difficult to understand why students still could not read (or write) after one or two years of college instruction, or why they could not graduate on time if they failed a reading and writing test. The general public wondered what was being achieved at all levels of education. All these dissensions had to be dealt with as the basic skills and language skills assessments were implemented.

Conclusions

Using minimum competency assessments, the University System of Georgia has uncovered important educational deficiencies. Reactions to the test results have influenced curriculum, student selection, instruction, policies, and assessment itself. If proficiency testing is used by institutions of higher education, it is clear there will be impacts in many areas. The issues which arose in Georgia will have to be addressed and resolved in each new proficiency testing program. The experience in the Georgia system of higher education has shown that proficiency testing programs can be implemented; the dynamics of the process of change may vary in other settings in higher education.

Notes

1. This survey was conducted by Dr. Charles Nash, assistant vice chancellor for academic affairs, who kindly made these data available.

2. Personal communications: D. M. Monroe, Sept. 27, 1978; J. E. Anderson, Sept. 26, 1978; H. D. Probst, Sept. 21, 1978; L. C. Milledge, Sept. 26, 1978.

3. J. E. Anderson, personal communication, Sept. 26, 1978.

4. R. E. Carlile, personal communication, Sept. 26, 1978.

5. M. Austin, personal communication, Sept. 25, 1978.

References

Collins, D. Summary of SAC Major Area Exam Survey, 1976.

Simpson, G. L., Jr. Remarks by Chancellor George L. Simpson, Jr. to the Franklin College of Arts and Science faculty. Athens, Georgia, January 19, 1978.

20   Characteristics of Tests Used in a Minimum Competency Testing Program in Higher Education

R. Robert Rentz

The purpose of this paper is to describe certain characteristics of the instruments used in the Regents' Testing Program (RTP) of the University System of Georgia. The RTP includes reading and writing tests which are administered to sophomores in the thirty-three state-supported colleges and universities in Georgia. Students are required to pass the tests as one requirement for either the associate (two year) or baccalaureate (four year) degree. The tests used in the RTP are called the Language Skills Examination (LSE) and are interesting in at least three ways: (1) the tests were designed around the concept of "minimum competence in reading and writing"; (2) an item pool using Rasch model calibration techniques is used; and (3) a writing sample is used.

The RTP is a minimum competency testing program. While it is operated at the higher-education level, several aspects parallel considerations usually made in programs at the secondary-school level. Three of these considerations form the framework within which the tests used in the RTP are discussed. The three considerations are local development, continuity through multiple, equated test forms, and cutoff scores. However, before dealing with these specific issues a simple description of the instruments is in order.

The Language Skills Examination consists of two parts: a reading test and a written essay. The tests, administered four times a year, are taken one or more times by every student who has completed at least 45 quarter-hours of college credit. Approximately 25,000 students are tested each year. Each of the two parts has a separate cutoff score, but both parts must be passed at the same testing for the student to have demonstrated minimum competence in reading and writing. Students who fail the LSE may repeat it as many times as they choose, subject to specific conditions required by the local institution, such as participation in special remedial programs.[1]

The reading part of the LSE typically includes 70 multiple-choice items involving vocabulary and reading comprehension, and it is administered in 60 minutes. The essay test, also administered in 60 minutes, requires the examinee to select one of two specified topics and write an essay of, in general, 300 to 500 words. While the reading test is machine-scored, the essay must be evaluated by special procedures using trained raters. Our procedures involve holistic scoring on a 4-point scale using model essays to illustrate the dividing lines between the four points on the scale. This scale automatically incorporates a cutoff score (1 = fail; 2, 3, and 4=pass) by virtue of its development.

Each essay is rated independently by three different raters. Since the final score is the median of the three ratings, an examinee cannot score a "1" (failing) unless at least two of three raters rated the essay "1." The reliability of these essay scores averages around .80, and on 95 percent of these essays at least two out of three ratings are identical. The essays are scored at six scoring centers around the state on two consecutive Saturdays (each quarter) by a total of about one hundred raters. Raters receive a small honorarium and rate, on the average, 30 essays an hour. The raters are all faculty members at system institutions; most of them are members of English departments, and they constitute an important part of the local involvement in the RTP.

Local Development and Content Validity

All test development, scoring, and reporting are conducted by the program staff. System faculty are particularly used for test development activities such as item writing and reviewing, as well as for minimum competency determination. The emphasis is on local development and local control. This issue of local test development is an important one; local development represents one of the options available to an organization contemplating an assessment program similar to the RTP in Georgia.

The other options for developing an assessment program are usually variations of one of two types that can be conveniently called "off-the-shelf testing" and "contract testing." "Off-the-shelf testing" can be thought of as simply purchasing an existing test from a commercial test publisher. This option has the advantages of the test's being readily accessible; it usually has been carefully developed technically and probably has national norms. "Contract testing" involves the development, to local specifications, of the tests (and may include test administration) by some outside firm under contract with the local organization. This option is popular, since many organizations prefer to have test development done by outside testing professionals. Another advantage of this method is that many of the "headaches" are borne by the contractor.

Because minimum competency testing requires a pass or fail decision, particular demands are placed on the test selection and development process. Since the test results usually have an important effect on the examinee (such as graduation or certification), issues of test security and content relevance are important factors in determining program credibility, and credibility is as important here as the usual issues of reliability and validity. Credibility is enhanced only when there is a strong and obvious match between test content and the program's purpose (which is an aspect of validity), as well as an assurance that examinees cannot pass for reasons other than a fair demonstration that they are indeed competent—hence the insistence on test security. Thus, credibility requires that the testing program be secure and that the tests be highly content valid. The concomitant requirements for test development for a program of this sort involve provisions for multiple test forms and a continuous and flexible content review process (which means the ability to add, delete, and/or modify test items). This content review process, organized and conducted at the local level, probably does more to enhance the credibility of a testing program than any other activity.

There are two dimensions of this content review process along which the three test development approaches might vary; these dimensions might be called local involvement and content specificity. The degree of local involvement in specifying test content can vary from: (1) the general specification of content at the local level with an outside firm doing item writing and test development; to (2) the complete test construction task being done at the local level. Obviously, the latter procedure is the ultimate in local involvement and control. Content specificity can vary from: (1) the situation where a test contains some items that are not considered a good match with the testing program's intent; to (2) the situation where every item has the approval of the responsible local officials.

"Off-the-shelf testing" is low on both dimensions, local involvement and content specificity. That does not necessarily mean that it is inadequate; just that, relative to the other types, it is lower. With this type of testing, the instruments are often nationally standardized and generally are designed to represent broad content areas which may not correspond exactly to the local content requirements. (It seems axiomatic that whenever any committee reviews any test, at least one person will dislike some items.)[2] Local test development, on the other hand, is high on both local involvement and content specificity, for obvious reasons. Contract testing is usually located somewhere between the two extremes of both dimensions. An organization under contract never has quite the flexibility to match the situation that can be achieved by local test development; the mere fact that the contractor is from the outside diminishes local involvement. Moreover, there is usually a limit to the revisions in content a contractor can make without exceeding the conditions of the contract.

All these factors might argue for the immediate superiority of local test development; however, the most compelling arguments against local development are the degree of staff expertise required, together with the fact that in many locations it is much easier to contract with an outside firm than it is to hire staff. Yet, on balance, the more local control in specifying content the greater the credibility is likely to be.

Multiple Equated Forms and Test Security

In addition to acceptable content, the credibility of a minimum competency testing program rests on test security. In the Georgia program, testing occurs four times a year with tests administered at each institution as often as four times a day over two or three days. The only way to insure a degree of test security is to change test forms fairly frequently. This means that whatever test development option is chosen, it must provide for multiple test forms that are equated to one another. Several state testing programs discovered the multiple forms requirement after plunging headlong into elaborate test development. They also found that not all development options lend themselves equally well to the creation of alternate test forms.

Although there are several ways in which tests can be equated, I will describe here only the process by which Georgia's RTP has dealt with the test equating problem. The reading test, which is a multiple-choice test, is based on Rasch model calibrations of an item pool (Rentz, 1978). Such techniques permit the use of large item-pools from which sufficient numbers of items are drawn to compose a test form. The Rasch model calibrations of the items in the item pool serve to automatically equate any test forms devised from the pool. Thus, any number of test forms can be composed with a system of this sort, limited only by the total numbers of items in the item pool. Incidentally, another advantage of the item-pool approach to test development is that individual items may be added or deleted whenever the content review process so dictates.

The problem of equating multiple forms of the RTP essay test is different. Recall that an essay test requires the examinee to write an essay on one of two assigned topics. If, for example, topics 1 and 2 were paired on one test form, then an alternate form could consist of topics 3 and 4. In other words, to create multiple test forms it is only necessary to have pairs of different topics. However, the equating question is whether or not the resulting scores on different topics represent equivalent levels of performance.

Since the scores an essay receives depend on the holistic scoring procedure that uses model essays, our initial attempt to create equivalent test scores consisted of carefully selecting sets of model essays for each topic used on a particular test administration. With a 4-point scale and with model essays at each of the dividing points between scale values, this meant three models for each topic (we designate the models "2/1," "3/2," and "4/3" to show which scale values they separate).

The process of model selection involved a panel of experts whose membership remained fairly constant over several years. The committee members began their model selection by reviewing a list of criteria for essay quality that they had developed during the initial year of the program, as well as by scoring models used in previous quarters. They then read a number of papers written by examinees for that quarter, selecting from those new essays potential candidates for the scoring models. These potential models were then independently rated by each committee member; only those essays with high rater agreement were retained for further consideration. There followed an extensive period of discussion on the candidate models, the outcome of which was the selection of models for a particular topic based on the unanimous judgment of the committee that the chosen models represented the desired standards of quality. The strength of this process was the insistence on unanimity of judgment. The result was a score scale that could very well be considered criterion referenced.

Because a different set of models was chosen for each topic, there was no guarantee of model equivalence, in spite of the elaborate selection process. Thus, in an effort to achieve a higher degree of equivalence, the rating procedure was modified to use a set of standard models. Our data, indicating comparable reliability and comparable score distributions across the topics, showed that raters could use the rating process just as well without having different models for each separate topic. In other words, one set of common models could be used to rate any essay regardless of its topic.

The use of standard models makes possible the use of more forms of the essay test each quarter, since topic-specific models do not have to be chosen (that process required about three-fourths of a day per topic).

In addition, standard models are likely to produce greater equivalence across test forms; however, more direct evidence of this equivalence needs to be obtained.

Determining Cutoff Scores

The determination of a cutoff score on the essay test is a direct outcome of the model selection process. The "2/1" model constitutes the definition of minimum competence, which is further elaborated in the statement of scoring procedures and in the description of criteria that define an essay's quality (Rentz and Steller, 1979). Although a good deal of judgment is involved in the definition of competence, there seems to be considerable confidence in the outcome. On several occasions, groups comprised of faculty, administrators, students, and outside individuals have reviewed the standards and found them satisfactory and reasonable.

The strategy for determination of the cutoff score on the reading test was quite different from that used on the essay test. The reading test was administered for three quarters (winter, spring, and summer 1972) before students were required to pass the test. When the passing requirement became effective, those first three quarters became the baseline or norm period. The reading test cutoff score was defined at the 10th percentile of the combined score distributions for the three quarters. The rationale at the time for what might seem to be an arbitrary decision was that: (1) the performance level represented by the 10th percentile did in fact represent a very low level of performance in reading; (2) the 10th percentile of the baseline norms would represent a fixed standard for subsequent test administrations, and these failing students in all likelihood would also fail the essay test (the failure rate on the essay was 25 - 30 percent); and (3) after gaining experience with the consequences of the cutoff scores, effects of remediation, and so on, needed adjustments could eventually be made.[3]

Summary

Experience with the Regents' Testing Program since 1972 has pointed out certain characteristics of the tests that require the attention of anyone contemplating a minimum competency testing program. In this paper, I have reviewed three such considerations, including whether or not tests should be developed locally, the need for multiple equated test forms, and the process by which cutoff scores were set for this statewide minimum competency testing program in higher education. As far as the Georgia program is concerned, no fundamental changes are contemplated. There is some concern about the impact of the "105 hour rule" on students transfering into the system, but since that change does not go into effect until fall 1979, an evaluation of its impact will have to await further data.

Notes

1. In the fall of 1978, the Board of Regents of the Georgia system modified the policy such that, on a systemwide basis, students who have not passed the test by their 105th quarter-hour must participate in remedial work and may not take further college-credit courses until they have passed the test.

2. The distinctions being drawn here may be inconsequential; however, real or imagined, these distinctions bear directly on the credibility issue.

3. Based on subsequent years' experience, additional research, and considerable review, the reading test cutoff scores were raised effective fall, 1978. The consequence of this change was that 86 percent passed the reading test, and the total passing the LSE (both parts) was 61 percent, compared with the fall of 1977 when the percentages were 99 and 63 respectively.

References

Rentz, R. R. Monitoring the quality of an item-pool calibrated by the Rasch model. Paper presented at the Annual Meeting of the National Council on Measurement in Education, Toronto, Ontario, March 1978.

Rentz, R. R., and Steller, N. A. A description of certain aspects of the Regents' Testing Program. Mimeographed. Atlanta: University System of Georgia, Georgia State University, January 1979.

Cases in School Systems

21   A School-District-Developed,
Rasch-Based Approach to
Minimum Competency
Achievement Testing

Walter E. Hathaway

Introduction

In accord with a state mandate and in response to requests from parents, teachers, and administrators, the Portland, Oregon, School District has developed a new Rasch based citywide minimum competency achievement testing program. The program's reading and mathematics tests for grades 4 through 8 were administered districtwide for the first time in fall 1977. Reading and mathematics tests for grade 3 and language usage tests for grades 3 through 8 were completed by fall 1979. Research and resource development efforts have been mounted to prepare the way for the possible extension of the program to the secondary level and to other content areas such as writing, science, and social studies.

The people responsible for the education of Portland students felt that their minimum competency achievement testing program should have the following characteristics.

It should help students become competent beginning as early as the

The author gratefully acknowledges the contributions of numerous colleagues to this paper and, more importantly, their leadership and participation in the work the paper describes. Special acknowledgment is made to the following members of the Portland Public School's Evaluation Department: Victor Doherty (Department Head), Dean Forbes, Fred Forster, George Ingebo, Jim Holmes, Ron Houser and Bill Matson.

third grade rather than denying diplomas to students who had arrived at the late stages of their secondary education without acquiring required competencies.

It should focus on basic skills competencies initially since these were the first competencies in which students were to be certified under the State mandate and since these were the highest priorities of the school system.

It should assist teachers, parents and students in instructional decision making by giving clear, accurate and unbiased information about student performance on specific major competencies and goals within the local curriculum leading to further diagnosis and prescription in areas in which a student's progress toward meeting district graduation competencies appeared unsatisfactory.

It should assist administrators, board members and citizens in administrative and policy decision making by giving clear, accurate and unbiased information about how Portland schools are doing in comparison with others and whether performance levels within the District are heading upward, remaining constant, or decreasing over time.

It should give every student a chance to be measured at his or her individual functional level and thus avoid discouraging some students while failing to challenge others.

There should be as little testing as possible and each test required should be short enough to be administered in approximately one 50 minute period.

With the support of the Board of Education and Superintendent Robert Blanchard, Portland teachers, curriculum specialists, and evaluators have worked together with the Tri-County Goal Development Project and with the Northwest Evaluation Association (NWEA) to build such a testing program. The measurement procedures are based on the logistic model first proposed by Rasch (1960; 1961; 1966a; 1966b). The Portland School District's application of Rasch's model to minimum competency achievement testing suggests that it leads to better basic skills measurement and reporting than is possible with traditional approaches to testing. This paper describes the process used in developing the tests, the tests themselves, and the distinctive features and advantages of the program, the reports, and their uses.

Test Development Processes Using Rasch Calibrated Item Banks

Each of the series of tests in reading, mathematics, and language usage was constructed according to blueprints in which the major competencies to be measured were identified along with subcompetencies selected by

Total Range in Rasch Units (RIT)

155 ⟶ 255

Competency	Test 817 Range 158 - 177 No. Items	Test 818 Range 171 - 190 No. Items	Test 819 Range 184 - 203 No. Items	Test 820 Range 197 - 216 No. Items	Test 821 Range 210 - 229 No. Items	Test 822 Range 223 - 242 No. Items	Test 823 Range 236 - 255 No. Items
1. The student can add whole numbers.	5	5	5	0	0	0	0
2. The student can subtract whole numbers.	5	5	5	5	0	0	0
3. The student can multiply whole numbers.	0	5	5	5	5	0	0
4. The student can divide whole numbers.	0	5	5	5	5	5	0
5. The student can order, compare, rename and represent whole numbers.	5	5	5	5	5	5	7
6. The student can order, compare, rename and represent fractional numbers (fractions, decimals, percents).	0	5	5	5	5	5	5
7. The student can compute with fractions.	0	0	0	5	5	5	5
8. The student can compute with decimals and percents.	0	0	0	5	5	5	5
9. The student can use knowledge of geometry.	5	5	5	5	5	5	5
10. The student can use knowledge of measurement.	5	5	5	5	5	5	5
11. The student can interpret and use graphs, statistics, and probability.	5	5	5	5	5	5	8
12. The student can solve story (word) problems.	5	5	5	5	5	5	5
13. The student can use the strategies and processes of problem solving.	5	5	5	0	0	5	5
Total of Items	40	55	55	55	50	50	50

Figure 1. Grades 4 through 8—Mathematics Test Plan

Total Range in Rasch Units (RIT)

155 ← → 250

Competency	Test 317 Range 158 - 177 No. Items	Test 318 Range 171 - 190 No. Items	Test 319 Range 184 - 203 No. Items	Test 320 Range 197 - 216 No. Items	Test 321 Range 210 - 229 No. Items	Test 322 Range 223 - 242 No. Items
1. The student can interpret meanings of commonly used words. (Context Clues; Synonyms, Antonyms; Structure Components; Multiple Meanings)	14	16	12	12	11	11
2. The student can comprehend the literal meanings or explicit content of written materials. (Recall of Details, Interpreting Directions; Sequence of Details; Classification of Facts; Recall Stated Main Idea)	16	16	17	16	14	11
3. The student can interpret implied and related meanings from the content and presentation of written materials. (Drawing Inferences; Recognizing Cause and Effect; Prediction of Events; Summary and Synthesis)	10	7	10	9	10	12
4. The student can evaluate the intent, validity, and worth of written materials. (Fact and Opinion; Merit, Accuracy and Persuasion; Internal and External Validity; Conclusion & Resolution; Bias and Underlying Assumptions)	5	6	6	8	10	11
Total of Items	45	45	45	45	45	45

Figure 2. Grades 4 through 8 — Reading Test Plan

Total Range in Rasch Units (RIT)

155 →   → 250

Competency	Test 617 Range 158 - 177	Test 618 Range 171 - 190	Test 619 Range 184 - 203	Test 620 Range 197 - 216	Test 621 Range 210 - 229	Test 622 Range 223 - 242
	No. Items	No. Items	No. Items	No. Items	No. Items	No. Items
1. The student can recognize and use fundamental sentence and paragraph structures.	6	6	6	6	6	6
2. The student can use basic grammar correctly.	6	6	6	6	6	6
3. The student can punctuate correctly.	6	6	6	6	6	6
4. The student can capitalize correctly.	6	6	6	6	6	6
5. The student can spell correctly.	12	12	12	12	12	12
6. The student can recognize and use the elements of effective written expression (e.g. co-herence, clarity, economy, and consistency).	6	6	6	6	6	6
Total of Items	42	42	42	42	42	42

Figure 3. Grades 3 through 8—Language Usage Field Test Plan

teacher committees. The number of items needed to represent each competency is shown on the blueprints.

During the four years preceding the development of the tests, Portland and other member districts of the NWEA carried on intensive field testing of items in reading, mathematics, and language usage. Rasch analysis and linking procedures were employed to create three banks, each containing more than a thousand goal and competency referenced test items that were Rasch calibrated and scaled. This made it possible to select appropriate levels of items related to the goals and competencies to be measured. The end result was the development of a flexible, valid, and reliable set of tests in a relatively short time.

Many of the competencies in the test blueprints prepared by Portland curriculum and evaluation specialists were completely covered by the NWEA bank items. The initial calibration of items in the banks was redone on the larger populations of students taking the tests in the Portland program. This provided the district, as well as the NWEA bank, firmer and more reliable calibrations for future use. Also, as Portland teachers, curriculum specialists, and evaluators filled out the test blueprints by selecting and writing items for competencies not covered by the bank, additional items were calibrated and made available to the bank. When other districts use the bank in similar fashion, they derive the same benefits and are able to make similar contributions.

The Tests

There are currently 7 levels of reading tests and 7 levels of mathematics tests in the Portland grade 4 through 8 minimum competency testing system. These test levels are matched to students not on the basis of their grade level, but on the basis of their approximate performance level within the subject area. The match of test to student is determined by previous test results or by short locator tests for students new to the system. This permits the accurate measurement of each student's achievement in a single, approximately 50-minute test period for each subject. The relative brevity of the tests makes possible both fall and spring testing in all these subject areas, thus making available the instructional and administrative advantages of testing at each of these times.

Rasch Scale Based Reporting

The first distinctive feature of the Portland tests is that results are reported in terms of an equal interval scale representing a range of achievement in each subject extending from the simplest to the most complex levels of performance. The Rasch scale is independent of a norming sample, since the scaling procedure partials out the effect of ability of groups performing on an item, leaving an estimate of the true relative scale level of the item compared with that of other items with which it is associated in a test.

It should be noted that by combining the Rasch scaling feature with the competency referencing feature, the flexibility exists to substitute items or to add or eliminate competencies and items from the tests while maintaining comparability of the measures from year to year. This important feature is not available with traditional norm-referenced measurement systems.

Functional Administration

The second distinctive feature of the tests is that they are designed to make it possible for a student of any level of ability to get at least half of the items right on the test taken. Placement of a student is predicted from performance on the last previous testing. New students are located by administering a short Rasch calibrated test designed for that purpose. By standardizing instructions, it is possible to test all students in a class at a single session even though they take different level tests. An added benefit is that absent or invalidly tested students from several grade levels can be retested in a single session for each subject with one proctor.

The Reports and Their Uses

The tests and their reports were designed to meet two district needs— first, to provide curriculum-sensitive survey measurement to support administrative decisions; and second, to provide competency-referenced measurement to support instructional decisions needed to lead students toward competency.

A special committee of principals and teachers was formed to advise the test developers on the testing program as a whole, and on the reporting of results in particular. Students and parents were also consulted. Two forms of reporting have been used to date. The first shows for every student whether or not the criterion for each minimum competency has been passed (figure 4). The second identifies all students who did not reach the criterion (see below) on each competency (figure 5). These reports have been valuable to teachers in working with students and parents to help students attain district competencies. Certification of competencies is done at the secondary level using test results as one among other factors.

School Lakeside   Teacher Jones   Grade 9   10/07/78

Fall 1978 Reading Level Test
Class Report - 24 Students in this Class

Goal	Students Passing	Students possibly needing additional work on this goal.	
1. The student can interpret the meaning of commonly used words.	19	Kristy Alfred M.	Pamela Loisregin
2. The student can comprehend literally stated written materials.	17	Denise Brian D. Kristy	Pamela Loisregin Alethea A.
3. The student can interpret implied meanings in written materials.	19	Denise Kristy	Pamela Loisregin
4. The student can evaluate the intent, validity and worth of written materials.	17	Kristy Julie L. Mary K.	Pamela Loisregin Alethea A.

Figure 4. Form Showing Reading Level Test Results, Class Report

School 100   Teacher Jones   Grade 9   10/07/78

Fall 1978 Reading Level Tests
Student Report

Student	Word Mng	Lit Comp	Int Comp	Eval Comp
Lesia E.	Pass	Pass	Pass	Pass
*Denise	Pass			Pass
Marcia A.	Pass	Pass	Pass	Pass
Sheri M.	Pass	Pass	Pass	Pass
Brian D.	Pass		Pass	Pass
*Kristy				
Julie L.	Pass	Pass	Pass	
Alfred M.		Pass	Pass	Pass
David N.	Pass	Pass	Pass	Pass
Yin Nyan	Pass	Pass	Pass	Pass
Kimberly D.	Pass	Pass	Pass	
Mary K.				
*Pamela	Pass	Pass	Pass	Pass
Tracy E.	Pass	Pass	Pass	Pass
Tammy J.	Pass	Pass	Pass	Pass
Kelly N.	Pass	Pass	Pass	Pass
Ovia D.	Pass	Pass	Pass	Pass
Joanne L.	Pass	Pass	Pass	Pass
Karen	Pass	Pass	Pass	Pass
Sharon D.	Pass	Pass	Pass	Pass
*Loisregin				
Alethea A.	Pass		Pass	

*Indicates a minimum standards target student

Students who were absent   Students marked invalid   Students needing a lower test
Vickie R.

Figure 5. Form Showing Reading Level Test Results, Student Report

If the test reports illustrated in figures 4 and 5 indicate that a student may have problems with a required competency, teachers are expected to do further diagnostic testing and inquiry. If a problem is confirmed, remedial measures are taken, such as: assignment to learning resource centers for individual instruction; tutoring; grouping of students with common difficulties for work with teachers and aides; and planning with parents and tutors for home instruction.

Research is being conducted on the identification of the most appropriate criterion levels for "passing" each competency. In the interim, the district is using the Rasch scale equivalent of one standard deviation below the fall 1977 district grade-level mean for the minimum competency level requirement.

A second type of report shows, for each subject and class, the achievement position of every child in relation to a distribution curve for the

School Lakeside   Teacher Jones   Run Date 1/07/78
Fall, 1977   Achievement Level Test Student Report   Grade 05

Rank	Mathematics	RIT Scale:	170	178	185	189	200	207	215	222	230

M=40   M=60

Student Name	P Score	RIT	Very Low	Low	Low Average	Average	High Average	High	Very High
Meridith	65	223							X
Nathan	63	219						X	
Missy	62	218						X	
Heather	61	216						X	
Randy	59	214					X		
Darcy	59	214					X		
Scott	59	214					X		
Betty	56	209					X		
Parrish	56	209					X		
Ronald	53	204				X			
Mark	53	204				X			
Bryce	51	201				X			
Kelly	59	200				X			
Charles	49	198				X			
Ronald	48	197				X			
Michelle	48	197				X			
Mike	47	196				X			
Demetri	47	195				X			
Adrienn	45	193			X				
Lonnie	45	192			X				
Adam	44	191			X				
Tiffany	43	190			X				
John	43	189			X				
Donald	41	187			X				
Lance	39	184		X					
Eric	39	184		X					
Chrissy	33	174	X						

**Figure 6. Form Showing Achievement Level Test Results,
by Rank, Student Report**

grade level to which the student belongs. This information is provided both by rank order and alphabetically (see figures 6 and 7).

In addition to plotting each student's position in the grade-level distribution, this second set of reports gives the Rasch achievement score and a standard score (mean of 50, standard deviation of 10) for each student. The standard score is based on the distribution of Rasch scale scores for all students in the grade-level group to which the student belongs. These

School Lakeside			Teacher Jones					Run Date 1/07/78		
Fall 1977		Achievement Level Test Student Report				Grade 05				
Alpha	Mathematics	RIT Scale:	170	178	185	193	200	207	215	222	230
					P=40				P=60		

Student Name	P Score	RIT	Very Low	Low	Low Average	Average	High Average	High	Very High
Ronald	48	197				..X.			
Kelly	50	200				..X.			
Ronald	53	204				..X			
Adrienn	45	193			..X				
Donald	41	187			..X..				
Chrissy	33	174	..X..						
Lance	39	184		..X.					
Adam	44	191			..X.				
Nathan	63	219						..X.	
Mike	'47	196				X			
Tiffany	43	190			..X..				
Eric	49	184		..X..					
Parrish	56	209					..X..		
Meridith	65	223							..X..
Bryce	51	201				..X.			
Mark	53	204				..X			
Heather	61	216						..X.	
Missy	62	218						..X	
Demetri	47	195			X.				
Randy	59	214					..X.		
Scott	59	214					..X.		
Darcy	59	214					..X.		
Michelle	48	197			..X.				
Betty	56	209					..X..		
John	43	189			..X..				
Lonnie	45	192			..X.				
Charles	49	198				..X.			

Figure 7. Form Showing Achievement Level Test Results, Alphabetically, Student Report

reports have been found valuable for examining achievement patterns
and variations within groups, for grouping students, and for program
evaluation.

In addition to teacher reports, student competency and subject achievement are reported in other forms and at different levels of aggregation to
assist administrative decision making. Reports giving student rank within
grade rather than class are provided to principals who use them, for example, in Title I and gifted-student identification and in parent consultation. And grade, building, area, and district means and standard deviations are reported longitudinally by subject area to assist administrators
in program management. Longitudinal reports of the progress of individual
students are being developed for parents and students. Just one of the many
current administrative reports is shown in figure 8. Regression methods
of comparing actual performance to predicted performance are also being
prepared.

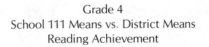

Grade 4
School 111 Means vs. District Means
Reading Achievement

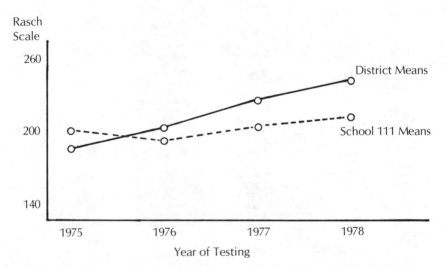

Figure 8. Longitudinal School Progress Report

Summary and Conclusion

The Portland achievement level tests have the following advantages: (1) the tests accurately reflect the Portland curriculum; (2) each child can be given a test in which he or she is likely to succeed; (3) student performance can be reported on major goals as well as on total score; (4) it is possible to describe student growth on an "absolute" rather than comparative scale; (5) the tests can be improved without destroying longitudinal data; and (6) shorter tests can be used, yet with greater accuracy of measurement. These advantages make it possible to secure more accurate individual test scores, more useful measures of group progress, and more sensitive measurement of the effects of instructional improvements.

While the developments described in this paper have been exciting and the results gratifying, the path to Rasch based minimum competency achievement testing has not been an easy one to travel. Mounting such a program has been more complicated and difficult than purchasing available instruments or settling for simple, locally developed criterion measures. The planning and development have required coordination of such disparate responsibilities as computer programming, item writing, test formatting, test blueprinting, development of scoring and reporting formats, in-service education, development of support manuals for principals, teachers, and test coordinators, editing and reviewing items for race and sex bias, Rasch analysis, linking, field testing, test scoring, answer sheet design, development of placement procedures for functional level testing, statistical analysis of item information to screen out poor items, and test packaging and distribution. Nevertheless, the evaluation staff believe that the results of the program and its benefits more than justify the effort that has gone into its development.

The Portland School District looks forward to continued sharing, with other school systems, of the results of its efforts in the area of Rasch based minimum competency achievement testing and reporting. It is our hope that the benefits of this approach will become more generally available.

References

Rasch, G. *Probabilistic models for some intelligence and attainment tests.* Copenhagen: Danish Institute for Educational Research, 1960.

———. On general laws and the meaning of measurement in psychology. In *Proceedings of the fourth Berkeley Symposium on mathematical statistics.* Berkeley: University of California Press, 1961, IV, pp. 321-334.

———. An item analysis which takes individual differences into account. *British Journal of Mathematical and Statistical Psychology* 19 (1966a): 49-57.

———. An individualistic approach to item analysis. In P. F. Lazarsfeld and N. W. Henry (eds.), *Readings in mathematical social science.* Chicago: Science Research Associates, 1966b, pp. 89-108.

22 Competency Tests: Decisions for Educators

Robert Sallander

There are two critical areas of concern in the competency testing movement which have caused those of us who are involved in the development of such tests to stop, ponder, and soul-search for solutions. That is not to say that these problems are the only ones, but they are always present, and dealing with them always involves critical concern.

These areas of critical concern are: first, the conflict which arises between instructional supervisors and assessment personnel when competency tests are introduced. Although "basic skills" are being measured, they are not usually presented in terms of life-role applications, as is required in California by legislation. Thus, while the skills being measured are the same as those which have been measured over the years on norm-referenced tests, the setting is different; and it is this difference that has caused curriculum developers to feel that evaluators have stepped beyond their turf. When curriculum developers speak of competency tests, evaluators are often accused of setting or changing the curriculum.

Second, what is the cutoff score? Who decides? Who will be affected? How much will a given cutoff cost? Such questions define the other dilemma facing evaluators who have responsibility for competency-based testing. This paper focuses on the second concern, that of establishing an acceptable cutoff score for the competency tests currently being used in the Los Angeles Unified School District (LAUSD). Some background information is necessary to report properly and meaningfully about cutoff scores.

Competency testing became a reality in the LAUSD during the summer of 1974. This predates the inception of the California proficiency test by a year and a half and the Hart legislation by nearly two years. The California proficiency test is the one that 16 and 17 year-old students may take as an alternative to the usual high school attendance. By successfully passing this test, a student is awarded the State Certificate of Proficiency— by law defined as equivalent to the high school diploma. The Hart legislation (AB 3408, 1976) requires all California secondary school students (grades 7-12) to acquire the knowledge, skills, and confidence required to function effectively in contemporary society. The Hart legislation has been superseded (AB 65, 1977), but the testing requirements have not substantially changed (except for being extended into the elementary grades).

The LAUSD began test development ahead of the legal mandates because of a report issued in July of 1974 by the Los Angeles County Grand Jury. That report was based upon a study of four large, urban, Los Angeles County high schools, one of which was located in the LAUSD. The report stated that up to 56 percent of the graduates of these schools were functionally illiterate. I must confess that I do not know the meaning of the term, functionally illiterate. It is not, as far as I know, an educational term, and I suspect that it is not a legal term. The grand jury did not define it except to mention some areas of poor performance. For example, the jury said such students were not able to fill out job applications. Both the grand jury and the legislature mentioned life-role applications as the context of their concern for poor performance in basic skills.

The reaction to the report issued by the grand jury was to begin development of a new testing system to improve instructional effectiveness. This system was to supplement current high school graduation requirements. The plan was simple. Our first effort was in reading and was called SHARP (Senior High Assessment of Reading Performance); in addition, we now have a plan for computational skills called TOPICS (Test of Performance in Computational Skills), and WRITE: SR a test of language usage and composition skills requiring actual writing samples.

Let me describe the plan for improving reading performance. Upon entering the tenth grade, all students are required to take a reading test. The test is designed to measure how well these students are able to apply their reading experience to certain contemporary life-role tasks which they would be expected to encounter after graduation from high school. Students passing the test go on with the regular high school curriculum, as in the past. Those not reaching an acceptable level of performance also continue with the usual course of study, except that they are also programmed into a special diagnostic and prescriptive program which teaches the application of reading to the specific skills being measured. These students and their parents are advised of the graduation requirement concerning the passing of the reading test. Those students who do not reach an acceptable level of competency as tenth graders are retested as they enter the eleventh grade. This cycle is repeated for twelfth graders except that those who do not pass at the beginning of the year repeat the test a possible fourth time just before graduation.

The establishment of a cutoff score was not as easy as it might seem. From a technical point of view, there is a fine article on proper procedures to determine cutoff scores by John Meskaukas in the winter 1976 *Review of Educational Research*. We studied several of these techniques, particularly Bob Ebel's method of passing-score estimation. We were also concerned about false positives and false negatives. However, the cutoff dilemma presented us with two basic considerations, which had to be resolved before a definite cutoff score could be established.

First, since the competency-based tests are primarily instructional devices, the instructional division had to decide at what point students performed at an acceptable level. (The tests are used to determine an acceptable level of student performance in basic skills and in life-role situations and to indicate the specific remediation necessary for those failing to meet such acceptable standards.) The instructional staff felt that success with 70 percent of the items on a test was a satisfactory level of competency, based on these instructional criteria.

Second, how much could the district afford to spend for the remedial program, especially after Proposition 13 curtailment of local monies for public schools? In a district which has over 47,000 entering tenth grade students, the cost of materials as well as the necessity for adequate human resources are vital concerns. It was decided that the district could financially support diagnostic, prescriptive instruction for about 25 percent of tenth graders plus all eleventh and twelfth graders who had not yet achieved an acceptable level of performance. In addition, students of all grades transferring into the district would need instruction. The number of students who might need diagnostic, prescriptive instruction could run as high as 15,000.

It just so happened that a raw cutoff score which failed 25 percent of the tenth grade students also fell at approximately 70 percent of the test items correct. In addition, a raw cutoff score which failed 25 percent of the tenth graders did not exceed the financial capability of the district for remedial costs. Thus, the cutoff score at the 25th percentile met both the desire of the instructional division (70 percent of the test items correct) and also the financial limitations of the district in its remediation program (approximately 25 percent of the students).

Another facet of the cutoff dilemma concerns test security. We have had a different form of the test each year, and each form is equivalent to the first. We now have six tests in use, and all need passing scores that can be discussed in similar terms. We have now moved to a standard score which has a common passing point for all of the secondary tests. The total development of the Los Angeles competency-based testing program has been long, complex, and, we believe, defensible.

PART V
Identifying Competencies, Developing Instruments, and Setting Standards

The papers in this section address three of the most vexing problems associated with minimum competency testing: how to specify competencies, how to develop instruments for measuring them, and how to establish minimum standards. All three problems are considered in *Competency Test Development, Validation, and Standard Setting* by Ronald Hambleton and Daniel Eignor. The authors begin by defining a minimum competency test as one "designed to determine an examinee's level of performance relative to each competency being measured." They require that each competency be "described by a well-defined behavior domain."

Hambleton and Eignor next present a twelve-step model for identifying competencies, developing measurement instruments, and validating the instruments. They draw parallels between the development and validation steps needed for minimum competency tests and those needed for any criterion-referenced test. Only four steps in the process—specification of competencies, development of test items, validation of test items, and assembly of tests—are discussed in detail, because they are claimed to involve tasks that are unique to minimum competency testing. Definition of competencies is said to require both clarity and specificity. Hambleton and Eignor endorse the use of "domain specifications," as proposed by Popham (1978). In a domain specification, a general description of the competency to be measured is given first. Next, a sample test item is prepared. The two remaining elements include definition of the content to be included in the domain, and the characteristics of acceptable response modes and (in the case of multiple-choice items) acceptable distractors. Examples of domain specifications are provided. If domain specifications have been generated successfully, they provide operational rules for writing test items. Generation of test items then consists of a writing task, with regular checks to ensure that the boundaries of the domain specification have not been violated.

Hambleton and Eignor view competency test validation as a content-validation task. They suggest using subject-matter experts to judge the match between test items and domain specifications. In keeping with the writings of Cronbach (1971) and others, Hambleton and Eignor suggest that reviewers ask whether the characteristics of test items match the requirements of the domain specification in all respects, and whether the domain has been sampled adequately by the set of items intended for use in the competency test. Empirical item-review methods are also suggested as useful validation tools, but are not to be used as final determiners of the content of minimum competency tests.

If domain specifications have been constructed carefully, Hambleton and Eignor suggest that the test can be readily assembled by using a probability sampling procedure to select items from each domain to be represented. They emphasize the need to include a sufficient number of items to measure each competency and suggest that the judged importance and desired reliability associated with each competency determine the number of items included.

In their next section, Hambleton and Eignor review nineteen procedures for setting competency test standards that have appeared in the measurement literature. These methods are classified as judgmental models, empirical models, combination models, Bayesian methods, or decision-theoretic models. Upon reviewing each of the proposed procedures, Hambleton and Eignor apply a stringent practicality criterion, and thus narrow the field considerably. They conclude by recommending two "judgmental" procedures and one "combination" procedure over all others. Although Hambleton and Eignor acknowledge that all standard-setting methods are arbitrary, they hold to the positive definition of "arbitrary": reflective of choice or discretion, as in "arbitration." Thus they reject the notion advanced by some authors that all standard-setting methods are not only arbitrary, but capricious as well.

Hambleton and Eignor conclude with a menu of technical topics in minimum competency testing that need further research. Reflecting the themes of their paper, they divide the list into competency test development and validation issues, and standard-setting issues.

In *A Taxonomy for Competency Testing Programs*, Fredrick Finch suggests that semantic confusion causes a large part of the difficulty that states and school systems are experiencing in defining competencies. This semantic confusion surrounds the domain of skills and knowledge which various publics expect the schools to address. He recounts expectations that the schools serve as college preparatory academies, basic-skills educators, job training institutes, credential granting institutions, behavior modification clinics, sports and social clubs, and even baby-sitters. Some of these expected roles lead to competencies defined in terms of basic skills; others require so-called "competencies for life"; still others would require behavioral and social competencies.

Finch proposes that the semantics of competency definition would be aided by adopting the following definition: "a competency [is] the ability to use a specific skill or set of skills to meet the needs of a specific situation." He then suggests a three-dimensional taxonomy for operationally defining the content of a competency measure. The dimensions are: (1) the context of the competencies measured (such as school applications or job applications); (2) the enabling skills required by the competencies (such as reading or writing); and (3) the measures and criteria used to assess the competencies (such as performance observation or pencil-and-paper tests). The use of this taxonomy is illustrated with an example involving a school system's competency tests.

The final paper in this section is Selina Ganopole's *Using Performance and Preference Data in Setting Standards for Minimum Competency Assessment Programs*. In addition to presenting a judgmental standard-setting procedure that is not included in the Hambleton and Eignor review, Ganopole suggests a practical procedure for identifying competencies to be assessed and for selecting measurement instruments.

One of the principal debates among proponents of various standard-setting procedures concerns the use of empirical or normative test data in determining appropriate standards. Ganopole adopts the stance advocated by Popham (1978), that performance data from a variety of groups be used to inform standard-setters of the rationality and/or consequences of their actions. She illustrates a procedure that involves performance data for a group of high school seniors (who presumably have received instruction in the competency areas assessed), a group of seventh and ninth-grade students (who presumably are uninstructed in the competency areas of interest), and a group of adults (who presumably possess the relevant competencies at a functional level). The first group, Ganopole claims, will provide standard-setters with data on the likely consequences of their actions, while the second and third will suggest reasonable lower and upper bounds, respectively, on standards.

In contrast to several judgmental standard-setting methods reviewed by Hambleton and Eignor (in which judges set standards for each item or for entire competency tests), Ganopole's method has judges set standards for each competency. Judges are shown sample items, but these are to be viewed only as *representing* particular competencies. Potential problems are obvious: low item-domain correspondence, and the influence of low correspondence on selected standards. Whether these potential problems are of sufficient gravity to invalidate the proposed method can only be determined through empirical studies, as is true for many of the methods cited by Hambleton and Eignor.

The papers in this section lead us to conclude that much progress has been made in grappling with major development and measurement problems of minimum competency testing, but that considerable work remains. The papers, and the problems they treat, are reminiscent of a cartoon that appeared in a measurement journal several years ago. The cartoon showed an unbalanced "measurement" cart going down a road with a decided list to starboard, its right side supported by a wheel representing progress in test design, item construction, and content validation, and its left side supported by a far larger wheel representing progress in statistical procedures for item analysis and reliability estimation. Perhaps the unequal degree of attention that measurement theorists have paid to problems amenable to statistical attack, in contrast to those requiring purely conceptual or definitional work, is now becoming even more apparent. Having interpreted the results of our measurements normatively for so long, we are ill-prepared to respond to the demand that we apply absolute or judgmental standards. Yet these papers are a good beginning, and perhaps they define the boundary of the present state of the art in ways that will inspire clearly needed research.

References

Cronbach, L. J. Test Validation. In R. L. Thorndike (ed.), *Educational measurement.* Washington: American Council on Education, 1971, pp. 443-507.

Popham, W. J. Key standard-setting procedures for minimum competency testing programs. Paper presented at the 1977-78 Winter Conference on Measurement and Methodology, University of California, Los Angeles, January 1978.

23   Competency Test Development, Validation, and Standard Setting

Ronald K. Hambleton
Daniel R. Eignor

The establishment of minimum competency testing programs for elementary and secondary school students, and for many professions, has reached immense proportions (or epidemic proportions, if you view the trend negatively). Well over half (33 to be exact) of our states have passed legislation requiring assessment of the "competence" of their elementary and high school students (Pipho, 1978). Further, many of these states require that students demonstrate at least a minimum level of performance on a set of competencies in order to receive a high school diploma. Why are so many state legislatures mandating minimum competency testing? It appears that it is to discourage schools from promoting all students and awarding high school diplomas based on school attendance only. It is common for legislators and parents to say that minimum requirements in the "basic skills" must be set, so as to graduate students with a diploma that has some meaning. Perhaps it is not surprising that participating states are approaching the task of establishing minimum competency testing programs differently. Some states are emphasizing "life skills," others "school skills," and yet other states have incorporated both types of skills into their competency testing programs. Also, the

Preparation of this paper was supported, in part, by a grant from the National Institute of Education, Department of Health, Education, and Welfare. However, the opinions expressed herein do not necessarily reflect the position or policy of the National Institute of Education and no official endorsement by the National Institute of Education should be inferred.

school years in which testing is done vary from one state to the next. Finally, there are variations in the ways competencies are identified and measured, and standards are set (Haney & Madaus, 1978).

The rapidity of change in school, district, and statewide testing programs and the demand for high quality tests have dictated that substantial research and development work be undertaken. Included among the more important research and development topics are: identification and definition of competencies, management of competency testing programs, development and validation of competency tests, methods of determining standards, and uses and interpretations of competency test scores (Brickell, 1978).

Other papers in this volume consider the philosophy and assumptions of competency testing programs, as well as their potential (and in some cases, demonstrated) effects on student performance and school curricula. Our contribution is to consider some ways of developing and using competency tests to insure that competency testing programs achieve their full potential, whatever that potential may be. Specifically, this paper was prepared to accomplish three purposes: first, to introduce a model for developing and validating competency tests; second, to review several promising methods of determining "standards" or "minimum performance levels"; and third, to offer several suggestions for future research and development.

We do not debate the merits of competency testing in this paper. Others are far more informed about the issues and capable of articulating them to those who have an interest. Our work begins at the point where a decision has been made to initiate a competency testing program and a set of competencies has been identified, so that tests to measure individual performance on the competencies are required.

Three other points concerning our work are, first, that attention is focused on the use of competency tests for making decisions about individuals. When groups are of primary interest (as in program evaluation studies or many statewide testing programs), approaches to competency test development and test score usage are somewhat different. (For example, individuals and test items can be sampled—that is, matrix sampling is used—and "standards" are set for group performance.) Second, many of our examples are from elementary and secondary school settings, although most of the testing technology discussed applies equally well to the development of competency tests in other content areas. Third, we focus on the construction of paper-and-pencil tests. Steps for constructing performance tests are basically the same, but special attention must be given to topics such as the design and use of behavioral checklists, and inter-rater reliability.

The remainder of the paper considers the development and validation of competency tests, suitable methods of standard setting, and suggestions for future research and development.

Development and Validation of Competency Tests

A Competency Test

We begin with a definition of a competency test: A competency test is designed to determine an examinee's level of performance in relation to *each* competency being measured. Each competency is described by a *well-defined behavior domain.*

The definition makes clear that the purpose of a competency test is to measure an individual examinee's level of performance on each tested competency. There will be as many test scores as there are competencies measured by a test. Also, competencies are clearly written so that there will be a high level of agreement among users of the test about the content (behaviors) defining the competency. This desirable goal can be accomplished through the use of "domain specifications" (Popham, 1978a). (This term will be described in more detail later.) There is nothing inherent in the definition of a competency test which requires test scores to be compared to standards. In fact, percentage scores (reported by competency) provide excellent descriptive information about an examinee's performance. Since it is common, however, to interpret an examinee's test performance relative to standards (an examinee who scores equal to or above a standard set at 70 percent, say, on the set of test items included in a competency test is described as a "master" or "competent"), it is necessary to introduce a new term, minimum competency testing.

A minimum competency test is designed to determine whether an examinee has reached *a prespecified level* of performance relative to *each* competency being measured. The prespecified level, or standard, may vary from one competency to the next. Also, each competency is described by a well-defined behavior domain. A standard (sometimes it is called a "cutoff score" or a "minimum proficiency level") is a point on a test score scale which is used to separate examinees into two categories. It is common to assign labels such as "master" or "competent" to those persons in the higher-scoring category and "nonmaster" or "incompetent" to those persons in the lower-scoring category. Note that if a test measures more than a single competency, and if examinees are to be classified as masters or nonmasters based on their performance on each set of items measuring a competency (as is often the case) a standard is set for each competency measured by a test. There will be as many competency decisions as there are competencies measured by a test.

It is important at this point to separate three types of standards. Consider the following statement: school district A has set the following target—it desires to have 85 percent or more of its students in the second grade achieve 90 percent of the reading objectives at a standard of performance equal to or better than 80 percent. Three types of standards are involved in the example: first, the 80 percent standard is used to interpret examinee performance on each of the objectives measured by a test; second, the 90 percent standard is used to interpret examinee performance across all of the objectives measured by a test; and third, the 85 percent standard is applied to the performance of all second-graders on the entire set of objectives measured by a test. Only the first use of standards will be considered in this paper.

From the definitions above, it is clear that minimum competency tests are a special type of competency test (tests where standards are introduced to interpret examinee performance), and as we shall see later, competency tests are a special type of criterion-referenced test (tests which are usually used in certification and licensing situations).

Finally, there is nothing inherent in the definition of competency testing (or minimum competency testing) which precludes the measurement of school skills (for example, arithmetic, spelling, and reading) or life skills (for example, balancing a checkbook, following directions, or answering a job advertisement).

Competency Tests and Criterion-Referenced Tests

Competency testing technology would be in an embryonic stage were it not for work done in developing a criterion-referenced testing technology since the late 1960s. A competency test is simply a particular kind of criterion-referenced test, and therefore, like a criterion-referenced test, it must be developed and used in ways somewhat different from better-known norm-referenced tests. Glaser (1963) and Popham & Husek (1969) introduced the notion of criterion-referenced testing so that test score information of the type needed to make a variety of individual and programmatic decisions would be available. Norm-referenced tests are designed, principally, to provide scores that facilitate the making of comparative statements about individuals. This is not the primary type of information required by those who implement competency testing programs. They require information about levels of individual performance relative to well-defined content domains (referred to as "domain specifications").

Considerable progress has been made during the last ten years toward the establishment of a practical and usable criterion-referenced testing technology. The existence of this technology (see, for example, Hambleton

& Novick, 1973; Hambleton & Eignor, 1978; Hambleton, Swaminathan, Algina, and Coulson, 1978; Millman, 1974; Popham, 1978a) makes possible, among other things, development of criterion-referenced tests for use in diagnosing student learning deficiencies, monitoring student progress, and evaluating school programs. The same basic technology is useful also for development and validation of minimum competency tests for, say, high school graduation, although matters such as the selection of competencies to be tested and approaches to developing and validating tests will be handled somewhat differently.

What is the current stage of development of competency testing technology? There would be considerable agreement among measurement specialists on the statements offered below. First, definitional problems have been sorted out (for example, distinctions among norm-referenced, criterion-referenced, competency-based, domain-referenced, and objectives-referenced tests are clear). Second, the need for "domain specifications" is clear, and adequate methods for developing them do exist. Third, an adequate technology is available for developing and validating competency tests. Fourth, the problem of test-score reliability has been articulated clearly, and approaches now exist for determining reliability of scores for various intended uses. Fifth, methods for using and reporting performances on competency tests are available. The interested reader is referred to Hambleton, Swaminathan, et al. (1978) and to Popham (1978a) for further discussion of the points above.

Of course, there remains a considerable amount of work to be done. Four topics are especially important: improved guidelines for preparing domain specifications; guidelines for evaluating competency tests and test manuals; research on relationships among test length, test score reliability, and test score validity; and further consideration of issues and methods for determining standards, as well as of guidelines for implementing each method.

Steps in Test Development and Validation

A twelve-step model for developing and validating competency tests is presented in figure 1. The importance of each step in the model depends upon the size and scope of the test development and validation project. An agency with the responsibility of producing a competency test for statewide use will proceed through the steps in a rather different way than will a small consulting firm or a school district.

In brief, the twelve steps are as follows:

Step 1—Competencies must be prepared or selected before test development can begin.

Step 2—Test specifications are needed to clarify the test's purposes,

1. Preparation and/or Selection of Competencies
2. Preparation of Test Specifications (for example, Specification of Item Formats, Appropriate Vocabulary, and Number of Test Items/Competency)
3. Writing Test Items "Matched" to Competencies
4. Editing Test Items
5. Determining Content Validity of the Test Items
   a. Involvement of Content Specialists
   b. Collection of Student Response Data
6. Additional Editing of Test Items
7. Test Assembly
   a. Determination of Test Length
   b. Test Item Selection
   c. Preparation of Directions
   d. Layout and Test Booklet Preparation
   e. Preparation of Scoring Keys
   f. Preparation of Answer Sheets
8. Setting Standards for Interpreting Examinee Performance
9. Test Administration
10. Collection of Reliability, Validity, and Norms Information
11. Preparation of a User's Manual and a Technical Manual
12. Periodic Collection of Additional Technical Information

Figure 1. Steps for Developing and Validating Competency Tests

desirable item formats, number of test items, instructions to item writers, and so on.

Step 3—Items are prepared to measure competencies included in the test (or tests, if there are going to be parallel forms, or levels of a test varying in difficulty).

Step 4—Initial editing of items is completed by the individuals writing them.

Step 5—A systematic assessment of items prepared in steps 3 and 4 is conducted to determine item validities. Essentially, the task is to determine the content validity of the test items.

Step 6—Based on the data from step 5, it is possible to do further item editing, and in some instances, discard items that do not adequately measure the competencies they were written to measure.

Step 7—The test (or tests) must be assembled.

Step 8—A method for setting standards to interpret examinee performance is selected and implemented.

Step 9—The test (or tests) must be administered.

Step 10—Data addressing reliability, validity, and norms should be collected and analyzed.

Step 11—A user's manual and a technical manual should be prepared.

Step 12—This step is included to emphasize the point that it is necessary continually to compile technical data on the test items and tests as they are used in different situations with different examinee populations.

Whether a competency test or a minimum competency test is being developed, steps one through six will be the same. At step seven, it is possible (although not essential) that different methods be used to select test items. Step eight is unique to minimum competency testing. Remaining steps in the model are essentially the same for the two types of tests. About the only differences concern approaches to validating test scores; since the two types of tests are intended to accomplish different purposes, approaches for validating test scores will, in general, be different.

Four of the steps (1, 3, 5, and 7) in developing a competency test will be discussed next. Useful references that present an expanded discussion of the other steps are Hambleton and Eignor (1978); Hambleton, Swaminathan, Algina, and Coulson (1978); Millman (1974); and Popham (1978a).

1. Statement of Competencies

It is popular to write competencies in "behavioral terms." However, although behavioral statements have some desirable features (for example, they are relatively easy to produce), they often lack the clarity necessary to permit unequivocal determination of the domain of test items measuring the behaviors defined by such a competency. If the proper domain of test items measuring a competency is not clear, the task of preparing valid test items is more difficult. Also, it is impossible to select a representative sample of test items from a domain that is not clearly specified. Since it is often desired to interpret examinee performance on a sample of test items measuring a particular competency as an estimate of that examinee's level of performance on the larger domain of items, it is essential to have the domain specified clearly and to choose a representative sample of test items.

Domain specifications are an important new development in competency testing (Popham, 1978a). Domain specifications clarify the intended content specified by a competency. Such information is invaluable to teachers (they must teach the competencies defined by the domain specifications), to parents (they often wish to have information about the competencies), and to item writers (they must produce "valid" test items; that is, test items that are representative of the domain of items measuring each competency).

There are at least four steps outlined by Popham for the development of domain specifications. The first involves the preparation of a general description, which could be a behavioral objective, a detailed description of the competency, or a short cryptic descriptor. Next, a sample test item is prepared. This will help to clarify the domain of test items and to specify item format. The third step is perhaps the most difficult. It is necessary to indicate the content included in the domain. In the final step, characteristics of response alternatives or response limits are specified. An example of a domain specification is shown in figure 2.

The important result of implementing the steps is that they lead to specified item domains; it is not necessary, however, that homogeneous content domains be produced. Specificity and homogeneity are different concepts. Millman (1974) makes this point, "The domain being referenced by a [criterion]-referenced test may be extensive or a single, narrow objective, but it must be well defined, which means that content and format limits must be well specified" (p. 314).

3. Generation of Test Items

Once domain specifications are defined, the test constructor must generate test items. If the domains were defined with absolute precision, the items themselves would not have to be generated. The items would simply be a logical consequence of the domain definitions (for example, see Hively, Patterson, & Page, 1968). Unfortunately, such precision will seldom be achieved in practice, so test items must be produced, and procedures like those described in step five must be used to check the adequacy of the test items.

Principles of item writing used in constructing norm-referenced achievement tests apply to competency tests as well. However, it is necessary that item writers attend closely to the domain specifications. Test items should be written to "tap" behaviors in the domain of behaviors defined by the domain specifications. After editing the test items, the next step is examining item validities.

5. Determination of Content Validity

Generally speaking, the quality of competency test items can be determined by the extent to which they reflect, in terms of their content, the domains from which they were derived. The problem here is one of item validation; unless one can say with a high degree of confidence that the items in a competency test measure the intended competencies, any interpretation of the test scores is questionable. When domain specifications are used, the domain definition is never really precise enough to assume, a priori, that the items are valid. Thus the validity of the items must be

SKILL: The student will identify the tone or emotion expressed in a paragraph.

SAMPLE ITEM:

Directions: Read the paragraph. Underline the best word to complete the sentence.

Jimmy had been playing at the beach all day. It was time to go home. Jimmy sat down in the back seat of the car. He could hardly keep his eyes open.

Jimmy felt _____ .

A. afraid   B. friendly   C. tired   D. kind

CONTENT:

1. The paragraph will contain situations which are familiar to the students being tested.
2. The paragraph will contain no less than three and no more than six sentences. The readability level will be no higher than Second Reader.
3. The tones or emotions expressed will be from the following list:

sad	mad	angry
tired	scared	friendly
happy	lucky	smart
kind	excited	proud

RESPONSE MODE:

1. Responses will be one word in length.
2. The items will contain one correct and three incorrect responses.
3. Distractors are to be words describing a feeling and may be taken from the list above.
4. Avoid using reasonable answers as distractors. (i.e., in the sample item, "mad" would not be a good choice for a distractor. Jimmy could feel mad about leaving the beach.)

Figure 2. An Example of a Domain Specification from the Reading Area
(The authors are grateful to Marlene Teichert for the example.)

determined in a context independent from the process by which the items were generated. This is an a posteriori approach to item validation. Some procedures have been designed to assess whether a direct relationship between an item and a domain or objective exists, through analysis of data collected after the item is written (Hambleton & Eignor, 1978; Hambleton & Fitzpatrick, in preparation; Popham, 1978a).

There are two approaches which may be used to establish the (content) validity of test items. The first approach (the approach we feel holds the most merit) involves the judgment of test items by content specialists. The judgments concern the extent of "match" between the test items and the domain they are designed to measure. Questions asked of content specialists about content validity of test items can be reduced to these two important ones: Is the format and content of an item appropriate to measure some part of the domain specification? Does the available set of test items adequately sample a particular domain?

A second approach to analyzing content validity makes use of empirical techniques to examine performance data in much the same way empirical techniques are applied in norm-referenced test development. In fact, several norm-referenced test item statistics can (and should) be used together with some recently developed empirical procedures for competency tests. The problem is to ensure that these statistics are used and interpreted correctly in the context of competency test development. Item statistics should be used to detect aberrant items that need to be reworked, but not to make final decisions about which items are to be included in a competency test. An excellent review of item statistics for use with competency tests has been prepared by Berk (1978).

7. Test Assembly

The length of a competency test (or more important, the number of test items measuring each competency in a test) is directly related to the usefulness of the scores obtained. Short tests typically produce imprecise competency score estimates and lead to competency decisions which prove to be inconsistent across parallel-form administrations (or retest administrations). (An examinee's competency score is the proportion of items in the pool of items defined by a domain specification that the examinee can answer correctly. A competency score estimate is obtained by administering a sample of items to the examinee and calculating his/her proportion-correct score.)

Two factors should be considered in determining the number of test items to measure a competency: (1) the relationship between the number of test items and the importance placed upon the particular competency, and (2) the relationship between the number of test items and the minimum acceptable level of test score reliability.

Consider factor one. Some competencies may be more important than others in relation to the goals of the competency testing program. If the test developer desires that the test measure several competencies, he/she should plan, when drawing samples of items from each domain of items "keyed" to a competency, to sample more thoroughly the most important competencies.

Guidelines are not readily available to assist in coping with factor two, the relationship of the number of test items to minimum reliability requirements. The Spearman-Brown formula, which relates test length to reliability, is reasonable to use only with norm-referenced tests. Similar relationships need to be developed for competency tests. The following procedure should be helpful to those attempting to determine a test length appropriate for competency score estimation. The solution is a conservative one; test lengths determined by this method will be a little greater than they need to be to obtain the degree of precision required by the test developer. The formula[1] is:

$$\text{Test Length} = \frac{.25}{(\text{degree of precision})^2}$$

Ask yourself (or interested others): What degree of precision is required of the competency score estimates? For example, if you required the competency estimate to be within .15 of the true value with 67 percent confidence (degree of precision $= .15$), the needed test length would be $\frac{.25}{(.15)^2} \cong 11$ items.

At present we are working on tables relating test length to reliability when a test is used for making decisions about the competence/incompetence of examinees. The research is just beginning; thus, we are unable to report any results at this time. However, two points can be made. First, it is unlikely that fewer than five or six items measuring a competency will produce acceptable levels of reliability unless the competency is narrowly defined. Second, while no tables or formulas exist to connect test length to reliability (or consistency) of decision making, reliability can be studied empirically following the administration of a pool of test items to a group of examinees (step 5b). "Post-hoc" test forms of varying lengths can be constructed, and reliability estimates may then be calculated, based on the assumption that examinees would have responded in the same way had they been presented with the "parallel forms" rather than a single large pool of test items. By varying the length of the forms and the formation of parallel forms (that is, which items are placed in which forms), the relationship between test length and reliability for a specified sample of examinees and a pool of test items measuring a particular domain specification can be studied.

The item-selection process is straightforward, provided the competency test developer has been careful in defining competencies and in constructing test items. That is, the test developer must have defined the size of his/her domains so as to be consonant with the test's purpose. If the purpose of testing is to make decisions on, for instance, broad school competencies, large domain sizes can be tolerated. If, however, the purpose of testing is to indicate areas for remedial instruction, a smaller domain size is needed. Popham (1978a) has offered some suggestions for ascertaining domain size. The critical point for item selection is that the domain be of reasonable size, so that proper sampling from the domain can occur. If the domain is so large that it is difficult to see how to generate a set of items from the domain, then the domain must be divided into subdomains and items must be generated for each of the subdomains. The sampling process should be clear for each subdomain. Thus, it is critical that the domain be sized so that a set of items can be clearly constructed from it. If so, the sampling process can be carried out without complications.

Having defined a domain size that is manageable for sampling is not enough; the test developer must also be careful to ascertain that all the items constructed for the domain do indeed "tap" the behavior specified. The items must adhere to the restrictions imposed on the domain specifications.

If the size of the domain is manageable and the test developer is sure that the items generated "tap" the specified behaviors, then the item selection process is straightforward. The test can be constructed by taking either a random or stratified random sample of items from the domain.

One advantage of choosing representative sets of test items is that examinees' test scores (or proportion-correct scores) provide "unbiased" estimates of their "true" competency scores. It is possible also to set standards and interpret test performance in relation to those standards. Unfortunately, when the number of test items is small (as is frequently the case), the consistency of decisions (competent/incompetent) across a retest administration or across a parallel-form administration of a test may be distressingly low. Increasing the number of test items measuring each competency is helpful, but it is not often feasible to do so. One answer to the dilemma is: When the primary purpose of the testing program is to make dichotomous decisions about examinees, a better test can be produced if test items are selected from the validated pool of items measuring each competency on the basis of their statistical properties. For example, if a competency standard is set at 80 percent correct, it would be best to select test items which have p-values (item difficulty levels) in the region of .80 *and* which have the highest discrimination indices. A test constructed in this way will have maximum discriminating power in the region where decisions are being made; therefore more reliable and valid decisions will result. One possible drawback is that scores derived from the test cannot be used to make descriptive statements about examinees' levels of performance on the competencies measured by the test. This is because test items measuring each competency will not necessarily constitute a representative sample. In theory, there is at least one way to make descriptive statements about examinees' levels of performance on the competencies measured by a test when nonrandom or nonrepresentative samples of test items are chosen. It can be done by introducing concepts and models from the field of latent trait theory. However, the feasibility of such an approach has not been tested.

Methods of Standard Setting

Numerous researchers have catalogued many of the available standard-setting methods (Glass, 1978a; Hambleton & Eignor, 1978; Hambleton, Swaminathan, et al., 1978; Jaeger, 1976; Meskauskas, 1976; Millman, 1973; Popham, 1978b; Shepard, 1976). If one fact is clear it is that all standard-setting methods are arbitrary. This point has been acknowledged by nearly every contributor to the area. All of the methods are arbitrary because they involve judgments of one kind or another (for example, raters may be asked to identify test items which a minimally competent examinee should be able to answer) and because selections (for example, selection of a standard-setting method) must be made. But the "arbitrariness" of standard-setting methods is not a satisfactory reason for rejecting the methods. A quote from Popham (1978a) is especially appropriate here:

Unable to avoid reliance on human judgment as the chief ingredient in standard-setting, some individuals have thrown up their hands in dismay and cast aside all efforts to set performance standards as *arbitrary*, hence unacceptable.

But *Webster's Dictionary* offers us two definitions of arbitrary. The first of these is positive, describing arbitrary as an adjective reflecting choice or discretion, that is, "determinable by a judge or tribunal." The second definition, pejorative in nature, describes arbitrary as an adjective denoting capriciousness, that is, "selected at random and without reason." In my estimate, when people start knocking the standard-setting game as arbitrary, they are clearly employing Webster's second, negatively loaded definition.

But the first definition is more accurately reflective of serious standard-setting efforts. They represent genuine attempts to do a good job in deciding what kinds of standards we ought to employ. That they are judgmental is inescapable. But to malign all judgmental operations as capricious is absurd. (p. 168)

In a recent review of the standard-setting literature, Hambleton and Eignor (1978) discussed six different sets of methods for setting standards. This review was an expansion of some earlier work by Millman (1973) and Meskauskas (1976). Rather than expanding that review merely by adding some standard-setting methods that have appeared in the literature more recently (such as Jaeger, 1978; Zieky & Livingston, 1977), we will restrict our attention to methods that appear to be useful for setting standards in minimum competency testing programs. Those methods that appear to us to be applicable will be discussed in some detail. Also, a number of comparisons will be made in this "sifting out" of relevant methods, the first being the useful distinction made by Meskauskas (1976) between continuum and state models.

Continuum and State Models

The basic difference between continuum and state models has to do with the underlying assumption made about ability. According to Meskauskas, two characteristics of continuum models are: First, mastery is viewed as a continuously distributed ability or set of abilities. Second, an area is identified at the upper end of this continuum, and if an individual equals or exceeds the lower bound of this area, he/she is termed a master.

State models, rather than being based on a continuum of mastery, view mastery as an all-or-none proposition—either you can do something or you cannot. Three characteristics of state models are: test true-score performance is viewed as an all-or-nothing state; the true-score standard is set at 100 percent; and after a consideration of measurement errors, observed-score standards are often set at values less than 100 percent.

There are at least three methods for setting standards that are built on a state-model conceptualization of mastery. The models take into account measurement error, deficiencies of the examination, and other discrepancies in "tempering" the standard from 100 percent. These methods have been referred to by Glass (1978a), in his review of methods for setting standards, as "counting backwards from 100%." State model methods advanced to date include the mastery-testing evaluation model of Emrick (1971), the true-score model of Roudabush (1974), and some recently advanced statistical models of Macready and Dayton (1977). Since state models are somewhat less useful than continuum models in elementary and secondary school minimum competency testing programs, they will not be considered further in this paper. Our failure to consider them here should not be interpreted as a criticism of this general approach to standard setting. It appears to be especially appropriate for many performance tests.

Traditional and Normative Models

Before discussing the various continuum models of standard setting, two other models will be mentioned. These methods, which seem to have limited value in setting minimum competency standards, have been referred to by a variety of names. We will call them "traditional standards" and "normative standards."

Traditional standards are standards that have gained acceptance because of their frequent use. Classroom examples include the decision that 90 to 100 percent is an A, 80 to 89 percent is a B, and so on. It appears that such methods have been used occasionally in setting standards for minimum competency tests.

"Normative" standards refer to any of three different uses of normative data, two of which are, at best, questionable. In the first method, use is made of the normative performance of some external "criterion" group. As an example, Jaeger (1978) cites the use of the Adult Performance Level (APL) tests by Palm Beach County, Florida, schools. Test performances of groups of "successful" adults were used to set competency standards for high school students. Such a procedure can be criticized on a number of grounds. Jaeger (1978) points out that society changes, and that standards should also change. Standards based on adult performance may not be relevant to high school students. Shepard (1976) points out that any normatively determined standard will immediately yield many counter-examples. Further, Burton (1978) suggests that relationships between skills in school subjects and later success in life are not readily determinable; hence, observing the test performance of some "successful" norm group makes little sense. Jaeger (1978) goes on to say: "There are no empirically tenable 'survival' standards on school-based skills that can be justified through external means."

A second way of proceeding with normative data is to set a standard based solely on the distribution of test scores. Such a procedure circumvents the "minimum test score for success in life" problem, but it is still not useful for setting standards. For example, Glass (1978a) cites the California High School Proficiency Examination, for which the 50th percentile of graduating seniors served as the standard. What can be said of a minimum competency testing procedure that passes or fails an individual, depending upon the performance of other individuals taking the test? In California, the standard was set with no reference at all to the content of the test or the difficulty of the items.

The third use of normative data discussed in the literature concerns the supplemental use of normative data in setting a standard. Shepard (1976), Jaeger (1978), and Conaway (1976, 1977) all favor such a procedure. Recently Jaeger (1978) advanced a standard-setting method which requires judges to make competency judgments partially on the basis of item content. In his method, Jaeger calls for incorporation of some tryout test data to aid judges in reconsidering their initial assessments. Shepard (1976) makes the point that:

Expert judges ought to be provided with normative data in their deliberations. Instead of relying on their experience, which may have been with unusual students or professionals, experts ought to have access to representative norms . . . of course, the norms are not automically the standards. Experts still have to decide what "ought" to be, but they can establish more reasonable expectations if they know what current performance is than if they deliberate in a vacuum. (p. 30)

We agree with Jaeger, Conaway, and Shepard about the usefulness of normative data when used in conjunction with a viable standard-setting method.

Consideration of Several Promising Standard-Setting Methods

Other methods for setting standards to be discussed in this paper are built either on a continuum model of ability or on some other, unexpressed model. For convenience, the methods under discussion were organized into three categories or "models." These models and methods are presented in figure 3. The models were labeled "judgmental," "empirical," and "combination." In judgmental methods, data for setting standards are collected from judges, or a judgment is made about the presence or lack of a variable (for instance, guessing) that would affect the standard. Empirical methods require the collection of examinee-response data to aid in standard setting.

Empirical Methods

A number of empirical methods require a criterion measure, performance measure, or true-ability continuum. Livingston (1975) presented a procedure that incorporates linear or semilinear utility functions. He uses these functions in viewing the effects of decision-making accuracy, based upon a particular performance standard. Livingston (1976) presented a method for choosing standards by stochastic approximation techniques. Once again, the procedure depends upon a performance measure, and for this method, a standard is first set on that measure. Huynh (1976) also bases a standard-setting method for competency tests on an external criterion. Finally, the work of Van der Linden and Mellenbergh (1977) depends upon the existence of a latent ability variable that can be dichotomized into two categories, labeled "competent" and "incompetent." The standard is then set by using a risk or expected-loss function.

These methods have only been mentioned briefly because all are

Judgmental Models	Combination Models		Empirical Models[1]	
Item Content	Judgmental-Empirical	Educational Consequences	Data—Two Groups	Data-Criterion Measure
Nedelsky (1954)	Contrasting Groups (Zieky & Livingston, 1977)	Block (1972)	Berk (1976)	Livingston (1975)
Modified Nedelsky (Nassif, 1978)	Borderline Groups (Zieky & Livingston, 1977)			Livingston (1976)
Angoff (1971)				Huynh (1976)
Modified Angoff (ETS, 1976)				Van der Linden & Mellenbergh (1977)
Ebel (1972)	Bayesian Methods			
Jaeger (1978)	Hambleton & Novick (1973)		Decision-Theoretic[2]	
	Novick, Lewis, & Jackson (1973)		Kriewall (1972)	
Guessing	Schoon, Gullion, & Ferrara (1978)			
Millman (1973)				

[1]Involve the use of examinee-response data.

[2]In addition, there are a number of decision-theoretic models that deal with test length considerations. These are also applicable to cutoff score determination (see, for example, Millman, 1974).

Figure 3. A Classification of Models and Methods for Setting Standards

difficult to apply in practice; they require a criterion variable upon which success and failure (or probability of success and failure) can be defined. It would be difficult to gain agreement on external criterion variables which would be appropriate for validating high school certification tests. Such variables would probably be even more difficult to measure. For example, how would one go about defining "life success" and measuring it? Reading experts, for instance, are not going to have the same idea about what a minimally competent person can read. Should he/she be able to read at the 12th-grade level, or the 8th-grade level? Jaeger (1978) has noted, "Educators would no sooner agree on the proportion of *New York Times* front page passages eleventh-graders should be able to comprehend and explain, than they would the proportion of multiple-choice test items those eleventh-graders should answer correctly, so as to be labeled "minimally competent." Thus, the gist of this reasoning is that if agreement cannot first be reached on the criterion measure, then this will not aid in setting standards on the test. One may therefore want to go ahead and try to set the standards on the test without considering criterion measures. Such a recommendation seems especially relevant for promotion and high school certification examinations.

One example of a decision-theoretic procedure was developed by Kriewall (1972). This procedure is based upon the definition of (usually) two mastery states. The standard is then selected as the point that minimizes "false-positive" and "false-negative" errors in classifying individuals into the defined mastery states. Once again, the problem with this method is evident. The mastery categories "competent" and "incompetent" are essentially undefined. Until people can agree on a definition of "competence" in a given situation, it is not possible to use the method. One cannot minimize errors of prediction if the categories to be predicted cannot be established. Jaeger (1978) has noted that many of the methods allow different utilities to be associated with false-positive and false-negative errors, in this case passing the "minimally incompetent" person or failing the "minimally competent" person. However, there are no guidelines for establishing these utility values, so another problem exists with the methods.

Berk (1976) presented a method that is very similar to the decision-theoretic methods just discussed. Rather than setting the mastery states arbitrarily and observing the probabilities of false-positive and false-negative errors on the criterion, Berk suggests the optimal standard be based on response data from samples of instructed and uninstructed students. Berk offers a number of procedures to be used in conjunction with his method. We feel that the procedure holds great merit for classroom instructional settings, and we devoted a great deal of space to it in our recent review (Hambleton & Eignor, 1978). The problem involved with using the procedure for setting standards on minimum competency tests is that there is no simple way of establishing whether groups of students were or were not instructed on the competencies included in the test. Other extreme groups might be formed (for example, "successful" adults and "unsuccessful" adults), and their performances on the test might be compared for the purpose of setting a standard. Clearly though, results from such comparisons can be explained in numerous ways, and therefore they have limited practical value.

Block (1972) introduced a method referred to as "educational consequences." In this method one looks at the effect that setting a proficiency standard has on future learning or on other related cognitive or affective success criteria. Block conducted an experimental study to consider the effect of different standards on several outcome measures. That standard for which the valued outcome is maximized (it could be a combination of valued outcomes) becomes the standard when the test is next used. Glass (1978a) likened this approach to a general objective of operations research; the concern is for maximizing a valued commodity by finding an optimum point on a mathematical curve. To locate a maximum, Glass has pointed out the need for non-monotonic curves that relate performances to valued outcomes, which are not likely. Glass also talks about the problem of how to weight individual outcomes to form a composite outcome. There is yet another problem, perhaps even more serious than the non-monotonicity problem. One cannot maximize a valued outcome if the outcome cannot be defined in any reasonable manner. In sum, to utilize Block's method, there would have to be agreement on what is a valued outcome of being competent. This would seem to be as difficult as trying to get people to define behaviors associated with minimum competency.

Finally, Millman (1973) has suggested that standards be adjusted for the effects of guessing. A systematic error is introduced when an item format allows a student to increase his/her score by guessing. Millman suggests raising the standard to take into account the expected contribution attributed to pure guessing. Educational Testing Service has corrected the standards on the National Teacher Examinations (NTE) to take care of guessing. The problem here is that on minimum competency tests, we expect that purely random guessing rarely occurs. Because of this, the effects of raising standards, as though it had, is unknown. Clearly, more work in this area is needed.

Bayesian methods will not be discussed, because they allow standard setters to augment the setting of standards with prior information and/or group information on the examinees. Bayesian methods also provide a statement of the probability that an examinee's true level of competency exceeds the standard. To use Bayesian methods, however, a standard must first exist. Any one of the methods to be discussed next could be used to set the standard.

Judgmental Models

What follows is a brief discussion of several judgmental methods. Comments, comparisons, and recommendations for use will also be offered. Table 1 provides a summary of some of the similarities and differences among the methods.

Nedelsky's Method

In Nedelsky's method, judges are asked to view each item in a test with a particular criterion in mind. The criterion for each item is: Which of the response options should the minimally competent student be able to eliminate as incorrect? The minimun passing level (MPL) for that item then becomes the reciprocal of the remaining alternatives. For instance, if on a five-alternative multiple choice item, a judge feels that a minimally competent person could eliminate two of the options, then for that item, MPL = ⅓. The judges proceed with each item in a like fashion, and upon completion of the judging process, sum the MPL values for each item to obtain a standard on the total set of test items. Next, the individual judge's standards are averaged. The average is denoted $\hat{\pi}_o$.

Nedelsky felt that if one were to compute the standard deviation of individual judge's standards, this distribution would be synonymous with the (hypothesized or theoretical) distribution of the scores of the borderline students. This standard deviation, σ, could then be multiplied by a constant K (decided upon by the test users) to regulate how many (as a percent) of the borderline students pass or fail. The final formula then becomes:

$$\hat{\hat{\pi}}_o = \hat{\pi}_o + K\sigma.$$

How does the K σ term work? Assuming an underlying normal distribution, if one sets K=1, then 84 percent of the borderline examinees will fail. If K=2, then 98 percent of these examinees will fail. If K=0, then 50 percent of the examinees on the borderline should fail. The value for K is set prior to the examination by, say, a committee.

The final result of the application of Nedelsky's method will be an absolute standard. This is because the standard is arrived at without consideration of the score distributions of any reference group. In fact, the standard is arrived at prior to using the test with the group one is concerned about testing. However, while the standard can be called absolute, there is a great deal of judgment involved in applying the method.

Table 1. A Comparison of Several Standard-Setting Methods

Question	Judgmental						Combination	
	Nedelsky	Modified Nedelsky	Angoff	Modified Angoff	Ebel	Jaeger	Contrasting Groups	Borderline Group
1. Is a definition of the minimally competent individual necessary?	Yes	Yes	Yes	Yes	Yes	No	No	Yes
2. What is the nature of the rating task—items or individuals?	Items	Items	Items	Items	Items	Items	Individuals	Individuals
3. Are examinee data needed?	No	No	No	No	No	No	Yes	Yes
4. Do judges have access to the items?	Yes	Yes	Yes	Yes	Yes	Yes	Usually, but don't need to	Usually
5. Are the judgments made in a group setting or an individual setting?	Both	Both	Both	Both	Both	Both	Individual	Individual

Modified Nedelsky

Nassif (1978), in setting standards for the competency-based teachers' education and licensing systems in Georgia, utilized a modified Nedelsky procedure. A modification of the Nedelsky method was needed to handle the volume of items in the program. In the modified Nedelsky task, the entire item (rather than each distractor) is classified in terms of two levels of examinee competence. The following question was asked about each item: "Should a person with minimum competence in the teaching field be able to answer this item correctly?" Possible answers were "yes," "no," and "I don't know." Agreement among judges can be studied through a simple comparison of the ratings judges give to each item. A standard may be obtained by computing the average number of "yes" responses judges give to the entire set of test items.

Ebel's Method

Ebel (1972) arrives at a standard in a somewhat different manner, but his procedure is also based upon the test items rather than an "outside" distribution of scores. Judges are asked to rate items along two dimensions: relevance and difficulty. Ebel uses four categories of relevance: essential, important, acceptable, and questionable. He uses three difficulty levels: easy, medium, and hard. These categories then form (in this case) a 3 x 4 table. The judges are next asked to do two things. First, they locate each of the test items in the proper cell in the table, based upon relevance and difficulty. Second, they assign a percentage to each cell, that percentage being the percentage of items in the cell that the minimally qualified examinee should be able to answer. Then the number of items in each cell is multiplied by the appropriate percentage (agreed upon by the judges). The sum of all the cells, when divided by the total number of items, yields the standard.

Three comments about Ebel's method should be sufficient to suggest caution when using it. One, Ebel offers no prescription for the number or type of categories to be used along the two dimensions. This is left to the judgment of the individuals judging the items. It is likely that a different set of categories applied to the same test would yield a different standard. Two, the process is based upon the decisions of judges; while the standard could be called absolute (in that it is not referenced to a score distribution), it cannot be called "objective." A third point about Ebel's method has been offered by Meskauskas (1976):

In Ebel's method, the judge must simulate the decision process of the examinee to obtain an accurate judgment and thus set an appropriate standard. Since the judge is more knowledgeable than the minimally-qualified individual, and since he is not forced to make a decision about each of the alternatives, it seems likely that the judge would tend to systematically over-simplify the examinee's task. . . . Even if this occurs only occasionally, it appears likely that, in contrast to the Nedelsky method, the Ebel method would allow the raters to ignore some of the fine discriminations that an examinee needs to make and would result in a standard that is more difficult to reach. (p. 138)

Angoff's Method

When using Angoff's technique, judges are asked to assign a probability to each test item directly, thus circumventing the analysis of a grid or the analysis of response alternatives. Angoff (1971) states:

. . . ask each judge to state the *probability* that the "minimally acceptable person" would answer each item correctly. In effect, the judges would think of a number of minimally acceptable persons, instead of only one such person, and would estimate the proportion of minimally acceptable persons who would answer each item correctly. The sum of these probabilities, or proportions, would then represent the minimally acceptable score. (p. 515)

Modified Angoff

Educational Testing Service (ETS, 1976) modified Angoff's method for setting standards. Believing that probability estimation may be overly difficult for the items on the National Teacher Exams, ETS instead supplied a seven-point scale on which certain percentages were fixed. Judges were asked to estimate the percentage of minimally knowledgeable examinees who would know the answer to each test item on the following scale: 5, 20, 40, 60, 75, 90, 95, DNK. ("DNK" stands for "do not know.")

ETS has also used scales with the points fixed at somewhat different values; the scales are consistent, though, in that seven percentage choices are given.

Jaeger's Method

Jaeger (1978) recently presented a method for standard setting on the North Carolina High School Competency Test. Jaeger's method incorporates a number of suggestions made by Stoker, Jaeger, Shepard, Conaway, and Haladyna at a 1976 National Council on Measurement in Education annual meeting symposium in San Francisco. The method is iterative, uses judges from a variety of backgrounds, and employs normative data. Further, rather than asking a question involving "minimal competence," a term which is hard to conceptualize and implement, Jaeger's questions are instead: "Should every high school graduate be able to answer this item correctly?____Yes, ____No"; and "If a student *does not* answer this item correctly, should he/she be denied a high school diploma?

_____Yes, _____No." After a series of iterative processes involving judgments from experts in various areas, and after the presentation of some normative data, standards determined by all experts in the same area are pooled, and a median is computed for each type of expert. The minimum median across all groups is selected as the standard.

Comparisons among Judgmental Models

We are aware of two studies that compare judgmental methods of setting standards; one study was done in 1976, the other is presently underway at ETS.

In 1976, Andrew and Hecht carried out an empirical comparison of the Nedelsky and Ebel methods. In that study, judges met on two separate occasions to set standards for a 180-item, four-options-per-item exam to certify professional workers. On one occasion the Nedelsky method was used. On a second occasion the Ebel method was used. The percentage of test items that should be answered correctly by a minimally competent examinee was set at 69 percent by the Ebel method and at 46 percent by the Nedelsky method. Glass (1978a) described the observed difference as a "startling finding." Our own view is that since directions to the judges were different, and since procedures differed, the results from using these two methods would likely differ as well. The authors themselves report: "It is perhaps not surprising that two procedures . . . would result in different examination standards. Such examination standards will always be subjective to some extent and will involve different philosophical assumptions and varying conceptualizations" (p. 49). Ebel (1972) makes a similar point: "It is clear that a variety of approaches can be used to solve the problem of defining the passing score. Unfortunately, different approaches are likely to give different results" (p. 496).

Possibly the most important result of the Andrew-Hecht study (this result was not reported in the Glass paper) was the high level of agreement in the determination of a standard using the same method across two teams of judges. The difference was not more than 3.4 percent within each method. Data of this kind address a concern raised by Glass (1978a) about whether judges can make determinations of standards consistently and reliably. At least in this one study, it appears that they could. From our interactions with ETS staff who conduct teacher workshops on setting standards, we have learned that teams of teachers working with a common method obtain results that are quite similar. And this result holds across tests in different subject matter areas and at different grade levels. We have observed the same result in our own work. Of course, certain conditions must be established if high agreement among judges is to be obtained.

Donald Rock at ETS is presently pursuing research on the use of the

Nedelsky and Angoff methods for standard setting on Real Estate Certification Examinations. His results which have not been released, should clarify the comparability of the two judgmental procedures used most frequently to date.

Combination Models

Two very attractive methods, which we will refer to as combination methods, will be considered next. They were first proposed by Zieky and Livingston (1977). In these methods, judges are asked to make judgments of the mastery levels of students, rather than judgments about test items. Teachers would be the most reasonable choice to serve as judges, since the judgments concern a student's mastery level in the area being tested. Judges must identify students as "adequate," "inadequate," or "borderline." The task of imagining a minimally competent student or group of students is thus circumvented, and for this reason alone, these methods are in favor. Readers interested in a more thorough discussion of the two methods, along with helpful hints for applying them, should refer to Zieky and Livingston (1977) and to Popham (1978b).

Borderline-Group Method

Once teachers have identified a group of students whose achievement is judged to be borderline in the area being tested, the test is administered and the median test score for this group becomes an estimate of the standard.

Contrasting-Groups Method

Once teachers are certain that they have identified students who are masters or nonmasters of the skills being measured, the test is given, and score distributions are plotted for each group. The point of intersection of the score distributions becomes the first estimate of the standard. This can then be adjusted up or down to obtain the required balance between "false-positive" and "false-negative" errors.

The contrasting-groups method is very similar to a method offered independently by Berk (1976). Berk assumes that the students being assessed are masters or nonmasters on the basis of whether or not they have been instructed on the content measured by the test. In contrast, Zieky and Livingston ask teachers to judge the students on the skills measured by the test. The major point is that procedures offered by Berk for analysis of the data (a validity coefficient, utility analysis) are also applicable to the contrasting-groups method.

Some Final Remarks

Our review of the literature identified a variety of methods for setting standards. However, when one tries to apply these methods to minimum competency tests, problems arise. The empirical methods require an external criterion measure which often is very difficult to obtain. When external criterion measures can be obtained, methods proposed by Livingston (1975, 1976), Huynh (1976), Van der Linden and Mellenbergh (1977), Kriewall (1972), and Berk (1976) will be very useful. At present, the best methods for setting standards on elementary and secondary school minimum competency tests are those that deal directly with the test. These methods do require judgments, and therefore they lead to arbitrary standards. Given the state of affairs in standard setting, we can only suggest that any method be used carefully, and that the expressed concerns and recommendations of researchers on this topic (for example, Conaway, 1976, 1977; Glass, 1978a, 1978b; Haladyna, 1976; Jaeger, 1976; Shepard, 1976) be carefully considered.

Suggestions for Future Research and Development

We have so far introduced a model for developing and validating competency tests and considered several methods of setting standards. In this final section our suggestions are organized around these two major topics.

Competency Test Development and Validation

First, technical guidelines are needed for the evaluation of competency tests and test manuals. The AERA/APA/NCME *Test Standards* have some value for this purpose, but are incomplete. What relevant material there is in the *Test Standards* is scattered throughout a 75-page document.

Second, usable guidelines for determining test lengths (number of test items per competency) are needed. There are several technical contributions on the problem in the literature, but these are rather complex mathematically and therefore not readily usable by practitioners.

Third, more needs to be learned about the development and validation of performance tests, since many of the competencies being discussed by designers of competency testing programs can be measured best by performance tests.

Fourth, considerable attention should be given to the development of guidelines for writing domain specifications. Also, their use in developing competency tests and in facilitating proper test score interpretations should be evaluated. Finally, the merits of domain specifications in comparison with other approaches for describing item pools (for example, algorithmic transformation of sentences from written instruction into test items, facet designs, and others) should be considered.

Fifth, latent-trait models are being used in the development of some norm-referenced tests and in the interpretation of norm-referenced test scores. The models appear to have potential for use with competency tests as well. Equating scores from one form of a competency test to another is one of the more promising applications. Clearly, more research on the feasibility of using latent-trait models with competency tests is called for.

Standard-Setting Methods

First, there is a need for considerably more work on both the moral and technical issues involved in standard setting. Second, there needs to be considerably more study of the term, "minimally competent," because if the term is better understood, it may be possible to link existing standard-setting methods to the intended meaning or meanings of the term, thereby greatly facilitating the selection of a standard-setting method (or the development of new methods). Third, for "acceptable" standard-setting methods, implementation strategies need to be developed, evaluated, and made ready for wide use. At present there are few guidelines or procedural steps available for applying any of the standard-setting methods. (An exception to this is the excellent work by Popham [1978b] and Zieky and Livingston [1977].)

The purposes of competency testing programs can only be accomplished if quality competency tests are constructed and if scores derived from the tests are interpreted and used correctly. We hope our paper will facilitate the accomplishment of both objectives.

Note

1. This formula can be derived from the binomial test model.

References

Andrew, B. J., & Hecht, J. T. A preliminary investigation of two procedures for setting examination standards. *Educational and Psychological Measurement* 36 (1976): 45-50.

Angoff, W. H. Scales, norms, and equivalent scores. In R. L. Thorndike (ed.), *Educational measurement*. Washington, D.C.: American Council on Education, 1971.

Berk, R. A. Determination of optimal cutting scores in criterion-referenced measurement. *Journal of Experimental Education* 45 (1976): 4-9.

— — —. Criterion-referenced test item analysis and validation. Paper presented at the First Annual Johns Hopkins University National Symposium on Educational Research, Washington, D.C., 1978.

Block, J. H. Student learning and the setting of mastery performance standards. *Educational Horizons* 50 (1972): 183-190.

Brickell, H. M. Seven key notes on minimum competency testing. *Phi Delta Kappan* 59 (1978): 589-592.

Burton, N. Societal standards. *Journal of Educational Measurement* 15 (1978): 263-271.

Conaway, L. E. Discussant comments: setting performance standards based on limited research. *Florida Journal of Educational Research* 18 (1976): 35-36.

———. Setting standards in competency-based education: some current practices and concerns. Paper presented at the annual meeting of National Council on Measurement in Education, New York, 1977.

Ebel, R. L. *Essentials of educational measurement.* Englewood Cliffs, N.J.: Prentice-Hall, 1972.

Educational Testing Service. *Report on a study of the use of the National Teachers Examination by the State of South Carolina.* Princeton, N.J.: Educational Testing Service, 1976.

Emrick, J. A. An evaluation model for mastery testing. *Journal of Educational Measurement* 8 (1971): 321-326.

Glaser, R. Instructional technology and the measurement of learning outcomes. *American Psychologist* 18 (1963): 519-521.

Glass, G. V. Standards and criteria. *Journal of Educational Measurement* 15 (1978a): 237-261.

———. Minimum competence and incompetence in Florida. *Phi Delta Kappan* 59 (1978b): 602-605.

Haladyna, T. Comments: measurement issues related to performance standards. *Florida Journal of Educational Research* 18 (1976): 33-34.

Hambleton, R. K. On the use of cut-off scores with criterion-referenced tests in instructional settings. *Journal of Educational Measurement* 15 (1978): 277-290.

Hambleton, R. K., & Eignor, D. R. *A practitioner's guide to criterion-referenced test development, validation, and test score usage.* Laboratory of Psychometric and Evaluative Research Report No. 70. Amherst: School of Education, University of Massachusetts, 1978.

Hambleton, R. K., & Fitzpatrick, A. Review techniques for criterion-referenced test items. Manuscript in preparation.

Hambleton, R. K., & Novick, M. R. Toward an integration of theory and method for criterion-referenced tests. *Journal of Educational Measurement* 10 (1973): 159-170.

Hambleton, R. K., Swaminathan, H., Algina, J., & Coulson, D. B. Criterion-referenced testing and measurement: a review of technical issues and developments. *Review of Educational Research* 48 (1978): 1-47.

Haney, W., & Madaus, G. *Making sense of the competency testing movement.* National Consortium on Testing, Staff Circular No. 2. Cambridge, Mass.: The Huron Institute, 1978.

Hively, W., Patterson, H. L., & Page, S. A. A "universe-defined" system of arithmetic achievement tests. *Journal of Educational Measurement* 5 (1968): 275-290.

Huynh, H. Statistical consideration of mastery scores. *Psychometrika* 41 (1976): 65-78.

Jaeger, R. M. Measurement consequences of selected standard-setting models. *Florida Journal of Educational Research* 18 (1976): 22-27.

— — —. A proposal for setting a standard on the North Carolina High School Competency Test. Paper presented at the 1978 spring meeting of the North Carolina Association for Research in Education, Chapel Hill, 1978.

Kriewall, T. E. Aspects and applications of criterion-referenced tests. Paper presented at the annual meeting of American Educational Research Association, Chicago, 1972.

Livingston, S. A. *A utility-based approach to the evaluation of pass/fail testing decision procedures.* Report No. COPA-75-01. Princeton, N.J.: Center for Occupational and Professional Assessment, Educational Testing Service, 1975.

— — —. *Choosing minimum passing scores by stochastic approximation techniques.* Report No. COPA-76-02. Princeton, N.J.: Center for Occupational and Professional Assessment, Educational Testing Service, 1976.

Macready, G. B., & Dayton, C. M. The use of probabilistic models in the assessment of mastery. *Journal of Educational Statistics* 2 (1977): 99-120.

Meskauskas, J. A. Evaluation models for criterion-referenced testing: views regarding mastery and standard-setting. *Review of Educational Research* 46 (1976): 133-158.

Millman, J. Passing scores and test lengths for domain-referenced measures. *Review of Educational Research* 43 (1973): 205-216.

— — —. Criterion-referenced measurement. In W. J. Popham (ed.), *Evaluation in education: current applications.* Berkeley, Calif.: McCutchan Publishing Corp., 1974.

Nassif, P. M. Standard-setting for criterion-referenced teacher licensing tests. Paper presented at the annual meeting of National Council on Measurement in Education, Toronto, 1978.

Nedelsky, L. Absolute grading standards for objective tests. *Educational and Psychological Measurement* 14 (1954): 3-19.

Novick, M. R., Lewis, C., & Jackson, P. H. The estimation of proportions in m groups. *Psychometrika* 38 (1973): 19-45.

Pipho, C. Minimum competency testing in 1978: a look at state standards. *Phi Delta Kappan* 59 (1978): 585-587.

Popham, W. J. *Criterion-referenced measurement.* Englewood Cliffs, N.J.: Prentice-Hall, 1978a.

— — —. Setting performance standards. Los Angeles: Instructional Objectives Exchange, 1978b.

Popham, W. J., & Husek, T. R. Implications of criterion-referenced measurement. *Journal of Educational Measurement* 6 (1969): 1-9.

Roudabush, G. E. Models for a beginning theory of criterion-referenced tests. Paper presented at the annual meeting of National Council on Measurement in Education, Chicago, 1974.

Schoon, C. G., Gullion, C. M., & Ferrara, P. Credentialing examinations, Bayesian statistics, and the determination of passing points. Paper presented at the annual meeting of American Psychological Association, Toronto, 1978.

Shepard, L. A. Setting standards and living with them. *Florida Journal of Educational Research* 18 (1976): 23-32.

Van der Linden, W. J., & Mellenbergh, G. J. Optimal cutting scores using a linear loss function. *Applied Psychological Measurement* 1 (1977): 593-599.

Zieky, M. J., & Livingston, S. A. *Manual for setting standards on the Basic Skills Assessment Tests.* Princeton, N.J.: Educational Testing Service, 1977.

24   A Taxonomy for Competency Testing Programs

Fredrick L. Finch

Tests of "everyday skills" were originally developed with the modest expectation that they would provide relevant measures of literacy and of mathematical competency. They were designed to assess the results of schooling in a way that would indicate whether a student could transfer academic training to life-role situations. The tests were immediately embraced by parents and students, who perceived them as providing a useful method of assessing performance, and as establishing a literacy criterion that was more readily understood than a grade-equivalent score.

During recent years, a media blitz and several lawsuits (asserting that schools have failed to meet the needs of students) have focused an intolerable level of attention on the failure of diplomas to certify excellent, or even average, performance. Some schools have turned to everyday skills tests for an answer to the problem. In addition, many state legislatures have forced the schools to take action by imposing minimum competency testing or some other accountability measure. However, the results of such testing have tended to exacerbate already inflamed emotions because the critics' worst fears seem to have been confirmed. Is it possible that so many have learned so little? Or, is this the right question? Perhaps the questions we should be considering have been suggested by Jeanne Chall (1978, p. 5), who asks:

Was John Doe a functional illiterate after 12 years of schooling because the achievement tests he took in school failed to reveal his reading problem? Or did his severe reading problem suffer from failure on the part of school personnel to implement the test findings? If so, might not the same occur with the best of the state competency tests?

Spady (1977, p. 9) characterizes adherents and practitioners of competency based education (CBE) as "marching (or parading) in different uniforms, to different drummers, playing different tunes." In responding to Spady's call for "basic definitions, conceptual clarity, and analysis of the organizational and social implications of various CBE approaches," many educators have suggested a fundamental need to develop a universally acceptable definition of competency, a best method for testing competency, and a proper criterion for distinguishing between competent and incompetent individuals.

It could be useful now, or at least palliative, to acknowledge that there may be no single best definition for competency, no best way of measuring competency, no ultimate criterion for competency, and no simple way of solving the literacy problem. As Sitton (1978) sagely suggests, opposition to competency testing and confusion regarding the meaning and purpose of competency measurement stems from our failure to recognize that "the real issue is disagreement over the basic purpose of public education among educationists, teachers, students, and parents." Sitton points out that it is not reasonable to expect unanimous agreement regarding the nature and purpose of competency testing when individuals or groups expect schools to serve a multitude of functions. For instance, the school has been perceived by different groups as: a college preparatory academy; a basic education service; a job training institute; a nonevaluative, credential-granting institution; a socializing or behavior-modification clinic; a sports and social club; and a baby-sitting service.

The competency testing movement appears to be fueled by the rhetoric of back-to-basics advocates who assert that a small but unacceptable number of students have endured twelve or more years of schooling without developing sufficient skills (whatever that means) in reading, writing, and mathematics. Others join Jencks (1978, p. 52) in opposing the competency testing movement because it seems to ignore "other necessary skills, such as learning to think critically and dealing with complex ideas."

Before a positive direction can be established, diverse views on what constitutes "competency" must be accommodated by a theoretical framework that provides a method for organizing the domain. There is no reason to restrict definitions of competency to basic skills or even "life skills," when some educational programs may emphasize oral competency, social competency, and the like. The diversity of needs and opinions makes it essential to describe competencies operationally in a way that allows rational discussion. Information to support this point of view is provided by Chall's report on a 1978 survey in which she found that although 80 percent of the states were planning, developing, or giving competency tests, only 23 percent of the chief state school officers (CSSOs) knew how to define and measure competency. Chall further reported that 30 percent of the CSSOs said that they could define competency, but had not yet decided how to measure it, and another 40 percent were working on definitions and procedures.

Out of the considerable debate about the nature of competency, there appears to be some agreement (although not a unanimous opinion) that competency tests should measure a student's ability to transfer academic training to life-role situations. Brickell (1978) provides a cogent analysis of many of the major issues. However, his implication that life skills and school skills represent two different domains creates a problem. It is not reasonable to expect schools to prepare students "for the shopping center" by teaching to the kind of "life skills" items represented by his example: "To saw very hard metal, should you buy a hacksaw blade with few teeth or many teeth?" (p. 589)

This item is an excellent example of some of the attempts that have been made to separate "school" skills and "life-role" skills. The competency being tested by this item may be important for plumbers and hardware salespersons, but it would have little general application. While it might be desirable to teach such specific solutions to all of the problems that an individual could encounter, it is obviously impossible to do so. The most one can expect of schools is that they provide a basic foundation of skills that can be applied to a wide variety of situations.

The competency testing movement, like any new phenomenon, is plagued with problems of semantics. Practitioners of competency-based education and evaluation are using a fairly small core vocabulary to describe a wide variety of situations; communication is hampered by the false assumption that similar terms have similar meanings. For example, the term "competency test" is frequently used to identify a paper-and-pencil test that includes questions about situations a person might encounter in the "real world." In contrast, some educators insist that competency tests used as graduation requirements should measure "school skills." This semantic problem could be partially solved if everyone agreed to use a descriptive adjective along with the word "competency." A "life-role competency test" could identify a measure of ability to function in a nonschool environment, and could be defined as a measure of application of skills, learned in school or elsewhere, to simulations of situations that occur in life. Another kind of competency test might be designated a "job skills competency test" or a "basic academic skills competency test."

Although descriptive labels could greatly improve the accuracy of communication, it is still essential to develop methods by which the content of competency tests could be operationally described. As a starting point, we might define a competency as "the ability to use a specific skill or set of skills to meet the needs of a specific situation." Note that this definition suggests that a competency has two aspects: the enabling skills, and the context in which these skills are applied. Figure 1 shows how these two components could provide a framework for describing competency tests.

Each item in a competency test could be described in terms of its context (based on a specific definition of competency) and its enabling skills (needed by the individual to meet the performance demands of a specific situation). This approach obviates the need to decide whether competency tests, as a general class, measure school-developed skills or life-related abilities. Many CBE practitioners might choose to describe the enabling-skills dimension in terms of basic skills such as addition, subtraction, literal comprehension, and the like. Alternatively, enabling skills could be described in terms of cognitive taxonomies, such as those developed by Bloom (1956), Metfessel, Michael, and Kirsner (1969), or Nelson (1978). It is not appropriate to suggest a single best method of classifying the enabling-skills aspect of competencies. However, if enabling skills were based on instructional classifications, reporting the sums of both rows and

Enabling Skills	Competency Context				
	1	2	3	4	Etc.
1	Item 1			Item 2	
2			Item 3		
3	Item 4				
Etc.					

Figure 1. Skill and Context Matrix

columns of a single test would provide information about life-role competencies *and* basic skills achievement. Such information might prove useful in responding to legal challenges that "competencies" have not been taught in school.

Just as the rows of figure 1 could be used to identify skills, the columns could be used to describe the various contexts of competency measurement. These contexts might identify particular life-role applications such as income tax forms, business letters, want ads, and other content associated with a single competency test. Alternatively, the context columns could be used to describe broad classifications of competency for the purpose of classifying a variety of competency tests. Figure 2 provides an example of the latter.

As currently practiced, competency testing seems to emphasize everyday applications without reference to the enabling skills associated with the measurement context. As a result, the content of some competency measures cannot be described adequately. Students are often expected to meet a minimum standard based on an unclassified (and often unclassifiable) assortment of items for which there is no specified rationale. The use of a two-dimensional matrix would allow an educational planner to understand the implications of a specific definition of competency,

	Competency Contexts			
	School and College Performance (by Course)	Everyday Applications (by Situation)	General Work Skills (by Task) or Specific Career Requirements (from Job Analyses)	Etc.
Enabling Skills				
Reading				
Writing				
Mathematics				
Information				
Etc.				

Figure 2. General Classes of Competency Measures

and to develop a test that adequately measured the competencies subsumed by that definition. Such a matrix could also be used for ex-post-facto analysis of existing measures or definitions. An example of such an analysis is provided by figure 3, which shows the classification of sample minimum competency items presented by Findley (1978).

The context and skill classifications shown in figure 3 might not be the ones that Findley would have used, but they describe his set of items fairly well. It is apparent that at least two consumerism items (1 and 4A) require specific information that must be learned directly from expository teaching or reading, and that at least two items (2 and 4D) could be answered by using logical reasoning, or common sense. Two of the five consumerism items (3 and 5) require application of several mathematical skills to reach a solution. The skills associated with item 5 in the consumerism test and item 3 in the mathematics test differ only in the mathematical operations (multiplication vs. division) and the units of measure used. A closer look at these two items confirms the similarity between calculating the price-per-ounce of cola and the price-per-foot of chain link fencing, and suggests that the items do not represent two different classes of competency. One item asks for the lowest price-per-ounce of cola and the other asks the approximate cost for 50 feet of fencing. The specific wording of the items

Enabling Skills	Competency Contexts					
	Consumerism Items				Mathematics Items	
	Group Health Insurance	Credit and Banking	Consumer Protection Agencies	Purchasing	Purchasing	Math School Skills
Specific Information	1*		4A, 4B, 4C?			
Logical Reasoning		2	4C?, 4D			
Addition						2
Subtraction		3				
Multiplication		3			3	3, 4
Division				5		
Place Value						1
Math Conversions						4, 5
Identify Math Process		3		5		

*Numbers denote specific test items.

Figure 3. Sample Minimum Competency Questions

changes neither the context (purchasing behavior) nor the required application of specific computational skills. Although these items could be classified in a variety of ways, it would be a minor error to assert that there is an important difference in the competencies they measure, and a grievous error to argue that one measures a school skill and the other a life skill.

Although the context and skills competency matrix could be used to analyze existing competency tests, it would be most useful in the planning stages of test development to specify the content to be measured. In order to adequately assess performance in life-role situations, competency test developers should first describe the contexts, or situations, that apply to their definition of competency, and then analyze each context to identify the skills needed by an individual to make an appropriate response. This procedure would result in a description of skills to be measured which, when compared to the school curriculum, typically would show that some basic academic skills were overrepresented, some were underrepresented, and some were omitted because they did not pertain to the selected applications. For example, items associated with balancing a checkbook would be limited to the skills required to perform this task. If, on the other hand, competency evaluators wanted to determine whether students could transfer basic skills to life-role situations, the important basic skills would be listed first and nonschool situations that required application of these skills would be selected. This procedure would result in a test that sampled a broader range of skills than would competency tests based on a ubiquity criterion for including a skill or life-role application.

Enabling skills could be classified in the proposed taxonomy in various ways, ranging from school-skill descriptions to cognitive processes. Competency contexts could be based on broad classifications or on descriptions of specific applications. Regardless of the system of classification used, it is essential that the CBE practitioner develop and use a competency framework that provides operational definitions that are consistent with the philosophy of the program.

In addition to enabling skills and competency contexts, one other parameter must be considered in describing competency measurement. Fitzpatrick and Morrison (1971, p. 239) have discussed the importance of "fidelity of simulation" in performance tests. Brickell (1978) has also discussed this issue, and Kasun (1978, p. 17) has succinctly summarized the typical lack of congruence between theory and application: "Just how different the real world is from classroom descriptions of it is a lesson that eventually comes to most of us, usually with a degree of shock." Life-role competency tests, and appropriate remediation of demonstrated deficiencies, can minimize this shock only if the competency tests provide a reasonable simulation of desired life-role behaviors.

We frequently hear assertions of the magnitude of prevailing illiteracy rates (for example, a recent article in *U.S. News and World Report* claimed that "13% of all 17 year-olds are functionally illiterate"), but such statements are meaningless unless they are based on an operational definition of literacy. Descriptions of the skills and contexts measured can help to give meaning to such statements, but an operational definition is not complete unless it also states how competency has been measured and what performance levels have been established as criteria.

For convenience, the term "test" has been used in this discussion, but it should not be assumed that multiple-choice and paper-and-pencil tests can or should be used as the sole measure of competency. Figure 4 shows only a few of the possible measures that could be related to the proposed model.

If it were possible to illustrate a fourth dimension, the criteria for acceptable performance might be plotted. However, since the criteria are so closely related to the type of measure used, it is appropriate not to distinguish them. Figure 4 suggests a few of the descriptors that might be used to describe competency. The actual terms used may not be important, as long as the CBE practitioner is able to define competencies in terms of these three dimensions. The three dimensions of figure 4 identify the information required to produce an operational definition of competency. They can be used as a starting point in the development of a

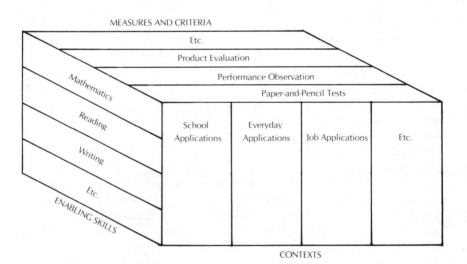

Figure 4. Competency Dimensions

competency framework, or for an ex-post-facto analysis of an existing program, test, or philosophy. Either use requires the following steps: Define the context—competent to do what? Describe the skills—what enabling skills are required? Describe the measures and set the standards—how are they measured and how much is enough?

Debating whether or not basic academic skills are more important than life-role applications, or even trying to determine which type represents a "higher level" skill, may be futile—or may be solely of academic interest. Unlike the chicken or egg problem, it seems obvious which comes first. The problems of day-to-day living are solved by the application of basic skills. The manner in which these skills are measured may vary, but the test developer and the test user must develop a reasonable method of describing the skills which are measured and the problems to which they are applied. The taxonomy described above may serve to meet this need.

References

Bloom, B. S. (ed.) *Taxonomy of educational objectives*. New York: David McKay, 1956.

Brickell, H. M. Seven key notes on minimum competency testing. *Phi Delta Kappan* 59, no. 9 (1978): 589-592.

Chall, J. S. *Informal survey on minimum competency testing to chief state school officers*. Unpublished manuscript, Harvard University, 1978.

Findley, J. Westside's minimum competency graduation requirements: A program that works. *Phi Delta Kappan* 59, no. 9 (1978): 614-618.

Fitzpatrick, R. and Morrison, E. J. Performance and product evaluation. In E. L. Thorndike (ed.), *Educational measurement*. Washington, D.C.: American Council on Education, 1971.

Jencks, C. Cited in quest for better schools. *U.S. News & World Report*, Sept. 11, 1978, pp. 50-52.

Kasun, J. A pipe too far: The story of clean water in Humboldt County. *USA Today* 107, no. 2398 (1978): 17-19.

Metfessel, N. S., Michael, W. B., and Kirsner, D. A. Instrumentation of Bloom's and Krathwohl's taxonomies for the writing of educational objectives. *Psychology in the Schools* 6, no. 3 (1969): 227-231.

Nelson, G. E. A proposed taxonomy of student assessment techniques in the cognitive domain. *Educational Technology* 18, no. 8 (1978): 24-26.

Sitton, C. (ed.). Behind the competency test debate. *Raleigh N. C. News and Observer*. Aug. 13, 1978.

Spady, W. G. Competency based education: A bandwagon in search of a definition. *Educational Researcher* 6, no. 1 (1977): 9-14.

25 Using Performance and Preference Data in Setting Standards for Minimum Competency Assessment Programs

Selina J. Ganopole

In response to widespread concern voiced by parents, colleges and universities, and the business community about low levels of pupil performance in basic skills, an increasing number of states are requiring that students pass a minimum competency test as a prerequisite to a high school diploma. The laws that have been enacted vary from state to state. In some states, legislatures have established minimum state standards which all students must meet. In others, the devices and standards to be used to assess students' competence are left to the discretion of educators in local school districts.

While the notion that high school graduates should be able to demonstrate proficiency in the basic skills certainly cannot be faulted, it raises certain related issues that are considerably less palatable. Of these, the most perplexing may well be the setting of standards to be used in determining whether students have attained adequate proficiency in the basic skills. Adding significantly to the already complex nature of this issue is the fact that failure to meet a given standard will result in denying some students a high school diploma. The situation becomes even more vexing because these standards are currently being set, not only in the absence of empirically validated procedures, but also without a definitive set of standard-setting procedures upon which standard-setters can rely.

Practitioners are still groping for answers to such seemingly basic questions as: What kinds of information are needed for setting sensible standards? What is the best way of getting this information? How can this information be used most effectively? And, where is the best place to start in the standard-setting process?

A number of standard-setting models exist in the measurement literature, each supposedly having certain attributes that makes it the method of choice in particular situations. However, as Shepard (1976) aptly noted, those particular attributes or distinctions are quite fuzzy, and it appears that a single composite plan for setting standards would be useful.

The purpose of this paper is to outline an organizational plan that attends to the basic questions listed above. The procedures described here are intended to help standard-setters obtain relevant data so as to proceed in a systematic manner in setting justifiable performance standards.

Several assumptions underlie this approach. The first is that any determination of who is (or is not) competent must ultimately be made by someone or some group responsible for making such decisions. That statistical techniques are capable of providing valuable assistance is not disputed. However, in the end, such determinations must be made on the basis of human judgment.

The second assumption is that such judgments can be rendered more defensible if standard-setters have access to the broadest and most relevant information base possible. And, carrying this assumption a step further, it is believed that a relevant information base must include both performance and preference data from a variety of relevant groups.

Third, it seems reasonable to assume that an approach that is open and visible at all levels of decision making would enhance acceptance of the standards by those directly affected.

Selecting the Competencies

The determination of competencies to be required for high school graduation is, justifiably, one of the key issues in the competency testing movement. It seems reasonable, therefore, to begin the standard-setting process with the selection of competencies. Although such selection may be a reasonable place to begin, it is by no means a simple task!

From amidst the tangle and controversy surrounding this issue can be heard such catch phrases as basic skills, academic skills, intellectual skills, reality-based skills, school-oriented skills, life-role skills, survival skills, and minimum essential skills. And, no doubt, more are being created as I commit these to paper.

As much as I would like to believe otherwise, I am convinced that no tablet shall be delivered onto us proclaiming specific competencies, which, if duly mastered, will lead our youth to everlasting effectiveness in real-life tasks. With no such perspicacious prophecies anticipated, who then must determine which competencies are important enough to be labeled "minimum essentials"? The state? The school? The taxpayers? The business community?

Since the demand for competency-based assessment may have had its origins in perceived differences in values and priorities between the schools and these various groups, the wisdom of depending solely on the preferences of any one group is highly doubtful. In light of the potential educational and legal implications (not to mention the social, political, and psychological implications) of any assessment program that could result in the denial of high school diplomas, decisions regarding the selection of competencies should reflect a majority viewpoint. That is, the competencies selected should be those most widely accepted as essential by such concerned groups as parents, students, educators, and members of the business community. Consideration of the views and preferences of these groups, while important in a variety of educational settings, appears to be absolutely necessary in establishing a minimal competency testing program and setting graduation requirements.

Having stated my case for the necessity of attending to the views and preferences from as wide a variety of relevant groups as possible, I will proceed to outline some suggestions for gathering such data. The first step in the process requires the preparation of a comprehensive list of specific, assessable competencies in the area(s) of concern (such as reading). Because of the significance of this step, those given the responsibility for preparing the list must be selected with care.

In addition to subject-matter specialists and individuals experienced in test development, it would be prudent to include educators from a variety of minority groups, as well as identified leaders from parent, student, and business groups. Dialogue among these individuals should produce a comprehensive and representative list of competencies.

In considering potential competencies to be included on the list, the following suggestions may be helpful. First, review the skills and content measured by such sources as the National Assessment of Educational Progress, state assessment programs, and surveys of adult performance on everyday tasks; for example, the Adult Performance Level Study (Northcutt, 1975). Second, explore existing collections of competencies (refer to state departments of education, objectives banks, and curriculum guides). Third, investigate the competencies adopted by other states. Fourth, attend to the concerns and preferences of citizens, educators, and special interest groups.

A volume could be devoted to a discussion of the nature and composition of the competency statements themselves. Space limitations preclude this luxury, so I will restrict my comments to three major points. The first pertains to the importance of clear, unequivocal competency descriptions. It is essential that the competencies be defined with sufficient clarity to permit common understanding of their content and the skills they encompass, by parents, teachers, students, and any others involved in the judging process.

The second point is that the competencies should reflect consolidated, terminal behaviors in which lower-level or en-route skills have been subsumed. Any other approach will only complicate the task of judging which competencies are most essential.

And third, in assessing minimum competencies for high school graduation, emphasis should be placed on students' abilities to apply basic skills to reality-based content. I see no advantage to being a "purist" and insisting upon a dichotomy between basic skills and reality-based content. Lindheim (1978, p. 4) was quite on target when she wrote, "All intellectual skills need to be exercised on content of some sort, and that content of any sort needs to yield to one or more intellectual skills."

Once the competency list has been completed, but prior to submitting it to the various groups, the list should be submitted to a small group that will rate and respond to the competencies, as a precaution against possible ambiguities and/or omissions.

Jaeger (1976) contends that the validity of standards depends, in part, on the sampling of judges. Therefore, in preparing to submit a list of competencies to representatives of various groups, consideration must be given to three factors: (1) representativeness—Are all relevant groups included? (2) randomness—Does each person in the population have the same chance of being selected for the sample? and (3) sample size—Is the sample of adequate size to provide acceptable estimation precision?

The format of competency statements should facilitate the rating or ranking process used. (An illustration of a ranking sheet for reading competencies appears in the Appendix.) And all respondents should be provided with an opportunity to augment the list of competencies if omissions are noted. Rankings or ratings can then be averaged for each competency for each group. This will provide information on the competencies most valued by each particular group. To appraise overall preferences, compute the mean of these averages across all groups, for each competency.

Suppose that it had been previously decided that only the six to eight highest-rated competencies (in a given subject area) would be selected for assessment. If the ratings from the various groups were fairly consistent, the selection task would be relatively easy. If, however, sizeable discrepancies between groups were evident, it would be advisable to meet with the leaders from the various groups in order to explore reasons for the high or low values placed on particular competencies. With information and insight gleaned from such meetings, standard-setters would be in a better position to make decisions regarding the inclusion or exclusion of particular competencies.

Selecting the Test

Once competencies have been selected, attention can turn to obtaining appropriate criterion-referenced measures to assess those competencies. Because many definitions and interpretations are associated with criterion-referenced measurement, certain aspects of its definition will be clarified, at least as it is used in this paper. Of concern is the interpretation of the word "criterion." Criterion is not to be interpreted as a standard of performance inherent in the test itself. The term "criterion-referenced test" is meant to signify a test containing items developed in accordance with a precise descriptive scheme. Such a descriptive scheme specifically delineates the class of behaviors being assessed by the test; it is to this descriptive scheme that an examinee's performance is referenced.

In recent years, the use of standardized achievement tests for educational evaluation has met with increasing criticism (Glaser, 1963; Popham, 1975). In spite of this, we still find school districts turning toward norm-referenced tests for use in competency-based assessment programs. Ironically, it is in such programs that their use may be especially unwarrantable. Such tests are typically constructed to measure generalized abilities, and they are intended to meet a wide variety of educational and administrative purposes. It is very unlikely that the content of a standardized test will exactly match the specific competencies a district wishes to assess. In addition, most norm-referenced tests lack an adequate descriptive scheme. When it is difficult to discern precisely what is being measured, we court the likelihood of a mismatch between what is tested and what is taught.

A second problem with norm-referenced tests is that they usually provide only a single summary score for measures of very general objectives. Further, item scores are frequently combined on an arbitrary basis, so that even if the content of such a test were to match the specific competencies emphasized by a district, the summary score would fail to reveal which competencies were mastered and which were not achieved. This lack of specificity makes teaching of the competencies incorporated in the test extremely difficult. If a district intends to minimize the number of students failing the competency test, it is essential that effective instruction be designed around the competencies assessed. Unfortunately, standardized achievement tests do not provide the guidelines needed to plan effective instructional programs.

And a third problem is that norm-referenced achievement tests frequently tend to function more like IQ tests than like measures of what has been learned. Popham (1978) points out that unless districts set indefensibly low performance standards for such tests, many students will fail to achieve associated proficiency levels required for graduation.

Although not a panacea for the competency testing movement, the increased clarity provided by criterion-referenced tests should permit educators to plan more effective instructional programs designed around designated competencies. And is that not a primary purpose of competency testing?

Undoubtedly, the intricacies of test construction and validation are best left to experts in test development. However, there are two test-related factors for which those overseeing a competency testing program should take responsibility. These factors are briefly described below.

Curricular Validity

This refers to the degree to which the objectives of a test reflect the objectives specified in a district's curriculum. Tests measuring objectives not incorporated in a curricular plan are unjustifiable in a competency testing program. Nothing short of a rigorous examination of the curriculum objectives and the objectives of the test can provide assurance that a match exists between the two.

Instructional Validity

This involves the degree to which the curriculum objectives are actually implemented in a district's instructional program. It is quite possible for a test to possess curricular validity and yet lack instructional validity. Classroom observation and dialogue with teachers are frequently the only ways of assessing the degree to which this kind of validity exists.

Using Performance Data in Setting Standards

The basic premise throughout this paper is that standard setting is ultimately a judgmental operation. Clearly, such judgments are not infallible. But they can be rendered more defensible if standard-setters avail themselves of a variety of relevant information. Such information should certainly include performance data on the measure actually used in the assessment program. There are those who insist that standard-setting decisions be made prior to seeing performance data, in order to avoid the circularity of having the judgment based on the test scores. But the use of performance data in setting standards has also been supported. Glass (1978), for example, points out that such use is "the only hope that could ever exist for setting sensible and safe standards." Popham (1978), too, supports the use of performance data and goes a step further in advocating the use of performance data from several relevant groups. He identifies three categorical groups—the uninstructed, the just instructed, and the previously instructed—each of which is capable of providing a particular type of information potentially useful to standard-setters in determining an appropriate passing level.

The logic inherent in Popham's scheme, plus its practical nature, is appealing. As with most plans, modifications can be made to fit the circumstances of the situation. As such, the basic procedure will be described as it is planned for implementation in a particular California school district. In this district, the plan will first be used to set a standard for reading competence. The Fundamental Reading Competencies Test (Ganopole, 1978) will be administered to three groups: the district's high school seniors; a random sample of seventh and ninth-grade students in the district; and adults seemingly capable of functioning effectively in day-to-day living. The Fundamental Reading Competencies Test consists of seven subtests, each representing one of the following competencies: (1) comprehends the main idea in news sources; (2) comprehends safety warnings; (3) comprehends graphic illustrations; (4) comprehends technical documents; (5) comprehends information and instructions presented on forms and applications; (6) comprehends consumer appeals in advertisements; and (7) uses common reference tools.

Sampling High School Seniors

The test will be administered to all high school seniors in the district, toward the end of the school year. Representing "the end of instruction," these students also represent the group that would be most directly affected by the standards set. Data obtained from this group will permit standard-setters to see how well their seniors are actually performing with respect to the designated competencies. The data will also permit estimates of potential failures in each competency, depending on the proficiency level that is set. For example, using a current group of high school seniors' average performance on the test, it is possible to estimate how many students would fail, depending on where the passing level was set. Table 1 illustrates this kind of data.

Although data such as these are useful, standard-setters must rigorously avoid being overly influenced by such numbers. It must be remembered that such data reflect only how things are at the present time. Plainly left undetermined are such questions as: Must students meet minimum proficiency levels on all of the designated competencies or only on a given number of them? If a student is very strong in some competency areas and weak in others, should his/her performance be considered holistically?

Table 1. Projected Failure Rates for High School Seniors
at Three Passing Levels*

Reading Competency	Proficiency Level (Percent Correct)	Probable Percent of Pupils Failing
Comprehends News Items	80	21
	70	11
	60	6
Comprehends Safety Warnings	80	19
	70	12
	60	3
Comprehends Graphic Illustrations	80	33
	70	18
	60	9
Comprehends Information on Forms and Applications	80	37
	70	23
	60	8

*Hypothetical data.

And, ultimately, what level of proficiency on designated competencies is indeed adequate to enable individuals to function effectively in contemporary society? Clearly, such data must serve only as guidelines in the standard-setting process. Standard-setters who permit such data to dictate the standards are, in essence, evading their responsibilities.

Sampling Lower-Grade Students

Consisting of a total of 200 students—100 seventh and 100 ninth-graders randomly selected from their respective grade-level populations—this group is representative of the "uninstructed learners" category. Toward the end of the school year, the same measure (the Fundamental Reading Competencies Test) administered to the seniors will be administered to this group. Data obtained from this group should provide standard-setters with guidelines for isolating a lower limit for their expectations. For example, if the average performance for seventh-graders on one of the competencies was 50 percent, and was 70 percent on the same competency for tenth-graders, standard-setters would likely reconsider any decision to set passing levels for graduation (for that competency, anyway) much below 70 percent. On the other hand, if the average scores for seventh-graders was 30 percent, and was only 40 percent for tenth-graders, lower passing levels may be more justifiable.

Sampling Adults

This group will include 100 first-year college students, 50 district teachers and administrators, 100 citizens' committee/advisory council members (includes parents and community business people), and 50 students attending a local trade school. Data from this group provide a "reality check" to help standard-setters determine whether their aspirations for pupil performance are realistic; that is, in accord with the kinds of proficiencies actually needed to function effectively in the real world.

Using Preference Data in Setting Standards

In determining passing levels on designated competencies, the views of relevant groups should be obtained once again. Whereas before, the focus was on determining which competencies would become the basis for the test, the focus now is on ascertaining what passing levels are deemed most appropriate. It is not suggested that standard-setters base their decisions solely on such data. However, to reiterate an earlier point, consideration of the preferences of those directly affected is a responsibility of those charged with setting standards.

Informed judgments are distinctly more beneficial than judgments made in the absence of pertinent information. Therefore, it is recommended that representatives of relevant groups be provided with information which includes a general description of each competency, plus a sample item from the test. (See below.)

Comprehends Safety Warnings

General Description
Students will be presented with safety warnings such as those found on labels for various medications, household and garden products, and on publicly posted signs alerting individuals to potential danger. Students will select from a set of alternatives the statement which describes a course of action appropriate to the instructions and/or recommendations given in the safety warning.

Sample Item
Directions to students
Safety warnings should be carefully read and followed. Otherwise, you risk hurting yourself and/or someone else. The example below was taken from an actual warning found on a medicine label. Read the warning, then decide which course of action is most appropriate.

Caution: Apply topically three times daily for relief of mild sunburn. For external use only. Do not apply to large areas of body.

a. Apply to skin once every third day.
b. Take by mouth three times daily.
c. Put on skin three times a day.
d. Apply topically for three days only.

Of course, judicious selection of the sample item is imperative in view of the fact that it is typically viewed as representative of the entire test. Analysis of performance data for each test item may be helpful in identifying items of intermediate difficulty.

Judges should also receive performance data for each competency, reported as average percent correct, for each of the groups that took the test. An example of such data appears in table 2.

Standard-setters may also wish to include the predicted percentage of students failing the test, based on varying passing levels (that is, such data as presented in table 1).

With this information at hand, members of the various groups will be better equipped to respond to the question: What percent correct must a high school senior have in each competency in order to pass the test? By averaging the individual responses from each group for each competency, standard-setters will be able to ascertain the passing levels preferred by each of the groups. More general preference data can then be obtained by computing the mean of the averages across all groups, for each competency.

Consequences of Setting Standards

It is a well-recognized fact that even the best data cannot guarantee infallible judgments. Standard-setters, therefore, must be prepared to analyze and reconsider their decisions in light of possible implications and consequences. It may be helpful to consider these implications and consequences with respect to six categories. These are listed below together with some issues and questions that are representative of each category.

Table 2. Average Test Performance by High School Seniors*

Competency	Percent Correct
Comprehends News Items	68
Comprehends Safety Warnings	75
Comprehends Graphic Illustrations	65
Comprehends Technical Documents	60
Comprehends Information and Instructions on Forms and Applications	64
Comprehends Consumer Appeals in Advertisements	69
Uses Common Reference Tools	79

*Hypothetical data.

Instructional Considerations

How will increased emphasis on the basic skills affect the concept of the comprehensive high school?

In an already crowded curriculum, where, when, and by what methods will students who have failed the minimum competency test receive remediation?

Are the competencies assessed by the test truly amenable to improvement through instruction?

Legal Considerations

A potentially explosive situation exists when students are denied the diploma because they have failed a competency test. There is an obvious need for careful attention to false positives (those who pass the test, but who do not actually possess "competence") and false negatives (those who fail, but who actually possess the requisite skills). Standard-setters will have to be prepared to defend the standards against pressure to lower them, or to bypass them altogether. Conaway (1977) suggested that standards failing to stand up under critical review, although currently regarded as minimal, will nevertheless be lowered or bypassed. It is also conceivable that the competency testing movement, which was intended to assure that most students attain essential skills before leaving school, could have the opposite effect—providing an escape route for many students who have acquired only a marginal education.

Some questions to be pondered here are:

Are the designated competencies of justifiable importance to a wide variety of educational clientele?

Are the competencies relevant to the needs of the students?

Were the proficiency standards set in a systematic and defensible manner?

Does the school provide for early detection and notification of weaknesses in the designated competencies?

Are the competencies assessed by appropriate measures?

Does the school provide an effective remedial program?

Is it legal to deny diplomas to students in one district (or state) where proficiency standards are high and award diplomas to students in another district (or state) where proficiency standards are lower?

What is the extent of a school's liability in cases where students pass the test but cannot function effectively in society?

Financial Considerations

What is the cost of holding students back for an additional year (perhaps longer) in order to ensure mastery of designated competencies?

How many students can the school afford to remediate at one time?

Psychological Considerations

Psychological impact is generally difficult to assess or predict. However, questions such as the following merit careful consideration.

How will failing the competency test affect a student's future learning?

How will failing the competency test affect a student's self-concept?

Is there any assurance that the advantages of a more stringent standard sufficiently outweigh the consequences of a lower standard? And the converse of this must also be considered.

Societal Considerations

What positions in society will be open or denied to those failing to meet proficiency standards?

Will society be able to make sense of the various proficiency standards adopted by districts or states?

These and other equally serious issues remain to be pondered in efforts by standard-setters to set sensible and more defensible standards. However, there is every reason to believe that individuals who confront the standard-setting task systematically, avail themselves of a wide variety of relevant information, and then critically evaluate potential decisions in light of possible consequences, are eminently capable of setting realistic and hence defensible standards.

References

Conaway, L. Setting standards in competency-based education: Some current practices and concerns. Paper presented at the National Council on Measurement, New York, April 1977.

Ganopole, S. The construction and validation of a criterion-referenced test of fundamental reading competencies. Paper presented at the National Council on Measurement in Education, Toronto, March 1978.

Glaser, R. Instructional technology and the measurement of learning outcomes. *American Psychologist* 18 (1963): 514-521.

Glass, G. V. Postscript to "Standards and Criteria." Paper presented at the 1977-78 Winter Conference on Measurement and Methodology, Center for the Study of Evaluation, University of California, Los Angeles, January 1978.

Jaeger, R. Measurement consequences of selected standard-setting models. *Florida Journal of Educational Research* 18 (1976): 22-27.

Lindheim, E. Developing measures for minimal competency assessment. Paper presented at the National Council on Measurement in Education, Toronto, March 1978.

Northcutt, N. Functional literacy for adults. In D. M. Neilsen and H. F. Hjelm (eds.), *Reading and career education*. Newark: International Reading Association, 1975.

Popham, W. J. *Educational evaluation*. Englewood Cliffs, N.J.: Prentice-Hall, 1975.

Popham, W. J. Key standard-setting considerations for minimum competency testing programs. Paper presented at the 1977-78 Winter Conference on Measurement and Methodology, Center for the Study of Evaluation, University of California, Los Angeles, January 1978.

Shepard, L. Setting standards and living with them. *Florida Journal of Educational Research* 18 (1976): 28-32.

Appendix

FUNDAMENTAL READING COMPETENCIES

Ranking Sheet

Place a check by the category that describes your position.

_____PARENT   _____STUDENT   _____TEACHER   _____OTHER

Directions: Read carefully each of the reading competencies listed below. Then rank the competencies from 1 to 14 in order of their importance as minimum basic requirements for high school graduation. Use each number from 1 to 14 in ranking the competencies. Do not use any number more than one time.

      1 is the **HIGHEST** rank (most important)
      14 is the **LOWEST** rank (least important)

COMPETENCIES	RANK	COMMENTS
NEW ITEMS. Is able to comprehend idea(s) expressed in such materials as newspapers, magazines, and business or personal letters.		
ADVERTISEMENTS. Is able to comprehend the appeals, requirements, and obligations contained in advertisements.		
SIGNS AND LABELS. Is able to determine the meaning of vocabulary and symbols in order to comprehend safety warnings found on signs and labels such as medicine bottles, household products, and road signs.		
MAPS. Is able to interpret terminology and symbols used on maps in order to locate specific locations and make appropriate decisions regarding travel routes.		

COMPETENCIES	RANK	COMMENTS
GRAPHIC ILLUSTRATIONS. Is able to extract needed information from graphic illustrations such as tables, graphs, and charts.		
NONACADEMIC REFERENCE MATERIALS. Is able to extract needed information from nonacademic reference sources such as the newspaper index, telephone book, airline, bus, and train schedules.		
ACADEMIC REFERENCE MATERIALS. Is able to extract needed information from standard academic reference sources such as the dictionary, encyclopedia, library card catalog, thesaurus, and almanac.		
GOVERNMENT DOCUMENTS. Is able to extract needed information from government documents such as voter pamphlets, sample ballots for state and local elections, income tax forms, Department of Motor Vehicle publications, and employment-related materials published by the United States Government Printing Office.		
CONSUMER DOCUMENTS. Is able to extract needed information from consumer documents such as warranties, sales contracts, insurance policies, leases, loan and credit agreements, bank statements, and bills.		
FORMS AND APPLICATIONS. Is able to comprehend what is required to complete standard forms and applications such as an application for employment, credit application, application for medical assistance, car registration, accident report, insurance claims, application for social security, and application for a driver's license.		
SETS OF DIRECTIONS. Is able to comprehend and follow directions such as those found in maintenance manuals and labels on household products.		
NONVERBAL MEDIA. Is able to comprehend the meaning of nonverbal media messages such as political cartoons, posters, and photographs.		

COMPETENCIES	RANK	COMMENTS
SUBJECTIVE NEWS SOURCES. Is able to infer the author's point of view when presented in such materials as editorials, commentaries, and letters to the editor.		
LITERARY SELECTIONS. Is able to infer the theme of a short story, play, essay, or poem.		

Please answer the following questions about the reading competencies you have just ranked.

1. Are there any additional basic reading competencies that you feel are essential in order for an adult to function effectively in normal everyday living?

_____

_____

_____

2. Should any of the competencies listed be eliminated completely? If so, which competencies?

_____

_____

_____

3. Should any of the competencies be combined (for example, are there any competencies that overlap)? If so, please indicate which competencies, and explain.

_____

_____

_____

PART VI

Alternatives to Present Conceptions of Minimum Competency Testing

A majority of the papers contained in this volume elucidate the present status of minimum competency testing and the issues related to it. However, the papers in this section represent attempts to search beyond the present status of these programs and their related technical problems. Their authors pursue either a broader view of the state's responsibility for providing education or an alternative view of what it means to have competency-based *education* as opposed to minimum competency testing programs.

Robert A. Feldmesser, in *Minimum Competency as an Individual Right*, develops an issue first raised in previous papers concerned with minimum competency testing of handicapped children. In that context, it was pointed out that the right to achieve a minimum competency is different from the other rights guaranteed in the Constitution, such as due process and equal opportunity, and this right would impose very different responsibilities on educational institutions. After considering the current minimum competency testing programs, Feldmesser suggests that the present alternatives for handling students who have not met minimum standards by the end of their high school education are not satisfactory. To simply offer remedial instruction, when schools have not yet brought students to the point of competence, seems futile. Similarly, denying students their diploma or providing a certificate of attendance (alternative) diploma is another instance of "blaming the victim," which also disproportionately penalizes students from minority and low-income families.

He contends that endowing minimum competency as an individual right would entitle everyone to the social resources necessary to bring her or him up to the specified level of competence. Feldmesser's arguments are provocative and deserve study, particularly his recommendation to use community colleges for further adult education—to provide free educational counseling and remedial instruction for those who wish to attain minimum competency. The community college would be entitled to award a Certificate of Minimum Competency, which would not substitute for the high school diploma nor surplant the local school's requirements for graduation. Feldmesser raises what are likely to be the major objections to his plan, and he attempts to counter them.

The paper by Mitchell and Spady and the following paper by Spady attempt to recast our frame of reference for the concept of competence. Rather than being concerned with minimum competency testing, these authors desire to clarify the nature of outcome-based education and to suggest that what happens in schools is more important than what happens in testing programs. In the paper, *Organizational Contexts for Implementing Outcome Based Education*, Douglas E. Mitchell and William G. Spady attempt to define competency-based education programs and other outcome-based alternatives, such as development, social integration, or social-responsibility-based education. They examine the aspects of school organizations which favor or disfavor these four alternative, outcome-based programs. These authors also speculate on, and attempt to contrast, alternative operational models of competency-based education, development-based education, social-integration-based education, and social-responsibility-based education. They make the important point that increasing the intensity of demands for measurable results will not necessarily enable the schools to produce the desired outcomes.

Spady enlarges the argument that competency-based education is a misused and misapplied concept. He suggests that, in all but a few cases, competency-based education is no more than a testing and remediation program focused on basic literacy and mathematical skills. However, competencies actually involve the ability to create effective results in one's life. Competence means both succeeding in existing social role structures and having the ability to create new roles for oneself in response to changing social conditions. Spady argues that schooling is time-based at present, but that a true competency-based (or any outcome-based) approach to schooling would shift the focus to achieving standards, rather than to fulfilling time-in-school requirements. At the very least, the reader will find Spady's distinction between competency-based education and minimum competency testing reflective of the earlier discussions of Jenne Britell and Maxine Greene on competence and standards of excellence, and thus provocative of our need to constantly keep in focus the goals of the educational system.

Thomas G. Sticht reexamines minimum competency testing in terms of a functional literacy approach. He suggests that the Department of Defense has provided, in its detailed studies of the literacy demands of various military jobs, an example of how to define minimum competencies. A study of "reading-to-learn" tasks and "reading-to-do" tasks showed that, for many entry-level jobs, the former demands far exceeded the latter. This discovery suggested the revision of job-training programs to reduce excessive emphasis on learning from textual materials. Sticht describes the development of a reading inventory to estimate the reading requirements of jobs, and he considers threats to its validity. With its implications for further tracking of students, the idea of establishing "reading demands" of jobs as an approach to establishing minimum competencies is highly debatable. Yet, such data may be very useful for giving a more realistic perspective to the reading tasks in school and to the nature of remedial programs.

26   Minimum Competency as an Individual Right

Robert A. Feldmesser

Efforts to establish minimum competency (MC) standards for high school students are bound sooner or later to run into a troublesome dilemma: how to deal with students who have not yet met the standard as they near graduation. To date, three ways of handling the problem have emerged, but all of them have major deficiencies.

First, one could do nothing at all about the failing students. Schools with large proportions of them might be required to institute remedial instruction or revise the remedial instruction already offered. But as far as the students themselves were concerned, the standards would simply "be there"; no tangible consequences would flow from not having met them, and no one other than the students in question (and perhaps their parents) would even know that they had failed. Though it may seem pointless to have standards that no one has to meet, this course of action — or inaction — does have the merit of avoiding the problems connected with the other procedures, which gives it a certain political appeal; and indeed it is the procedure that was adopted in New Jersey in 1975 (although legislation is now pending to change it to the one which will be described next). Its obvious defect is that, precisely because it does not require students to meet the standards, this procedure would greatly weaken the ability of the standards to increase the proportion of students who acquire the

The author is grateful for the helpful comments made by Henry S. Dyer and Earl G. Medlinsky on an earlier version of this paper.

skills and knowledge they represent—and that ability is, of course, the ultimate justification for establishing MC standards. In short, doing nothing about the students who fail undercuts the rationale for having the standards.

Second, such students could be denied their diploma, or awarded a diploma that in some fashion attests to the fact that they have not measured up. This would put "teeth" into the standards, and it is the strategy that has received the greatest attention. A serious objection is that it imposes a penalty upon students that is not only harsh but unfair, because some of the fault may lie with poor instruction; and the injustice is compounded by the high probability that the students so penalized would come disproportionately from minority and low-income families. Thus, this second option is subject to the valid criticism that it is another instance of "blaming the victim."[1] There is a way of escaping this difficulty, and that is to set the standards (the passing scores on the MC tests) low enough that the vast majority of students can meet them. It is very likely that such a lowering of standards would happen in states where attaining some specified MC test score is prerequisite for award of the diploma, since it would be intolerable, for reasons both humane and political, to deny high school diplomas, or issue "second-class" ones, to large proportions of students. But if the standards are low enough to allow nearly all students to meet them at the outset, then clearly they will exert little pressure toward improving student performance in the subjects tested. Again, the purpose of having the standards would be defeated.[2]

The third procedure—probably the one most commonly recommended and perhaps the one most frequently adopted—is to require that students who do not meet the standards take remedial instruction before receiving their diploma. This might reduce the number of below-standard students, though that is not a certainty. If a school has been unable to bring a student up to the standards before the senior year, why would it suddenly be able to do so during the senior year? At any rate, in principle this approach, rather than solving the problem, merely puts off having to deal with it for a while. If the student gets the remedial instruction, but then fails the MC test again, we are back where we started. If the student does not have to take the MC test again, but has only to receive a passing grade in the remedial course, what is to be done about students who fail the course? The teachers of these courses would be under great pressure to pass everyone, regardless of performance, to allow them to get their diplomas—the equivalent of setting a very low passing score on the MC test. And if—as is the case in some jurisdictions—students are required to take the remedial course but need not earn a passing grade in it, we have a replication of the situation in which students do not have to meet the MC standards, and the same consequences would follow. We are still presented with the same dilemma—a choice between useless enactment and distasteful enforcement.

What I propose is that we slip between the horns of the dilemma by establishing MC standards not as a requirement imposed upon individuals, but as a right which they enjoy. Actually, this approach is a logical corollary to the concept of MC standards as a set of "survival skills" or "functional necessities." If we declare that people really do need to acquire whatever we call "minimum competencies" in order to survive or function, then surely they have a right to that level of competence. Of course, achievement in reading or mathematics cannot be made a "right" like voting, in the sense that it can be conferred upon individuals when they reach the age of 18. But there is a meaningful sense in which every person can be given an entitlement to social resources, an entitlement which could be reasonably called a "right to minimum competency " The mechanisms for establishing such a right, the advantages it offers, and the questions that might be raised about it will occupy succeeding sections of this paper.

Creating MC as a Right

The right to minimum competency would be created by two provisions of state legislation. First, a Certificate of Minimum Competency (CMC) would be established which would be awarded to any resident of the state who met educational standards set by appropriate authorities. The standards would represent the desired minimum levels of performance in reading (or language arts) and mathematics, and they would be expressed as specified scores on designated tests. Award of the CMC would be entirely separate from the high school diploma, which local school districts would continue to grant under whatever conditions and in whatever manner they were already doing. No one would be required to take the test leading to the CMC, but anyone would be permitted to take it whenever it was offered. It might be helpful to think of the CMC as being analogous to a driver's license: a credential issued by the state to any person who passes tests with content and passing scores determined by state authorities. Many people, especially young people, receive in their high schools the instruction that would enable them to pass the exams (though they may get it elsewhere if they wish), but the document would have nothing to do with the high school diploma; and no one would be compelled to seek or possess it, although employers may make the CMC a prerequisite for certain jobs.

In the second provision, the state would declare that every resident of the state would have the right to receive instruction, in suitable and reasonably convenient form and at public expense, *until such time as he or she had attained the specified score, however long that might take.* To implement this right, the state would designate a public agency or agencies which would have the duty of responding to any resident's request for instruction leading to the CMC. (The question of what agency this might be is discussed below.)

In practice, the CMC program would work as follows. Students would go through high school in the same way as at present. The MC tests would be offered several times a year, and any students who wanted to could take them. A student who attained the necessary score would receive a certificate (the CMC) attesting to that fact. The high schools would presumably offer some sort of remedial instruction to students who did not attain the necessary score, but they could take it or not, as they wished. Such students would still receive their diplomas, or would be permitted to leave school prior to graduation, under whatever conditions already existed—that is, without regard to whether they had earned the CMC. However, at any time after they had left school (whether with or without a diploma), they would be able to apply to the designated agency for further instruction in order to prepare for the MC test, and the agency would be obliged to offer educational counseling and to arrange, within a reasonable period of time, for suitable instruction at a convenient time and place. When these students felt ready, they would take the MC test. If they passed, they would be awarded their CMC; if not, they could resume instruction, immediately or at any later time, until they did attain the necessary score. No charge would be made for any of these services.

For the agency designated to furnish the services, there are several possible choices. One would be the local school district, but this choice has several drawbacks. The major one has already been alluded to: it seems unlikely that a school system which has not enabled some students to reach the MC standard by the time they are nearing the end of high school will be able to do so in another year, or two, or three. Certainly the students themselves would be justified in being skeptical, and that in itself would diminish their motivation for utilizing the schools. The inauspiciousness would be highlighted if the students were merely to be readmitted to the high school's remedial classes—which would probably be regarded dimly by both the school administration and the students anyway, if only because of the age heterogeneity that would result. Moreover, it would be expensive and inefficient for a school district to arrange for the special instruction of what might be a relatively small number of students. A second possibility would be the creation of a wholly new agency for this specific purpose, but it would be a long time before a new agency could be functioning smoothly, and there is also the question of where its staff would come from. And why add to the governmental bureaucracy when a very promising alternative already exists?

That alternative is the public community college, which commends itself on a variety of grounds. It is indeed a college, not a high school, and it is attended by people of all ages, thus lending some dignity to those who want MC instruction, rather than causing them embarrassment. Yet unlike other collegiate institutions, the community college has traditionally been open to all persons at little or no cost and with few or no prerequisites. Many community colleges already accept educational counseling and remedial instruction as being among their primary missions; they often have, or can be expected to acquire, the faculty and the facilities for conducting such instruction effectively. Community-college campuses are not as numerous or accessible as high school buildings (though in rural areas even that might not be true), but the other side of that coin is that the community colleges draw students from a wider area and so can offer specialized services more efficiently. At the same time, however, many community colleges, in keeping with their character and their mission, do conduct outreach programs to bring their services closer to the people who need them, at convenient times for those who may be working or caring for a family. Such efforts could be further encouraged if the state were to pay the full cost of the staff and facilities connected with MC instruction—a reasonable expectation if the state designates the community colleges as the agency obligated to offer MC instruction without charge.[3]

The nature of the instruction (including instruction in test-taking skills, where useful) would be worked out in discussions between an educational counselor and the student. It might be intensive, occupying several hours a day for a few weeks or months. It might be given for a few hours a week over a longer period of time. It might be offered through conventional classes, though some of them would presumably be held in the evening or on weekends, and they would take place not only at the community college but also in storefronts, community centers, or church basements— possibly even in high schools, like many adult-education classes at present. Self-instructional and self-paced programs, or televised instruction, would also be acceptable, provided that students had ready access to a counselor or teacher who was willing and able to answer questions and to help in other ways. Referral by the community colleges to other institutions— such as private or proprietary schools—would be permitted as long as they were suitable to the purpose and the student did not have to pay.

Advantages of MC as a Right

The establishment of MC as a right seems to overcome the objections that arise when MC is a requirement. The existence of the certificate provides an incentive for students to perform at the MC level, because employers and college admissions officers will presumably begin to inquire if applicants have their CMC, much as they now ask about the high school diploma. Yet at the same time, the pressure to keep the competency scores low would be relieved, for two reasons: First, students who fail to meet the standards before leaving high school would not have an irrevocable penalty imposed upon them; and second, seeking the CMC would be a voluntary act.[4] Even if prompted by inquiries from employers or colleges, the decision to seek the CMC will have been arrived at by the individual, on the basis of his or her own experience. The initiation and termination of instruction—to some degree even its form—would be under the control of the students, something they can make choices about rather than a hurdle they have to jump at someone else's bidding and on someone else's schedule. All of these factors surely enhance motivation, which in turn makes the necessary mastery more likely and makes the setting of higher standards more feasible. By the same token, the MC entitlement places some of the responsibility for learning on the student, where indeed some of it inescapably belongs; yet it retains and even extends the educational system's obligations to teach.

It is true that, even now, most school districts offer high school equivalency courses, often without charge, so that a person without a diploma can voluntarily return for further instruction. In jurisdictions where meeting MC standards is made a prerequisite for the diploma, the courses would presumably have to include appropriate basic-skills instruction. But in addition to the deterrents already mentioned, the idea of returning to high school to earn one's diploma is more daunting than the idea of going to a school (and a community college at that) with the shorter-term and more limited goal of earning a CMC. Still, one would hope that a successful experience with the CMC would lead on, when necessary, to resumption of study for the high school diploma. Certainly the aim of "lifelong learning" is utterly unrealizable without mastery of the basic skills.

Besides meeting the objections to establishing MC as a requirement, the right to competence has some advantages of its own. The most important of them is that it is intrinsically nondiscriminatory. Enactment of the right is a commitment by the state to give each individual whatever assistance he or she needs to reach the MC standards, without regard to "disadvantagement" or "handicap." Implicit is the premise that every person can be helped to attain the MC level, and a civilized nation should permit no other premise to be at the foundation of its educational system. The right to competence is the embodiment of equality—not merely equality of educational opportunity, but actually equality of educational outcome, at least at a minimum level.

A second virtue of the CMC provisions is that they continue to leave the conditions for awarding the high school diploma in the hands of the local school district. The CMC would be a supplement to the diploma, not a substitute for it. More will be said about this below; the point here is that it is politically advantageous to be able to say that local autonomy has remained unsullied.

Third, when the principle has been accepted that every person has a right to instruction at public expense until attaining the CMC, a solution emerges to another problem which haunts all MC programs: How are appropriate MC standards to be determined? Those who have tried to answer this question have usually proposed some sort of criterion-referenced score arrived at by consensus among relevant groups (for example, Zieky and Livingston, 1977; Hambleton, 1978; Linn, 1978), but this procedure is unsatisfactory because one must first assume that there are "absolutely necessary" competencies and then, when different individuals and groups put forth different versions of what they are, one must inconsistently call for a compromise among them. Indeed, Glass (1978) and Burton (1978) have opposed the setting of MC standards altogether on the ground that, from a psychometric point of view, they are inevitably nonrational and capricious. With the establishment of the CMC, however, it would make eminently good sense to derive standards from political and economic considerations. The MC standards would be the test scores corresponding to the proportion of the population for which the state legislature is willing to appropriate the funds needed for additional instruction. If, for example, the legislature were to decide that the state can afford to remediate the basic-skills performance of the lowest 20 percent of the population, the MC standards would become the scores at the 20th percentile of the score distributions at the norming administrations of whatever tests were used. As experience showed the cost to be higher or lower than the legislature had anticipated, and as the political and economic climate changed, the MC standards could be changed accordingly.

This method makes no pretense to psychometric rationality, for that is an irrelevant concern. Perhaps there *are* absolute levels of performance that a group of judges can agree are in some sense "necessary." But if those levels are higher than the levels to which the legislature is willing to try to raise everyone, it would be pointless to set them as the MC standards; to do so would place the state in the inadmissible position of asserting that a given level of educational performance is "necessary" for everyone while refusing to help everyone to reach it. On the other hand, suppose that the levels the judges agree upon are *lower* than what the state is willing to finance. Why should anyone object to the state's effort to educate people beyond what is "necessary," since the policy would be democratically adopted, and especially since "necessary" is only a term of human judgment anyway? Thus, in the last analysis, legislative action, reflecting public opinion, should determine the MC standards.

This procedure for setting the standards is obviously norm-referenced and so might well give rise to the cry that it would "condemn to failure" a fixed proportion of the population—that is, 20 percent, if the MC score were set at the 20th percentile. Such criticism is often voiced in discussions of the defects of norm-referenced tests, but it is simply incorrect. Once a score has been selected as a standard, there is no *statistical* reason why all members of a population cannot rise above it. The only limits are those imposed by lack of educational ingenuity, of individual motivation, of economic means, and of political will. In other words, surprising as it may seem at first glance, it is quite possible for "everyone to be above the 20th percentile" (or even, for that matter, for everyone to be above the median), so long as that percentile refers—as it generally does in discussions of norm-referenced tests—to the score distribution of a *previously* tested population. Of course, in the happy event that 100 percent of a later population does attain the original standard, the state legislature could, if it wished, authorize a new standard or a new test, presumably striving for a higher level of performance. It would not be unreasonable to call that educational progress.

If the community colleges serve as the vehicle for implementing the right to MC, two additional favorable consequences might follow. The first of these is suggested quite tentatively. Many members of the administrations and faculties of community colleges are concerned that their institutions are often identified with the high schools rather than with colleges. This identification is connected with the common perception that the community colleges are attended by "low-ability" students and have relatively "low academic standards"; many community-college people would be reluctant to reinforce that perception by enlarging their remedial function. At first glance, this would seem to be an obstacle to having the community colleges become the centers for MC instruction after high school. However, there is a countervailing force that might convert the obstacle into an inducement.

The open-access tradition is a source of great pride in the community colleges, and few of those involved with them would want to do anything to weaken it, even though it might mean that academic standards are thereby lower than might otherwise be possible—thus contributing to the "glorified-high-school" image. But if the community colleges were to become the agencies for carrying out the MC-entitlement program, they might then be justified in making possession of the CMC a condition of admission into their degree-credit programs. This would allow them to make greater demands on their students, and thus raise standards, without attenuating the open-admissions policy.

The community colleges would say, in effect: "It is unreasonable to expect students who cannot perform at the MC level to benefit from degree-credit courses, and so students who lack the CMC cannot be admitted to those courses. However, we welcome them as students into our CMC program. We pledge to instruct them in ways and at times and places that correspond to their needs. We will not charge them for this instruction, and they may remain enrolled in the program for as long as necessary. When they have earned their CMC, we will be happy to enroll them in our degree-credit courses."

The score on the MC test, in short, would be the basis for a placement decision rather than for an admission decision. At the same time, it may be hoped that becoming the instrument of a pioneering concept like the right to competence would give a strong sense of purpose, perhaps even of inspiration, to the staff charged with the remedial education function.

The other potential advantage can be stated with more confidence. The opportunity to earn a CMC, and the right to receive preparatory instruction, must obviously be open to all residents in a state—that is, to those who have left high school as well as to those who are still enrolled (as is the case for the driver's license). Undoubtedly, many adults will want to have a CMC. Some will feel a need for instruction, which will put them in contact with the community college; others will feel they can take the MC test without instruction, but they, too, could be brought to the community colleges by having the colleges be the test-administration centers. Thus, a large part of the population will become aware of the colleges and could be encouraged to make use of their other facilities— vocational counseling and other guidance services, occupational training and other kinds of continuing education, degree-credit and recreational programs, and exhibits, lectures, and concerts. It might not be too much to expect that the community colleges, building on the base of the right to competence, would become—more often than is now the case—genuine, comprehensive educational centers for the areas they serve. If nothing else, the example of parents seeking a CMC is bound to have an effect on their children.

Grounds for Opposition

Finally, here are some of the objections that could be raised to the concept of the MC as a right, and the ways in which those objections might be answered.

First objection: the MC entitlement would "take the schools off the hook"—that is, it would relieve them of any responsibility for their students' acquisition of basic skills, because those in charge would know that the students would always have another chance later at no financial cost to themselves. Those who make this argument would presumably favor making MC a graduation requirement, so that the schools would "have to do something" about low achievement. But, as was explained at the outset, making it a requirement will almost certainly lead to the setting of a very low standard, one that probably 90 or 95 percent of present-day high school students can meet—and that is *really* "taking the schools off the hook." This is not to say that it is impossible to hold schools accountable; rather, it is to say that school accountability ought to be kept quite separate from a minimum competency requirement for students, for in the absence of such a separation, either accountability will not amount to much or students, not educators, will pay the penalty for failure to meet the accountability standard. In any event, the primary goal of educational policies should be to educate people rather than to allocate blame.

Second objection: the MC entitlement would require that the state pay again—perhaps several times over—for what the elementary and secondary schools were supposed to accomplish in the first place (in part, at least, with state aid). There is some truth in that; and in the long run, it is to be hoped—for the sake of all concerned—that the high schools and, what is more to the point, the elementary schools will be strengthened and improved so that children will be enabled to master the basic skills well before the 12th grade. Meanwhile, however, the alternative to a refusal to pay a second or third or fourth time for what was not accomplished the first time is to allow people to perform at an extremely low level of basic skills, and that is surely the less tolerable alternative for a democratic and a technologically complex society, which is still—despite all the current complaints—comparatively wealthy.

Third objection: the MC entitlement would further undermine the significance of the high school diploma, because the CMC, based as it would be on "hard data," would become the really meaningful document.[5] If that were to happen, it would admittedly be unfortunate. The high school diploma has independent value that ought not be diminished. Despite the many criticisms, it does represent some accomplishments and qualities besides the (perhaps minimal) knowledge of some kinds of subject matter: namely, a degree of punctuality and reliability, of cooperativeness, and of willingness and ability to follow instructions and to conform to the rudiments of a moral code—the sorts of things that can be learned from the judgments of teachers (as summed up in the award of a diploma) far better than from the responses to items on objective tests. It would be irrational to ignore such information in favor of scores in reading and math, however important the scores may be. However, for that very reason, employers and college-admission officers are unlikely ever to disregard the diploma altogether.[6] If it is held important to assure that such disregard does not happen, then the diploma could continue to be, or could be made (along with the CMC), a prerequisite for taking certain civil service and occupational licensing examinations.[7] Another step in the same direction would be to include on the diploma information about courses, grades, and number of days absent.

Fourth objection: the MC entitlement would lead the high schools to neglect all subject matter other than that which is covered by the MC test. This rests on the belief that subjects in which the results are quantitatively measured and publicly reported will of necessity divert attention from those in which measurement is impossible or merely more difficult. One way of compensating for this would be to list courses and grades on the diploma, as suggested above. Actually, though, the belief itself does not seem to be well grounded. It is analogous to believing that since speed of running is more readily measurable than grace or agility of movement, having students run footraces will drive out the teaching of basketball and dance. There is no sign that this has occurred.

Fifth objection: the MC entitlement would create a class of professional students, who would take an insufferably long time to learn the basic skills, entailing unlimited expense on the part of the state and therefore rendering the whole scheme impracticable. This argument may refer to two quite different categories of people. On the one hand, there are those who might be pictured as being comparable to a permanent welfare class, forever dependent on handouts and open to suspicion of malingering. This comparison is not warranted. MC instruction would be free, but students would not be receiving financial assistance and so could hardly live off the instruction. There is no apparent reason for them to deliberately fail the MC test; and once they have passed it, they would no longer be eligible for free preparatory instruction, nor would they need it.

The other category is that of the mentally deficient or handicapped. For them, taking a long time to acquire the basic skills is not an artful ploy but a symptom of a condition beyond their control. But this is a small group, and so the expense involved would not be insupportable; and as long as such persons are willing to keep on trying to learn, for society to do anything other than try to teach them would surely be ignoble.

Summary

Establishment of minimum competency as a right seems to have much to recommend it. It would allow society to set moderately high standards of minimum competency—perhaps even constantly rising standards—while keeping open to all persons the possibility of reaching those standards. It would be nondiscriminatory by its very nature. It would clearly place the responsibility for acquiring basic skills with the student, yet it would also impose upon the educator a continuing obligation to search out effective ways of teaching those who have not yet acquired them. It would lead readily to a sensible way of setting minimum standards. It could enable the community colleges to raise their standards while preserving open admissions, and it could bring a larger proportion of the adult population into touch with them. Is it too much to hope that establishing this right may help to end irrational disputes over the structure of competency testing programs and become the instrument by which American society begins to rejuvenate its faltering educational system?

Notes

1. Florida's MC law is an example of this type, and the Miami chapter of the NAACP has threatened a legal challenge to the state's MC test on the ground that the proportion of black students scoring below the standards was substantially higher than the proportion of white students (NAACP may file suit, 1978). It has also been reported from Florida that the law has led to an increase in the dropout rate; some students, realizing that they may not receive their diploma anyway, decided that there was nothing to be gained by staying in school.

2. The Committee on Testing and Basic Skills of the National Academy of Education has said: "any setting of state-wide minimum competency standards for awarding the high-school diploma . . . is basically unworkable because in many populous states cut-off points for a passing grade that are politically and educatively acceptable to parents, pupils, and educators would have to be so low that an overwhelming majority of students would be allowed to pass. This would make the diploma standard almost meaningless" (National Academy of Education, n.d., p. 9).

3. If the community-college option is chosen, the community-college authorities, and perhaps higher-education officials in general, would have to have a voice in determining the level of the MC standard.

4. Having the MC standards as a right rather than a requirement that must be met at some fixed time eases another problem: the excruciating one of what to do

about a student who misses the MC score by only a few points. If attainment of the standard were a right, the student would be able to take the MC test another time.

5. Note that this and the following criticism are applicable to making MC scores into diploma requirements as well as to making MC into a right.

6. This is admittedly a speculative statement. But it is also true that we know remarkably little about how people outside the school system, and particularly employers, presently interpret the possession of a high school diploma, especially in the absence of a detailed transcript. Some useful and very interesting research could be done on this topic.

7. A legal challenge to such requirements, on the grounds that they were irrelevant to job performance, could well be met by the response that the attributes mentioned above as being reflected in the diploma, and the capacity for further learning that is indicated by mastery of the basic skills, are pertinent to virtually any job. For some evidence of their lasting importance in facilitating later acquisition of information, see Hyman, Wright, and Reed (1975).

References

Burton, N. W. Societal standards. *Journal of Educational Measurement* 15 (1978): 263-271.

Glass, G. V. Standards and criteria. *Journal of Educational Measurement* 15 (1978): 237-261.

Hambleton, R. K. On the use of cut-off scores with criterion-referenced tests in instructional settings. *Journal of Educational Measurement* 15 (1978): 277-290.

Hyman, H. H., Wright, C. R., & Reed, J. S. *The enduring effects of education*. Chicago: University of Chicago Press, 1975.

Linn, R. L. Demands, cautions, and suggestions for setting standards. *Journal of Educational Measurement* 15 (1978): 301-308.

NAACP may file suit charging Florida Proficiency Test discriminatory. *Education Daily*. February 7, 1978, p. 1.

National Academy of Education. *Improving educational achievement: report of the National Academy of Education Committee on testing and basic skills to the assistant secretary for education*. Washington: The Academy, n.d.

Zieky, M. J. & Livingston, S. A. *Manual for setting standards on the Basic Skills Assessment Tests*. Princeton, N.J.: Educational Testing Service, 1977.

8

27   Organizational Contexts for Implementing Outcome-Based Education

Douglas E. Mitchell
William G. Spady

The "Competency Based Education Movement," described by Spady (1977) as a bandwagon in search of a definition, appears to be here to stay—at least for a while. According to an update of state legislative and policy action by the Education Commission of the States (Pipho, 1978), some type of "CBE approach" is now underway in at least thirty states, and several others appear to be headed in this direction. Based on the proceedings compiled from four regional conferences on this topic which ECS and the National Institute of Education sponsored in October, 1977, however, there is considerable confusion among educators, researchers, policy-makers, and the public regarding the meaning, desirability, and implications of various CBE approaches.[1]

Nonetheless, the general tenor of public concern about schooling which underlies this groundswell of educational policy reform is clear, and it provides a vehicle for reassessing the purposes and activities of the public schools from some new perspectives.

Major Themes in the CBE Movement

Three dominant themes can be identified in the diversity of recent CBE policy initiatives. These themes involve: 1) the belief that the school has

Reprinted with permission from Mitchell, Douglas E. and Spady, William G., "Organizational Contexts for Implementing Outcome-Based Education." *Educational Researcher*, Vol. 7, No. 7 (July-August, 1978) pages 9-17. Copyright 1978, American Educational Research Association, Washington, D.C.

failed to fulfill its major purposes, 2) an endorsement of *explicit expectations* for enhanced student outcomes, and 3) a conviction that schools lack an adequate *base* for program design and operation. The failure theme, frequently articulated in terms of declining test scores or the inadequate preparation of high school graduates for either jobs or college level academic work, lies at the heart of public concern with an apparent decline in standards of *technical competency*. This concern has led many states to seek some type of "objective," external assessment of student performance, and accounts for the popularity of the "Minimum Competency Testing" approaches to CBE.[2] Some critics, however, with broader definitions of the purposes of schooling, see school failures more in terms of the lack of student *social responsibility, social integration*, or *personal development*. Failure in these areas, though less well documented, is a persistent source of pressure on the schools to concern themselves with the *outcomes* as well as the processes of education.

The endorsement of explicit expectations regarding the kind and quality of student outcomes represents a sharp movement away from trusting educators to produce schooling results based on broad generalized goal statements and an increased specification of both the concrete ends of schooling and the means for achieving them. This emphasis is what Wise (1977 and 1978) calls the "hyper-rationalization" of education and is a serious effort to improve school accountability systems.

The conviction that educational program design is improperly based, refers, as noted by Spady (1977) and Spady and Mitchell (1977b), to the belief that educational organizations need to shift away from program structures based on time and role concepts, to ones based on the outcomes or goals to be reached.

Taken together these three themes provide an impetus for examining more carefully the nature of the "demands" schools face and the responses they develop to them. They imply that the current bases of school operations are neither clear nor effective, that they need to become more explicit, and that they need to be grounded on the accomplishment of outcome goals rather than on the provision of means.

In the analysis that follows, we shall consider four distinct sets of expectations for school outcomes, each of which forms a potential base for school operations and student responses.

Outcome Expectations and the Alternative Bases of Education

As suggested in previous work (see Spady & Mitchell, 1977c; Mitchell & Spady, 1977; Mitchell, 1978) there exists a set of broad societal expectations which are responsible for the creation and maintenance of schools.

These expectations can best be described in terms of certain character-istics thought to be important for adult citizens to possess in order to enter and participate in a society which is productive, orderly, and attractive to its members. There are four major contributions which schools have been expected to make to these adult characteristics. They are: 1) to facilitate and certify the achievement of technical *competence*, 2) to en-courage and enhance the fullest possible *development* of physical, emo-tional, and intellectual skills and abilities, 3) to generate and support *social integration* among individuals across cultural groups and within institutions, and 4) to nurture and guide each student's sense of *social responsibility* for the consequences of his/her own personal actions, and for the character and quality of the groups to which the student belongs. In other words, each of these four conditions can be viewed as an important outcome domain in its own right.[3]

Which of these four outcome expectations will be seen as the most important depends both on one's views about the nature of an ideal society, and on one's judgment about how the schooling of children specifically contributes to the improvement of current social conditions. If, for ex-ample, the maintenance of social order seems to be threatened, nurturing social responsibility may seem more important than promoting personal development. If, on the other hand, social alienation or loss of personal creativity seems to be the more pressing social issue, fostering social integration or personal development may become priorities.

When one of these major societal outcome expectations becomes dominant and serves as the primary basis or context for school program development and organization, it is useful to think of education as being *based* on that expectation. Thus, Competency Based Education programs are ones in which the demand for competence is dominant and school operations are organized around student attainment of explicit achieve-ment goals. As shown in table 1, there are three other outcome based alternatives to be considered. They are: Development Based Education, Social Integration Based Education, and Social Responsibility Based Education.

Although each of these four basic expectations for schooling outcomes contributes to at least some aspects of all school programs, school or-ganizations do not favor all equally. Major strategies for improving school performance can be developed by concentrating on one of these primary outcome domains and subordinating the others to the realization of the dominant one. These four different approaches tend to draw social and political support from different groups both within and outside the schools, creating tension and competition around the various alternatives.

Compounding the tensions related to these four alternative bases of

Table 1. Characteristic Features of the Alternative Bases of Education

	Competency Based Education	Development Based Education	Social Integration Based Education	Social Responsibility Based Education
Dominant Societal Expectation	Performance Competency	Personal Development	Social Integration	Social Responsibility
Dominant Functional Process	Certification	Instruction	Acculturation	Supervision
Central Student Activities	Qualifying	Learning	Participating	Adjusting
Primary Condition of Motivation	Opportunity	Adventure	Identity	Status
Central Problems in Social Organization	A. Standards B. Production	A. Production B. Engagement	A. Engagement B. Maintenance	A. Maintenance B. Standards
Alternative Operational Emphases	A. Utility of Outcomes B. Quality of Outcomes	A. Intellectual Development B. Affective Development	A. Social Service B. Integrative Living	A. Loyalty and Respect B. Appropriate Conduct
Most Pertinent Social Science	Economics	Psychology	Sociology	Political Science
Mode of Inquiry				

education are the organizational difficulties associated with translating typically diffuse and abstract societal expectations into more specific functional processes and activities that engage both staff and students in behavior that ultimately produces the outcomes sought. As noted in table 1, this means that the realization of each outcome expectation is predominantly dependent upon a specific set of functional activities within the school organization. Each of these dominant organizational functions in turn facilitates a corresponding set of student behaviors. Thus, for example, in responding to demands for student competency, the schools highlight student technical performance by employing *certification* criteria and mechanisms which both emphasize and validate a student qualifying for rewards, promotions, or certificates by meeting explicit and agreed upon standards. In other words, assuring that student outcomes will involve technical competence depends upon the centrality and integrity of the certification procedures used to validate them. Similarly, societal expectations for personal development require an emphasis on the school's instructional function and corresponding expectations for student learning activities. Expectations for social integration elevate the importance of the acculturation function and its corresponding emphasis on student participating activities; and finally, basing school operations on the expectation for social responsibility means that supervisory processes and student adjusting responses are to be given top priority.

Because schools are institutions and must develop integrated and workable procedures, the activity patterns in any school or classroom will always reflect the presence of some elements of all four major functional processes and all four student responses—regardless of whether or not one particular outcome expectation becomes dominant. That is, schooling always involves the supervision, acculturation, instruction, and certification of students and always seeks from youngsters adjustment, participation, learning, and qualifying responses, regardless of which, if any, outcome base is used to judge whether the schools are realizing societal expectations.

Motivating student compliance with, and engagement in, any of these functional activities is, of course, crucial to its success. Students must be attracted by the outcomes to be achieved and be responsive to the functional processes within the school which are intended to embody these outcomes. Table 1 suggests that there is a particular motivational condition associated with each of the principal outcome domains which serves as the key to student engagement and involvement. We are suggesting, for example, that from the student's perspective, certification processes, which embody socially endorsed performance standards, are only attractive if they enable the student to qualify for desirable and real future *opportunities*. Lacking a sense that their efforts in meeting performance demands will have positive consequences for their (immediate or long term) future, students are unlikely to invest the effort or risk the frustration associated with hard work that has little promise of payoff.[4] Unless educators can convince the students that better educational, occupational, or financial opportunities will result from their meeting certification standards, competency based programs may encounter serious problems of compliance and participation which educators have little capacity to control.

Given the stress among Development Based Education advocates on the emergence of student learning and growth from the child's natural curiosity and motivation, it is not surprising to find that the key motivational condition governing instructional effectiveness is *adventure*. From the student's perspective, interest, stimulation, wonder, excitement, and the promise of enhanced personal effectiveness are all important elements in creating and sustaining engagement in tasks that lead to real discovery and learning. Without an accompanying sense of adventure, instructional tasks and experiences run the risk of alienating students rather than capturing their attention.

The key motivating factor governing the realization of social integration outcomes is *identity* formation. Response to acculturation activities aimed at facilitating student participation in the school depends on the confirmation of their worth and attractiveness. Participation is valuable to the extent that it affirms one's personal value, both to oneself and to other group members.

Similarly, adjusting to the prevalent rules and norms of the social group and subordinating one's personal interests to the general welfare depends fundamentally on the individual holding a place of real *status* in the group. Consequently, Social Responsibility Based Education programs will inspire student responsiveness to the extent that student rights, prerogatives and prestige are distributed in relation to the adequacy of their adjustments. If they are without recognition and influence in a valued social order, students will lack a basis for viewing their personal welfare as inseparable from the welfare and integrity of the group as a whole.

Taken together, then, these relationships suggest some important starting points for examining school effectiveness issues. In particular, they identify four major conditions that may underlie school system success in reaching primary outcome goals. That is, opportunity, adventure, identity, and status are the essential preconditions for student involvement and engagement in the school's major operational functions.

Note, however, that the four outcome domains which serve to create alternative outcome-based education programs are not isolated ends in themselves. In various combinations they help resolve four fundamental social problems faced by every society and institution: norm or *standard setting,* the creation of *individual engagement, societal maintenance,* and the stimulation of *productive capacity.*[5] For example, the development of both competency and social responsibility combine to enable a social group to set and maintain visible standards of personal conduct and performance, while personal development and social integration enable social group members to be responsive to, and fully engaged in, the societal system. Similarly, social integration and social responsibility outcomes, when combined, contribute to group and organizational stability or maintenance, and competency and development outcomes combine to create a group's productive capacities.

Thus, each outcome domain, taken by itself, contributes to the solution of two basic social problems. For example, as shown in table 1, competency outcomes enable the society to set standards for performance and to expect citizens to meet them, and they also facilitate the capacity of individuals to be productive, contributing members of the social system. Similarly, developmental outcomes contribute both to enhancing individual productivity and to promoting fuller engagement in the societal system. Social integration outcomes, which obviously strengthen the engagement of individuals in the society by enhancing their sense of involvement and participation, also play a key role in maintaining social institutions and value systems by reducing alienation and discontent within the societal system. Similarly, social responsibility outcomes assist with societal maintenance by nuturing respect for the rights of others, even when individuals are unhappy or alienated, and by contributing to the establishment of high standards of personal and group conduct—thereby going beyond maintenance to the creation of order where it would otherwise not exist.

As suggested in table 1, there are two educational program models inherent in each of the four major outcome bases just discussed—one related to each of the two fundamental social problems to which that outcome domain may be directed. For example, when advocates of CBE expect schools to raise the level of performance standards for all citizens, they usually emphasize the practical social *utility* of the competencies to be achieved. But when the focus is on increasing individual and aggregate productivity, CBE emphasizes the *quality* of outcome competencies and their contribution to improved effectiveness, inventiveness, or creativity on the part of individuals.

Development Based Education advocates also differ. When they see the most pressing problem as social productivity (as occurred under NDEA programs in response to the 1957 Sputnik launching), they emphasize *intellectual* development. But when they are more concerned with alienation and social disengagement, they tend to emphasize *affective* rather than intellectual outcomes.

Policymakers who support Social Integration Based Education programs and see social engagement as the central problem, often emphasize outcomes which lead students to identify with a life of *social service*. However, when the central problem is viewed as the deterioration of the social institutions or an inability to maintain social patterns, Social Integration advocates tend to emphasize the need for student outcomes which facilitate the desire and ability for *integrative living*.

Social Responsibility Based Education programs emphasize the development of *loyalty and respect* for social institutions and norms when their central concern is social pattern maintenance. When the central issue has more to do with the development and maintenance of social order and standards, Social Responsibility enthusiasts focus more attention on the nuturing of *appropriate conduct* among students.

It is also helpful in understanding the differences among these four alternative approaches to outcome based education to see them in relation to the conceptual frameworks or approaches to social problem definition and resolution found in various social science disciplines. As suggested by the terms in the bottom row of table 1, each alternative base is closely associated with a particular social science discipline. For example, CBE, with its emphasis on social utility and rewarding high quality performances, closely reflects an *economic* perspective on society. Economic concerns with establishing market values for goods and services, assessing programs in terms of the "value added" to the materials which pass through them, and the development of production functions for social institutions, provide an important framework used in both understanding and measuring the success of CBE programs.

Personal development approaches to education are much more compatible with the theoretical perspectives of *psychology*. Psychologists are concerned with the consequences to the individual of exposure to institutions and their programs, and (in industrial psychology, at least) with the conditions under which individuals become intimately engaged in, and contribute effectively to, organizational outputs. Both in its therapeutic and experimental concerns, psychology is concerned with the developmental process, its problems, and its facilitation.

Social Integration is the most fundamental of all *sociological* themes. Sociology is concerned with the creation of social groups and institutions, with the maintenance of these social entities, and with the engagement and/or alienation of individuals from them. Sociologists emphasize the creation of meaningful identities for individuals and social groups, and study the acculturation or socialization processes by which these identities are acquired.

Social responsibility is the central province of *political science*. Whether politics is seen primarily as rulemaking, authoritative allocation of values, legitimation of power and coercion, or realization of normative beliefs and values, it is always seen as delineating the nature and limits of social rights and responsibilities for citizens. On the one hand, political theory articulates the basis for demanding social responsibility from citizens, and on the other, it attempts to analyze the processes through which this social responsibility can be nurtured and guided.

The parellelism between the alternative approaches to outcome based education and these four social science disciplines not only suggests that educators could benefit significantly from a closer scrutiny of the concepts and approaches to explanation found within the social sciences, but also that each discipline could contribute much more to our understanding of school operations than has generally been the case. Except for psychology, most social science disciplines have been largely ignored by those responsible for the training of teachers and school administrators. One reason educators have found recent pressures for educational reform so confusing and difficult to understand has been their woefully inadequate training in the perspectives and assumptions of these other three social science disciplines. Of equal concern, however, is the fact that scholars from these disciplines have paid scant attention to education as an arena of study. Even when looking at the schools, economists, sociologists, and political scientists have generally emphasized the relationship of the school to other social institutions, rather than the internal workings of the school itself. The foregoing suggests that classrooms contain not only a psychology of learning, but also an exchange economy, a governance system, and a sociology of group life. Too little is known about these vital processes and how they might become the basis for structuring and controlling teaching and learning.

Alternative Operational Models of Outcome Based Education

As noted earlier, the expectations for basing schooling on a particular outcome can give rise to alternative interpretations of, and approaches to, the realization of that outcome depending on its assumed relation to a given social problem. What follows is a more detailed treatment of the eight outcome alternatives identified in this way in table 1. The analysis reveals how each alternative is operationalized by a unique ordering of functional priorities, how each functional process is reoriented to support the dominant outcome domain, and that some specific trends in school personnel management and structural arrangements are implied by each model.

Competency Based Education

The operational characteristics of the two major approaches to CBE are summarized in table 2. Both reflect attempts to elevate and significantly reorient the certification function of the school. The thrust of this reorientation shifts the certification function itself away from having students satisfy time based course requirements (by meeting the often vague, variable, and frequently suspect standards of individual teachers), to validating the attainment of known, explicit, criterion referenced performance goals. What really counts in such a system is documenting that students have reached explicit performance levels.

Table 2. Operational Models of Competency Based Education

Dominant Functional Process	Certification	
Significant Reorientation of Functional Purpose	From Satisfying Course Requirements to Reaching Criterion Referenced Performance Goals	
Major Operational Models (Central Problem)	Utility of Outcomes (Standards)	Quality of Outcomes (Production)
Primary Supporting Function	Supervision	Instruction
(Major Reorientation)	(From process sanctions to outcome sanctions)	(From subject based textbooks to performance handbooks)
Secondary Supporting Function	Instruction	Supervision
(Major Reorientation)	(From concept based textbooks to content based workbooks)	(From time structured course enrollment to multiple learning opportunities)
Tertiary Supporting Function	Acculturation	Acculturation
(Major Reorientation)	(From friendship to opportunism)	(From assigned classmates to workgroup membership)
Implied Emphasis in Personnel Management	Practitioner Certifiers	Measurement Specialists
Implied Structural Emphasis	Non-School Instructional Sites	Learning Laboratories

The two alternative models of CBE differ in their contrasting emphases on the *utility* as distinct from *quality* of the competencies desired. Those who emphasize the utility of outcomes are primarily concerned with the potential harm to the society as a whole that would occur from tolerating a deterioration of standards of personal performance by high school graduates in either economic, political, or social affairs. Consequently, they seek outcomes with high economic and social utility in order to maintain or reestablish desired standards, and they see the utilization of the supervision function as the primary means for supporting this goal by tying sanctions to the actual accomplishment of specific outcomes rather than administering them on the basis of behavior and deportment.

Once the standards and appropriate sanctioning mechanisms are established, the instructional system can be used to provide the explicit and pragmatic content needed by students. This may require the use of specific content based workbooks instead of more general concept based texts, and may precipitate a reorientation of student social relationships away from spontaneous friendship choices to more calculative and opportunistic associations based on their capacity to facilitate outcome attainment.[6]

In addition, this focus on the utility of outcomes requires that the school have access to individuals in the society who know the practical value of given competencies and who could serve as more valid certifiers of student performance. Such an approach also benefits from structural arrangements that give students access to non-school instructional sites that will enhance the linkage between learning and its actual applications. It is clear that many vocational and career education programs closely resemble this model.

When the emphasis on student outcomes is motivated primarily by a desire to improve individual achievement and productivity (rather than maintain group standards), the pressure for competencies focuses on their quality rather than direct application. This orientation is supported through the natural alignment of the certification and instruction functions as the means for facilitating student accomplishment, and involves a shift in instructional approach from the use of conventional subject based textbooks to handbooks designed to develop specific performance capacities.

The supervision function is used in this model to support this realignment of instructional mechanisms by restructuring patterns of student access to instruction and certification. This restructuring replaces fixed time boundaries for course enrollment with a framework in which multiple opportunities for learning and performance are available. It also allows for a shift in acculturation processes by altering the student's primary group membership, emphasizing relationships with fluid work groups rather than with more permanently assigned classmates.

Accompanying this focus on improving the quality of student outcomes are personnel and structural emphases designed to maximize both opportunities for achievement and the validity of their assessment. Such an approach places substantial importance on the availability of both measurement specialists to handle matters of certification and on specialized learning laboratories designed to facilitate competency development. This model is characteristic of CBE approaches designed to raise the ceiling of accomplishment for the individual student rather than assuring a minimum standard for the cohort as a whole.

Development Based Education

The primary thrust of a development based approach to school operations involves concentrating on expanding student learning and capacities for

Table 3. Operational Models of Development Based Education

Dominant Functional Process	Instruction	
Significant Reorientation of Functional Purpose	From Pursuing Structured Curriculum to Expanding Awareness and Quality of Experience	
Major Operational Models (Central Problem)	Intellectual Development (Production)	Affective Development (Engagement)
Primary Supporting Function (Major Reorientation)	Certification (From Prescribed Standards to Unique Excellence)	Acculturation (From Getting Along to Significant Encounters)
Secondary Supporting Function (Major Reorientation)	Acculturation (From Accepting Social Identity to Creating Personal Identity)	Certification (From Performance Level to Quality of Endeavor)
Tertiary Supporting Function (Major Reorientation)	Supervision (From Routinization to Experimentation)	Supervision (From Controlling and Directing to Guiding and Facilitating)
Implied Emphasis in Personnel Management	Subject Matter Specialists	Therapeutic Specialists
Implied Structural Emphasis	Achievement/ Ability Grouping	Age/Interest Based Grouping

self-fulfillment. While instruction would appear to be the most obvious of the school's central functions and a natural operational priority, adopting an outcome based approach to student development means paying less attention to the pursuit of the structured components of the instructional curriculum and focusing more sharply on developing enhanced awareness and quality of experience.

The two operational models or approaches to Development Based Education analyzed in table 3 differ with regard to their central conception of learning and development. A focus on intellectual development results when learning is centrally regarded as a societal achievement and production issue. When seen primarily as a matter affecting the quality of encounter and engagement between an individual and his/her environment, personal development stimulates a concern with the affective dimensions of learning and growth.

The operational thrust of the intellectual development model rests on a close linkage between instruction and certification as processes affecting personal achievement and productivity. The certification function is used to support a developmental focus on learning outcomes by validating accomplishments reflecting unique personal excellence rather than by assessing and verifying student compliance with prescribed minimum standards. In this model, the acculturation function also reinforces the unique achievement and excellence of each student by promoting personal identity rather than stressing group attributes. Supervision is used in the same vein to facilitate whatever experimentation may be necessary to maximize student accomplishment rather than to assure routinization of instructional activities.

Among the more important administrative implications of this intellectual development based model are the importance of subject matter specialists in expanding students' awareness and conceptions of excellence, and the use of achievement or ability grouping as a basis for structuring students' engagement with the curriculum. Overall, this approach essentially marries a clear orientation toward cognitive development and the primacy of excellence with a flexible, humanistic approach and regard for the individual.

The humanistic character of the development based approach appears to be even clearer, however, when development is seen primarily as a basis for enhancing the quality of the individual's engagement with his physical and social environment. This orientation toward affective rather than cognitive development is facilitated through the natural linkage of the instruction and acculturation functions in expanding the social and experiential capacities of students. When used in direct support of the learning process, the acculturation function is used to heighten the student's sensitivity to the importance, depth, and significance of social encounter rather than to support a more passive orientation to "getting along" with others.

Given the dominant concern within this model of expanding the boundaries of students' capacities to experience and encounter themselves and their environment, the school is required to revise both the certification and supervision functions in support of these goals. The typical concern of certification procedures with performance levels gives way to a focus on the quality of the student's engagement and endeavor within a learning experience; and supervision shifts from an orientation toward controlling and directing behavior, to guiding and facilitating the student's exposure to new and significant experiences.

In such a model specialists with a therapeutic orientation to student development acquire a prominent role in facilitating an expansion of awareness and experience, and structural arrangements using age and interest groupings as frameworks for developmental activities take on added importance. Many free schools, alternative schools, and elementary school programs embody the dominant features of this operational model.

Social Integration Based Education

To adopt a social integration based approach to schooling is to establish acculturation as the most important operational activity and to create a significant basis for social interaction and involvement for students in the larger social milieu. As suggested in table 4, this requires a reorientation of purpose away from accepting the passive participation of youngsters in the social life of the classroom and the school, to one in which they actively contribute to and shape the social order. The alternative operational models of this approach depend on whether social integration outcomes are essentially seen as elements for facilitating the engagement of the individual with others or as preconditions for maintaining the coherence and stability of the social order itself.

When viewed primarily as a contribution to the school's engagement goals, the acculturation function takes on a social service and developmental thrust. That is, the instruction function is used to develop in students capacities for role based, socially referenced growth that can be used to promote the viability of the social system through effective service to it. By acquiring significant learning experiences in the context of important social roles, students associate their own growth with effective role performance.

In such a model, the supervision function shifts away from a reliance on external bases of student control to a focus on self-regulation acquired through active role engagement. Similarly, the important criteria for certifying student progress focus less on personal knowledge and intellectual prowess and more on the contribution which the student's role engagement makes to the integrity and effectiveness of the group.

The personnel management strategies highlighted by the social service

Table 4. Operational Models of Social Integration Based Education

Dominant Functional Process	Acculturation	
Significant Reorientation of Functional Purpose	From Accepting Passive Participation to Creating Significant Social Involvement	
Major Operational Models (Central Problem)	Social Service (Engagement)	Integrative Living (Maintenance)
Primary Supporting Function (Major Reorientation)	Instruction (From Curriculum Content to Life Role Engagement)	Supervision (From Managing Orderly Classrooms to Reconstructing Social Reality)
Secondary Supporting Function (Major Reorientation)	Supervision (From External Control to Self-Discipline)	Instruction (From Mastering Academic Disciplines to Acquiring Relevant Social Experience)
Tertiary Supporting Function (Major Reorientation)	Certification (From Personal Knowledge to Social Contribution)	Certification (From Achievement Level to Quality of Participation)
Implied Emphasis in Personnel Management	Activity Advisers/ Coaches/Directors	Non-Instructional Community Aides, Multicultural Teacher
Implied Structural Emphasis	Extracurricular, Community Based Activities Programs	Integrated Classrooms, Bilingual/ Biculturalism

model emphasize the central contributions of activity advisers, coaches, and project directors of various kinds; and structural conditions are developed which provide an abundance of extracurricular and community based activities and programs. There are strong parallels between this model and Dewey's conceptions of schooling that led to the Progressive Education Movement.[7]

By contrast, when social integration is regarded mainly as a contribution to the maintenance of orderly patterns of social cohesion among often diverse cultural or socio-economic groups, the primary goal of the acculturation function is to facilitate integrative living. Such an approach typically involves the close alliance of both the acculturation and supervision functions in an attempt to reconstruct important conditions in students' social environment and the bases of their interactions within it.[8] These new contexts allow new possibilities for significant social interactions between otherwise dissimilar students to emerge and for pluralism to become an operational reality.

The instructional focus of this model relies less on academic mastery and more on students' acquisition of a broader range of social experience and the capacity to work and play compatibly with youngsters different from themselves. Similarly, what is assessed and certified pertains more to the quality of students' participation with others than to their personal academic achievement.

Given the focus on social and cultural pluralism in this model, its priorities for both personnel and structural management focus on the heterogeneous composition of staff and student groups. Noninstructional community aides, multicultural teachers, integrated classrooms, and bilingual/bicultural instructional approaches are all significant elements. The Social Interaction Based Education model has played a visible role in attempts to erase racial and cultural stereotyping during the past two decades.

Social Responsibility Based Education

For the school to adopt the demonstration of student social responsibility as its principal base of operation, supervision and the reorientation of students' relationships to the social order must be the central focus in the network of essential staff functions. Being social responsibility based entails a major shift in student orientation which moves beyond mere compliance with rules, norms, and institutional pressures, to an internalization and actual embracing of the values and norms that underlie orderly social intercourse. Only when students believe in and embody these rules and obligations is their status in, and identification with, the social order clear.

The two operational models described in table 5 vary according to the centrality of the problem of preserving and maintaining important social values on the one hand, or of establishing specific standards of behavior on the other. When responsibility is seen primarily as a contributor to the maintenance of social institutions and values, the operational thrust of the supervision function involves the nurturing of loyalty and respect for existing norms and patterns. Here the natural linkage between supervision and acculturation combine to shift the basis of personal relationships in a direction in which the reputation of others, defined in terms of their propriety and worthiness, is used as the major criterion in choosing friends and associates.

Table 5. Operational Models of Social Responsibility Based Education

Dominant Functional Process	Supervision	
Significant Reorientation of Functional Purpose	From Complying with Institutional Pressures to Embracing Social Norms	
Major Operational Models (Central Problem)	Loyalty and Respect (Maintenance)	Appropriate Conduct (Standards)
Primary Supporting Function (Major Reorientation)	Acculturation (From Enjoyable Relationships to Reputable Associates)	Certification (From Achieving Solutions to Accepting and Following Formal Directions)
Secondary Supporting Function (Major Reorientation)	Certification (From Achievement Level to Quality of Citizenship)	Acculturation (From Unrestricted Friendship Choices to Status Based Relationships)
Tertiary Supporting Function (Major Reorientation)	Instruction (From Skill Development to Attitude Development)	Instruction (From Development of Abilities to Propriety of Conduct)
Implied Emphasis in Personnel Management	Guidance Specialists	Student Disciplinary Specialists
Implied Structural Emphasis	Staff Centered Programs/Procedures	Closely Structured Classrooms and Schools

This strong link between the individual and the dominant values of the social order is further reinforced through the assessment and certification of qualities of citizenship rather than levels of performance, and in the instructional priority for attitude development rather than skill development. In short, grounding an operational model around loyalty and respect for existing social arrangements precipitates a set of functional activities that reinforce students' conceptions of their personal integrity as inseparable from the integrity of the company they keep and institutions they maintain.

The personnel and structural policies used to facilitate this model include extensive use of guidance counselors in cases where student adjustment to established norms is problematic, and staff centered programs and procedures which continually remind students of their relationships to established authority. The current Fundamental School movement appears to embody many features of this operational model.

A second operational model for Social Responsibility Based Education identifies social responsibility with the establishment of orderly social behavior standards and emphasizes the contribution of schooling to the development of appropriate conduct. In this model, certification processes provide the most immediate support for the supervision function by shifting the criteria for assessment and evaluation away from concern with achievement of solutions to problems or demonstration of skills, and onto the student's willingness to follow formal directions. When the objective is proper conduct, compliance is more important than results.

Acculturation processes in this model also support conduct norms by shifting participation processes away from unrestricted friendship choices and toward status based relationships for student social groupings. Associating with members of one's own status group or class reinforces the acceptance of the behavior norms of that group. In this model, instruction shifts from development of abilities to the specification or propriety of conduct. Lessons tend to stress following prescribed instructions and procedures rather than identifying emergent abilities or skills.

This appropriate conduct model also implies the development of both student disciplinary specialists on the school staff who will maximize the impact of the school on conduct norms, and closely structured classrooms and tightly organized schools. Traditional military academies symbolize the optimal development of this model of Social Responsibility Based Education.

Organizational Tensions and the Alternative Outcome Models

Educational outcomes, as the foregoing analysis has emphasized, involve much more than technical competencies. Not only are outcomes related to personal development, social integration and social responsibility different in principle from those emphasized by the Competency Based Education movement, they are also achieved in ways which require different and frequently contradictory emphases in school operations. In responding to demands for enhanced educational outcomes, it is important for educators and policymakers alike to keep in mind that increasing the intensity of demands for measureable results will not necessarily enable the school to produce the desired outcomes. There is every reason to believe that, at some point, increasing attention on competency will mean a reduction in other schooling outcomes.

Although little is known about the effects of organizational processes and activity structures on student outcomes, it is quite clear that alternative outcome approaches imply dramatic shifts, both in the essential character and in the relative emphasis placed on the central school functions and structures. If the pressures for school reform and redirection are to be creative rather than merely disruptive, it is vitally important that research and policy analysis focus on the relationship between the increasingly explicit political demands for educational outcomes and the specific organizational changes required if the schools are to pursue those outcomes. Without a clear understanding of how organizational mechanisms facilitate or inhibit desired student outcomes, pressure for improved performance can only lead to frustration and disappointment.

A close look at the history of educational policy could provide an effective means for identifying the operational variables which affect schooling outcomes and for exploring tensions between alternative outcome based education models. Over the past century, articulate spokespersons for all of the operational models described in this paper have proposed specific reforms in the instruction, supervision, certification and acculturation functions of the school. Although, as Tyack (1974) suggests, the search for the "one best system" has given contemporary schooling a rather monotonous sameness, attempts to operationalize all of the various models, either alone or in combination, can be identified. Although the historical view is helpful, it is also limited. As Cremin (1964) so ably documents, "the transformation of the school" through reform has always been partial and incomplete, producing organizational and program elements which are inconsistent and contradictory. Only if the historical alternatives are understood within a theoretical framework and subjected to systematic research, can educationally effective and politically acceptable outcome based education programs be developed.

Real variations which exist at the classroom level are rarely manifested within entire schools or districts. Thus research which is insensitive to qualitative differences in both the outcomes and the functional processes enumerated here will obscure rather than illuminate the full range of the effects and effectiveness of schooling.

Notes

1. A report of the proceedings of these conferences has been published by the Central Midwest Regional Educational Laboratory. See Miller (1978).

2. The vast majority of the recent policy initiatives by state legislatures have

focused quite narrowly on the development or adoption of competency tests. In fact, the appeal of this testing approach is so widespread that some congressional leaders have given serious consideration to the development of a national competency testing program.

3. While his articulation of these four types of schooling outcome expectations is focused rather narrowly on the alternative hypotheses regarding the effects of desegregation, Levin (1975) identifies each of these four types of expectations in his article on "Education, Life Chances and the Courts: The Role of Social Science Evidence."

4. Stinchcombe (1964) has looked closely at the effects on students when they find schooling activities unrelated to personal opportunities. Tuinman, et al., (1972) has demonstrated that student motivation to score highly on tests may not be the same for all students, and may be affected by such external motivational factors as paying for high scores. Hence, the opportunity for palpable rewards appears to be very closely connected with the motivation to perform well.

5. These problems are treated widely in the literature, although many different concepts are used to describe the basic problems of social organization. Among the analysts using concepts close to our own are Charters (1964), who distinguishes the problem of productivity from the problem of organizational maintenance, and Durkheim (1951) whose treatise on suicide is a classic treatment of the relationship between social standard setting and the engagement of individuals in meaningful social relationships.

6. Bossert's (1978) provocative work on the activity structures of the school clearly indicates that the structure of the teacher/student relationship within the classroom has important consequences for competitiveness among students, and the nature of their social relationships with peers.

7. The impact of the Progressive Movement is detailed in Cremin (1964).

8. This approach was characteristic of Durkheim's (1961) concern in *Moral Education*. Derkheim and Dewey differed sharply in their approach to social integration. While Dewey focused on both social integration and personal growth through self-discipline, Durkheim emphasized the need for social discipline to control unbridled desires, and the use of close supervision to secure student integration.

References

Bossert, S. T. *Activity structures and student outcomes*. Prepared for the National Institute of Education's Conference on School Organization and Effects, January 1978.

Charters, W. W., Jr. An approach to the formal organization of the school. In D. E. Griffiths (Ed.), *Behavioral science and educational administration*. 63rd Yearbook, NSSE, Part II. Chicago: The University of Chicago Press, 1964, 243-261.

Cremin, L. A. *The transformation of the school: Progressivism in American education, 1876-1957*. New York: Vintage Books, a division of Random House, 1964.

Durkheim, E. *Suicide: A study in sociology*. Translated by J. A. Spaulding and G. Simpson. New York: Free Press, 1951.

Durkheim, E. *Moral education: A study in the theory and application of the sociology of education.* New York: Free Press of Glencoe, 1961.

Levin, H. M. Education, life chances, and the courts: The role of social science evidence. *Law and contemporary problems,* 1975, 39, 217-240.

Miller, Barbara S. (ed.), *Minimum competency testing: A report of four regional conferences.* St. Louis: Central Midwest Regional Educational Laboratory, January 1978.

Mitchell, D. E. *Expectation, evaluation and reward systems in schools.* Prepared for the National Institute of Education's Conference on School Organization and Effects, January 1978.

Mitchell, D. E., & Spady, W. G. Authority and the functional structuring of social action in the schools. Unpublished manuscript, 1977.

Pipho, C. State activity related to minimal competency testing. Unpublished report. Education Commission of the States, Denver: January 1978.

Spady, W. G. Competency based education: A bandwagon in search of a definition. *Educational Researcher,* 1977, 6, 9-14.

Spady, W. G. & Mitchell, D. E. Authority, power and expectations as determinants of action and tension in school organizations. Unpublished manuscript, 1977a.

Spady, W. G., & Mitchell, D. E. Competency based education: Organizational issues and implications. *Educational Researcher,* 1977b, 6, 9-15.

Spady, W. G., & Mitchell, D. E. The uses of authority and power in the organization and control of school task performance. Unpublished manuscript, 1977c.

Stinchcombe, A. *Rebellion in a high school.* Chicago: Quadrangle Books, 1964.

Tuinman, J. J., Farr, R., & Blanton, B. E. Increases in test scores as a function of material rewards. *Journal of Educational Measurement,* 1972, 9, 215-223.

Tyack, David B. *The one best system: A history of American urban education.* Cambridge, Mass.: Harvard University Press, 1974.

Wise, A. E. The hyper-rationalization of American Education. *New York University Education Quarterly.* Summer 1977, 8, 2-6.

Wise, A. E. Minimal competency testing: Another case of hyper-rationalization. *Phi Delta Kappan,* 1978, 9, 596-598.

28   The Concept and Implications
of Competency-Based Education

William G. Spady

Competency-based education (CBE) ranks as one of the most misused and misapplied concepts in American education today. Since 1973, a major ground swell of policy action has emerged in over 30 states imposing some kind of "competency demonstration" as a condition for student promotion or graduation. In all but a few cases, what has come to be called CBE is no more than a testing and remediation program focused on basic literacy and mathematical skills. It misses the point in terms of the meaning and importance of competency in life-role activities, what it means to base a program on competencies, and in what respects the term education extends beyond the boundaries of student certification alone. In short, competency-based education, if adequately understood and flexibly applied, could be an exciting and valuable concept. However, in order for it to be so, educators, policy makers, and the public will have to be willing to entertain some substantial departures from traditional educational assumptions and practices. The following offers a broader view of this concept and some of its important implications for school systems.

William Spady. "The Concept and Implications of Competency-Based Education." *Educational Leadership. ASCD Journal*, Volume 36, Number 1, October, 1978. Reprinted with permission of the Association for Supervision and Curriculum Development and William Spady. Copyright 1978 by the Association for Supervision and Curriculum Development. All rights reserved.

The Concept of Competency

As noted in an earlier paper (Spady, 1977), I share a viewpoint with many others who have worked with the CBE concept in institutions of higher education that competencies are "indicators of successful performance in life-role activities" (p. 10). Framed in a slightly different way, competencies involve the ability to create effective results in one's life. According to Block (1978), this means both succeeding in existing role structures and having the ability to create new roles for oneself in response to changing social conditions. While there are small differences in the implications of these two definitions, their common elements are most important.

First, they suggest that the focus and context of competencies are real life and the various roles we occupy, which require a broad range of individual capabilities. To be competent in a life role (such as breadwinner, consumer, mate, parent, or political citizen) is to create the quality of experience and success one seeks in that role. This means that the curricula developed to facilitate competencies must take as their starting points an assessment of the demands and contingencies associated with major life roles, not the logic and substance of academic subjects. There are, for example, no life roles called language arts, mathematics, or social studies.

Second, life-role success fundamentally requires coping with the ever-changing realities of social conditions. The environments, resources, regulations, and individuals that are an integral part of modern life are often troublesome and continually changing, which suggests that one of the most essential attributes of a generally competent person will be adaptability.

Third, competencies are formed through the highly complex integration and application of many discrete capacities. These capacities represent the essential building blocks or foundation on which competencies rest. Some of these capacities are, of course, quite apparent and measurable; others are extremely subtle or even invisible to many people. The essential point, however, is that competency requires tapping this reservoir of individual capacities, integrating them in complex ways, and applying them based on the contingencies present in specific social contexts. Competency rarely involves the simple mechanical application of simple cognitive or manual capacities.

Fourth, the integration and application of capacities that underlie competency clearly reflect both the cognitive and manual skills directly supported in most school instruction and a broad repertory of affective capacities, which may, on balance, actually be the attributes that most facilitate life-role success. That is, while knowledge, skills, and concepts are important components of success in all life roles, they do not ensure it. Successful role performance is at least equally facilitated by the attitudes, values, feelings, expectations, motivation, independence, cooperation, endurance, and intuition people possess. Affective capacities cannot be left implicit in a life-role oriented program as they now are in so many schools. In many life situations, these affective capacities may be both "the medium" and an essential component of "the message" itself.

Fifth, competencies ultimately require role performance, not just the acquisition of skills or knowledge of appropriate methods. They are, in other words, reflections of both what one is and what one can do. Competency-oriented programs should, therefore, develop assessment tools that focus on the more qualitative aspects of performance as well as the more concrete demonstrations of cognitive and manual skill tapped by conventional measurement devices.

When taken together these implications represent a major departure from the typical capacity-building orientations of most school programs. Social reality and enlightened projections about life in the twenty-first century become our guides to conceptions of life roles, competencies, curricula, appropriate instructional settings and agents, and assessment tools. The role of segmented school subjects taught in the generally sheltered environment of school buildings will have to be altered substantially if we choose to foster and assess competency outcomes. Capacities must indeed be developed if competencies are to emerge, but the methods, contexts, and timing of their development could alter significantly if life roles were made a more central vehicle in curriculum and instruction.

The issues on which all of this is focused are the transferability of school learning to life and the extent of the school's responsibilities for fostering the moral and technical socialization of youngsters. Although debates have raged over these two related problems for decades, some of the general domains of agreement will be explored in the following section.

The "Bases" of School Operations

School systems, like all formal organizations, must contend with two competing sets of forces: those focused on system productivity and those that stress maintenance and preservation of the organization. In general, the productivity subsystem of an organization requires adaptability, flexibility, and responsiveness to changing demands and technologies, whereas the maintenance system is concerned with ordering, routinizing, and stabilizing activities and procedures. The challenge to administrators is to manage and support both systems without impairing the impact and effectiveness of either. Given the inherent differences between them, this is an extremely challenging task. (See Spady and Mitchell, 1979.)

When we examine the actual organization and operations of schools more closely, we find elements of these two competing subsystems imbedded in classrooms as well as administrative offices. To a large extent, these elements reflect two major bases of organizing school functions and activities: one is time and the other is outcomes (or results). CBE implies a major shift from time as the primary "base" of operations to outcomes (or competencies) as that base, and from vaguely referenced standards of accomplishment to more specific criterion-referenced ones.

At present, schooling is time-based. Major procedures, operations, decisions, and opportunities for both staff and students are dictated by the clock, the schedule, and the calendar. Fixed periods of time such as class periods, grading periods, semesters, and school years impose arbitrary constraints on the ways in which we organize instruction, and when and how often we evaluate and certify student performance. In the time-based system as we know it, time is fixed, students are usually given single opportunities to "pass," and the standards used are usually personal, subjective, variable, and vague. Grades represent a vague and unknown mixture of achievement, ability, motivation, deportment, attendance, "attitude," contextual, and background factors. The high school diploma is merely a certificate of attendance and an indicator of the student's willingness to "satisfy" the particular minimal expectations and standards of a series of teachers. Society's expectations for the year-by-year social promotion of students have reinforced the fixed time basis of schooling, even though we know that the achievement differences among our high school graduates are enormous (and their general standards of social and technical competency are quite disappointing). A time-based system stresses roles rather than goals, emphasizes maintenance rather than productivity, and encourages orientations concerning "having things run smoothly" and "getting through the day" rather than "creating results."

An outcome-based approach to schooling—which is what CBE represents—would reverse the relationships between time and standards. Goals and objectives take on new importance as they are made more explicit, defined in terms of the actual competencies and capacities students will develop and demonstrate, and made the basis of operations and decisions regarding student assessment and movement through the instructional program. In such a system, schooling will no longer be determined by time; instead time is used in more flexible ways, and multiple opportunities for instruction and assessment are provided. This means that much more small-group and individualized instruction is needed to foster student mastery of given outcome goals. In addition, courses, credit, report cards, and standards will be defined on a criterion-referenced basis so that actual levels of skill are known. "Promotion" is not from grade to grade with a total cohort of students at a fixed or final point in time, but a continuous movement through an instructional program. Courses will be units of content representing levels of mastery, not units of time.

To use the term "competency-based" to describe a major approach to education is to treat the framing and attainment of outcomes as the primary base of school operations. But even a nodding acquaintance with the politics and sociology of schools is sufficient to suggest that there is considerable diversity and disagreement among both educators and segments of the public regarding which outcomes should be given priority in school programs. It is doubtful, therefore, that if schools actually wished to become outcome-based that a sufficient consensus could be obtained in most places regarding the particular outcomes around which they could really organize.

According to Mitchell and Spady, who discuss these competing alternatives in some detail elsewhere in this volume, there are four broad themes that characterize the expectations of educators and the public regarding the contributions schools make to the development and socialization of youngsters capable of entering and participating in a society that is orderly, productive, and attractive to its members. These themes include: (a) nurturing in students a sense of *social responsibility* regarding the consequences of their actions for the welfare of others and the society as a whole; (b) generating and supporting *social integration* among individuals from varying social and cultural groups through direct interaction and participation in collective activities; (c) stimulating and fostering the fullest possible *development* and expression of the individual's physical, affective, and mental capacities; and (d) promoting and certifying the achievement of necessary and important *technical competencies*. Each theme has had a major place in the evolution of American education, and each has its visible and vocal contemporary advocates as well.

What is particularly germane to this analysis is that each theme represents an alternative conception of what constitutes "real competency" for individuals, each has the potential for becoming the dominant outcome base for a given school or school system, and each represents an agenda to which every teacher and administrator must be sensitive, irrespective of the pressures imposed by the others. Attention given to one theme often means overlooking others. Consequently, with staff attention divided in four directions at once, it is often true that none of the outcomes desired in each domain is fully realized. The result is both potential and actual staff vulnerability for failing to meet either someone's or everyone's expectations.

It is also important to note that there are major philosophical differences among the advocates of each major theme that further contribute to policy and operational strain in school systems. For example, to some social responsibility means developing loyalty and respect for social institutions and adjusting one's moral and legal conduct to prevailing rules and norms. For others it means showing sensitivity to others, and being willing to serve and support those in need. Similarly, to some social integration means learning appropriate social roles, fostering a sense of belonging, and appreciating and participating in existing social structures and groups. To others it means exercising leadership and initiative in promoting group cohesion and purpose, or establishing close and significant ties to other individuals or cultural groups.

There are also differences among the advocates of personal development. Some would concentrate on intellectual and physical development, others on affective capacities. Within each group, some would stress "trainable and proven" capacities, others would advocate "discovering" emergent capacities and promoting creative expression. Similarly, some advocates of technical competency are primarily concerned with basic language and mathematical proficiency; others with a broader range of technical skills. Among each of these, some stress the utility and minimum standards of competencies, while others seek high standards of excellence and innovative performance capabilities.

Given the tremendous range of qualitative and quantitative differences sought by various groups in terms of school outcomes, it is not surprising to find most state "CBE" policy initiatives reflecting a "lowest common denominator/basic skill" orientation to required student outcomes. The major exceptions, such as Maryland, Oregon, and Pennsylvania, have emerged largely as the result of strong state board of education/state department of education leadership rather than legislative mandate. Yet it is these nearly three dozen other "testing bills" that have substantially turned an educational effectiveness issue into a potential accountability nightmare.

Implementing Competency-Based "Education"

To many of its advocates, imposing new performance requirements for high school graduation is an attempt to re-establish "the credibility of the high school diploma." Now that over 90 percent of an age cohort stays in school a full twelve years and "social promotion" within an age-graded system is accepted policy, we have a large proportion of "graduates" today who would have not finished school in previous eras. However, a distressing proportion of these graduates are conspicuously deficient in basic literacy skills as well as in more advanced aspects of development and achievement.

What lies at the heart of this dilemma is not the diploma or social promotion, it is the system of teacher-referenced standards that we use along with time as the basis for establishing grades and Carnegie units of "credit." As noted earlier, the combination of individual subjective judgment, mixed criteria, and floating standards leads to a labeling and credit system that is best described as vaguely referenced. That is, the letter or numerical grades dispensed by teachers convey far more symbolic value than actual content. Twelve years of vaguely referenced symbols provide one with a transcript and diploma, but not necessarily a good education.

The paradox in all of this, of course, is that employers and college admission officers—the people who need to make selection decisions about graduates based on what they know, can do, and are like—are generally staunch opponents of abandoning the Carnegie unit credit system even though it contributes to the problem of applicants with only paper qualifications. They are "getting stuck" with the same evaluation-certification system they continue to perpetuate by using time and letter grades as the primary criteria for graduation.

There are, of course, alternative approaches to setting and defining standards that could be considered, two of which could be made criterion-referenced rather than vaguely referenced. They are curriculum-referenced and societal-referenced standards.

Curriculum-referenced standards would apply to the acquisition of specific kinds and levels of subject matter mastery. The content and criteria of the standards would be based on the logic and content of the subject, and would be set by experts in each respective field. We could expect the outcomes in such a system to reflect cognitive and psychomotor capacities.

Societal-referenced standards would reflect the judgments of a broader array of citizens regarding the competencies needed to facilitate success in life roles. In this case, the social, political, and economic demands of life would constitute the frame of reference for both curriculum building and standard setting. Mastery of individual capacities could be included among the array of competency standards selected.

The third major alternative, norm-referenced standards, has been the popular choice of nearly every state that has chosen to implement a standardized testing program. Depending on how measurement is actually done and reported, the advantages of norm-referenced testing may be little better than teacher-referenced. In this system, standards are fundamentally comparative and peer-based, and performance in many different knowledge and skill areas is usually reduced to a single numerical score. While you may know that a student scored at the "eighth-grade level" in reading, you may still not know what the student can and cannot read, or what his or her particular strengths and deficiencies may be.

The use of norm-referenced testing to create an accountability system for students will not solve the problems of educational effectiveness that lie within the instructional system. The basic orientation of account-ability approaches is to use some reliable form of student performance data as the basis for making judgments and decisions about either students or staff. This often means reward, placement, or promotion decisions. While remediation for "substandard" performers may be required, that remediation generally consists of providing these students with the content and approaches that have not worked for them in the first place. Nearly every example of current state "CBE" policies either declares or presumes that the existing time-based, age-graded structure of schooling shall remain unchanged. [This is a nonsolution.]

If the problem is seen as an effectiveness issue, two complex, but more valuable, activities would have to be undertaken. The first is examining and improving the nature of and interrelationship between two major factors that affect instructional effectiveness. One factor is the bearing that school structures—that is, the organizing principles for school activity—have on the techniques, procedures, mechanics, and content affecting student involvement, learning, and performance. The other has to do with the quality and character of expectations and social process that characterize the interaction between staff and students. These factors lie at the heart of school effectiveness and cannot be ignored.

The second activity that needs to be undertaken in order to improve school effectiveness is to create *close articulation* between student assessment and instruction. This means continual diagnosis, monitoring, feedback, and correction of student progress based on regular contact. This does not mean the once-a-year administration of "the big standardized test" that may not correspond with the curriculum the students have been pursuing. It is not clear what we expect these tests to tell us about the levels of student achievement that the teachers who interact with them on a daily basis do not already know. If this information *is* missing, it is due to the inadequacies of the classroom assessment system, and that is what needs to be strengthened. If this information is available but not used effectively to improve student learning, the fault may lie in our typical use of classroom assessment to manage and control students rather than to manage and improve instruction. Also, in most states where such testing programs have been installed, it is the students who are penalized for program weaknesses by having promotion or diplomas withheld.

In a genuine competency-based program, the danger of poor articulation between assessment and instruction would be averted. CBE is built around the close integration of three essential components: (a) outcome goals; (b) instructional experiences that directly reflect those goals; and (c) assessment devices that represent the operational definition of the goal itself. To build maximum flexibility and responsiveness into such a program, all three need to be *explicit* (that is, criterion-referenced and clear); be *known* (that is, public and visible—without secrets and surprises); be *agreed upon* by all those with a direct interest in the student's progress; *allow choice* (that is, be framed and developed with several equivalent alternatives to choose from); and be *adaptive*. Being adaptive means to use student performance data as the basis for modifying and improving four major things: (a) the student's subsequent performance, (b) the content and quality of instruction provided, (c) the assessment tools used to measure goal attainment, and (d) the content and sequencing of goals and curricula.

Since there are dangers of such a goals-means educational approach becoming inflexible and mechanistic, care must be taken to create as many choices and as much flexibility as possible. There are, as Spady and Mitchell (1977) point out, two distinctly different conceptions of how a goal-based (or outcome-based) approach such as this might work. One is to prescribe and delimit at the outset both the goals to be pursued and the role opportunities available to students. This has been characterized as the "whips and chains" approach to schooling. The other is to expand both the goal and role choices available, particularly when outcomes are defined in competency terms, and engagement in realistic life-role pursuits is desirable. In a goal-based program the important and determining principle of operation is *reaching the goal*. The means, locale, resources, agents, time, and number of opportunities given for reaching the goal are open to far greater choice than in a role-dominated program in which time and means are often taken more seriously than the outcomes attained.

From this perspective CBE can be fundamentally geared to improving student opportunities in several ways: (a) by dealing with time and opportunities for meeting goals more flexibly and realistically; (b) by articulating goals and the purposes of instruction clearly and openly; (c) by giving a specific content referent to assessment, evaluation, certification, and promotion criteria; and (d) by bringing schoolwork closer to the real factors affecting success and fulfillment in life.

What it does in the process is influence the entire range of accepted school structures and practices, including: the structure and use of goals and objectives; the meaning and bases of standards and credit; the definition, organization, and delivery of the curriculum; the criteria and methods of student evaluation, record keeping, and reporting systems; student grouping and promotion practices; the criteria and timing of "graduation"; methods of student supervision and control; role expectations and relationships between staff and students; and staff interdependence and cooperation.

In a phrase, CBE means a continuous progress approach to instruction and certification for all students. As a California school administrator recently remarked, "It makes perfect sense from an educational standpoint, but we'll all be afraid to try it. Instead, we'll keep giving kids standardized tests and ask teachers to grade tougher all twelve years." CBE does, indeed, ask both educators and the public to give up decades of habits and assumptions regarding the structures and methods of schooling, just at the time when accountability looks cheaper and safer than another version of school reform. The "CBE testing movement" has reached bandwagon proportions in just a few years, but CBE in practice may become this century's major nonevent in public education.

References

William G. Spady. "Competency Based Education: A Bandwagon in Search of a Definition." *Educational Researcher 6* (1): 9-14; January 1977.

William G. Spady and Douglas E. Mitchell. "Competency Based Education: Organizational Issues and Implications." *Educational Researcher 6* (2): 9-15; February 1977.

William G. Spady and Douglas E. Mitchell. "Authority and the Management of Classroom Activities." In: Daniel L. Duke, ed. *Classroom Management.* National Society for the Study of Education Yearbook, Part 2, 1979. In press.

29   Minimum Competency in Functional Literacy for Work

Thomas G. Sticht

Under the fire of public criticism, fueled by the many reports of student incompetence even after twelve years of education, over half the nation's states have initiated efforts to establish "minimum competency" standards. They hope to provide students with literacy skills needed to cope with the world of work, home, and community outside of the school.

In the pursuit of minimum competency, many have discovered that it is not a simple matter to identify the literacy tasks people encounter outside of school, nor to identify a "level" of competence which might be considered "minimal" yet "functional" enough to be set as a standard for achievement.

Functional Literacy for Work

One of the aims that citizens have for their schools is that they prepare students with the literacy skills needed to get, hold, and achieve in a job. Most aspire to more than unskilled labor for their children. They want the schools to develop literacy skills needed for access to responsible, well-paying jobs. They do not necessarily demand preparation for jobs for which extensive

The findings and opinions expressed in this report do not necessarily reflect the position or policy of the National Institute of Education or the U.S. Department of Health, Education and Welfare. The research reported herein was conducted while the author was a staff member of the Human Resources Research Organization, Western Division, Monterey, California. I am indebted to Lynn Fox, Diana Welty Zapf, Robert Hauke, John Caylor, Richard Kern, Kent Huff, and John Joyner for their outstanding work as members of the research team who conducted the research projects summarized here.

higher education is required, but jobs for which a good high school education—that takes 12 years!—should prepare one: a good trade, a craft, or
a white-collar managerial job.

Yet many efforts to develop minimum literacy standards lack a clear
understanding of what is meant by literacy and of the ways literacy skills
are used in various occupational settings. The latter problem was recognized by the National Institute of Education's Study Group on Linguistic
Communication, chaired by Professor George Miller of Rockefeller University, when it recommended that two types of data be gathered for a
random sample of occupations in the society: data on the level of reading
skills required to have access to an occupation; and data on the level of
reading skills necessary to gain the knowledge to perform adequately in
the occupation (Miller, 1974).

Though this recommendation is now over four years old, it has yet to
be followed in any systematic way by the National Institute of Education.
However, other organizations (notably the Department of Defense) have
been studying the literacy demands of various military jobs for some time.
Much of the Department of Defense work has been reviewed elsewhere
(Sticht, 1975; Sticht and Zapf, 1976). However, some of the more recent
research to identify reading tasks and necessary reading levels for jobs in
the military has not been reviewed outside of the military setting. This
paper will discuss this recent work so that its relevance to the civilian
sector can be observed, and so associated conceptual and methodological
problems may be aired and taken into consideration by others who are
concerned with job and task analysis, literacy, and minimum competency
testing. The report here is a summary; a complete description of the
research can be found in technical reports obtainable from the Navy Personnel Research and Development Center, San Diego (Sticht, Fox, Hauke,
and Zapf, 1977a, b).

The Nature of Job Reading Tasks

Written language differs from spoken language in two major features;
written language is more permanent, and it is visual and can hence be
arrayed in visual space. These features make possible the use of written
materials for two broad classes of reading tasks: *reading to do* something,
and *reading to learn* something. Because printed language is permanent,
it forms an external memory that can be consulted for reference pruposes.
Therefore the information it contains does not have to be learned; it can
simply be looked up if needed again. It is this type of reading task that I
refer to as a reading-to-do task.

Reading-to-learn tasks also draw upon the permanence of printed
language, in that they employ various strategies for learning from textual

materials that involve repeatedly reading and studying the test. Additionally, the fact that printed language is visual is used to advantage in such study strategies as underlining, outlining, making figures, schematics, and so forth.

Information regarding the performance of reading-to-do and reading-to-learn tasks in job settings was obtained in interviews with some 180 navy personnel in ten job fields and for three job roles: students, instructors, and active workers (Sticht, Fox, Hauke, & Zapf, 1977a). Personnel were interviewed at their school or job sites. An attempt was made to get citations of one reading-to-do task and one reading-to-learn task from each interviewee. Thus, for students, instructors, and job incumbents we wanted 50 percent reading-to-do and 50 percent reading-to-learn tasks.

However, as figure 1 shows, with increasing distance from the school setting, the proportion of reading-to-learn tasks which people could report performing in the last 24 hours decreased, and the proportion of reading-to-do tasks increased to the point that three-fourths of the tasks obtained from job performers were reading-to-do tasks.

The fact that students who have just entered the navy perform proportionately more reading-to-learn tasks is consistent with their role as students. In confirming what we would expect of students, the findings also suggest that, in many trades and skilled jobs, the cognitive demands of job training are likely to exceed those of job performing. This is so because reading is common to both reading-to-do and reading-to-learn tasks, while the latter make additional demands on information-processing strategies for learning from textual materials. To ensure that job training does not act primarily as a screening test to select those with high verbal ability and well-developed strategies for learning from text—skills that may not be so necessary for job performance—the design of training programs should reflect the requirements of the job itself as faithfully as possible. Jobs which essentially are hands-on and performance-oriented should not involve excessive requirements for learning from textual materials during job training.

Identifying Reading Demands of Jobs

The research reviewed above clearly shows the importance of reading in job training programs and in job performance. The identification of reading-to-learn and reading-to-do tasks provides a rough indication that, in many cases, training programs may make considerably more demands on literacy skills than the jobs themselves make. This is because training programs involve the complex strategies used in studying—that is, transforming the store of information in textbooks into a store of knowledge in memory that can later be used to complete course examinations.

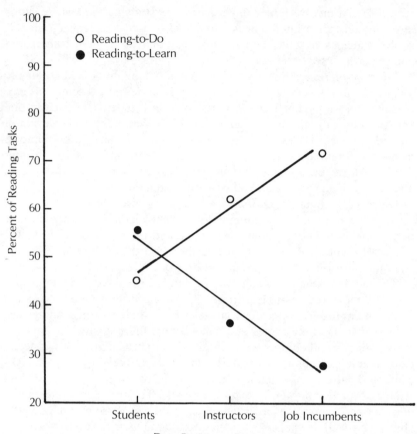

**Figure 1. Percentage of Reading Tasks Cited by Three Groups
of Navy Personnel**

A more precise determination of the reading demands of jobs is required
if we intend to use such information in establishing objectives and curricula
which provide students with the literacy skill levels needed to perform
reading tasks in the world of work—that is, if we are to render students
vocationally literate. In this case, what we would like to know is: What are
the reading tasks people have to perform in various jobs, and what level
of reading skill is needed to perform those tasks?

In exploratory research for the U.S. Navy, we attempted to develop an
inventory tool which job analysts could use to (1) identify the reading
tasks people perform in various jobs, and (2) determine the percentage of

people reading at different levels (expressed in reading grade-levels, as determined by a standardized reading test) who could be expected to accurately perform the job reading tasks (Sticht, Fox, Hauke, and Zapf, 1977b).

The foregoing report presents a detailed discussion of the methodology and a critique of several different methods for estimating the reading requirements of jobs. Here I will briefly summarize the outcomes of our efforts and discuss certain methodological difficulties inherent in any attempt to define literacy demands of jobs, and hence to establish minimum competency levels for work.

To define job-related reading tasks in this exploratory work, no attempt was made to consider reading-to-learn tasks. Rather, attention was restricted to the reading-to-do tasks identified in the interviews described above. For purposes of developing the Navy Reading Task Inventory, we grouped the ten jobs into three clusters, as shown in figure 2.

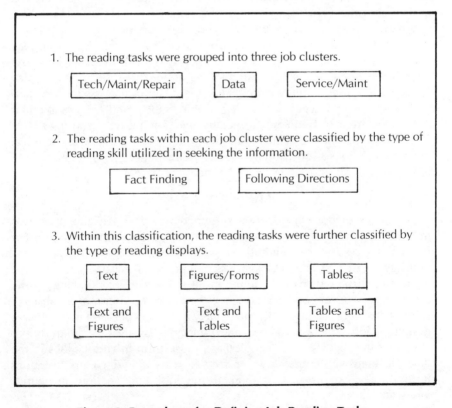

Figure 2. Procedures for Defining Job Reading Tasks

The next step in our procedure was to identify (1) the type of information sought in performing each task, and (2) the type of display in the reading materials. Type of display was further classified as text (which would be written language); figures (including line drawings, photographs, and schematic diagrams); tables (including both numerical and verbal tabulations); text plus figures; texts plus tables; or tables plus figures.

This analysis of displays revealed that the information sought was usually some type of factual data; the person was trying to find out how to do something. Thus, two categories of reading skills—fact finding and following directions—were identified (see figure 2).

Analysis of the reading-to-do tasks for students, instructors, and job performers, summed over the three vocational clusters, showed that 110 required fact-finding skills and 76 required following-directions skills. Instructors and job incumbents utilized fact-finding skills 2 to 4 times more than following-directions skills, whereas students used following-directions skills 2 times as often as fact-finding skills (though this differed in the data-oriented jobs).

Analysis of materials by display types revealed that the combination of tables plus figures was only very rarely used; hence this type of display was not used in the subsequent research. Texts constituted the most frequently used type of display and made-up about one-third of the display types, with figures running a close second, at somewhat less than 30 percent of the display types. Tables, texts plus figures, and texts plus tables fell in that order of frequency of occurrence, behind texts and figures.

Jobs differed in the relative frequency of uses of displays; technical maintenance jobs used proportionately more figures, and data-oriented jobs used figures and tables to about the same extent.

The Reading Task Inventory

By means of the classification system outlined above and presented in figure 2, generic reading tasks were defined as the application of either fact-finding or following-directions skills to texts, figures, tables, text plus figures, or text plus tables. Tasks composed of the two skills applied to the five display types were found in all ten of the jobs making up the three career clusters of figure 2. They therefore represent, at an abstract level, the types of reading tasks which navy personnel perform in the course of doing a job. In an abstract manner, this analysis answers the question: What are the reading tasks people have to perform in various jobs in the navy? The answer is: they look up facts in texts, they look up directions in texts, they look up facts in figures, they look up directions in figures, and so forth.

Conceivably, we could develop an inventory simply by asking people whether they look up facts in texts, figures, tables, and so forth. In work for the Department of Manpower and Immigration in Saskatchewan, Smith (1975) and associates used a somewhat similar inventory approach in which they attempted to discover both the kinds of materials that were read in a number of occupations (such as notes, memos, letters, directions, instructions, policy manuals, and the like) and the reading tasks that were performed in those jobs (for example: read to locate facts, to follow directions, or to discover the main idea). To obtain this information, interviewers showed displays of the general type of material they were talking about. For instance, in determining if a given job required the reading of graphs, two graphs were shown as examplars, and interviewees were asked to indicate whether they read similar graphs in performing their jobs.

A problem with the inventory approach (in which people simply indicate whether they read some type of material) is that it fails to distinguish among complexities of materials, and it provides no indication of the level of general reading skills required to perform the set of reading tasks in a given occupation.

To overcome these difficulties in the navy research, a reading-task inventory was constructed which included three levels of complexity for each type of display. The displays were taken from the navy's *Bluejacket's Manual*. This 617-page manual is the basic manual for navy recruits. Therefore it is meant to be read using only general reading skills and knowledge, and its content is familiar to all navy personnel. These features are important, because a primary type of information desired for the analysis of occupational reading requirements is "data on the level of reading skills required to have access to the occupations." (Miller, 1974). Since *The Bluejacket's Manual* is an entry-level manual, it represents the type of material that one must be able to read to have access to all navy job training and occupational fields.

To develop an inventory that we could use to identify the kinds of reading tasks recruits perform, and to discover the general level of reading skill needed to perform those reading tasks, we searched *The Bluejacket's Manual* to locate three concrete instances of each of the five abstract categories of generic reading tasks identified in figure 2. Having three examples of each generic reading task permitted us to distinguish three levels of complexity for each reading task. These levels were confirmed by two judges.

Figure 3 shows the types of displays included in the inventory. On the left-hand side is a sample of text plus table material from *The Bluejacket's Manual*. On the right-hand side are the inventory questions. This particular page from the inventory is for fact finding, so job incumbents were asked: In your job, would you ever have to perform reading tasks using material

All ships are assigned *designations*—a group of letters which indicate their type and general use—and *bull numbers*, which are usually assigned in sequence to ships of a type as they are built. These identifying designations are used in correspondence, records, plans, communications, and sometimes on ships' boats, because letter and number designations are shorter than the ship's name — *Mission Capistrano*, (AC 162)—and help to avoid confusion between such similar names as *Home* (DLG 30) and *Hornet* (CVS 12) or *Phoebus* (MSC 199) and *Phoebus* (YF 294).

The first letter in a designator is a general classification: *D* for destroyers, *S* for submarines, *L* for amphibious vessels, *M* for minewarfare vessels, *A* for auxiliaries, *W* for Coast Guard vessels, *T* for Military Sealift Command ships. and *Y* for service and yard craft. In combatant designations, the letter *N* means nuclear powered and *G* means the ship is equipped to fire guided missiles. A listing of most ship designations follows; minor yard craft and service craft have been omitted.

AD	Destroyer Tender	AKR	Vehicle Cargo Ship
ADG	Degaussing Ship	ANL	Stores Issue Ship
AE	Ammunition Ship	AO	Net Laying Ship
AF	Store Ship	AOE	Oiler
AFS	Combat Store Ship	AOG	Fast Combat Support Ship
AG	Miscellaneous	AOR	Gasoline Tanker
AGDE	Escort Research Ship	AP	Replenishment Oiler Transport
AGEH	Hydrofoil Research Ship	AR	Repair Ship. Salvage Ship
AGER	Environmental Research	ARS	Submarine Tender
AFG	Miscellaneous Command Ship	AS	Assault Support Patrol Boat
AGM	Missile Range Instrumentation Ship	ASPB	Submarine Rescue Ship
AGMR	Major Communications Relay Ship	ASR	Auxiliary Ocean Tug
AGOR	Oceanographic Research Ship	ATA	Armored Troop Carrier
AGP	Patrol Craft Tender	ATC	Fleet Ocean Tug
AGS	Surveying Ship	ATF	Salvage and Rescue Ship
AGSS	Auxiliary Submarine	ATS	Seaplane Tender
AGTR	Technical Research Ship	AV	Guided Missile Ship
AH	Hospital Ship	AVM	Heavy Cruiser
AK	Cargo Ship	CA	Command Ship
AKD	Cargo Ship Dock	CC	Command and Control Boat
AKL	Light Cargo Ship	CCB	Guided Missile Cruiser
		CC, CGN	Light Cruiser
		CL	Cruiser
		CLG	

(1) In your job would you ever have to perform reading tasks using material like this to look up facts?

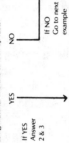

YES   NO

If YES   If NO
Answer   Go to next
2 & 3   example

(2) How *frequently* do you perform a reading task similar to this?

1	2	3	4	5
1 to 3 times a year	1 time each month	2 to 3 times a month	1 or more times each week	Daily

(3) What might be the consequence of a reading error with this type of reading task?

1. No consequence.
2. I would be disciplined and some time would be wasted.
3. The job would have to be done over again and some time would be wasted.
4. The job would have to be done over and some material would be wasted.
5. The job would have to be done over and some people would be inconvenienced.
6. Equipment would be damaged or lost.
7. I might be injured or other personnel might be injured.

Figure 3. Sample Page from the Navy Reading Task Inventory

like this to look up facts? If they said yes, then they were asked questions about the frequency of performance, and then questions about the consequences of making a reading error. These data are used to make decisions about the criticalness of a reading task.

To identify the general level of literacy required to perform each reading task, we wrote fact-finding and following-directions questions for each of the display types in the inventory. The resulting job-related reading tests were administered to some 250 Navy personnel, along with a standardized reading test. With these two sets of data, we could then determine how well young adults of differing reading skills could perform on the job-related, reading-task test items.

Figure 4 shows the results of asking a following-directions question using the same material that was shown in figure 3 as a fact-finding inventory item. This type of display shows the job-related reading material on the left side of the page; and, on the right side of the page, presents the type of reading task, its form (in this case E for easy), the question, and the test results (the percentage of personnel at each reading grade-level who got the correct answer to the test item). In figure 4, we see that 10 persons read at the 6th-grade level, and that 40 percent of those 10 answered the question correctly, using the material on the left side of the page. (In the actual test, the material was in *The Bluejacket's Manual*. Examinees were given page references, and then had to locate the material in the 617-page manual. By using the intact *Bluejacket's Manual* we hoped to obtain greater fidelity to the actual job-related reading situation.)

Results of the use of the material in the inventory format are presented at the bottom of the right side of the page. In our exploratory study, only four persons from four jobs tried out the inventory. The results show differences in the reported frequency of use by these four personnel for this type of material. Obviously, large numbers of personnel are needed to obtain a reliable, normative view of the performance of various reading tasks in different jobs.

Figure 5 shows how general reading skill is related to performance on the job-related reading tasks considered as a set. The percentage of test items on which 50 percent or less of the examinees scored correctly is plotted for each reading grade-level group. The figure shows that for all of the reading tasks attempted by 6th-grade-level readers, 42 percent of the tasks had accuracy rates of 50 percent or lower. The proportion of reading tasks having this accuracy rate decreased to 6 percent when averaged over persons with 12th, 13th, and 14th-grade reading levels. Thus, the probability that more than half of the people at a reading grade level of skill will be able to perform a given reading task shows a 36 percent increase from the 6th-grade level of reading skills to the 12th- 14th-grade levels.

All ships are assigned *designations*—a group of letters which indicate their type and general use—and *hull numbers*, which are usually assigned in sequence to ships of a type as they are built. These identifying designations are used in correspondence, records, plans, communications, and sometimes on ships' boats, because letter and number designations are shorter than the ship's name—*Mission Capistrano*, (AC 162)—and help to avoid confusion between such similar names as *Home* (DLG 30) and *Hornet* (CVS 12) or *Phoebe* (MSC 199) and *Phoebus* (YF 294).

The first letter in a designator is a general classification: *D* for destroyers, *S* for submarines, *L* for amphibious vessels, *M* for minewarfare vessels, *A* for auxiliaries, *W* for Coast Guard vessels, *T* for Military Sealift Command ships, and *Y* for service and yard craft. In combatant designations, the letter *N* means nuclear powered and *G* means the ship is equipped to fire guided missiles. A listing of most ship designations follows: minor yard craft and service craft have been omitted.

AD	Destroyer Tender	AO	Net Laying Ship
ADG	Degaussing Ship	AOE	Oiler
AE	Ammunition Ship	AOG	Fast Combat Support Ship
AF	Store Ship		Gasoline Tanker
AFS	Combat Store Ship	AOR	Replenishment Oiler
AG	Miscellaneous	AP	Transport
AGDE	Escort Research Ship	AR	Repair Ship, Salvage
AGEH	Hydrofoil Research Ship	ARS	Ship
AGER	Environmental Research	AS	Submarine Tender
	Ship	ASPB	Assault Support
AFG	Miscellaneous Command		Patrol Boat
	Ship	ASR	Submarine Rescue
AGM	Missile Range Instru-		Ship
	mentation Ship	ATA	Auxiliary Ocean Tug
AGMR	Major Communications	ATC	Armored Troop Carrier
	Relay Ship	ATF	Fleet Ocean Tug
AGOR	Oceanographic Research	ATS	Salvage and Rescue
	Ship		Ship
AGP	Patrol Craft Tender	AV	Seaplane Tender
AGS	Surveying Ship	AVM	Guided Missile Ship
AGSS	Auxiliary Submarine	CA	Heavy Cruiser
AGTR	Technical Research Ship	CC	Command Ship
AH	Hospital Ship	CCB	Command and
AK	Cargo Ship		Control Boat
AKD	Cargo Ship Dock	CG, CGN	Guided Missile Cruiser
AKL	Light Cargo Ship	CL	Light Cruiser
AKR	Vehicle Cargo Ship	CLG	Cruiser
ANL	Stores Issue Ship		

NAVY READING TASK TEST/INVENTORY—RESULTS OF EXPLORATORY STUDY

Type of Task: Following Directions Using Texts and Tables (Form E, Item 16)

Question: Situation — You are on watch and have been told to report all ships that you see. When reporting, you have been told to first give the ship's general classification and then the designation. You have sighted a light cargo ship.

What do you report?

Test Results: Percentage of personnel at each reading grade level who got the correct answer.

				READING GRADE LEVEL						
	6	7	8	9	10	11	12	13	14	TOTAL
N	10	8	7	8	11	8	7	6	17	82
%	40	50	86	62	55	62	71	83	82	66

Inventory Results: Frequency with which this type of task is performed.

	1 (1 to 3 times a year)	2 (1 time each month)	3 (2 to 3 times a month)	4 (1 or more times each week)	5 (Daily)	Not Used
Electronics Technician		x				
Electrician's Mate				x		
Gunner's Mate						x
Boatswain's Mate						x

Figure 4. Performance of Personnel at Various Reading Grade-Levels on a Test of Following Directions Using Text and Tables

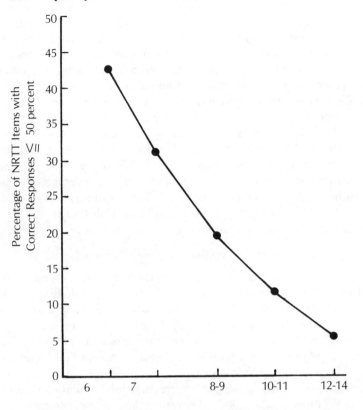

Reading Grade-Level on Nelson-Denny Test

**Figure 5. Percentage of NRTT Items for Which Correct Responses
Were Obtained by 50 Percent or Less of the People
at a Given Reading Grade Level**

To identify the reading demands of any navy job using this inventory approach, one would first administer the inventory to job incumbents in order to determine frequency and criticalness of performance for each reading task. Then, to determine the reading grade-level of difficulty for each type of reading task in the inventory, the job analyst would consult expectancy tables which showed how well people of differing reading grade-levels performed the reading task. At this point, a management decision would have to be made about what percentage of people should be able to perform the reading task. If it were determined that only 40 percent of the people should be able to perform the task, then, using the example of figure 4, a 6th-grade level of reading skill would be deemed sufficient, and the task would be assigned a 6th-grade level of difficulty. However, if it were determined that 80 percent of the people should be able to perform the task, then in the example of figure 4, it would be placed at the 13th-14th grade level, where 80 percent of the persons got the item correct (it is assumed that with larger numbers of persons taking the test, fluctuations in the percentages correct as a function of reading-skill level would be greatly reduced. Here we have regarded the 86 percent correct for 8th-grade readers as a sampling fluctuation, to be ignored.)

To determine the reading difficulty for a job, the reading grade-level of each reading task would be weighted by its frequency and criticalness. These weighted figures would be summed, and the average, weighted reading difficulty level would be computed. The resulting average reading grade-level would be the level of general reading skill that is needed, on the average, to perform the reading tasks of a given job.

Critique of the Reading Inventory Approach

A variety of methodological and procedural problems are encountered in any attempt to develop an assessment instrument for evaluating the skill/ knowledge levels required for successful performance in a domain. The experimental development of the Navy Reading Task Inventory is no exception. A discussion of some of these problems may be instructive to others who would set out to identify reading demands or "minimum competencies" for vocational literacy.

Key requirements of the inventory are that job incumbents respond to the generic aspects of a task display rather than to the specific content; that they respond to the levels of complexity; and that they respond to the distinctions between fact finding and following directions. In the research described, however, no good basis was established for assuring that designated levels of complexity or types of uses (fact finding; following directions) actually entered into the interviewee's responses. There was evidence that, of the four people who tried out the inventory, two responded to more than the generic aspects of the displays; they responded in part to the specific content. In the work by Smith (1975) this was not reported to be a problem. But neither was it detectable because of the methodology used in that study.

Several problems are associated with the job-related reading-task test. Technical problems involved with some items could be remedied by careful redesign of questions. A major problem is in knowing how close the reading-task questions approximate real reading tasks. It may be that the reading test imposes unrepresentative information-processing demands which are not involved in the real execution of reading tasks on the job. Indeed, the most difficult question to answer is that of the validity of the reading inventory/test as a measure of the reading demands of jobs. Is there any way to be certain that this entire procedure presents a valid estimate of the reading demands of jobs? This raises the question of how we would know. It may be easier to demonstrate lack of validity than to support a claim to validity. For example, sole use of a readability formula could be challenged because it in no way involves figures and tables in forming reading difficulty estimates; and, as we found in the navy research, only 30 percent of the reported reading tasks involved texts alone; two-thirds used figures or figures plus texts.

In a review of seven different approaches for estimating the reading demands of jobs, Sticht and McFann (1975) show that all seven approaches provide different estimates. Indeed, the very definition of a reading task differs from one to another approach. From the present discussion, and the analysis of Sticht and McFann, it should be apparent that there is no such empirical "condition" or "event" or "thing" known as "*the* reading demands of a job". Hence there is no one "sure" way to establish "minimum" competency levels of literacy for vocational preparedness. Reading demands of jobs are not to be discovered; rather, they must be estimated by procedures which are systematically performed according to specifiable rules. The validity of any estimate can only be assessed with respect to a model or theory of job-related reading, which would define systematic procedures for estimating the reading demands of jobs.

It should be noted, however, that the foregoing problem of validity is not specific to the determination of job-related reading requirements. Indeed, such problems permeate all aspects of job analysis and all psychometric approaches to the evaluation of skills and knowledge. Within these limits—and they are formidable limits which ought to conduce humility amongst psychometricians, job and task analysts, and educators—I believe that the inventory approach can, with refinements, offer useful information about the reading demands of jobs and contribute to the development of more useful vocational literacy training programs, thus permitting higher levels of vocational competence.

Summary

In this paper I have discussed the nature of literacy in work settings. I have offered a view of the written language that distinguished written language from spoken language in two critical ways: it is permanent, and it is capable of being arrayed in space. Because of these features, written language can be consulted as an "external memory"; and hence reading-to-do tasks are possible, in which a person reads to obtain some information which can be immediately applied and then forgotten. If needed again, it can be looked up again. Additionally, the permanence of print permits reading-to-learn tasks, wherein written material is studied and transferred to the memory for subsequent use.

The importance of the fact that written language can be arrayed in space showed up in analyses of the materials used by job incumbents, where it was found that two-thirds of the reading tasks involved either figures or figures plus textual material. Such figures usually include written language placed as labels at various points in space, and the reader searches the visual space for information.

An exploratory study was discussed which attempted to use reading-to-do tasks, composed of looking up information in texts, figures, tables, and combinations of these materials, to develop a job reading inventory that could be used to (1) identify the reading tasks performed in various jobs and (2) to determine the level of general reading skill needed to perform the job-related reading tasks. Results of the study showed a strong relationship between reading ability and ability to perform job-related reading tasks, with persons who read at the 6th-grade level performing only one-seventh as well as those reading at the 12th-14th-grade levels. Yet, more than half of the reading tasks were still performed correctly by more than half of those reading at the 6th-grade level.

A critique of the inventory approach to understanding the reading requirements of jobs revealed that significant questions remain unanswered regarding the validity of the approach. The need for solid theory was noted, so that methods of assessing vocational literacy competencies which have construct validity might be developed. In the absence of a sound theory of literacy in vocational settings, any approach to establishing "minimum competency" levels for ensuring that students achieve literacy skills needed for successful participation in a meaningful vocation will remain largely arbitrary and open to skepticism.

References

Miller, G., ed. *Linguistic Communication: Perspectives for Research*. Newark, Del.: International Reading Association, 1974.

Smith, A. *Generic Skills for Occupational Training*. Prince Albert, Saskatchewan: Training Research and Development Station, 1975.

Sticht, T., ed. *Reading for Working: A Functional Literacy Anthology*. Alexandria, Va.: Human Resources Research Organization, 1975.

Sticht, T. and McFann, H. Reading Requirements for Career Entry. In D. Nielsen and H. Hjelm, eds. *Reading and Career Education*. Newark, Del.: International Reading Association, 1975.

Sticht, T. and Zapf, D., eds. *Reading and Readability Research in the Armed Services*. HumRRO FR-WD-CA-76-4. Alexandria, Va.: Human Resources Research Organization, September 1976.

Sticht, T., Fox, L., Hauke, R., and Zapf, D. *The Role of Reading in the Navy.* Technical Report NPRDC TR 77-40. San Diego, Calif.: Navy Personnel Research and Development Center, September 1977(a).

Sticht, T., Fox, L. Hauke, R., and Zapf, D. *Integrated Job Skills and Reading Skills Training System.* Technical Report NPRDC TR 77-41. San Diego, Calif.: Navy Personnel Research and Development Center. 1977(b).

Epilogue

A Summing Up

In a recent *New York Times* article (March 19, 1979), Edward Fiske concluded that minimum competency testing has had little effect on schooling in the United States and is unlikely to have much effect in the future. His conclusions were based on early studies of a few state programs and on longer-term reports from a few school systems (such as Denver) that have had some form of minimum competency testing for a decade or more. He admitted that the data were sparse and his conclusions were, perhaps, premature.

The papers contained in this volume suggest that Fiske's conclusions are, indeed, premature. With few exceptions, the authors warn of many serious, if not dire, consequences of minimum competency testing. The movement has its strong proponents and opponents, but only a rare few would suggest that it is likely to be benign in all of its effects.

In papers on topics as diverse as philosophy (Cohen and Haney), policy (Baratz), and curriculum (Broudy), we find the suggestion that the political effects of minimum competency testing may be the most profound. Although the legal right to prescribe the content and process of schooling has always been reserved to state governments, delegation of this authority to local school systems has long been a tenet of public education in United States. (Only in special situations, such as schooling of American

Indian children, has control been centralized. Minimum competency testing may signal the beginning, or the acceleration, of a move to centralize control of all public education. True, some states (such as Oregon and California) merely require school systems to establish competency requirements and determine corresponding assessment methods, with no state proscriptions on their choices. But as Marshall Herron reports, the resulting problems have yet to be squarely faced. When equality of educational opportunity is guaranteed by state statute or in a state's constitution, between-system variation in graduation requirements is difficult to justify and is certainly open to challenge through equal protection suits. The alternative exemplified by Florida and North Carolina, where the state government adopts uniform competency criteria and state-mandated tests, is somewhat more popular.

With the state controlling the extrinsic rewards of schooling, control of instructional content and process cannot long remain in local hands. Indeed, several authors in this volume (Amarel and Bardon) conclude that minimum competency testing will disfranchise teachers and reduce them to pawns in a sterile, lockstep system of schooling. So the political results of minimum competency testing may well have important instructional consequences.

Although minimum competency testing and basic skills instruction are not synonymous, a review of the content of minimum competency tests currently in use suggests otherwise. Minimum competencies are most often expressed as rote-learning objectives or direct application of facts to supposedly practical situations. If, as suggested in this volume, the content of the tests comes to define the content of our high school curricula, we are indeed in danger of "having the minimum become the maximum." More than one author represented here (Broudy, Amarel, Cohen and Haney, Greene) warns that public education may revert to the equivalent of a kindergarten through sixth-grade curriculum for the children of the masses, while the children of parents who can afford private schools may enjoy an enriched college-preparatory curriculum that adequately spans the content of secondary as well as elementary instruction. So one social consequence of minimum competency testing may well be the exacerbation of our current social and economic class differences. Even if the curriculum is not changed materially, imposition of a test-based standard for high school graduation will likely have profound effects on the racial composition of college attendees. Bruce Eckland's paper leads to the conclusion that minimum competency testing could triple the gap between the college attendance rates of black and white high school graduates, while having limited effects on the employment and wage rates of those who manage to squeak by the cutoff scores.

Economic data suggest that the certification value of a high school diploma is very high, although test data suggest that basic skills performance has almost no functional value when measured against fundamental economic criteria. By imposing minimum competency testing, then, we may well be "blaming the victim," a term used by Blau in describing students' perceptions of the purposes of such tests.

In sum, minimum competency testing is social and political dynamite. Whether its power will result in some positive outcome for the schools, for students, or for society is an open question. But the force of logic and the limited data gathered to date suggest that caution is certainly warranted. It is disquieting to see so many states and school systems embracing this vast social experiment, when a sound pilot study has yet to be conducted.

Where to Now?

A myriad of questions—educational, technical, and socio-political—surround minimum competency testing. The field is ripe for solid study, evaluation, and research. The National Institute of Education has made a small beginning by funding the design of a nationwide evaluation study (see Shoemaker's paper), but the resources invested in that study are a pittance compared to the need and the gravity of the problem.

Among the educational issues demanding investigation are questions surrounding the effects of minimum competency testing on the organization and control of school curricula; the content of school curricula; mechanisms for the change of school curricula; teachers' instructional practices, their morale, and their modes of interaction with children and peers; students' psychological and social reactions; and allocation of school resources to various educational purposes. The remediability of competency deficiencies in high school students must also be investigated.

Technical questions yet to be resolved concern all facets of the design and operation of minimum competency testing programs—from the dynamics and practice of competency identification, to the development and validation of measurement instruments, to the linkage between measurement goals and practices, to the establishment of defensible competency standards, to the use of test results toward some worthwhile instructional ends.

Political and social issues are apparent in the summary provided above. We must study the effects of minimum competency testing on graduation rates, dropout rates, college-going rates, career choices, employment opportunities, and choices of high school courses—by race, national origin, and social class of students. In addition, we must carefully monitor the actions of state legislatures and local school boards in setting instructional and curricular policies and in allocating resources for various educational purposes. In these ways, we can learn about important process as well as outcome effects of minimum competency testing.

So this book must end as do so many research reviews: with a list of questions rather than a list of answers; with a plea for investment in further research; and with the fervent hope that its warnings will be heeded before too many students, teachers, and schools are made victims of the latest popular craze in U.S. education, and too much money that is sorely needed to improve the educational attainment of all students is wasted on shortsighted regulatory policies.